EDUCATIONAL AND
PSYCHOLOGICAL MEASUREMENT

CONTRIBUTIONS TO THEORY AND PRACTICE

A Blaisdell Book in Psychology

CONSULTING EDITOR

Raymond G. Kuhlen, *Syracuse University*

Educational and Psychological Measurement

CONTRIBUTIONS TO THEORY AND PRACTICE

EDITED AND WITH INTRODUCTIONS BY

David A. Payne / Syracuse University

Robert F. McMorris / State University of New York at Albany

BLAISDELL PUBLISHING COMPANY
A Division of Ginn and Company
WALTHAM, MASSACHUSETTS · TORONTO · LONDON

BF
39
P3

PREFACE

After many years of neglect, the behavioral sciences are receiving important notice from both public and private quarters. Monies, for example, are being funneled in increasing amounts into research and research training programs. A "knowledge explosion" is one of the more apparent results of this funding. There has been a tremendous increase in knowledge in the form of research reports, theoretical papers, and numerous other types of publications. An obvious problem now evident is how to communicate and digest the increasing amounts of data being made available to the academic community.

Academic programers of both graduate and undergraduate courses are being required to increase the amount and speed with which updated information is introduced to students. Instructors of educational and psychological testing courses are particularly aware of this dissemination problem. It is, therefore, the primary purpose of the set of readings contained in this book to assist in the communication of knowledge by providing convenient and readily accessible discussions and research summaries of concern to the student of measurement.

This collection of papers represents a variety of topics and reflects several degrees of sophistication. It contains coverage of both theoretical and applied subjects. The primary audience for this volume was considered to be students in introductory tests and measurements courses at the college senior or first-year graduate level. These students might be found in departments of psychology or in schools of education. Advanced graduate students and instructors should also find valuable material for review or reference in this volume.

A book of this sort would probably be used most frequently as an adjunct to a general text. However, it could very well be used itself as the basic text, especially if supplemented by appropriate experiences such as test development (e.g., item writing and analysis), administration, and interpretation.

With only a few exceptions the papers have been edited and abridged. Extensive reviews of the literature have been condensed, statistical data summarized, and all but the major references deleted. The remaining references are listed alphabetically at the back of the volume.

It is difficult and perhaps presumptuous to edit articles which have already undergone review before their original publication. The likely presence of some loss in clarity and the introduction of some ambiguity may have resulted from editing rather than from the original writing. Where such communication problems have been created the editors beg the indulgence of the original authors, as well as students and instructors who may find this collection of papers useful.

The papers are grouped by chapters. Each chapter is introduced by a foreword which highlights its general significance and the contribution of the individual papers. In addition each paper is given a brief introduction to orient the reader and point up parallel and interrelated themes that recur in the various readings. The first six chapters parallel the development of a test from theory to construction and on through analysis, refinement and interpretation. The next two chapters consider a variety of applications of measurement data, with a focus on prediction and decision making. The final chapters focus on testing programs and on the state of the art and science in educational and psychological measurement.

The major acknowledgement goes to the publishers and authors of each paper. They were more than generous in permitting us to reproduce their publications. To our many colleagues and students who assisted in selection of the articles, but who are too numerous to mention by name, a sincere general acknowledgement is hereby made. To Miss Arlene Welles fell the major typing task of bringing order out of chaos. To these, to Mary Ann and Bobbie, and to many others we are indebted.

D.A.P.
R.F.M.

CONTENTS

"Examinations are formidable, even to the best prepared, for the greatest fool may ask more than the wisest man can answer."

C. C. Colton

LACON (REVISED EDITION), 1836

I
INTRODUCTION
FOR STUDENTS
AND INSTRUCTORS

This collection of readings is intended for use by students of educational and psychological measurement. It is concerned with many technical and philosophical problems which are encountered in any attempt to assess human behavior. The study of educational and psychological measurement might be undertaken on the basis of its academic merits alone. As a subject for study, measurement offers much to the individual interested in relating and integrating theoretical, research, and applied developments within the behavioral sciences. For without the availability of measurement devices, most of the significant behavioral research completed in the last 100 years could not have been accomplished. In addition the practicing educator and psychologist will derive much information from an extensive and intensive study of measurement which should prove helpful in meeting day-to-day problems.

This introductory chapter has several purposes: first to point up the significance of measurement; second to discuss some possible uses of the book and guidelines involved in selecting and editing the papers; and third, to set forth the major framework of the volume.

Our ability to quantify human behavior has many practical implications. But sound measurement practice must rest on a solid theoretical base. The use of theory allows us to integrate research findings as well as to derive hypotheses which, after testing, should stimulate further applications. A practitioner must be aware of both research results and theory.

1

THE SIGNIFICANCE OF EDUCATIONAL AND PSYCHOLOGICAL MEASUREMENT

The intelligent application of tests and measurements constitutes a powerful force which can be used to improve the human condition, particularly in the realm of education. The use of poor instruments, on the other hand, or the improper use of good ones can adversely affect individuals and society. Even though misuse sometimes occurs, the demonstrated and potential benefits that can be derived from scientific and valid assessment cannot be denied.

It is almost a truism that the results of measurement permeate the lives of all people. It would indeed be an unusual individual who has not taken a test and whose life has not in some way been directly influenced by a test. Tests have been devised to assist in the determination and analysis of individual differences primarily in the areas of general intelligence, specific aptitudes, educational achievement, occupational competency, and personality development. Tests are not limited to use only with individuals, but have also frequently been applied to groups and institutions in a variety of employment, educational, psychological, military, and sociological settings, often for the purpose of arriving at major policy decisions.

It is axiomatic in science that unless something can be measured it cannot be studied. Thus measuring procedures are an important base of science and provide means of testing scientific hypotheses. Consequently the research applications of measurement methods are receiving increased attention, especially in the behavioral sciences with which this book is primarily concerned. Some idea of the scope of the research applications can be seen in Freeman's (1962) enumeration of test uses in psychology. He notes that:

> Among . . . studies, the following have been most common and include the most important fields of investigation: the nature and course of mental development, intellectual and non-intellectual personality differences associated with age, sex, and racial membership; differences that might be attributed to hereditary or environmental factors; differences among persons at different occupational levels; intellectual and other personality traits of atypical groups such as the mentally retarded, the mentally gifted, the neurotic, and the psychotic.

The foregoing partial list, if extended and expanded to include other current and future applications, would become encyclopedic. Tests are probably used more extensively for educational classification, selection, and planning than for any other purpose. Furst (1958), for example, notes ten major purposes served by educational measurement and evaluation. These are (1) determining the effectiveness of courses and programs, (2) testing assumptions about instructional practices, (3) selecting, clarifying, and appraising objectives, (4) discovering and understanding learning difficulties, (5) planning instruction, (6) motivating learning, (7) guidance, (8) selection, (9) placement, and (10), certification. Obviously then tests influence the entire educational career of an individual.

Not to be overlooked are business, industry, and the military, where tests are helpful in selecting and classifying personnel for placement in positions ranging from semi-skilled to top-level management. In any decision making or evaluation situation, however, test data constitute only one source of valuable information.

It is clear that measurement methods have great utility. Many different procedures are available for use. The papers in this book deal almost exclusively with the so-called paper and pencil variety. Rating scales, checklists, sociometric and observational methods, and projective devices are, in addition, valuable components of the psychometrists' arsenal. All of these techniques have one thing in common; they are methods that can be used to quantify behavior. Stated in another way, they constitute procedures for assigning numerals to represent objects or events according to rules. The problem is that they are fallible and subject to error. Some of the methods used to reduce, control, or eliminate these errors of measurement, as well as related topics, are covered in this book of readings.

WHY A BOOK OF READINGS?

Textbooks are dull! How often have college and university professors heard this or similar comments from their students. Why is this the case? It is in part probably because of the author's style, perhaps to the selection of subject matter, or perhaps to level of instruction. Very frequently it is not just *what* one says but *how* one says it that influences communication. But communication is also how the basic concepts, principles, and pertinent research are integrated into the body of the text. Generally these are briefly summarized with scholarly footnotes attached. Frequently something is lost in the translation and interpretations. What is this "something"? Perhaps it is the transmitted enthusiasm of a researcher discussing his original investigation or experiment. Or the clarity with which a creative scholar presents his logical and well thought out contribution. It is indeed an unusual textbook author who can draw upon the thoughts and data from a variety of original sources and authors and mold them into a readable and concise communication. It would perhaps even be unreasonable to expect an author to be able to address himself with equal clarity to a large number of topics. Some writers, by virtue of their command of the language, and mechanics and style of expression can frequently "instruct" more effectively than others. And they may also be more knowledgeable about the subject matter. A book of readings which contains original presentations should then facilitate communication and learning.

The problem of motivating the student to seek and digest the original source is ever present. An instructor may assign readings in selected journals or go so far as to require an "integrative" term paper which will, hopefully, result in a meaningful learning experience. Such efforts most would probably agree fall short of intentions. This is due in part to the fact that many of the original sources may be difficult either to obtain or comprehend. It was a primary intention of the editors of this volume to collect some of the significant original research and theoretical discussions in the area of educational and psychological measurement and make these available for possible use as text materials.

SELECTION AND EDITING OF PAPERS

Several criteria guided the selection of papers. It was hoped that within the general sections papers of variable difficulty level could be placed and sequenced in such a way as to allow an instructor to select appropriate readings for his students.

The editors have included some papers presenting theory or research which represent the frontiers of knowledge; also some of the "classic" discussions in the area of psychometrics have been included. The research studies reported deal with both application and theory-testing. The student's exposure to original research should provide him with both perspective on current practices in measurement as well as justification for the various theoretical positions assumed. The approach taken in general was toward providing a broad perspective on measurement. If a bias exists, it is in the direction of placing greater weight on the assessment of learning outcomes, i.e., on educational measurement. Some attempt has been made to select articles which will generate discussion. This was done by including somewhat controversial material or unusual conceptualizations of certain topics.

To help insure appropriate selection many of the articles were "tried out" either in edited or original form with students in courses in tests and measurements. A large number of these articles have been rated by students on such factors as readability, aid in understanding course material, clarity of author's presentation of main points, number of readings necessary for comprehension, and relevance to professional needs. These data influenced the selection of the majority of the papers included in this book.

With only eight or nine exceptions, all articles in the present book have been edited in an effort to emphasize the most salient points in each of the authors' original presentations. It will be noted that the editing has often been quite extensive; by saving space it was possible to include a wide sampling of significant studies and discussions. The elaborate reviews and references to the literature that frequently accompany research articles have been abridged or eliminated. An attempt has been made to simplify the statistical presentation so as to minimize the knowledge of statistics required for comprehension of the material. One technique employed was the simplification of selected tables through elimination of all but descriptive data. Reference to various introductory statistics texts should provide the reader with sufficient background for comprehension of the research articles.[1]

Each group of papers (chapter) is introduced by a brief discussion of the general topic with which the papers are concerned for the purpose of providing a perspective in which the individual papers might be viewed. In addition each paper is introduced by a brief paragraph which may include several "focusing questions." It is hoped that these introductions and questions will serve to guide the reader through the papers and alert him to important ideas in each article.

ORGANIZATION OF THE VOLUME

The organization of the papers is somewhat unlike most of the topical outlines that might be found in traditional textbooks in the area of testing, measurement, or evaluation. The fifty-four articles included in this volume are *not* intended to serve as a systematic integration of either the theoretical or empirical literature of measurement. The book is intended to provide for student use a collection of research reports and discussions which have historical significance, represent contemporary thought, or will assist him in dealing with measurement concepts and devices.

What is measurement all about? The four articles of Chapter II present summaries of the thinking of a number of authorities about the purposes and processes of measurement. These papers also contain a synopsis of the characteristics of a "good" measuring instrument. The central measurement concepts of reliability and validity are treated in the next two chapters. Aspects of both the technology and theory associated with these topics are treated in detail. Chapters V and VI deal with test construction techniques. Subtopics such as planning the test, item writing, and test analysis are approached from both discussive and empirical angles. The reader is next introduced to a systematic consideration of the many factors in the test situation which influence the scores and their interpretation. In the following two sections, Chapters IX and X some applications of test and measurement data are illustrated. Examples of research drawn primarily from academic settings are presented. Various "do's and don't's" and "pros and cons" of testing programs are summarized in Chapter XI. And finally in Chapter XII an effort is made to present a balanced philosophical view of testing. Both positive and negative comments are made. In total this collection of papers represents a cross-section of measurement theory and practice. Close examination of them will bring about changes in cognitive behavior, and in addition will assist in developing critical attitudes toward testing. Bon Voyage!

---

[1] See for example Adkins, 1964; Blommers and Lindquist, 1960; Bradley and McClelland, 1963; Gotkin and Goldstein, 1964; Guilford, 1965; and McCullough and Van Atta, 1965, 1963. *Note:* All bibliographic references have been drawn together at the end of the book.

II
OVERVIEW OF THE
PURPOSES AND PROCESSES
OF MEASUREMENT

The study of individual differences is a fascinating and worthwhile endeavor. It is one field within the behavioral sciences which holds interest for both casual observer and scholar. Part of the fascination and value of such studies derives from the fact that information concerning individual differences touches on vital questions in all aspects of our lives. Educators and psychologists are particularly sensitive to the importance of individual differences as they are continually being called upon to make decisions and evaluations about people.

Many dimensions of human behavior are in need of assessment. The techniques that may be employed are many, and the task itself is complex and arduous. What is assessed will, of course, depend upon the requirements of the particular situation. It may be an on-the-job training program, ability to take shorthand at a specified rate, or effective teaching.

The standardized test is a frequently used technique to gather data reflecting individual differences. Cronbach (1960) notes that tests are used to make decisions with respect to the selection and classification of individuals, evaluation of educational or treatment procedures, and acceptance or rejection of scientific hypotheses. But what is standardized about a standardized test? Obviously the content is fixed; i.e., all examinees will be required to respond to the same stimuli. The administration and scoring procedures are also controlled. In addition virtually all manuals accompanying standardized

7

tests provide tables of norms which summarize the test performances earned by specified and representative subjects. The procedures involved in the process of standardizing a test are outlined by Doctors Angoff and Anderson in the first article in this chapter. Their presentation provides a good summary of the processes involved in the construction and refinement of a standardized test. When we hear the term "standardized" used in conjunction with a test, we generally think of an instrument published by a commercial organization. But there is no reason why a classroom test could not be considered as a standardized test. The only element lacking perhaps is the availability of normative data. Of course this kind of information could be accumulated over time, if desired. Norms may be thought of as providing frames of reference for interpreting test scores. But the type of norm developed will obviously depend on the "purpose of testing."

Just as the "purpose of testing" may dictate the type of normative data gathered, it will also determine the general approach taken to test development and interpretation. In the second article of this chapter Dr. Julian Wohl compares and contrasts two rather distinct philosophies of testing. He refers to these as the traditional (or psychometric) and the contemporary (or impressionistic) approaches. In both frames of reference testing is viewed as providing a situation in which useful information may be gathered to aid in making decisions. But there the similarity ends. Dr. Wohl claims that the traditional view of testing is focused on obtaining a quantitative indication of behavior, whereas the contemporary view is concerned with gathering test as well as non-test data and in viewing the individual in the total test and life situation. Both approaches have advantages and disadvantages; the reader should attempt his own evaluation.

One purpose of testing is to assess educational achievement. In the third article in this second chapter Dr. Robert Ebel has specified some of the knowledge and skills that a classroom teacher must possess if he is to adequately evaluate student learning. It is interesting to note that Dr. Ebel considers principles that range from the philosophical to the technical, thereby underscoring the complexity of the measurement task.

Most of the tests in use today by educational, industrial, and governmental agencies are objective paper and pencil instruments. Historically the term "objective," when used in conjunction with measurement, has meant consistency of scoring. It has required that a standard key be applied in the same way to all examinees. Ebel (1965, p. 296) takes this definition a little further by including the notion that not only must the scoring key be applied fairly, but also that the responses keyed as correct must in fact be correct. The keyed answers must therefore be evaluated by a number of experts in addition to the test constructor.

A somewhat different approach to defining objectivity particularly with respect to personality instruments is presented by Dr. Ivan Scheier in the final article of this chapter. Dr. Scheier takes a more examinee-centered, rather than instrument-centered, view of objectivity. The author artfully demonstrates how failure to consider this important characteristic of an instrument can distort the resulting measurement and destroy the validity of the instrument relative to the intended purpose.

1   The Standardization of Educational and Psychological Tests

....

WILLIAM H. ANGOFF AND SCARVIA B. ANDERSON

The development and standardization of a mental test is a very complex, expensive, and time-consuming project. In this article Doctors Angoff and Anderson present a lucid overview of the test development process. Although they are primarily concerned with tests which become commercially available, their comments apply equally well to any "homemade" instrument, be it for classroom or research use. The following questions should guide the reader through this article. What does the term "standardization" mean? What are the primary purposes of "scaling" a test? What might be some applications of scaling procedures for a classroom test or for a college qualification admissions test? What purposes might a teacher have in mind in developing norms for his classroom tests?

The development and application of standardized tests probably represent one of the major contributions to educational progress of the last fifty years. But its success has not come without criticism; indeed, some of the success would not have been possible without the constructive criticism which has spurred test makers into improving their procedures and seeking new methods of assessing human mental processes. Some of the least constructive of the criticisms have stemmed from a fundamental view that testing is motivated by a mechanistic philosophy by which all men are cast into one mold, without regard for their essential individuality. The test makers, on the other hand, take the view that not only do they *not* disregard the essential differences among individuals, but also that these differences are precisely what they seek to understand. They also maintain that the pursuit of this understanding is best accomplished by adopting the methods of scientific inquiry by which they imply that all aspects of measurement be held constant and uniform, except for the individual's own performance. Only then can the variability in performance from one person to another be taken as evidence of the *abilities* of the individuals and of nothing else.

The test makers will also take the position that because it provides *uniform*

Reprinted with permission of the first named author, and publisher (Ray Page, State Superintendent of Public Instruction) from the *Illinois Journal of Education*, (February) 1963, pp. 19–23.

methods and *uniform standards* for everyone standardized testing necessarily yields fair and equitable assessments of performance for everyone. Thus the process of standardization permeates all aspects of a test; the construction, administration, scoring, reporting, and evaluation of test results.

TEST CONSTRUCTION

Ordinarily a standardized test poses the same questions for all students. The test maker attempts to write questions that will be regarded in the same way by all students who take the test. He pretests his questions in an effort to weed out ambiguities that result in different meanings to different people. (Pretests are conducted for other reasons as well: to insure the proper degree of difficulty for the test and the highest degree of reliability.) In most cases he writes a variety of test questions in order to sample as widely as possible the distribution of knowledge covered in a particular test. In this way he avoids giving special advantage to a student for whom the test is heavily weighted with questions in which he happens to have special competence or for which he did special intensive preparation in an attempt to "beat the test." In order to achieve a test which gives uniform opportunity to all students, a test maker asks not one or three or five questions but fifty or a hundred, because only with large numbers of questions can he be confident of achieving an adequate sampling of knowledge. He also writes questions which will test specifically what he intends to test, say knowledge and understanding of the events leading up to World War II—not "test wiseness," not general intelligence, not handwriting ability, nor neatness, nor English composition. This is not to say, of course, that some of these other characteristics are unimportant; but fair assessment demands that they must be measured separately.

ADMINISTRATION AND SCORING

The test maker also prescribes that the test be administered under uniform conditions—the same directions for all, the same presentation of questions, the same time limits, and insofar as possible the same favorable environmental conditions: proper light, ventilation, and temperature; convenient working space; general quiet, with freedom from extraneous disturbances.

Uniformity is also achieved in the scoring process. By restricting the nature of the student's responses and by removing from the task any opportunity the student may seize upon to bias the grading of his paper, the test maker insures virtually perfect scoring reliability. On a subjectively scored test the teacher's ratings can be influenced by such diverse factors as neatness and legibility, good or poor prose, his own fatigue or boredom with the scoring task, his general feeling of well-being, and, not of least importance, *his prior biases toward the student.* The standardized test, on the other hand, is scored only for the student's performance on the questions that are asked him. Again this is not to say that such factors as prose style or legibility of handwriting should not be tested. But if they are considered important enough to be tested, they should be tested independently. They should not appear as unreliable riders to another purpose to be considered as part of the score or not, depending on the particular mood and predilections of the person who happens to be scoring the paper at the time. As in the administration of the tests, what is sought here is a fair and equitable score, uncontaminated by factors that can only be considered as irrelevant or biasing in terms of the stated purpose of the test.

Of course all standardized tests are not "multiple-choice" tests. There are numerous instances in which a student is asked an "open-ended" question, as in the Stanford-Binet, the Wechsler-Bellevue, and the Interlinear Section of the College Board English Composition Test. In such cases the rules for scoring are agreed upon in advance by a group of experts and set down to be followed rigidly in the scoring process. Thus, even with tests that call for some subjectivity in scoring, attempts are made in the standardized test to reduce to a minimum the influence of extraneous factors and to set uniform standards to be applied to all examinees without bias.

SCALING

Standardization is also achieved in the development of an appropriate score scale system. Very frequently tests are constructed in more than one form—to discourage students from memorizing the questions either for their own benefit on retest or to help other students achieve higher scores, to avoid the effects of practice in studies of educational change, and to allow a second measurement when the validity of the first is open to question. Even when the various forms are constructed according to common specifications and precautions are taken to adopt an item-sampling scheme that will yield a similar "mix" of items in all forms, there are almost certain to be small differences between forms. Occasionally the differences are large, not only with respect to the general level of talent for which the forms are appropriate, but also with respect to the range of talent for which they are appropriate. In such cases it would be grossly unfair to compare the raw score earned by one student who is given an easier form with the raw score earned by another student who is given a more difficult form. Therefore, in order to correct the differences between forms and to provide scores that are independent of the particular form that happened to be administered in any instance, scores on the various forms of a test are equated—or "calibrated"—and converted to a common reporting scale. (In order to avoid confusion this scale is made independent and different from the raw-score system for any single form.) Then, within the limitations imposed by the reliability of the equating method one can be confident that a student's score was unaffected by the difficulty of the particular form he took. Teachers, admissions officers, and counselors are relieved of the obligation of taking into consideration the difficulty characteristic of each test form.

There are other advantages to equating. If the reporting scale is maintained intact and without change over a period of time during which new forms are introduced, it is possible to trace the quality of successive groups of examinees, to make studies of trends, and to compare individuals and groups tested at different times, in different places, and for different purposes.

The methods by which a scale is established and the methods by which it is maintained in the face of multiple forms constitute a sizable field of study by themselves. Frequently a representative group of individuals ("representative" in terms of the population for which the test is designed) is tested to become the "standard group" on whom the scale is based. In later uses of the test the "standard group," whose average performance provides the focal point of the scale, is used as the basic reference or normative group for the purposes of evaluating individual scores. This procedure expresses the view that the "standard group" gives normative meaning to the scale. Multiple forms of the test that are introduced at later times are equated, by procedures to be described below, to the scale defined by the original group, a process which allows scores on all of the forms to be reported in terms of this single standard scale.

There are other approaches to the problem of scale definition. One of these is based on the philosophy that because of changes in the population it is not always possible to give the scale lasting normative meaning. Moreover, even in those instances when the characteristics of the group may be expected to remain fairly constant, there is some question whether the scale should have any normative meaning or whether it should be a purely arbitrary scale of measurement, like the commonly used scales of inches, pounds, and Fahrenheit. The proponents of this view maintain that a measurement should be just a measurement and no more; that the evaluation of that measurement, as of the measurement of physical objects, should come from other sources: from continued experiences and increased familiarity with the scale and from comparison with the performance of groups of individuals who are either known to the test user or easily characterized for him.

The methods of equating two forms of a test all pre-suppose that the conversion of scores from one form to another involves simply an adjustment of units to account for differences in difficulty of the forms. Ideally this adjustment would be determined by administering both forms to all members of a group and observing the differences in performance on the forms—after first removing the effect of practice or fatigue on the form administered second. Variations on the approach, necessitated by practical considerations, include a) dividing a large group of individuals into two random halves, administering one form to each half and observing the differences in the statistics on the test form that each group took; and b) administering the same "equating" test to two groups, each of which has been tested with one of the major test forms. Here, too, the differences in performance on the two test forms are observed, but with adjustments made for any differences in the two groups by use of the equating test.

NORMING

An essential characteristic of the test standardization process is the presentation of reference data for appropriate norms groups. In some cases, as was just noted, the characteristics of the norms sample are built directly into the test scale itself. Tests which yield I.Q. scores fall into this category. In other cases an arbitrary scale is maintained, and the test is accompanied by norms appropriate for the principal uses for which the test is intended.

Tests designed for general surveys of ability, aptitude, and achievement are frequently related meaningfully to "national" norms collected by grade or age. But for these tests and for other tests in specific areas other types of norms may be desirable—norms differentiated by sex, geography, type of curriculum, rural-urban-suburban, public-private-parochial, etc. It is then the task of the test user to choose the appropriate norms from those that are available and to apply them in evaluating the performance of the individuals he has tested.

The norms that are developed for a test may be as elaborate as the test demands or the test maker can afford. The process of norms development, however, is fundamentally the same, regardless of the number and type of norms that are constructed. The test maker defines the characteristics of the population from which he decides to sample, and proceeds to select a sample from this population which will be as nearly representative of the population as possible. Ideally this would mean selecting all individuals at random from the population; however, for practical reasons other procedures are ordinarily employed. Typically the schools in the nation are grouped into categories or strata, homogeneous by type, size, socio-economic level, or location, or by combinations of these characteristics; and entire schools are chosen at random from these strata. Sometimes multistage cluster sampling techniques are employed, involving several steps: random sampling of communities, random sampling of schools within those communities, random sampling of classes within those schools, and occasionally random sampling of students from those classes. When possible, the methods of stratified sampling and cluster sampling are combined to yield norms samples that are not only economical as to size, but also possess the desired levels of reliability and representativeness.

When any particular student is to be evaluated, the best comparison group is a group of students with whom he is in competition or with whom he aspires to compete (or a group as similar to one of these as possible). Thus, if a test is to be used for educational guidance, an appropriate norms group consists of those students with whom the student will be in competition if he undertakes a particular course of study. If the test is to be used for selection at a given college, the appropriate norms group is the group of candidates with whom the student is competing for a place. If a test is to be used for evaluation of achievement in a specific school course, then the ideal group is the rest of the class.

Increasingly the major test publishers are coming around to the point of view that the most valuable norms group may be one that is locally assembled by the test user himself. This does not relieve the publisher of the responsibility of providing more general norms; however, his norms may be considered only supplementary to the data collected on the local group.

OTHER TEST CHARACTERISTICS

Finally, the producer of a standardized test will make available to the test user for his information in selecting and using the instrument a set of data describing the various characteristics of the test: the use to which it is intended or for which it is recommended; an outline of the test content; the item difficulties and discrimination indices; data on the speededness of the test; its reliability and standard error of measurement; its predictive validity for various pertinent criteria; the pattern of growth if the test is designed for use at more than one level; relationships with other tests or forms; and, finally, an evaluation of the strengths and weaknesses of the test for various purposes to which it might be put. The makers of standardized tests are committed to the methods of scientific inquiry; they must also assume the obligations of science—making the results of their inquiry available to the public.

The procedures involved in the process of standardizing tests as they are discussed here are not by any means intended to constitute a set of minimum criteria for a test to be considered "standardized." Some highly useful tests follow the procedures of standardization in somewhat different ways from those that are outlined here. However, aside from the details of procedure, it is certainly reasonable to say that taken together the characteristic features of a standardized test are what make it a scientific measuring instrument, capable of precision and predictive of future achievement. For both human and practical reasons the standardized test is a necessary outcome of the philosophy of a modern democratic society in which large masses of individuals competing for educational awards, or simply seeking better self-understanding, assemble for an objective, unbiased evaluation of their abilities. No other method that we know of today can provide measurement for the tremendous number of individuals who demand objective consideration of their talents. Certainly no other method that we know of today can accomplish this measurement as equitably as can the standardized test.

2 Traditional and Contemporary Views of Psychological Testing

JULIAN WOHL

The following discussion provides a useful perspective on the variety of situations where tests are used and the reasons for using them. The two viewpoints discussed by Dr. Wohl parallel the testing philosophies Cronbach (1960, pp. 24–28) describes with the terms "psychometric" and "impressionistic." While this author clearly favors what he calls the "contemporary approach," the reader should recognize that strong arguments can be advanced for both viewpoints. How do the traditional and contemporary views of testing differ with respect to (1) the function of the tester, (2) the importance and influence of the testing situation, (3) the role of the examinee, and (4) the function and characteristics of the testing instrument? What shortcomings of the psychometric or traditional approach have led to the expansion of the contemporary or impressionistic approach? What implications for the training of psychological examiners are implicit in the article?

This paper attempts to describe two approaches to the activity known conventionally as psychological testing. Much of what is considered here under the "contemporary view" will seem obviously related to and is derived from clinical psychology; to make this identification, however, would be a mistake. The "contemporary view" and the "traditional" or "psychometric view" describe not areas of work but methodological and conceptual approaches to testing. The Stanford-Binet test began life as a psychometric instrument, but no competent professional uses it only in this way. The worker who spends an hour or so administering one and emerges only with an I.Q. score is not simply "psychometrically oriented"; he is making poor use of the test since he neglects much information available from this testing.

Any area or problem in the field of testing can be approached from either point of view or can use a combination of both. The contemporary view is broader than the traditional; it is also in some ways less exact. What is needed is to extend the precision of the psychometric approach to the wider field of study of the contemporary one. The closest one can come to allocating these approaches to areas is to assign psychometrics to group testing, and the contemporary view to individual testing, regardless of the purpose of the testing.

Reprinted and abridged with permission of author and publisher (the Society for Projective Techniques, Inc.) from the *Journal of Projective Techniques & Personality Assessment*, 1963, Vol. 27, pp. 359–365.

TRADITIONAL OR PSYCHOMETRIC VIEW

THEORY OF THE TEST ▪ The traditional conception of psychological testing follows Thorndike's dictum that if something exists, it does so in some measureable amount. Implicitly using this approach testing psychologists would select or create specific continua as dimensions, such as "honesty," "neuroticism," or "intelligence," which any individual would "have" in some quantity. A good test would be one that was a perfect measure of this unitary characteristic and of no other characteristic. People could be compared with respect to where they stood or fell on these various dimensions; conventional statistical techniques could be applied to the data obtained from such measurement. With the absence of contrary information, and for the purpose of achieving statistical simplicity, assumptions can be made that the characteristic in question is continuous and that in the general population this characteristic is universally found distributed according to the normal probability curve. In this sense and within such a context it is proper to speak of psychometric testing. Here an effort is made to measure; an individual performs in a standardized situation, said to be the mirror of some unidimensional human characteristic. A numerical score is obtained, indicating on a continuum of the characteristic the position occupied by the performer. The validity of the test is measured by the size of a correlation coefficient determined by comparing scores on the test with those on some criterion which by definition is a truer measure of the characteristic than the test. This criterion may be contemporary in time (concurrent validity) or some future event (predictive validity).

THEORY OF THE TESTEE ▪ The conception of a person within the psychometric tradition is of a bundle of points on continua in a multidimensional psychological universe. The person is thought of as the total variance contributed by the measurement of these dimensions. The goal of measuring is to account for all of the sources of variance in a person's performance. This would theoretically be done by devising valid tests for all variables, achieving extremely high reliability in the measuring process, thus reducing to a negligible amount unaccounted for variance, and thereby explaining performance. That "negligible amount" would be error variance attributable only to inexactness of a specific measuring process.

THEORY OF THE TESTER ▪ The theoretical tester working under these assumptions is the least significant element in the testing process. He is required as a necessary evil until the time when machine administration, scoring, processing, and interpreting results are achieved. His function is to present materials together with a standard set of instructions, permit the testee to respond according to standardization requirements, score, interpret (a minimal activity in this approach), and report the results. The tester is an impersonal factor in a mechanized measuring process. With this conception the best kind of test would be one that requires no administrator, for he, as well as the testee, might contribute to unreliability of measurement through momentary fluctuations in attention, motivation, administration error, fatigue, and preoccupation with things other than the testing. To eliminate the tester is to reduce at the source a contributor to random error. Since he is subject to the "personal equation," he is also a source of constant error, providing another justification to eliminate him. An underlying assumption followed here is that one can have measurement or observation without creating a disturbance or effecting what is being observed or measured.

THEORY OF THE TEST SITUATION ■ The dominating characteristic of the test situation in the psychometric tradition is the emphasis on *objectivity*, with this term taken in a very special sense.[1] In this sense it refers to measuring and/or observing with an instrument that does not affect what it observes. The psychometric tradition sees the actors in this interaction as responding to each other ideally not at all, and if this ideal cannot be realized, it would see the encounter as contributing distortion or error to the measuring process. The interaction is supposed to be limited to the tester's efforts to establish rapport, which usually means an atmosphere conducive to the testee's performing at his best. The tester should give necessary instructions, give occasional approval for good responses, note any unusual or particularly revealing behavior on the part of the subject, or any that might reduce the validity of test results. The establishment of rapport is supposed to insure that the subject's motivation in the situation is the same as the examiner's: i.e., to achieve a valid record of the subject's performance. This is the only interaction that is presumed to go on between them for the purposes of the testing, and the only interaction that is required to be considered by the examiner in evaluating his results. In the testing interaction the examiner is interested only in what is now measurable, or in what he can see might affect the precision of measurement.

CONTEMPORARY OR IMPRESSIONISTIC APPROACH

The "contemporary approach" extends in several directions the conception of a test. In doing so it almost automatically carries criticisms of the psychometric view. The following is a brief summary of these criticisms:

1. It has an overly restricted view of where relevant information is to be found and of what it consists.

2. It has an unduly narrow conception of a test.

3. It eliminates sources of information about the testee.

4. Its statistical conception of personality is less useful in interpreting and applying test results than some nonstatistical conceptions.

5. It has paid insufficient attention to the tester and to the testing interaction.

---

[1] See Paper #4 by Scheier (later in this chapter) for a different approach to the concept of objectivity.

CONTEMPORARY THEORY OF THE TEST AND TESTEE ■ The narrow psychometric definition of a test has been broadened to conform with the facts of life in testing. The conception of what a test evaluates or measures and of how one knows if the test is doing its job have similarly changed. Also enlarged upon are the nature of test results and events subsequent to obtaining the data.

These changes have been influenced by the expansion of the application of tests to new situations, and by increased understanding and consequent modification of statistical conceptions in testing. The new definition of a test goes beyond Thorndike in recognizing that many of the situations in which tests are used are not suitable to the idea that a test measures some dimension, the result of which measuring is recorded with a number. It is possible to use any situation as a test situation as long as it involves a "systematic procedure." Observations of such situations may or may not provide numerical results. But whether results are expressed in words or figures they constitute information which requires processing in order to be useful. Contemporary testing considers the raw data (immediate test results or scores) as being much closer to the beginning of the testing process than does the traditional view. Great emphasis is placed upon the issue of interpreting results to answer the question for which the tests were given.

The validity concept has been expanded through its association with the question: "Validity for what purpose?" We recognize that different purposes and different decision problems may require different tests for reasons which have nothing to do with a correlation coefficient. A score on an intelligence test just below the borderline range, no matter how valid an estimate this test provides, is inadequate for the decision regarding commitment of a person to an institution for mental defectives. Before making such a decision one would want also to know about the person's social understanding and ability, his home situation, and relative strengths and weaknesses in areas most related to living outside of an institution. On the other hand a counselor might feel relatively free to discourage the family of such an individual from planning a professional career for him, although even here it would be important to consider the etiology of the defective behavior.

The validity question has been broadened also with the introduction of the concept of construct validity.[2] This is particularly important for tests which do not purport to measure a single dimension, where complexity of personality functioning is accepted by the test, where a simple criterion-to-test comparison is not feasible, and where the test is bound up with personality theory. In construct validity the theory underlying the test is equally at issue with the test itself. Such validity is determined not on an all-or-none basis or by a single correlation, but on the strength of repeated studies exploring the reaches of the concept.

THEORY OF THE TESTER AND TEST SITUATION ■ The conceptions of the test situation and of the tester show a greater departure from the psychometric tradi-

---

[2] See a later article by Cronbach and Meehl in the present volume (Paper #14) for an expanded discussion of construct validity.

tion than any yet mentioned. Developments in psychoanalytic ego-psychology, interpersonal theory, and research on testing techniques demonstrating the need to consider the context in which testing occurs—these have been three prominent forces making for this departure. The tester has emerged from his shadowy, impersonal position as administrator and recorder and is given full equality with the testee and the test as a determinant of the outcome of the testing situation. The test situation includes all of the subtle determinants of behavior in the situation from the classic "random error" variables of lighting, attention fluctuation, etc., to the purposes of the testing and the interaction of the two people concerned. It has become the tester's responsibility to evaluate these factors so as to account for his results as completely as is possible. The tester's position is similar to that of the therapist in psychotherapy in that he is a participant observer who has to be aware of the testee's behavior, his reactions to the tester, to the test, and to the total context of the testing; he must try to understand the testee's frame of reference in entering upon testing, and he should be able to use his own reactions to the testee and to the situation as aids in understanding the total process.

The test situation is designed to obtain information about an individual which will be useful in making decisions about that individual. Looking at the test situation from this point of view it becomes obvious that if a tester is intent only upon obtaining a score, he is omitting a large amount of potentially useful information. No test that exists today is so adequate for any purpose for which it might be used that a tester can afford to ignore any additional useful information he might have.

The goal of testing is to account for all sources of variance in a set of measurements. The greater number of relevant variables accounted for, the less variance is there attributable to error. The position of the contemporary tester would be that much of the "error term" is based upon our ignorance of the effects of certain factors simply because we have been unwilling or unable to evaluate their effects.

Interpersonal patterns in the testing situation affect test results. They can provide another source of information which can be used together with formal test results in increasing accuracy of description, interpretation, and decision making. To complicate the picture further, if the testee can react to the total situation and to its parts, so can the tester; where there is transference there can be counter-transference. Here again appears a host of possibilities for distortion. All of this is very complex, but one reason testing has not been as useful as it could be in many areas is its failure to consider enough of the relevant variables and the tendency of testers to classify much potentially useful data as error.

The tester instead of being insignificant becomes indispensable, for he must be the synthesizer and integrator of all of these sources of information, and must be able to allow for his own effect upon the situation.

I shall close with some practical implications of this discussion. Where one cannot use the psychometric approach alone, testing becomes an extremely expensive operation. The tester must be an expert in personality appraisal, dynamic psychology, and be able to order and integrate findings from all of the various sources of data in the testing situation. The testing itself and the interpretation are time-consuming and because of the expense are not to be undertaken lightly. In current practice one does not simply test because some referral source asks that tests be given. The approach is to evaluate the situation and decide not only which tests would be most useful, but first whether testing is required or advisable.

Another practical implication has to do with the communication of test results. With so much more information available on the basis of an individually administered intelligence test it is not fair to an untrained recipient of test results to give only a score. It is the responsibility of the person communicating test results to interpret them so that the recipient will be able to understand their meaning. Here again skill and understanding of tests are vital. With the testing movement so widespread today in education and in other fields, and with people who want tests used relatively ignorant of how they can be used, it becomes the responsibility of the tester to communicate his understanding, and not attempt to abrogate it by substituting a safe number for a more extensive, and daring, but more realistic, complete and helpful interpretive effort.

3   Measurement and the Teacher

ROBERT L. EBEL

After reading this article, the reader may say to himself, "That's only common sense," or "Everyone knows that." Unfortunately the ten principles summarized by Dr. Ebel are not always considered in developing tests. He has spelled out tacit assumptions which form the basis for much of what we do in evaluating instructional outcomes. The principles are well worth reviewing. A teacher might ask himself how his tests and evaluation philosophy stackup against Dr. Ebel's requirements. Some of the author's statements might be considered controversial. For example, can every important educational outcome or classroom experience be practically assessed? Is the acquisition of useful knowledge the most important outcome? Are the listed criteria for judging the quality of a test exhaustive? What is the relationship between test reliability, item discrimination, and item difficulty? Many of the points covered in this article will be treated in more detail in presentations later in this volume.

Reprinted and abridged with permission of the Association for Supervision and Curriculum Development and the author. Copyright 1962 by the Association for Supervision and Curriculum Development. From an article which appeared in *Educational Leadership*, 1962, Vol. 20, (October), pp. 20–24 (43).

The principles of measurement of educational achievement presented in this article are based on the experience and research of a great many people who have been working to improve classroom testing. The particular principles discussed here were selected on the basis of their relevance to the questions and problems which arise most often when tests of educational achievement are being considered, prepared and used. While some of the principles may seem open to question, we believe a case can be made in support of each one.

1. *The measurement of educational achievement is essential to effective education.* Learning is a natural, inevitable result of human living. Some learning would occur even if no special provision were made for it in schools, or no special effort were taken to facilitate it. Yet efficient learning of complex achievements, such as reading, understanding of science, or literary appreciation requires special motivation, guidance, and assistance. Efforts must be directed toward the attainment of specific goals. Students, teachers, and others involved in the process of education must know to what degree the goals have been achieved. The measurement of educational achievement can contribute to these activities.

It is occasionally suggested that schools could get along without tests, or indeed that they might even do a better job if testing were prohibited. It is seldom if ever suggested, though, that education can be carried on effectively by teachers and students who have no particular goals in view, or who do not care what or how much is being learned. If tests are outlawed, some other means of assessing educational achievement would have to be used in their place.

2. *An educational test is no more or less than a device for facilitating, extending, and refining a teacher's observations of student achievement.* In spite of the Biblical injunction most of us find ourselves quite often passing judgments on our fellow men. Is candidate A more deserving of our vote than candidate B? Is C a better physician than D? Is employee E entitled to a raise or promotion on his merits? Should student F be given a failing mark? Should student L be selected in preference to student M for the leading role in the class play?

Those charged with making such judgments often feel they must do so on the basis of quite inadequate evidence. The characteristics on which the decision should be based may not have been clearly defined. The performances of the various candidates may not have been observed extensively, or under comparable conditions. Instead of recorded data, the judge may have to trust his fallible memory, supplemented with hearsay evidence.

Somewhat similar problems are faced by teachers as they attempt to assess the achievements of their students. In an effort to solve these problems, tests have been developed. Oral and objective examinations make it easier for the teacher to observe student behavior under controlled conditions.

The price that must be paid for a test's advantages of efficiency and control in the observation of student achievements is some loss in the naturalness of the behavior involved. In tests which attempt to measure the student's typical behavior, especially those aspects of behavior which depend heavily on his interests, attitudes, values, or emotional reactions, the artificiality of the test situation may seriously distort the measurements obtained. But this problem is much less serious in tests intended to measure how much the student knows, and what he can do with his knowledge. What is gained in efficiency and precision of measurement usually far outweighs what may be lost due to artificiality of the situation in which the student's behavior is observed.

3. *Every important outcome of education can be measured.* In order for an outcome of education to be important, it must make a difference. The behavior of a person who has more of a particular outcome must be observably different from that of a person who has less. Perhaps one can imagine some result of education which is so deeply personal that it does *not* ever affect in any way what he says or does, or how he spends his time. But it is difficult to find any grounds for arguing that such a well-concealed achievement is important.

If the achievement does make a difference in what a person can do or does do, then it is measurable. For the most elementary type of measurement requires nothing more than the possibility of making a verifiable observation that person or object X has more of some defined characteristic than person or object Y.

To say that any important educational outcome is measurable is not to say that every important educational outcome can be measured by means of a paper and pencil test. But it is to reject the claim that some important educational outcomes are too complex or too intangible to be measured. Importance and measurability are logically inseparable.

4. *The most important educational achievement is command of useful knowledge.* If the importance of an educational outcome may be judged on the basis of what teachers and students spend most of their time doing, it is obvious that acquisition of a command of useful knowledge is a highly important outcome. Or if one asks how the other objectives are to be attained—objectives of self-realization, of human relationship, of economic efficiency, of civic responsibility —it is obvious again that command of useful knowledge is the principal means.

How effectively a person can think about a problem depends largely on how effectively he can command the knowledge that is relevant to the problem. Command of knowledge does not guarantee success, or happiness, or righteousness, but it is difficult to think of anything else a school can attempt to develop which is half as likely to lead to these objectives.

If we give students command of knowledge, if we develop their ability to think, we make them intellectually free and independent. This does not assure us that they will work hard to maintain the status quo, that they will adopt all of our beliefs and accept all of our values. Yet it can make them free men and women in the area in which freedom is most important. We should be wary of an educational program which seeks to change or control student behavior on any other basis than rational self-determination, the basis that command of knowledge provides.

5. *Written tests are well suited to measure the student's command of useful*

knowledge. All knowledge can be expressed in propositions. Propositions are statements that can be judged to be true or false. Scholars, scientists, research workers—all those concerned with adding to our store of knowledge spend most of their time formulating and verifying propositions.

Implicit in every true-false or multiple-choice test item is a proposition, or several propositions. Essay tests also require a student to demonstrate his command of knowledge.

Some elements of novelty are essential in any question intended to test a student's command of knowledge. He should not be allowed to respond successfully simply on the basis of rote learning or verbal association. He should not be asked a stereotyped question to which a pat answer probably has been committed to memory.

6. *The classroom teacher should prepare most of the tests used to measure educational achievement in the classroom.* Many published tests are available for classroom use in measuring educational aptitude or achievement in broad areas of knowledge. But there are very few which are specifically appropriate for measuring the achievement of the objectives of a particular unit of work or of a particular period of instruction. Publishers of textbooks sometimes supply booklets of test questions to accompany their tests. These can be useful, although all too often the test questions supplied are of inferior quality—hastily written, unreviewed, untested, and subject to correct response on the basis of rote learning as well as on the basis of understanding.

Even if good ready-made tests were generally available, a case could still be made for teacher-prepared tests, the chief reason being that the process of test development can help the teacher define his objectives. This process can result in tests that are more highly relevant than any external tests are likely to be. It can make the process of measuring educational achievement an integral part of the whole process of instruction, as it should be.

7. *To measure achievement effectively the classroom teacher must be* (a) *a master of the knowledge or skill to be tested and* (b) *a master of the practical arts of testing.* No courses in educational measurement, no books or articles on the improvement of classroom tests are likely to enable a poor teacher to make good tests. A teacher's command of the knowledge he is trying to teach, his understanding of common misconceptions regarding this content, his ability to invent novel questions and problems, and his ability to express these clearly and concisely—all these are crucial to his success in test construction. It is unfortunately true that some people who have certificates to teach lack one or more of these prerequisites to good teaching and good testing.

However, there are also some tricks of the trade of test construction. A course in educational measurement, or a book or article on classroom testing can teach these things. Such a course may also serve to shake a teacher's faith—constructively and wholesomely—in some of the popular misconceptions about the processes of testing educational achievement. Among these misconceptions are the belief that only essay tests are useful for measuring the development of a student's higher mental processes; that a test score should indicate what proportion a student does know of what he ought to know; that mistakes in scoring are the main source of error in test scores.

8. *The quality of a classroom test depends on* (a) *the relevance of the tasks included in it,* (b) *the representativeness of its sampling of all aspects of instruction, and* (c) *the reliability of the scores it yields.* If a test question presents a problem like those the student may expect to encounter in his later life outside the classroom, and if the course in which his achievement is being tested did in fact try to teach him how to deal with such problems, then the question is relevant. If the test questions involve in proportion to their importance all aspects of achievement the course undertakes to develop, it samples representatively. If the scores students receive on a test agree closely with those they would receive on an independent, equivalent test, then the test yields reliable scores.

Relevance, representativeness, and reliability are all matters of degree. Procedures and formulas for calculating estimates of test reliability are well developed, and are described in most books on educational measurement. Estimates of representativeness and relevance are more subjective, less quantitative. Yet this does not mean that relevance and representativeness are any less important than reliability. The more a test has of each the better. While it is possible to have an irrelevant and unrepresentative but highly reliable test, it is seldom necessary and never desirable to sacrifice any one of the three for the others.

Either essay or objective test forms can be used to present relevant tasks to the examinees. Ordinarily, the greater the novelty of a test question, that is, the smaller the probability that the student has encountered the same question before or been taught a pat answer to it, the greater its relevance. Because of the greater number of questions involved, it is sometimes easier to include a representative sample of tasks in an objective rather than in an essay test. For the same reason, and also because of greater uniformity in scoring, objective tests are likely to yield somewhat more reliable scores than essay tests.

9. *The more variable the scores from a test designed to have a certain maximum possible score, the higher the expected reliability of those scores.* Reliability is sometimes defined as the proportion of the total variability among the test scores which is not attributable to errors of measurement. The size of the errors of measurement depends on the nature of the test—the kind and the number of items in it. Hence, for a particular test any increase in the total variability of the scores is likely to increase the proportion which is not due to errors of measurement and hence to increase the reliability of the test.

Figure 1 shows some hypothetical score distributions for three tests. The essay test consists of 10 questions worth 10 points each, scored by a teacher who regards 75 as a passing score on such a test. The true-false test consists of 100 items, each of which is worth one point if correctly answered, with no subtraction for wrong answers. The multiple-choice test also includes 100 items, each of

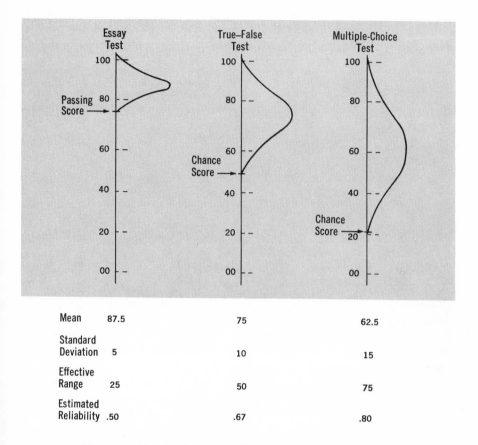

Mean	87.5	75	62.5

Mean	87.5	75	62.5
Standard Deviation	5	10	15
Effective Range	25	50	75
Estimated Reliability	.50	.67	.80

Figure 1. Hypothetical Score Distributions for Three Tests

which offers four alternative answer options. It too is scored only for the number of correct answers given, with no "correction for guessing."

Note in the data at the bottom of Figure 1 the differences among the tests in average score (mean), in variability (standard deviation), in effective range, and in estimated reliability. While these are hypothetical data derived from calculations based on certain assumptions, they are probably reasonably representative of the results most teachers achieve in using tests of these types.

It is possible to obtain scores whose reliability is above .90 using 100 multiple-choice items, but it is not easy to do, and classroom teachers seldom do it in the tests they construct. It is also possible to handle 100-point essay tests and 100-item true-false tests so that their reliability will equal that of a 100-item multiple-choice test. But again, it is not easy to do and classroom teachers seldom succeed in doing it.

10. *The reliability of a test can be increased by increasing the number of*

questions (or independent points to be scored) and by sharpening the power of individual questions to discriminate between students of high and low achievement. Figure 2 illustrates the increases of test reliability which can be expected

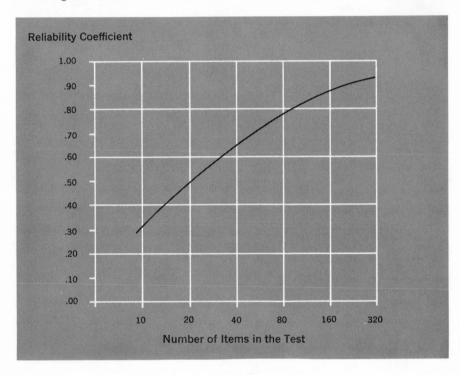

Figure 2. Relation of Test Reliability to Test Length

as a result of increasing the number of items (or independent points to be scored) in a test. Doubling the length of a 10-item test whose reliability coefficient is .33 increases the reliability to .50. Doubling again brings it up to .67 and so on. These estimates are based on the Spearman-Brown formula for predicting the reliability of a lengthened test. While the formula requires assumptions which may not be justified in all cases, its predictions are usually quite accurate.

Figure 3 shows how the maximum discriminating power of an item is related to its level of difficulty. These discrimination indices are simply differences between the proportions of correct response from good and poor students. Good students are those whose total test scores fall among the top 27 percent of the students tested. Poor students are those whose scores make up the bottom 27 percent. An item of 50-percent difficulty does not necessarily have (and usually will not have) an index of discrimination of 1.00. Its discriminating power may be zero, or even negative. But items of middle difficulty have higher ceilings on their discriminating power. What is more important, they not only can have, but

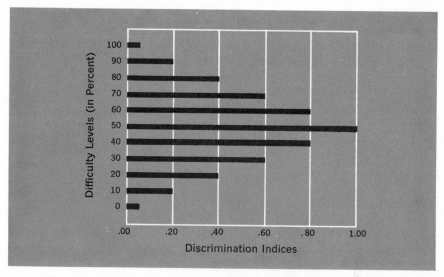

Figure 3.   Maximum Discrimination Attainable with Items at Different
Levels of Difficulty

usually do have greater discriminating power than very easy or very difficult
items. An item that no one answers correctly or that everyone answers correctly
cannot discriminate at all. Such an item adds nothing to the reliability of a test.

4   What Is an "Objective" Test?

IVAN H. SCHEIER

*One of the most frequently discussed characteristics of a test is "objectivity."
The term has traditionally referred to the methods and problems of scoring test
responses. It usually carried the connotation that an agreed upon key composed
of a standard set of acceptable responses would be applied in the same way to all
tests. In the following article Dr. Scheier expands on this idea and applies his
resulting schema to personality measurement. Why should both layman and
professional be concerned about objectivity? What advantages does objectivity
afford the test user? Although the criteria of objectivity are here discussed in
the context of personality assessment, how might they be applied to achievement
and intelligence tests?*

Reprinted and abridged, with permission of author and publisher, from *Psychological Reports*,
1958, Vol. 4, pp. 147–157.

A basic research strategy is that personality measurement must first be based on ratings of behavior in lifelike situations, then advanced through questionnaire measurement towards an ultimate goal of objective test measurement (Cattell, 1957a). The reason for starting with ratings is that the "face valid" content of behavior in the lifelike rating situation better enables us to develop suggestive hypotheses about the relationships and factors found. Questionnaire measurements achieve meaning with a directness almost equal to that of ratings, because they usually deal with lifelike material.

What, then, is an "objective" test; how is it related to the other two media of measurement; and why should it be the ultimate goal of personality measurement? According to Cattell (1957a), an objective test is "a test in which the subject's behavior is measured for inferring personality, without his being aware in what ways his behavior is likely to affect the interpretation" (p. 897). There is general agreement that objective tests deal with a person's behavior as contrasted with what he says about his behavior (in questionnaires), and that all observers will agree on the score to be assigned a given person's performance on an objective test (as contrasted with his rated performance).

A DEFINITION OF TEST OBJECTIVITY

INITIAL DEFINITION ■ Our basic definition holds that a test is objective only insofar as testing operations prevent distorting or obscuring processes from intervening between the tester and the events to be measured. More precisely, we mean that on an objective test a subject (S) cannot misrepresent himself on whatever behavior or characteristics are being measured by the test. Measurements of bodily dimensions such as height are objective because S cannot easily alter his score value from what it actually or naturally is. That is, testing operations and/or test-taking behavior are such that the relation between S and score is "determinate" in the sense that conscious conation or failure of memory cannot affect it.

TEST OBJECTIVITY AS DISTINGUISHED FROM TEST VALIDITY ■ Objectivity refers to a relation between S and score while validity is most intelligibly understood as based on or being an empirical relation between the test score and another measurement external to that test, e.g., another test score or performance, or predicted (vs. observed) performance on the test being validated.[1] Though the two concepts are easily confused, there is no necessary relation between them. For example, given proper instrumentation and scoring technique, a measurement of "average size of PGR (psychogalvanic response, a measure of skin resistance to weak external electric current) deflection to threat" will be objective, that is, S cannot misrepresent the natural size of his PGR. However, this measurement

[1] See Paper #11 in this volume for an overview of types of validity.

can still be *invalid* if uncorrelated with a validating criterion, e.g., "success as a 6th grade teacher." Similarly, a test can be valid though unobjective. As Meehl (1945) notes, a self-rating may have interesting correlations with other measures (including validity in our sense) even though it is not an accurate indicator of the characteristic on which *S* is rating himself. For example, if in attempting to measure frequency of crying we simply ask *S* how frequently he cries, the measurement is likely to be less than perfectly objective, for *S*'s answer may reflect poor memory and deliberate faking as well as his actual frequency of crying. However, the score of this unobjective measurement can still be valid, i.e., highly correlated with the "teaching success" criterion, if it happens that tendency to forget or lie about crying is related to teaching success.

ADVANTAGES OF TEST OBJECTIVITY ▪ Though the two are not necessarily related, test objectivity may often increase the probability of test validity, particularly as there is more *a priori* certainty that a given behavior is actually related to the validating criterion. The problem then becomes one of developing test operations to objectively measure relevant behavior so we can be certain that the test score reflects only this, and not other behaviors or characteristics which we have no reason to believe are related to the criterion. To the extent that a test is not objective, we cannot know exactly what is contributing to the test score; hence any relation of this test to the validating criterion will be more or less a lucky coincidence, rather than the result of guidance by enlightened hypothesis.

Test objectivity also adds precision to interpretations of whatever relationships do emerge. Thus, interpretation is more rigorous if, to take an hypothetical example, we know that what correlates with teaching success is actually a tendency to cry frequently, not this plus other influences (such as a tendency to lie), the type and degree of which cannot be certainly known. A third advantage to be expected from objective measurement is a greater stability of data through differences in motivating conditions incidental to the measurement itself. Thus, if a measurement *can* be faked, i.e., is not objective, it probably *will* be faked by some *S*'s under certain conditions, for example when the test is being used for job selection. Relationships (including validity coefficients) obtained under these conditions will differ from those obtained under conditions when *S* is less disposed to fake, e.g., when the test is being used for research purposes only, with all records confidential, etc. The above are the major reasons why personality measurement (which starts with ratings and questionnaires) should aim ultimately at objective measurement.

We have stated a working definition of objectivity and compared it with the concept of validity. Let us now compare objective tests as a medium of measurement with the rating and questionnaire media. Our method will be to contrast the media on each of several attributes of measurement in general. These criteria deal primarily with testing and scoring operations and test-taking behavior, and only indirectly with statistical operations and values (as in the definition of reliability and validity). As noted before, the criteria will be helpful in understanding possible ways measurements can differ from one another, even if one disagrees with the definitions offered by any one medium of measurement, or questions the overall value of the threefold classification which we aim to clarify.

CRITERIA FOR DISTINGUISHING BETWEEN THE THREE MEDIA OF OBSERVATION

THE NATURE OF THE TASK—SUSCEPTIBILITY TO MISREPRESENTATION ▪ *Deliberate misrepresentation or faking.* The first criterion applicable to the distinction between rating, questionnaire, and objective test media is: does the test situation allow S deliberately to change his response from what it would ordinarily or naturally be, i.e., does it allow him to fake? We assume here, as a minimum in all tests, that the test instructions are clear, that S is not confused as regards the actual operations the tester wishes him to perform on the test. However, S may or may not have insight into what the tester wants to find out from his behavior in the test situation. Insightfully directed faking may be more "effective" from S's point of view, but—and this is the important point for psychometricians—deliberately unnatural behavior, with or without insight, lowers measurement accuracy, confuses interpretation, and may even lower validity.

Unintentional distortion—failure to remember. Should objective test operations prevent unintentional ("unconscious") as well as deliberate misrepresentation? As noted before, test objectivity is the absence of any distorting or obscuring processes between the observer and the events we intend to observe. The previously discussed stipulation that objective test operations must prohibit deliberate faking is one application of this general rule. A second application is that objective test operations must also prohibit or minimize the possibility of "unintentional" forgetting of the event which we wish to observe whenever the measurement makes some person or persons responsible for recording that event. It is assumed that there is such a thing as "unintentional," dynamically unrelated forgetting; that there is a recognizable, definable, and potentially measurable event being studied; and that this event is not the distorting process itself. In such cases, unintentional forgetting can stand between the observer and accurate representation of the event we wish to study; hence a test is more objective insofar as time relationships between observer and observed are such as to facilitate accurate recall of the event. Thus, if we aim to measure "rate of speaking when 15 years of age," the following three measurements, all other things being equal, would be progressively less objective: (a) recording of S's speech under various conditions at 15 years of age, (b) S's statement made at 17 years of age about his rate of speech when 15 years old, and (c) S's statement made at 50 years of age about his rate of speech at 15 years of age.

Misperceptive or projective processes. Both unintentional forgetting and deliberate faking lower test objectivity because they can be distorting or obscuring processes between the observer and the events we wish to observe. What about unintentionally distorting processes other than simple forgetting, the so-called projective or misperceptive tendencies? Must such processes be removed before a test can be termed "objective"? Obviously not. In the first place, the above distinction between event and (distorting) process of observation does not easily apply to some projective tests, for when dynamically actuated misperceptive processes are assigned the role of "process of observation," it is often impossible to determine empirically or even define intelligibly the event or entity they are distorting, e.g., the "true" person, or the "real" self. But even where this classification is possible, for example, in measurements of tendency to misperceive (process of observation) the size of a coin (event), very often the misperceptive *process* itself is the event we wish to measure. Removing it as a distorting process will not make the measurement objective; it will remove the object of measurement, e.g., there will remain only an objective test of "ability to perceive coin size accurately," a measure of more interest to optometrists than to psychologists. On the other hand, if tendency to misperceive is understood as the event to be measured, objectivity lies mainly in S's inability to deliberately change his degree of misperception (over-or underestimation of coin size) from what it is naturally. Thus, projective tests may or may not be objective, but their objectivity obviously does not depend on the degree to which perceptual distortions are removed from the measurement.

INSIGHT INTO THE DIAGNOSTIC IMPORT OF THE TASK ▪ The question here is: does S know what we are trying to find out about him via the testing situation? Consider these two verbal items: (a) "Do you worry a lot?" and (b) "The atomic bomb has been overrated. After all, it's just another more powerful weapon." In both cases a "yes" response indicates a higher level of anxiety, but in (b) S is much less likely to "know what you're after."

In the writer's view "hidden meaning" is a necessary ingredient of objective tests only insofar as it reduces the probability of faking. Presumably, if S fails to perceive the diagnostic significance of a task, or even that it has any diagnostic significance at all, he is *less likely* to fake, even though it is physically possible to do so. But, as noted before, hidden meaning is not enough by itself, for deliberately controlled faking is just as damaging when undertaken in accordance with a misapprehension as to the significance of a task, or an otherwise undirected desire to fool the psychologist. The best conclusion at present is that hidden meaning never does any harm in an objective test and usually has positive value in reducing the probability of faking attempts. It is therefore to be looked for as a characteristic of objective tests.

LIFELIKENESS OF THE TASK ▪ The criterion here is: how similar to real life is the situation in which S is being tested? Our conception of "lifelike" parallels May and Hartshorne's (1925) conception of "natural," the naturalness of a situation being judged by the frequency with which it is likely to occur in the individual's ordinary run of experience. Technically it is possible to rate S's behavior in narrow "laboratory" situations, but ratings are usually made in lifelike situations. This provides the richness of manifest content which makes rating measurements so useful in the initial identification of personality factors and in the generation of hypotheses concerning personality. Questionnaires usually ask S to comment on what he believes he does or would do in lifelike situations, but the testing situation itself is not lifelike, and there may be a difference between what S says he does and what he actually does. At the present time objective tests tend to involve relatively narrow laboratory-type situations. Primarily this is because an agreed-upon numerical scoring system, hidden meaning, and unfakeability are difficult to attain in a lifelike situation.

DEPENDENCE ON VERBAL MATERIAL

In questionnaires both question and response are in verbal terms. Rating assessments are usually expressed in terms of common verbal categories such as "cheerfulness," "cooperativeness," etc., with some indication of "how much" of each. The behavior which is rated may or may not be verbal. For example, there will be a substantial verbal component if S is rated in an interview situation or when participating in group discussions, but the verbal element will be relatively unimportant when posture or expressive movements are rated. The tests which best meet objective test criteria tend to be non-verbal, e.g., physiological and physical measurements, but a test can be objective even though employing verbal material. Thus, "PGR deflection to threat" remains an objective test even though the threat stimulus is verbal, since the PGR *response* to threat is not easily subject to deliberate control. Even when the response itself is verbal, we can *approach* objectivity of measurement, if, as noted before, the nature of the task is well hidden, e.g., with innocuous-appearing verbal questions or problems whose diagnostic significance is well hidden. In this approximate sense it is possible to have a verbal objective test with verbal test material and/or verbally mediated responses.

SCORING

AGREEMENT AMONG OBSERVERS ▪ In both questionnaires and objective tests all observers will agree on the score to be assigned S, once the test rationale has been formulated and a scoring key or system has been agreed upon. But raters are notoriously prone to disagree on their ratings of a given person in a given situation. In other words, inter-observer reliability will be perfect in questionnaires and objective tests (within limits of clerical scoring errors), while disagreement among observers will produce less than perfect inter-observer reliabilities in rating measurements.

THE IMPORTANCE OF THE OBSERVER ▪ An observer is always *present* in any type of measurement, if only to apply a scoring key to S's test results and record them. The question here is: when and how is the observer important, in the sense that the score obtained depends on who the observer is? Thus, the rating observer is important, as just noted, insofar as different observers disagree in their evaluations of a given person's behavior.

An observer can be important in another sense, as an *interpreter* of S's actual behavior. In ratings the score is not what S actually does; it is an *interpretation* of what he does by an observer who may not want or be able to see everything. Thus he functions as a distortion between the actual event and accurate recording of the event. Clearly this is a defect in ratings over and above disagreement among observers, for even insofar as raters agree, it may be only on a systematically biased interpretation common to an entire group of raters. Thus a certain school of clinicians may tend to agree in imputing to S characteristics which he does not actually possess, at least in the alleged degree.

Only in objective tests is the observer unimportant as an interpreter of S's behavior. Here the test yields the actual behavior or characteristics in which we are interested. S's score *is* this behavior, e.g., his PGR response or his bodily dimensions, which the observer has only to record. Obviously the above distinction does not apply to all types of interpretation. The psychometrician will always interpret S's response in trying to understand its relation to other aspects of S's personality or even in deciding the method of scoring or scoring key. *The point here is that in objective tests, as contrasted with ratings and questionnaires, there is no interpretation of the degree to which the behavior or event in which we are interested actually occurred.*

PRESENCE OF A NUMBER SCORE ▪ In questionnaires and objective tests a numerical quantity is assigned as score. Evaluation of S's verbal responses by another person who does not use a scoring key is referred to more properly as a rating of verbal behavior. Rating evaluations almost always involve *some* recognition of amount, ranging from "presence or absence" and "more or less" to actual numerical values. However, numerical values are not a *necessary* characteristic of ratings and do not imply agreement among observers on the value to be assigned, as is the case in questionnaires and objective tests.

SUMMARIZING DEFINITIONS OF THE THREE MODES OF MEASUREMENT

Table 1 summarizes the relationships discussed between the three media of observation. These have been used to develop the definitions of each medium.

In a rating (Life-Record) S's behavior is observed and evaluated by others. The rated behavior may involve verbal or non-verbal components to any degree,

TABLE 1. *Summary of Relationships Among Rating, Questionnaire, and Objective Tests*

	Rating	Questionnaire	Objective Test
Content of variables directly helpful in understanding their nature and in forming hypotheses about personality characteristics, factors, and relationships	Good	Good	Not so good by themselves
Results subject to deliberate distortion by S	Yes	Yes	No
Conditions permit unintentional forgetting of event, if it is being studied via S's report on it	Maybe	Maybe	No
S has insight into diagnostic import of task	Maybe	Maybe	Not usually. Desirable that he does not
Behavior studied is lifelike, *in situ*	Usually	Usually S comments on this type of behavior for himself	Not usually but is possible
Dependence on verbal material	Maybe	Always	Maybe in stimulus. If in responses, can only approach objectivity
Observer is present as scorer	Always	Always	Always
Observers agree on score to be assigned (once scoring method or key is decided upon)	No	Yes	No
Observer (other than S) can misrepresent actual behavior, characteristic, or event studied	Yes	No	No
Observer (as S himself) can misrepresent his own actual or typical behavior	Yes	Yes	No
Score is a number	Not necessarily, but usually some indication of quantity	Yes	Yes

and is usually, but not necessarily a lifelike situation. Rating evaluations generally indicate the amount of a given verbally defined characteristic, but the score is not necessarily a number, and there is less than perfect agreement among observers on its value. S may or may not understand the diagnostic significance of the rating situation but is usually capable of behaving unnaturally in it. Distortion in ratings may arise both from faking by the observed and from bias in the observer. However, rating measurements have the sort of obvious or "face valid" content which facilitates hypothesizing concerning the factors or mechanisms involved.

Like ratings, *questionnaire measurements* (*Self-Rating*) tend to have useful "face valid" content. *S* rates himself on what he does or would do in various situations (usually of a lifelike nature). Both questions and responses are verbally mediated. *S* can deliberately control his responses in order to fake and may misperceive or unintentionally forget the events on which he is asked to report. He may or may not be able to perceive the diagnostic significance of the questions asked. Once the scoring rationale has been decided upon, all observers will agree on the numerical score to be assigned.

The concept of test *objectivity* refers to *a relation between S and the resultant score* as determined by the nature of testing operations and test-taking behavior. The concept of test *validity* refers to *a relation between one set of scores and another* (*criterion*) *set*, determined empirically and evaluated statistically. *Basically, the objective test aims at the elimination of distorting or obscuring processes between the final observer and the events he intends to study.* This requires minimization of the possibility of deliberate faking, and one way of doing this is to hide the diagnostic significance of the task from *S*. Objectivity further requires minimization of the possible unintentional forgetting of events which are the goal of measurement via *S*'s report on them. Dynamically actuated misperceptive processes are almost always intelligibly considered not as a hindrance to objectivity, but as themselves the goal of a measurement which on other grounds may or may not be objective.

Objective tests require agreement among observers on the numerical value assigned as score (an agreement which naturally would be expected in accurate perception of a real event). Physiological, physical, and other primarily nonverbal measurements best meet the criteria for objective tests, but such tests can involve verbal stimuli. Even when verbally mediated responses are used, a test can approach objectivity if the diagnostic significance of the task is well hidden. At present, objective test situations are usually not lifelike, but there is no reason why they might not eventually be so.

Most tests presently termed "objective" actually only approach the ideal as we have defined it to a degree which can be assessed by application of the criteria discussed in this paper. For example, most projective tests can be deliberately faked, and even ability tests permit malingering. Almost any test involving verbal responses is not fully objective since *S* can control these responses and *choose* to give an answer which is not true or natural for him. Though rare at present, perfectly objective tests may be expected to appear in greater numbers as personality measurement progresses.

III

DEFINING AND

ESTIMATING RELIABILITY

The term "reliability" as used in everyday language conveys a meaning which is somewhat parallel to the meaning ascribed to it by the measurement expert. An example may serve to demonstrate the similarities and differences in meaning. Suppose we said that a worker was reliable. What would this convey? It might be supposed that the worker reports at the same time every day, appears in the same condition, and performs consistently. This similarity of behavior from time to time would be comparable to one of the tester's approaches to reliability. Note, however, that for the tester no judgment of the appropriateness of the behavior is implied. Suppose the worker could be trusted to report to work one hour late, with the same amount of alcohol already consumed, and to fall asleep next to his machine. Following the measurement expert's approach, this man is reliable. His behavior is consistent from time to time, although it probably would not be deemed desirable. Similarly, a test can yield very dependable information but be inappropriate for the particular purpose for which we may be considering it.

For decades the concept of reliability has remained of crucial importance for describing the outcomes of the measuring process. The test manuals containing reliability information as well as the theoretical and research articles devoted to reliability constitute a significant proportion of yearly scholarly production and publication in the field of educational and psychological measurement. The first article in this chapter is a summary of recent authoritative thinking as to the reliability information which should be included in test manuals. It is the product of a joint committee representing the following three associations: American Psychological Association, American Educational Research Association, and National Council on Measurement in Education. The reading of these *Standards* will yield an overview of the chapter, especially with regard to the kinds of variation in test scores that may be considered "error."

The publication dates of the next two articles (1912–1913, 1928) should help "validate" the statement made at the beginning of the previous paragraph, i.e., "For decades ...". In one of these papers the late Dr. Percival Symonds presents a diagrammatic assist to the understanding of reliability and validity before discussing what factors affect the various sources of error. Not only should the producer of an instrument consider how to control its reliability, but also the consumer should interpret reliability information in view of the various factors which influence the reliability.

The other early paper represents a merger of three classic studies by Doctors Daniel Starch and the late Edward Elliott, and vividly illustrates the possible unreliability of scoring essay exams. Inconsistency of scoring is placed in a reliability context both by the Joint Committee in their *Standards* (the first paper in this chapter), and by Dr. Raymond Cattell[1] (the fourth paper in the chapter). Cattell's article again serves to summarize types of reliability and to present an alternative set of terms and relationships. It may be noted that another source of error not commonly considered in discussions of reliability—error due to different administrators—is discussed both by Cattell and by the Joint Committee.

In the above articles the emphasis has been more upon test selection and description than upon the interpretation of scores for an individual. But suppose one finds himself concerned with the accuracy of a score for a particular individual. While one knows that the greater the reliability for the group, the smaller the error to expect for him, how small an error would be expected if, for example, the correlation between alternate forms given a week apart were .83? One would want an estimate of the number of points the score is apt to be in error. This is the problem addressed by both Dr. Jerome Doppelt and Dr. Frederic Lord in the remaining two articles of the chapter.

Doppelt defines the standard error of measurement and discusses its interpretation. Lord next presents a quick and simple approach to estimating the amount of error expected in a single score. The concept of standard error of measurement is of prime importance when interpreting the results of either informal or standardized instruments, and studying these two articles should enable the reader to make more correct and more frequent use of this concept.

---

[1] Admittedly, the use of the term "reliability" in this sentence is inconsistent with Cattell's definition.

5 Standards for Reporting and Evaluating Test Reliability

NATIONAL COMMITTEE ON TEST STANDARDS

In 1954 the American Psychological Association published Technical Recommendations for Psychological Tests and Diagnostic Techniques. *The guidelines included in this document were to serve as criteria against which a test publisher would compare his product before it was to be made commercially available. Minimum and more desirable amounts and types of information to be included in the test manual were specified. The focus was on potential users of educational and psychological tests, and was to serve as a kind of "watchdog" for the psychometric fraternity. As with most suggested guidelines, the* Recommendations *have met with varying degrees of acceptance. Their influence can, however, only be evaluated as having been positive.*

The following excerpt from the newly revised Recommendations, *now called* Standards, *describes the essential reliability data required in any test manual for the user to make intelligent evaluations and applications of the instrument. It also represents an integration of the requirements specified by the American Educational Research Association and the National Council on Measurement in Education in their 1955 publication,* Technical Recommendations for Achievement Tests.

The following questions should guide the student's reading. What reliability information should a teacher be most interested in with respect to his classroom examinations? What specific influences would have the greatest impact on the score reliability of an individually administered intelligence test rather than a group administered intelligence test? If you were developing a test to predict success in medical school, what specific recommendations would you need to make about reliability? What are some possible ways by which a tester could control the reliability of the tests he administers? A factory uses a "work-sample" (actual job tryout with a drill press) as a predictor of success on the job. What are some possible sources of measurement error and how could you determine the magnitude of their influence? In a mental health clinic, a psychologist uses a "projective test" (e.g., Thematic Apperception Test) to make a diagnosis of the presence or absence of psychopathology. In what way would reliability be a significant factor in this situation?

Reliability refers to the accuracy (consistency and stability) of measurement by a test. Any direct measurement of such consistency obviously calls for a com-

Reprinted and abridged from *Standards for Educational and Psychological Tests and Manuals,* 1966, pp. 25–32. Copyright 1966 by the American Psychological Association and reproduced by permission.

parison between at least two measurements. (Whereas "accuracy" is a general expression, the terms "consistency" and "stability" are needed to describe respectively form-associated and time-associated reliability). The two measurements may be obtained by retesting an individual with the identical test. Aside from practical limitations, retesting is not a theoretically desirable method of determining a reliability coefficient if—as usual—the items that constitute the test are only one of many sets (actual or hypothetical) that might equally well have been used to measure the particular ability or trait. Thus there is ordinarily no reason to suppose that one set of 50 vocabulary items, for example, is especially superior (or inferior) to another comparable or equivalent set of 50. In this case it appears desirable to determine not only the degree of response-variation by the subject from one occasion to the next (as is accomplished by the retest method), but also the extent of sampling error involved in selecting a given set of 50 items. These two objectives are accomplished most commonly by one's correlating scores on the original set of 50 items with scores by the same subjects on another set of 50 items—an "alternate form" of the original 50. If the effect of content sampling alone is sought (without the effects of response-variability by the subject), or if it is not practical to undertake testing on two different occasions, a test of 100 items may be administered. Then the test may be divided into two sets of 50 odd-numbered items and 50 even-numbered items; the correlation between scores on the odd and the even sets is a "split-half" or "odd-even" correlation, from which a reliability (consistency) coefficient for the entire test of 100 items may be estimated by the Spearman-Brown formula.[1] Essentially the same type of estimated reliability coefficient may be obtained from item-analysis data through use of the Kuder-Richardson formulas.[2] It should be noted that despite the possible heterogeneity of content, the odd-even correlation between the sets of items may be quite high if the items are easy and if the test is administered with a short time limit.

It is clear that different methods of determining the reliability coefficient take account of different sources of error. Thus, from one testing to the other, the retest method is affected not only by response-variability of the subjects but also

---

[1] The general form of the Spearman-Brown formula employed to estimate reliability is usually expressed as follows:

$$r_{tt} = \frac{nr}{1 + (n-1)r}$$

where r_{tt} is the reliability of a test lengthened n-times and r represents the original reliability. If the test has been divided into comparable or equivalent halves, r would represent the correlation of these halves, and the formula could be rewritten as follows:

$$r_{tt} = \frac{2r}{1+r}.$$

[2] The most frequently used Kuder-Richardson formula is Number 21, and is usually expressed as follows:

$$KR_{21} = \left(\frac{K}{K-1}\right)\left(1 - \frac{\overline{X}(K - \overline{X})}{KS^2}\right)$$

where $K = \#$ of items in the test, scored as either right (1) or wrong (0), $\overline{X} =$ the mean, and $S^2 =$ the variance of test scores.

by differences in administration (most likely if different persons administer the test on the two occasions). Reliability coefficients based on the single administration of a test ignore response-variability and the particular administrative conditions: their effects on the score simply do not appear as errors of measurement. Hence "reliability coefficient" is a generic term referring to various types of evidence; each type of evidence suggests a different meaning. It is essential that the method used to derive any reliability coefficient should be clearly described.

As a generic term reliability refers to many types of evidence, each of which describes the agreement or consistency to be expected among similar observations. Each type of evidence takes into account certain kinds of errors or inconsistencies and not others. The operation of measurement may be viewed as a sample of behavior; in a typical aptitude or achievement test the person is observed on a particular date as he responds to a particular set of questions or stimuli, and his responses are recorded and scored by a particular tester or system. The occasion is a sample from the period of time within which the same general inquiry would be pertinent; some sampling error is involved in selecting any one date of observation. The items that constitute the test are only one of many sets (actual or hypothetical) that might have been used to measure the same ability or trait. The choices of a particular test apparatus, test administrator, observer, or scorer are also sampling operations. Each such act of sampling has some influence on the test score. It is valuable for the test user to know how much a particular score would be likely to change if any one of these conditions of measurement were altered.

There are various components that may contribute to inconsistency among observations: (a) response-variation by the subject, due to changes in physiological efficiency or in such psychological factors as motivation, effort, or mood— these may be especially important in inventories of personality; (b) variations in test-content or the test-situation; (In "situational tests" which include interacting persons as part of the situation this source of variation can be relatively large.) (c) variations in administration (either through variations in physical factors such as temperature, noise, or apparatus-functioning; or in psychological factors such as variation in the technique or skill of different test-administrators or raters); (d) variations in the process of observation. In addition to these sources of error, scoring error variance in test scores reflects variation in the process of scoring responses as well as mistakes in recording, transferring, or reading of scores.

The estimation of clearly labelled components of error variance is the most informative outcome of a reliability study, both for the test-developer wishing to improve the reliability of his instrument and for the user desiring to interpret test scores with maximum understanding.

Although estimation of clearly labelled components of error variance is the most informative outcome of a reliability study, this approach is not yet prominent in reports on tests. The more familiar reliability study obtains two measures and correlates them, or derives a correlation coefficient by applying one of several formulas to part- or item-scores within a test. Such a correlation is often interpreted as a ratio of "true variance" to "true variance plus error variance." Many different coefficients, each involving its own definition of "true" and "error" variance, may be derived from a multivariate reliability experiment with the presence of controls for such factors as those of content, time, and mode of administration. Hence any single correlation is subject to considerable misinterpretation unless the investigator makes clear just what sampling errors are considered to be "error" in the particular coefficient he reports. The correlation between two test forms presented on different days has a different significance from an internal-consistency coefficient, for example, because the latter allocates day-to-day fluctuations in a person's efficiency to the "true" rather than to the "error" portion of the score variance.

In the present set of *Standards* the terminology by which the 1954 *Technical Recommendations* classified coefficients into several types (e.g., coefficient of equivalence) has been discarded. Such a terminological system breaks down as more adequate statistical analyses are applied and methods are more adequately described. Hence it is recommended that test authors work out suitable phrases to convey the meaning of whatever coefficients they report; as an example, the expression "the consistency between measurements by different test-forms as determined by stability over a 7-day interval," although lengthy, will be reasonably free from ambiguity.

GENERAL PRINCIPLES

1. The test manual should report evidence of reliability that permits the reader to judge whether scores are sufficiently dependable for the recommended uses of the test. If any of the necessary evidence has not been collected, the absence of such information should be noted.

The test manual should furnish insofar as feasible a quantitative analysis of the total inconsistency of measurement into its major identifiable components; viz., fluctuations or inconsistency in responses of the subject; inconsistency or heterogeneity within the sample of test content (such as the stimulus items, questions, and situations); inconsistencies in administration of the test; inconsistency among scorers, raters, or units of apparatus; and mechanical errors of scoring.

With group tests of school achievement the principal sources of error to be evaluated usually include (a) inconsistency or heterogeneity within the sample of test content; (Although admittedly in an achievement test the content should be just as heterogeneous as the subject matter or the functions that are involved in successful use of knowledge.) (b) inconsistencies in test administration; and (c) inconsistency in responses of the examinee over time, i.e., instability. The collection of data should be designed to permit evaluation of these three factors. In the case of projective tests fluctuation or inconsistency in the responses of the subject is usually a major source of random error to be evaluated; inconsistency among scorers or raters should also be evaluated.

For instruments that yield a profile having a low reliability of differences between scores, the manual should explicitly caution the user against casual interpretation of differences between scores, except as a source of tentative information requiring external verification.

2. In the test manual reports on reliability or error of measurement, procedures, and samples should be described sufficiently to permit a user to judge to what extent the evidence is applicable to the persons and problems with which he is concerned.

The maturity of the group, the variation in the group, and the attitude of the group toward the test should represent normal conditions of test use. For example, the reliability of a test to be used in selecting employees should be determined by testing applicants for positions rather than by testing college students or workers already employed.

The reliability of a school intelligence or achievement test should generally be estimated separately for each of many classes at each of several grade levels within each of several school systems. The mean and standard deviation for each sample should be reported in the test manual along with its reliability coefficients.

The reliability sample should be described in the test manual in terms of any selective factors related to the variable being measured. Demographic information such as distribution of the subjects with respect to age, sex, socio-economic level, intellectual level, employment status or history, and minority group membership should be given in the test manual.

If reliability coefficients are corrected for range, both the uncorrected and the corrected coefficients should be reported in the test manual, together with the standard deviation of the group actually tested and the standard deviation assumed for the corrected sample.

3. Reports of reliability studies should ordinarily be expressed in the test manual in terms of (a) variances for error components (or their square roots), or (b) standard errors of measurement, or (c) product-moment reliability coefficients.

Reliability is a necessary, but not a sufficient condition of validity. Reliability coefficients are pertinent to validity in the negative sense that unreliable scores cannot be valid. But reliable scores are by no means *ipso facto* valid, since validity depends on what interpretation is proposed. Reliability is of special importance in support of, but not in replacement of, the analysis and estimation of content validity.

COMPARABILITY OF FORMS

4. If two forms of a test are published, both forms being intended for possible use with the same subjects, the means and variances of the two forms should be

reported in the test manual along with the coefficient of correlation between the two sets of scores. If necessary evidence is not provided, the test manual should warn the reader against assuming comparability.

Whenever feasible, the test manual should present a summary of item statistics for each form, such as a frequency distribution of item difficulties and of indices of item discrimination.

Whenever the content of the items can be described meaningfully, it is advisable that a comparative analysis of the forms be presented in the test manual to show how similar they are.

In the instance of two forms of an achievement test, a chart or table should be presented in which not only frequency distributions of item statistics are furnished, but also a tabulation of frequency of items by categories of subject-matter content and of behavioral or instructional objectives. The two forms should represent different samples of items within each category. Artificially close similarity between forms which could be attained by matching item for item from form to form is not desirable because it hides real errors of measurement associated with content sampling, and in this case the inter-item correlation is a spuriously high estimate of the reliability.

Whenever two sets of performances on a test are correlated to determine comparability, the interval of time between the testings should be specified in the test manual.

INTERNAL CONSISTENCY

5. If the test manual suggests that a score is a measure of a generalized, homogeneous trait, evidence of internal consistency should be reported.

Internal consistency is important if items are viewed as a sample from a relatively homogeneous universe, as in a test of addition with integers, a list of general high-school vocabulary, or a test presumed to measure introversion. Nevertheless, measures of internal consistency should not be regarded as a substitute for other measures. When alternate forms are available, alternate-form reliabilities should be reported in preference to coefficients based on internal analysis.

Estimates of internal consistency should be determined by the split-half method or methods of the Kuder-Richardson type, if these can properly be used on the data under examination. Any other measure of internal consistency which the author wishes to report in addition should be carefully explained in the test manual.

Whenever reliability coefficients based upon internal analysis are reported, the test manual should present evidence that speed of work has a negligible influence on scores. If speed is a consequential factor, the internal correlation measures will be too high by an indeterminate amount; in such cases, assuming that alternate forms are not available, the reliability coefficient should be based upon separately timed half tests.

COMPARISONS OVER TIME

6. The test manual should indicate to what extent test scores have stability: that is, how nearly constant the scores are likely to be if a test is repeated after time has lapsed. The manual should also describe the effect of any such variation on the usefulness of the test. The time interval to be considered depends on the nature of the test and on what interpretation of the test scores is recommended.

For most purposes in psychology and education fluctuations of test scores within a few hours, days, or even months will interfere with measurement. The intention in using educational and psychological tests is to draw conclusions about relatively lasting characteristics of the person tested; hence, instability over trails or observations within a short period is regarded as a source of error variance which lowers reliability. For example, a college entrance test which is administered once is intended to measure a characteristic of a person that is related to his accomplishments over the first year of college. To the extent that the test scores fluctuate from day to day about the person's average level, they are in error. In some situations, however, where the test is intended as a measure of a changing characteristic, fluctuation over a period of weeks or months is not to be regarded as a defect in the measurement. A reading readiness test used only once for an initial tentative assignment of first-grade pupils among instructional groups is an example. Even for this test, however, stability over a month perhaps is required if scores are to serve their intended purpose. In experiments on the effects of drugs, on the other hand, it may be desirable to measure meaningful changes in two sets of test scores that represent a time lapse of only a few minutes.

It seems reasonable to require an assessment of stability for projective techniques and other devices for assessing personality dynamics even though it is recognized in some instances that a low retest stability over a substantial period merely reflects true trait fluctuation and hence indicates desired validity. However, clinical practice rarely presumes that the inferences from projective tests are to be applied only on the very day the test is given. Realistically, one must recognize that pragmatic decisions are being made from test data which are meaningful only in terms of at least days, and usually weeks or months of therapy and other procedures following the test administration. If a certain test result is empirically found to be highly unstable from day to day, this evidence casts doubt upon the utility of the test for most purposes even if that fluctuation might be explained by the hypothesis of trait inconstancy.

In any report in the test manual concerning the determination of the stability of scores by repeated testing, alternate forms of the test should have been used to minimize recall of specific answers, especially if the time-interval is not long enough to assure forgetting.

6 Factors Influencing Test Reliability

PERCIVAL M. SYMONDS

The individuals who construct instruments have to be concerned with how reliably the instruments measure. These individuals, such as teachers, psychologists, and researchers, are concerned not only with how accurately an instrument functions with a specific type of group, but how that accuracy may be improved. For example, should the items be of varying difficulties? Does objectivity of scoring allow for higher reliability? Would making the content more homogeneous be apt to increase the reliability? What influence would each of the following factors have on test reliability: (a) guessing, (b) training, (c) speed, (d) testwiseness, and (e) physical condition?

Many of the comments included in the following article may appear to some readers as naïve and unsophisticated. It must be remembered, however, that when this summary was prepared, little definitive research had been completed. The paper has nonetheless been included in this collection because the generalizations presented are as viable today as they were in 1928. For more recent, comprehensive, or technical considerations of reliability, the reader is referred to any one of the following: Jackson and Ferguson (1941), R. L. Thorndike (1951), Cronbach (1947 & 1951), Cronbach, Rajaratnam, and Gleser (1963), and Tryon (1957).

This paper proposes to list and discuss the factors which influence the reliability of tests. Were psychologists more conscious of what it is that makes a test reliable, fewer blunders would be made in devising tests which have low and unsatisfactory reliability. The development of the natural sciences depended on the development of exact measurements, and the development of psychology as a science likewise depends on the perfection of its measuring instruments. Much of the recent work in the development of tests, particularly in the measurement of personality, is practically worthless because the tests do not tell a consistent story.

Reliability in this paper is defined as the correlation between two comparable tests. If a test is split so that one-half contains items 1, 3, 5, 7, etc., and the other half items 2, 4, 6, 8, etc., these two halves constitute in themselves comparable tests. Any two comparable tests may be thought of as being the split halves of a test double the length of either. If the test is an objective test containing homogeneous material, corresponding items of comparable tests may have little resemblance to one another in form, significance, or difficulty.

To use Kelley's (1924) terminology with reference to Figure 4 let the two

Reprinted and abridged from an article by the late Professor Percival M. Symonds entitled "Factors Influencing Test Reliability," which appeared in the *Journal of Educational Psychology*, 1928, Vol. 19, pp. 73–87. Copyright 1928 by the American Psychological Association and reproduced by permission.

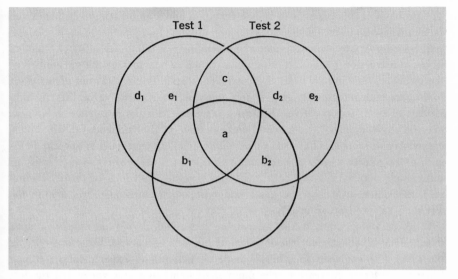

General Field
Figure 4.

upper circles represent the field measured by two comparable tests 1 and 2 and let the lower circle represent the field that the tests are intended to measure, such as intelligence, reading, algebra, or French.

Let a $=$ a factor common to test 1 and test 2 and to the field that the test intends to measure

$b_1 =$ a factor common to test 1 and the general field but not to test 2

$b_2 =$ a factor common to test 2 and the general field but not to test 1

c $=$ a factor common to test 1 and test 2, but not to the general field

$d_1 =$ a factor unique to test 1

$d_2 =$ a factor unique to test 2

$e_1 =$ a chance factor found in test 1

$e_2 =$ a chance factor found in test 2

Kelly defines the reliability of test 1 as

$$\frac{\sigma_a^2 + \sigma_c^2}{\sigma^2}.$$

The validity of test 1 is

$$\frac{\sigma_a^2 + \sigma_{b1}^2}{\sigma^2}.$$

NOTE: The symbol σ^2 represents a measure of variability referred to as the "variance." When unaccompanied by a subscript it is interpreted as "total variance."

The problem of this paper is to isolate factors a and c and distinguish them from factors d and e.

It is customary to group the factors influencing test reliability into: (1) factors in the construction of the tests themselves; and (2) factors in the variability of the individuals taking the tests. For certain factors this is a clear cut distinction; for others both irregularity in test and construction and the variability in individuals seem to be operative. Factors concerned with the construction of tests may be divided into: (a) general factors such as the influence of directions, objectivity of scoring, character of printing; and (b) character of specific items such as the affective tinge of items or catch questions. Likewise the variability of individuals may be divided into: (c) the general conditions of the individual such as excitement or nervousness; and (d) specific methods of attack on the test such as speed or accuracy.

1. A very important factor influencing test reliability is the *number of test items*. That is, *the greater the number of the items in a test, the more reliable the test*. The evidence for this is both deductive and experimental. It can be argued that an increase in the number of items in a test (provided the test retains identity in comparability with the original test) increases the reliability. This increase in reliability has a mathematical relationship as given by the Spearman-Brown formula.

The reliability of tests would increase exactly as predicted by the Spearman-Brown formula if the longer tests were exactly comparable to the shorter tests. Since this is never actually true there is deviation from the Spearman-Brown prophecy in actual practice.

Any factor which apparently tends to make a test have a greater or smaller number of items or which is correlated with number of items is a factor in test reliability. Among these factors may be mentioned:

2. Other things being equal, *the narrower the range of difficulty of the items of a test the greater the reliability*. If an item is so hard that no one in the group answers it, that item may be omitted without changing the score of any individual taking the test. Consequently it has no influence upon the reliability of the test and really makes the test equivalent to a test having one item less. Likewise a test including items so easy that everyone in a group answers them correlates perfectly with the same test minus those easy items Hence those items add nothing to the value of the test. That item which has the greatest influence on the reliability of a test is one answered correctly by 50 per cent of the group taking the test.

3. *Evenness in scaling is a factor influencing the reliability of a test*. Other things being equal a test evenly scaled is more reliable than a test that has gaps in the scale of difficulty of its items. Bunching items together in difficulty has the same effect on the reliability of a test as lowering the number of items. For instance, if an extreme case is taken so that items are divided into two groups, the items in one group being passed by the majority of pupils in a class and the items

in the other group being failed by the majority of pupils in a class, the test is reduced to little better than a test of two items.

4. Other things being equal, *interdependent items tend to decrease the reliability of a test.* If the answer to one item is suggested in another item, or if the meaning of one item depends upon a previous item, these items act to lower the reliability. For the tendency becomes to answer neither item or both items and thereby produces an effect equivalent to reducing the number of items in a test. Asking several questions on one paragraph in a reading test comes under this head, for if a pupil fails to understand the paragraph he has difficulty with all the items on that paragraph.

5. *The more objective the scoring of a test the more reliable is the test.* One factor which may influence the variability of test scores is the uniqueness of the answers which are given credit. If a test is perfectly objective, i.e., if answers which are given credit are sharply defined in a key and only those answers are given credit, this factor influencing reliability is eliminated. But where judgment of the scorer enters in determining the acceptability or fitness of an answer, as in the verbal completion test, there is a factor causing test unreliability.

6. As a corollary to the last point *scoring inaccuracy is a factor in test reliability.* This factor is eliminated with accurate scoring. But errors in scoring give rise to a variation in scores which lowers the reliability of the test.

7. *Chance in getting the correct answer to an item is a factor in test reliability.* Some of the most objective forms of tests offer the most opportunity for a chance to influence the score. The true-false test is a type in which chance plays a maximum part in determining the score. In the single-answer test and in subjective tests chance plays a negligible part in test reliability because the ratio of the one correct answer to the multitude of possible answers is so small. In the case of multiple-response tests the influence of chance in determining the correctness of any item is $\frac{1}{n-1}$ where n is the number of alternatives provided. A skillful test maker can lower this ratio by including misleading associations among the various alternatives. There has been much speculation as to the influence of chance in lowering test reliability. It is especially important to know the relative influence of chance in lowering reliability as against objectivity in raising it. This has been considered by Ruch, whose results are illustrated in the following reliability data (Form A–Form B) for comparable tests of 100 items.

Type of Test	Coefficient of Reliability
Recall	.950
7-response multiple choice	.907
5-response multiple choice	.882
3-response multiple choice	.890
2-response multiple choice	.843
True-false	.837

These data enable one to estimate the loss in reliability which is due to chance. Any factor that causes chance to play a part in determining whether or not an item is to be answered is also a factor that influences test reliability.

8. Other things being equal, *the more homogeneous the material of a test the greater its reliability.* The reason for this may be seen by referring back to Figure 4. If the items of a test are heterogeneous in subject matter or if the factors b, d, and e are more numerous than factors a and c, by definition the reliability becomes less. If a test maker purposely includes items of diverse character in a test in order to sample different phases of the function being measured, he does so at the expense of reliability as the increased heterogeneity of the material only works to lower the reliability.

9. Among chance factors may be mentioned the commonness or uniqueness of the experiences in the test. Other things being equal *the more common the experiences called for in a test are to the members of the group taking the test the more reliable the test.* For this reason tests of things learned in school are more reliable than things learned outside of school. In general, tests of conduct or character will always be less reliable than tests of ability in which there is universal agreement as to rightness or correctness. Tests using material taken from the common environment are the most reliable. A good example of this is found in the Stanford Achievement Test. Even though the test in language usage contains more items than test 1 (reading of paragraphs), test 2 (arithmetic computation), and test 3 (arithmetic reasoning), it has a lower reliability coefficient than these other tests. Part of this may be due to the form, for since each item of the language usage test is a two-alternative item, chance may play a considerable part in the score. But part of the lower reliability may be due to the fact that pupils learn their language habits mainly at home which has its own standard of correctness. On the other hand, tests on subjects learned at school usually have a common standard of correctness.

10. Variations of this factor of commonness or uniqueness of material occur frequently. Other things being equal *the same test given late in the school year is more reliable than when given early in the year.* Given early in the year much of the material of the test will not have been formally covered in class. Whether or not a pupil answers many items in the Powers General Chemistry Test at the opening of the school year will depend on such factors as whether he has read chemistry outside of class, or whether he has had a chemistry experimental set at home, or whether his family discusses matters of intellectual interest at the table.

11. *Another factor similar to the last is the inclusion of extraneous or dead material in a test.* If a test contains material not discussed in class or not given in the textbook, that test is less reliable than a test having the same number of items all of which are relevant. Such a test may be considered as the equivalent of a shorter test with a smaller number of items, with chance determining the answers to the extraneous or dead material. For this reason standardized tests

in a subject are probably less reliable than comparable tests, equivalent in form and length but containing only material relevant to the course as given.

12. Other things being equal, *catch questions in a test lower the reliability of the test.* A test answered by the systematic recall or recognition of orderly facts or experience is more reliable than a test answered by sudden insight because of novelty. Questions which must be answered by sudden insight tend to lower the reliability of the test. Thorndike has noted the incidence of this factor. He says: "The equalization of environmental influence obtained by novelty in and of itself has one notable practical disadvantage. Special coaching for the test is likely to produce many great inequalities in favor of those who receive it." The most reliable tests are those in which special coaching has the least influence.

13. *Subtle factors* in a test item which tend to be misinterpreted or over- or underemphasized help to make the test in which the item is included unreliable. Such factors are:

(a) *The Emotional Tinge of Words in Items.* If words are included in an item which cause the item to be misinterpreted or which lend false clues or associations, that item is a factor of unreliability in the test.

(b) *Length of a Test Item.* The longer a test item the more chance there is that it will be misinterpreted or that certain factors in the item will be over- or underestimated. Items which require extensive reading tend to be less reliable than items which require little reading.

(c) *Choice of Words.* If strange or unusual words are used or if words are used with unusual or technical meanings, they tend to increase the unreliability of an item. Any item which contains trade secrets tends to be less reliable than an item in which all terms are used with their ordinary connotation.

(d) *Poor sentence structure.* Particularly an unusual order of words tends to lead to misinterpretation of an item and is a factor in unreliability.

(e) *Inadequate or faulty directions* in a test or the *failure to provide suitable illustrations* of the task tend to lead to test unreliability.

(f) *Any factor which makes one misinterpret the intention in a test item* tends to make that item and hence the whole test unreliable. Matters of printing, spacing, paragraphing, etc., are all potent in this connection. If a term or phrase is split so that it occupies two lines, or if variations in type are used so that certain parts of the test stand out and others are diminished, the test is liable to be misinterpreted and become unreliable.

The factors to be discussed next are those which have to do with the variability of the individuals being tested.

14. It has been shown that the *speed of taking a test* is a factor in the reliability of the test. Individuals may vary in the speed with which they take a test. At one time they may work more slowly than at another time. Part of this is due to the matter of getting adjusted to the taking of the test. One has to learn how to work the test as well as the requirements of the exercises themselves. Pupils will

differ in the speed with which they adjust themselves to the taking of a test. This is due partly to general mental agility and partly to experiences in taking tests. Practice and experience with tests, particularly with the mechanics of taking the test, helps to diminish the unreliability of tests. A fore-exercise to a test which pupils may experiment with before taking the test itself helps to stabilize this factor of speed. In this connection the *accuracy with which a test is timed* is an important factor in test reliability,

15. *Accuracy in taking a test* is an important factor influencing reliability. A pupil will vary at times in his accuracy on a test. This may be due to the set which he is given by the directions in the test. It is often due to the fact that before a pupil understands what the test requires he will proceed with less accuracy than later when he understands the nature of the test exercises. Part of this factor is due to the way in which we teach pupils to interpret test results. Our insistence on speed and the length of the test leads a pupil to believe that he is expected to cover as much ground as possible, regardless of the accuracy of his work.

16. *Incentive or effort.* Differences in incentive and effort tend to make tests unreliable. The appeal of a test is stronger with some pupils than with others; and is stronger with a pupil at one time than at another. It is commonly assumed that tests have a uniform and a maximum appeal, but this must be far from the case. When one comes to character or personality tests this factor is greatly magnified. Such tests assume that the pupil is being impelled by the same forces of interest and purpose. In the case of achievement tests a strong motive is thrown into the field, like a magnet, and as in magnetization we assume that all of the molecules align themselves in the direction of polarity, so we assume that the motive of the test is equally effective on all pupils taking the test. But in a character or personality test we cannot even assume a uniform motivation. Probably this is as potent as any other factor in causing the unreliability of personality tests.

17. An unknown but probably powerful factor in determining unreliability is the *obtrusion of competing ideas.* This perseveration of previous experience is a factor that must be reckoned with. Children bring to school perseverating experiences from the movies, family life, happenings on the street, playground, and locker room. If a pupil is steeped in the sentimentality of a movie, or worried because of friction at home, or afraid because of a bully who promised to get him after school, his mental mechanism is surely less able to stick to the manipulations required on a test than if his mind is freed from such extraneous factors. Pupils probably differ in their ability to concentrate. Pupils differ also in the number or intensity of outside distracting influences which they encounter. Any one pupil will be more dominated by the compelling idea on some occasions than on others.

18. Following closely on this last point is the matter of *distractions* during the test itself. Any incident that occurs in the schoolroom during the taking of a test influences to some degree the taking of the test. If a test is given while noisy pupils are having recess on the playground under the window or in the school

corridors, or if a test is given at the end of the hour when the pupil is momentarily expecting the bell for dismissal, the conditions are unfavorable for the best results. Distracting incidents in the schoolroom also ought to be avoided. Pupils should not be allowed to leave their seats during a test. No questions from pupils should be permitted after the test is started. Directions should be given concerning what to do if the test is finished ahead of time. Under no conditions should pupils be allowed to leave the examination room early if confusion is to be the result.

19. *Accidents occuring during the examination,* such as breaking a pencil, running out of ink, or defective test booklets influence the reliability of the test. So far as possible accidents should be foreseen, prevented if possible, quickly remedied at any event.

20. *Illness, worry, excitement* probably are minor factors in test reliability. The pupil who has sprained a wrist so that he cannot write with his writing hand is at an obvious disadvantage. Likewise if the pupil is working with a splitting headache or high fever the average results should not be expected. The human machine can submit to marked variations in physical efficiency, however, with no marked change in mental efficiency. In general this factor of general condition of the individual has been much overemphasized in considerations of test reliability. Most persons believe that excitement, worry, and variations in physical efficiency markedly influence test results. Many teachers would entirely discard test results as measures of achievement because they believe that pupils are unable to do themselves justice on an examination. This superstition probably may be traced to one's own experience in taking tests and the rationalization that would excuse a test result on the basis of excitement, worry, or nervousness.

On the other hand experimentation shows that the general condition of an individual is of relative unimportance in influencing the results of a test. A number of experiments have been conducted studying various phases of work and efficiency. The general conclusion is that mental work has a remarkable consistency even during or following a variety of distracting influences. Continuous mental work or fatigue has been found to have little effect on the subsequent efficiency. Loss of sleep, fasting, atmospheric effects all seem to produce no immediate effect on the capacity to do mental work. Concerning this Gates says, "Such facts bear witness to the remarkable stability of the mechanisms involved in well habituated mental activities. It is surprising that those functions, which may be so readily allowed to operate below maximum in the absence of incentives, remain unimpaired in efficiency, during and after such extreme deprivations and exertions. The facts attest, also, to the remarkably effective and facile adaptability of the human organism to unfavorable conditions imposed upon it." In general, therefore, distractions on general conditions of the individual are relatively unimportant as factors in test reliability.

21. Indeed, so little potency have those individual variations in causing unreliability that Woodyard has found that there is little lowering of reliability for intervals up to a year. In other words, *an interval between repetitions of compara-*

ble tests up to a year has little influence on the correlation between comparable tests.

22. *Cheating* may be a factor in the reliability of a test. Cheating tends to make an individual score higher (or lower) than he otherwise would score and hence tends to lower the correlation between a test and the true score of individuals on that test.

7   The Reliability of Grading Work in English, Mathematics, and History

DANIEL STARCH AND EDWARD C. ELLIOTT

In these classic works, first published more than fifty years ago, Professors Starch and Elliott point vividly to the subjectivity in essay test grading. These articles undoubtedly had the effect not only of urging caution in the use of essay items but of encouraging the use of the "new" more objective type of test items.

The reader may find the results of the present studies rather startling; the contrasts shown are probably as applicable to the grading done by today's teachers as when the study was done. One of the difficulties in constructing, using, and grading essay items and exams is not that they are inherently unreliable, but that examiners usually do not put forth enough effort to evaluate them properly. What is the effect of lack of reliability in grading a test paper upon a course grade, or upon the results of a psychological experiment? Should this subjectivity necessarily rule out the use of the essay item? How might a teacher or experimenter estimate the subjectivity of his own procedures?

The reliability of the school's estimate of the accomplishment and progress of pupils is of large practical importance. For, after all, the marks or grades attached to a pupil's work are the tangible measure of the result of his attainments, and constitute the chief basis for the determination of essential administrative problems of the school, such as transfer, promotion, retardation, elimination, and admission to higher institutions, to say nothing of the problem of the influence of these marks or grades upon the moral attitude of the pupil toward the school, education, and even life. The recent studies of grades have emphatically

Reprinted and abridged with permission of the first-named author from three articles by Dr. Starch and the late Professor Elliott. The articles, all of which appeared in *School Review*, were as follows: "Reliability of the Grading of High School Work in English," 1912, Vol. 20, pp. 442–457; "Reliability of Grading Work in Mathematics," 1913, Vol. 21, pp. 254–295; and "Reliability of Grading Work in History," 1913, Vol. 21, pp. 676–681.

directed our attention to the wide variation and the utter absence of standards in the assignment of values.

METHOD

In order to determine precisely the personal equation in evaluating the work of pupils it is necessary to eliminate all other causes of variation. The mere comparison of marks assigned by different teachers to their classes will not reveal this personal factor stripped of the other variable elements, such as difference in amount and kind of work covered by the class, emphasis upon different topics, differences in teaching ability, and differences in the pupils themselves. To discover the variability in judging the merits of an examination-answer paper it is necessary to have the same paper graded independently by different teachers.

Concretely, the problem of this investigation was to determine the range of variation and the reliability of the marks assigned by teachers to examination-answer papers. For this purpose two examination-answer papers written by two pupils at the end of the first year's work in English, together with the questions, were obtained from one of the largest high schools in Wisconsin. Also, a geometry paper and a history paper were similarly obtained. Plates of these answer papers were made, and several hundred copies were printed. In this manner the handwriting, the errors and changes made by the pupils, the neatness, and so forth were reproduced exactly as in the original papers. The questions asked in the examinations were as follows:

ENGLISH ■ 1. Give five rules for the use of the comma, two for the period, and illustrate each use by a sentence.

2. Give five requirements to be observed in the structure of a paragraph.

3. Write a brief business letter.

4. Define narration, coherence, unity; classify sentences rhetorically and grammatically. Illustrate or define.

5. Name all the masterpieces studied this year and name the author of each. (Answer: Irving's *Sketch Book*, Hawthorne's *Mosses from an Old Manse*, Shakespeare's *Merchant of Venice*, Whittier's *Tent on the Beach*, Scott's *Ivanhoe*.)

6–10. Write a three-paragraph essay, narrative, descriptive, or both combined.

GEOMETRY ■ Choose 8, including one selected from 4, 6, and 8.

1. Two triangles having the three sides of one equal, respectively, to the three sides of the other, etc. Prove.

2. Prove that every point in the bisector of an angle is equally distant from the sides of the angle.

3. An angle formed by two intersecting chords is measured by, etc. Prove.

4. If the middle points of two opposite sides of a quadrilateral be joined to the middle points of the diagonals, the joining lines form a parallelogram.

5. To construct a mean proportional to two given lines. Explain fully.

6. AM is a chord of a circle, xy is a diameter perpendicular to AN and intersecting AM at O. XO is 10 inches and ax is 20 inches . Find the diameter of the circle.

7. The ratio of the areas of two similar triangles is equal to, etc. Prove.

8. Find the area of a right triangle whose hypotenuse is 1 ft. 8 in and one of whose legs is 1 ft.

9. The sum of the interior angles of a triangle is equal to, etc. Prove.

10. If two circles are tangent, and two secants are drawn through the point of contact, the chords joining the intersections of the secants and the circumferences are parallel.

HISTORY ■ Write on any five of the seven questions.

1. Contrast the motives and methods of settlement of the French and English colonists in America.

2. (a) Point out all the possible points of difference between what the English and American idea of representative government was about 1775. (b) Give two concrete illustrations of how the above difference caused open friction.

3. (a) Explain clearly what the British plan of attack for 1777 was. (May be outlined). (b) Point out why the date, October 17, 1777, was such an important date in American history.

4. Describe the "Period of Confederation." (a) Name of instrument of government used. (b) Defects in plan as proved by experience.

5. (a) Trace the steps leading up to the Federal Convention. (b) What objections were given to the ratification of the constitution? (c) Why is the constitution considered such a "wonderful instrument of government"?

6. (a) Contrast the personal characteristics and political policies of Hamilton and Jefferson. (b) What was Washington's policy relative to foreign alliances and how has it been observed since that time?

7. Describe industrial conditions in the United States in 1800 as to: (a) various industries engaged in; (b) their relative importance and why. (c) Define the various kinds of tariff. (d) Why did the South object to the protective tariff?

For each of the subject areas a set of questions and a copy of the answer paper (2 copies for English) were sent to approximately 200 high schools in the Middle West with the request that the principal teacher of that subject grade the paper(s) according to the practices and standards of the school.

SPECIFIC RESULTS

For English, 152 out of the 200 papers were returned; 10 were discarded. For geometry, 140 out of 180 papers were returned; 12 had to be discarded. For history, 122 out of 200 papers were returned; 8 could not be used.

The comments and criticisms on returned papers indicated that they were evaluated with much care and discrimination.

A frequency distribution of grades assigned by the teachers is presented below. Four papers are designated as English A and B, Geometry, and History.

TABLE 1. *Grades Assigned to English, Geometry, and History Examination Papers Using Two Different Passing Grade Criteria*

Grade Assigned	English A Passing Grade		English B Passing Grade		Geometry Passing Grade		History Passing Grade	
	75	**70**	**75**	**70**	**75**	**70**	**75**	**70**
98–99			1					
93–97	16	8	1	3				
88–92	33	16	12	3	1	2	3	1
83–87	21	14	22	6	8	1	7	
78–82	15	9	28	14	11	3	12	
73–77	1	3	16	12	16	7	10	3
68–72	2		6	7	6	8	15	2
63–67	2	1	3	4	15	7	7	6
58–62	1		1	2	11	4	4	2
53–57					3	3	4	1
48–52			1		1	5	7	2
43–47					1	2	3	1
38–42					2			
33–37								1
28–32								
23–27						1		
18–22								1
N	91	51	91	51	75	43	72	20
Median	88	87	80	79	70	67	71	65
Range	37	32	48	36	49	64	49	70

ENGLISH ▪ In one column are given the values assigned by ninety-one teachers to English paper A in schools whose passing grade is 75. In the adjacent column are given the values assigned by fifty-one teachers to the same paper in schools whose passing grade is 70. The ranges were 37 and 32 points, respectively. It will be noted that there is a difference of only 1 point between the medians (reported to the nearest whole number) of the two groups, although there is a difference of 5 points between the passing grades. Also, for English paper B there is a difference of only 1 point between the medians. Paper B is considerably poorer; it is judged 8 points lower by the first and second group of teachers. The ranges were 48 and 36 points.

GEOMETRY ▪ The grades assigned to the geometry paper also are presented in Table 1. For the teachers in schools whose passing grade is 75, the median was 70 with a range of 49. For the teachers from schools whose passing grade is 70, the median grade was 67 and the range 64. The marks assigned by ten schools whose passing grade is 80 are 50, 50, 58, 70, 72, 73, 75, 80, 80, 83.

The geometry paper was used because of the current assumption that a mathematical paper can be graded with mathematical precision. Our investigation shows that the marks of this particular geometry paper vary even more widely than the marks of either English paper used in the former study.

Why the marks of this particular paper vary even more widely than those of the English papers is to be sought in the fact that this geometry paper allowed for two fairly distinct ways of evaluation. The form, make-up, and appearance of the paper were of decidedly poor quality. Some teachers entirely disregarded these elements while others imposed a heavy penalty upon the paper on their account. In many instances this was indicated by the comments on the papers. But even this difference in viewpoint alone does not explain the extremely high or extremely low marks. For example, one teacher gave the paper a mark of 50 and said that he had deducted 4 points for spelling. Another marked it 45 and stated that he had made no deduction for poor form. Still another one marked it 75 including a penalty for form, or 85 excluding a penalty for form.

HISTORY ■ Turning now to the history grades, we see the values assigned where the passing grade was 75 are shown in Table 1. The scores extended from 43 to 92, with a median of 71. Where the passing grade was 70, the scores extended from 18 to 88, with a median of 65. (The values assigned by the twenty schools whose passing grade was 80 are 70, 70, 83, 84, 80, 75, 71, 85, 62, 50, 53, 65, 80, 76, 75, 72, 55, 75, 78, 75. The median is 75. The four schools whose passing grade was 65 returned marks of 66, 40, 76, and 52.)

GENERAL RESULTS

1. The first and most startling fact brought out by this investigation is the tremendously wide range of variation. The dramatic impact of the data reported in Table 1 would have been enhanced if the grades had been grouped into intervals of size 1 instead of size 5. The range and distribution of the marks of papers in these subjects are almost identical. The extremes in each case extend over nearly the entire marking scale.

Teachers usually state when asked about differences in marking that the grades of the same paper assigned by different teachers might differ at the most by 10 points. It is almost shocking to a mind with more than ordinary exactness to find that the range of marks given by different teachers to the same paper may be as large as 35 or 40 points.

2. The variability or unreliability of marks is as great in one subject as in another. Contrary to current belief, grades in mathematics are as unreliable as grades in language or in history. The variability of marks is not a function of the subject but a function of the examiner and of the method of examination.

3. The immense variability of marks tends obviously to cast considerable discredit upon the fairness and accuracy of our present methods of evaluating the quality of work in school. No matter how much anyone may wish to minimize the utility of marks, they have, nevertheless, an indispensable administrative value from the school standpoint and a personal value from the pupil's standpoint.

8 Suggested Restructurings of the Concept of Reliability

RAYMOND B. CATTELL

It is believed by many psychometric theoreticians that traditional definitions of test reliability as applied to present-day instruments and testing situations are often misleading and may result in inconsistent and invalid evaluations. Professor Cattell is a member of this group. He feels that although the massive literature concerning reliability does not lack for mathematical and statistical sophistication, it does perhaps suffer from an absence of common sense, logic, and psychological perspective. The suggested reformulations of the reliability concept which follow are the result of Professor Cattell's concern with both the theoretical and practical aspects of this important test parameter.

Since the original article is somewhat technical, the editors have extensively edited the more complex sections; formulas have been omitted. The interested reader is urged to consult the original paper and its references.

What does the author mean by test consistency, and how does his conceptualization differ from the more traditional views? (The reader may wish to refer to the previous three articles in order to identify comparative descriptions.) What are the three major dimensions which influence test consistency or generalizability? What are the subtypes within reliability, and of what practical import are these? To what characteristic of a test does the term homogeneity refer? What is the assumption underlying the assessment of transferability? Are correlation coefficients sufficient to describe consistency? How can one develop an index of total test consistency? What arguments does Cattell present for the view that reliability and homogeneity are not the same thing?

In what is generally called reliability the innovations to be proposed in this paper cover first that involved by the introduction of the generic, supraordinate term—*test consistency*—to express the test's total consistency along all dimen-

Reprinted and abridged from Raymond B. Cattell, "Validity and Reliability: A Proposed More Basic Set of Concepts," *Journal of Educational Psychology*, 1964, Vol. 55, pp. 1–22. Copyright 1964 by the American Psychological Association and reproduced by permission of author and publisher.

sions. Within this we recognize the three distinct forms of consistency presented by *reliability, homogeneity* and *transferability.* (See Figure 5) Let us examine

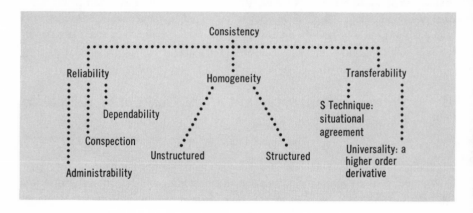

Figure 5.   Forms of Consistency

these separately leaving until later the derivation and definition of some single index corresponding to a test's total consistency.

There are three possible senses in which the consistency or generalizability of a test needs to be evaluated, viz:

1. Across occasions. The agreement of scores on the same test applied to the same people on different occasion conditions. This we shall call its reliability.

2. Across tests. The agreement on the same occasion and the same people of different subsets (or, commonly, single items) in the same test. This agreement among parts of a test (or battery) designed to measure some one thing we shall call its homogeneity.

3. Across people. The agreement in score meaning of the same test applied (on the same kind of occasion condition) to different sets of people we shall call its transferability (or hardiness, in the sense of a plant withstanding changes of climate).

Before proceeding to infer the proper operations for measuring these, we can say a word in a general way about their relations. In the first place we pay a heavy price, in terms of testing inefficiency, for mistaking homogeneity for reliability. Indeed, it is often indifferently designated reliability. A high reliability is almost always desirable, but homogeneity should be low or high depending on purpose and test structure. A good test, like a good engine, may perform its function best when its parts are differentiated. Whether water is better raised by a homogeneous sponge or a nonhomogeneous pump depends on the specific purpose. The aim of good test design is surely a properly functioning single instrument, and in many cases the optimum internal consistency for such an instrument is one which is made to fall below a certain homogeneity coefficient value.

A second lack in much current test evaluation practice, of which the above basic trinity reminds us, is that the transferability aspect of test consistency is entirely overlooked. Yet good transferability of a test, across age ranges convenient for use and across commonly encountered subcultural differences, is obviously a very important test property. Parenthetically, good transferability is also likely to be harmed by too high a test homogeneity.

The generic concept of *test consistency* from which the above three parameters derive can be verbally defined as the extent to which a test continues to measure the same psychological concept despite such changes as inevitably and normally occur in a test, its administration and the populations to which it is administered. These changes must be defined as a standard variance in types of people, test lengths and forms, and common conditions of administration and scoring. It will be noted that the word "normally" and the added clause define a distribution and standard deviation for each of the universe parameters—people, tests, and circumstances. In other words, published consistency values, to be helpful, must be known to apply to a defined, typical variability in populations of people, test elements, and occasion conditions—not to some artificial laboratory changes of condition or to inflated ranges of performance, etc., such as often determine published test parameters in handbooks.

Our estimate of the true reliability will be affected by a sampling of people and occasions; of the true homogeneity by sampling of items (or test elements) and people; and of the true transferability across populations by the sampling of people from various cultures and occasions.

OPERATIONAL MEASUREMENT OF THE CHIEF RELIABILITY COEFFICIENTS

Although it has been usual to think of consistency as the agreement of a test with itself, when two series of measures are taken, one should consider the possibility that a theoretically better (if practically more difficult) notion is the agreement of both testings with a third external standard. We might then ask, "How far does the test continue to measure the same psychological concept?" instead of the familiar "How far does it literally continue to agree with itself in score?" This integrates consistency more closely with validity.

Numerically we should, in any case, get somewhat different results from such a shift, because the degree to which a test agrees with itself is not necessarily exactly parallel to the extent to which it retains constancy of validity, though it is roughly parallel. Magnitude of change of composition and measured departure from perfect self-correlation are exactly parallel only if we include within the composition change the change on the contaminating, unwanted factors as well as the wanted, validating factor. But validity as such definitely refers only to the test's amount of the wanted factor and takes no account of the nature of the contamination. Consequently, it is a matter for choice in definition whether when we come to consistency, we want to ask about consistency not only in the amount of the wanted factor but also in the nature and amounts of the unwanted common and specific factors. Since the treatment here is only an introduction to the new concepts and has no space for these special issues, our first treatment of reliability handles the "third referent" approach to consistency in terms of the usual concept of self-agreement, i.e., of both wanted and unwanted factors remaining constant.

With this statement of principle the present section will now develop specifically the reliability aspect of consistency. At the outset let us be reminded that although psychologists commonly think of correlation coefficients as expressing validity and reliability, the full evaluation of consistency should actually include three indexes, respectively, to express the retention (across whatever change of testing is involved) of (a) rank order of subjects (or occasions) by correlation, (b) the mean score, and (c) the standard deviation of scores. Completely ignoring the last two, as is commonly done with reliability coefficients, is surely justifiable only in quite special circumstances.

Reliability is a subconcept within consistency. But it can itself be divided into several subtypes, and in practical psychological test evaluation it is extremely important to recognize their differences and to refer to them correctly by specific terms. The types derive from inclusion of varying combinations of conceivable sources of error variances. Actually, there is little point in employing ideationally conceivable sources of error when we cannot also operationally isolate them. On this basis of operational realism some six different reliability coefficients (and corresponding mean and standard deviation constancy measures) have been defined elsewhere (Cattell, 1957a) with a suggestion for specific titles. However, if one confines consideration to what are in factual experience the main sources of retest variability, one can perhaps advantageously cut down to even three: (a) that which estimates unreliability due to having different test administrators; (b) that evaluating unreliability due to different scorers; and (c) that expressing the unreliability due to the remaining unknown and uncontrollable conditions of the subjects' decision in the test and its situation. This is the unreliability remaining when the same administrator and same scorer handle the retesting.

From considering these three sources of error in relation to the true score variance, one issues with a total of five conceptual variances. Actually the three error terms could be combined in several ways, each defining a distinct and worthwhile type of reliability coefficient. However, probably only three of these— which can be called the *dependability* (immediate retest), *administrative* reliability (across administrators), and the *conspection* (across scorers) coefficients —are of major importance and justify sufficient description and definition here.

The dependability reliability coefficient $(r_{r(d)})$ has been defined as that obtained by an essentially immediate retest (using the same administrator and scorer). Obviously this is a correct statement of the meaning of the immediate test-retest coefficient only if there are no learning, no error in scoring, and no difference in administration.

The administrative reliability coefficient $(r_{r(a)})$ shows the extent of agreement between two different administrators (and like the conspection coefficient would best be averaged over several typical pairs of administrators).

The conspection reliability coefficient $(r_{r(c)})$ has been defined as the agreement usually found between two different scorers (from *con* and *spectare*, to observe together). If we choose to define it as that obtained when they are given the same batch of completed tests (from a single administrator, of course), then the observed variance nevertheless already contains experimental error. The value obtained for $r_{r(c)}$ would typically be unity for a fully conspective test, e.g., a multiple-choice, carefully stencil marked test, but much less for tests like the *Rorschach* and the *Thematic Apperception Test*.

A fourth coefficient which is frequently classed with the reliability coefficients, but does not actually belong there or, indeed, with the true test consistency coefficients at all is the stability coefficient. Measured simply as the correlation between a test and itself, readministered (same administrator and scorer) after an appreciable time interval, it may be called the uncorrected stability coefficient $(r_{s(r)})$.

Since the uncorrected stability coefficient reflects a mixture of trait and test qualities, it would be quite fallacious to conclude that a low stability value shows a test to be of poor consistency.

Consistent with the terminology and concepts here adopted, it is suggested that the notation for a reliability coefficient be r_r; for a homogeneity coefficient, r_h; and for a transferability coefficient, r_t. Subvarieties within these can be indicated by subscripts in parentheses as we have done for the main three (retest) reliability coefficients: $r_{r(d)}$, dependability; $r_{r(a)}$, administrative reliability; and $r_{r(c)}$, the scoring reliability or conspection coefficient among reliabilities.

OPERATIONAL MEASUREMENT OF HOMOGENEITY AND TRANSFERABILITY

The operational measurement of homogeneity (despite a fairly widespread semantic and even logical confusion with reliability) has been so competently treated by a succession of expert writers (Gulliksen, 1950a; Kuder & Richardson, 1937; Loevinger, 1948) culminating in the generalized alpha coefficient of Cronbach (1951) that little requires to be added except relationships. Also some very recent additional modifications have been proposed by Cattell and Radcliffe (1963) and Cattell and Tsujioka (1964).

As mentioned initially, there has been an uncritical tendency in test reviewers to criticize low homogeneity in a test as if it were a form of unreliability. A more complete analysis than can be given here has recently been made by Cattell and Tsujioka (1964) bringing out certain radical shifts in the evaluation of homogeneity, based on the algebraic demonstrations that: (a) if the items in two tests have the same mean correlation with their factor criterion (of validity), then the less homogeneous test will have a higher final validity for the test as a whole; (b) there is a high probability that high homogeneity is being achieved in many current tests by causing items to share what are really specific factors, over and above the general personality or ability factor which they claim to measure; (c) a highly "inbred" homogeneous test would be expected to show poorer transferability or hardiness across subcultures, age ranges, etc.

Among the varieties of homogeneity coefficients—the genus being symbolized as r_h—one may especially recognize four as of main importance. They are the familiar random split-half coefficient, $r_{h(h)}$; the generalized homogeneity coefficient, $r_{h(g)}$ (Cronbach's, 1951, alpha); the symmetrical or "herringbone" homogeneity coefficient, $r_{h(s)}$; and the equivalence coefficient, $r_{h(e)}$. The last two are special cases of the notion of a structured homogeneity coefficient, differing from the generalized or unstructured homogenity evaluation as in the Kuder-Richardson (1937) and Cronbach coefficients (split-half and generalized homogeneities).

In the symmetrical homogeneity coefficient each person's score on a total school achievement would be split in a special structured way. One-half of the items for arithmetic, for English, for social studies, etc. would score on one side and half on the other—hence the "herringbone" title. Similarly, the equivalence coefficient between two forms of a test, A and B, which are deliberately constructed for equivalence, will generally belong with the structured homogeneity coefficients. For in most modern tests there is in some sense an organic structure introduced in the construction of any unit or form to give a single score. The agreement between any two deliberately, organically constructed forms is therefore something different from any random split-half or general homogeneity coefficient, taken within one form. The design of construction may be such that the internal homogeneity of a broken form runs much lower than the equivalence coefficient between two forms that are designed and intended to measure the same thing.

Turning lastly to the measurement of transferability, we encounter a pioneer area where a little more space must be given to concepts and fundamental principles. For the sake of symmetry with reliability and homogeneity the transferability calculation should be indicated as the correlation between two persons from the application of the same test over a series of occasions where they are experiencing exposure to exactly the same series of stimuli. This is, of course, an indication of what would commonly be arranged instead as the application to two groups of persons (subcultures, for example) whose mean scores could be so compared.

While this is one theoretically satisfactory way of evaluating the extent to which a test retains its properties over different people and groups, namely, with respect to the effects of a varied set of stimulus occasions, it is not the only or the best evaluation of transferability. In fact, what is conceptually the most essential form of transferability measurement departs from simple symmetry to the reliability and homogeneity measurement operations. Transferability is essentially defined as the degree to which a test retains its properties constant across an agreed standard range of reference populations.

Although transferability is here introduced as a new psychometric parameter, it is obviously one which, though unmeasured, has always been of first importance to both the practicing and research psychologist. Experience must henceforth decide, however, whether psychologists will find it more convenient to apply the common meaning and measurement of the concept to (a) the constancy of the validity, or (b) some higher order derivative simultaneously giving weight to constancy in all test properties, viz: validity, reliability, homogeneity, standardization, etc.

Parenthetically, though high transferability is surely desirable if other things are equal, it is probable that it will commonly be gained at the expense of validity in one preferred group, so that a compromise between it and other properties will generally be desirable.

A weighting problem which cannot easily be avoided is that involved in combining r_r (reliability), r_h (homogeneity), and r_t (transferability) to give a single index of a test's consistency. It can well be objected to any single index that consistency is a logical not a functional concept, and that homogeneity and reliability, for example, are functionally and correlationally independent, bound only by being, generically, aspects of a concept of consistency. Two alternatives therefor present themselves: (a) to give equal weight, i.e., calculate a single total consistency coefficient as a (z transformed) mean of the three coefficients; (b) to name some specific purpose for which their relevance is being examined, e.g., obtaining maximum agreement with teachers' judgments, over several school systems, on which children need special class instruction (battery validities being initially equal). This latter, and more defensible "specific purpose" use would take the form of determining weights in the ordinary way in a multiple correlation, so that the equation maximizes R with the desired specific purpose.

SUMMARY

1. A logical and psychological re-examination of the concepts of reliability has been made with a view to arriving at more fundamental and practically effective parameters for evaluating tests.

2. A generic term for the total constancy of a test—quite apart from validity— is proposed as test consistency. This generic term covers reliability, homogeneity, and transferability.

3. If one considers experimental error as most aptly divided into error due to (a) different administrators or observers, (b) different scorers, and (c) other sources, seven reliability coefficients exist from the possible different combinations of these. Again, in practical importance, however, a restricted set of three

reliability coefficients stand out, namely, *dependability, conspection,* and *administrative* reliability. The stability coefficient is not a reliable coefficient, depending more on trait than test.

The reliability of a test includes constancy of mean and standard deviation as well as of the rank order of second administration scores, i.e., the value given by the usual coefficient.

4. *Homogeneity* in a test is conceivable either as test homogeneity or factor homogeneity. As test homogeneity it needs to be differently evaluated for unstructured tests (by split-half, Kuder-Richardson, Cronbach alpha, etc.) and for structured tests (symmetrical, equivalence, etc., coefficients).

5. *Transferability* (hardiness, durability) is a test's constancy across the typical range of age, subculture, status, etc., which a test is likely to encounter.

6. Whereas high reliability is almost always desirable, and high transferability is desirable if other qualities are not lost, an optimum rather than a high homoegeneity is commonly desired. Sufficient suppressor action, validity against a broad as opposed to a narrow factor, and adequate transferability are all likely to be impaired by too high a homogeneity, in degrees partly derivable from formulas.

7. A single index for consistency may be obtained by giving equal summation weight to the three logically, and largely correlationally, independent coefficients; but it is probably more meaningful to calculate a "special purpose consistency" weighting for each of the three according to the multiple correlation possible with the special criterion for which consistency is desired.

9   *How Accurate Is a Test Score?*

JEROME E. DOPPELT

The degree of relative precision of measurement or accuracy of a set of test scores has been defined as test reliability. This test characteristic may be expressed as a reliability coefficient (e.g., the correlation of scores from two forms of the same test administered a month apart), or in terms of the standard error of measurement as described in the following article. The reliability coefficient is a useful way to describe precision because it is an abstract summary index which is independent of the units of measurement and as such can be applied in making inter-test comparisons even though the score units are not comparable. It has a disadvantage in that it is not independent of the "range of talent" (i.e., the variability of individual differences measured by a particular test). In general the greater the spread of ability the higher the coefficient. On the other hand,

Reprinted and abridged with permission of the publisher from *Test Service Bulletin #50,* New York: The Psychological Corporation, 1956.

the standard error of measurement is relatively independent of the range of talent, and is therefore helpful in making judgments about the relative precision of measurement for intra- or inter-individual comparisons.

What is a "true" score? How does the standard error of measurement relate to an individual's "true" score? How would a teacher or counselor use the standard error of measurement to interpret a test score?

Every user of test scores knows that no test is perfectly accurate. The score on a test is determined principally by the ability or knowledge of the person who takes it, but the score is also affected by the inaccuracy of the test itself.

It would be helpful if we could know each time we see a score whether it is higher or lower than it should be, and by how much. Unfortunately, no one has ever figured out a practical way to determine the precise amount of error in an individual case. Statistics have been developed, however, for *estimating* the margin of error we should allow for in test scores. One of the most useful of these is the *standard error of measurement* (SE_M).

Let us consider a practical situation in which it would be useful to have a measure of the accuracy of a test score. Suppose we have an opening for a junior executive in our company. We have a large number of applicants and among them is Henry Smith. He looks good on most counts, but he has a score of 28 on a test of administrative knowledge. The test norms show that a score of 32 would place an applicant within the upper half of all executive applicants and we desire to make our choice from the upper half. Since Smith looks promising in other ways we begin to wonder about his test placement.

If we could test him again, would he get 28 or some other score? Just what is Smith's *true* score on this test? Before we can make sense in talking about the difference between the *true* score and the *observed* or *obtained* score, we need to specify what we mean by *true* score.

Imagine that we have a very large number of comparable forms of our test. (We need not go into the statistics of comparable forms here; let us simply agree that comparable forms are interchangeable. That is, if we had to choose only one form to measure administrative knowledge, we would be equally happy with any one of the forms.) Now suppose we were able to corner Henry Smith and test him with all our tremendous number of equivalent forms. We would find that our hero does not always get the same score. As the number of forms administered gets larger and larger, we would discover that the distribution of Smith's scores begins to resemble the familiar "normal" curve. In this situation we can reasonably decide that the average of the large number of scores is characteristic of Smith's performance on our test, and we will call this his *true* score.

At the beginning of the article we pointed out that the score on a test reflects primarily what the person tested brings to the task and partly it reflects the error of measurement in the test. The true score measures the performance that is characteristic of the person tested; the variations plus and minus around the true score describe a characteristic of the test.

When we use the standard deviation as a measure of the variation of observed scores around the true score, the result is called the *standard error of measurement*. Since this statistic has direct interpretable meaning in relation to the "normal" curve, we are in a position to make this statement:

> If we could know both an individual's exact true score and the SE_M which is characteristic of the test, we would know that about 68 percent of the scores the individual obtained on the vast number of comparable forms fall within one SE_M of his true score. A band stretching two standard errors above and below his true score would include about 95 percent of his obtained scores, and within three standard errors of the true score would lie over 99 percent of his scores on the many forms of the test.

Obviously it is useful to be able to say, putting it a little differently, that for about two-thirds of all people tested the observed scores lie within one SE_M of the true scores—and that for nineteen out of twenty cases the observed score will not be more than two standard errors away from the true score.

As explained in the Note at the end of this article, we must be quite careful how we make statements like the foregoing. It is not correct to say of an individual with a certain *observed* score that the odds are two out of three that his *true* score is within one SE_M of the score he got. But in the practical instance we can use the SE_M in defining limits around the observed score within which we would be reasonably sure to find the true score. Whether the "reasonable limits" will be one, two, or three times the SE_M will depend on the level of confidence the test user desires. The surer he wants to be of not making a mistake in locating the true score, the broader the margin of error he must allow for and therefore the less definite and precise will be the indication given by the test. The broader the score band we allow for each job applicant, for example, the greater the likelihood that his true score will be within it, but the harder it will be to tell the applicants apart.

Coming back to the case of Henry Smith, let us suppose that the test manual reveals that the SE_M is 3 points. If we establish "reasonable limits" of one SE_M on either side of the observed score, the band for Smith would extend over the score range 25–31. And since a score of 32 is needed before a person may be considered as belonging to the top half of executive trainees, we may decide that Smith does not belong in the top half of the group. We are not willing to act as if his true score is 32.

We could have established wider "reasonable limits," say 2 or 3 SE_M on either side of the observed score. We would then have greater confidence that our location of the true score within the band is correct. This extra confidence costs us something. We pay for it by having more people to be considered as possibilities. When there are many applicants, we usually want to reduce the number of eligible candidates even though we increase the possibility of making a wrong decision about the true score of some of them.

Since in practice we cannot give a large number of equivalent forms of a test in order to find the characteristic standard error of measurement, how do we determine it? The answer to this takes us back to the reliability coefficient.

As measured by the reliability coefficient, reliability means consistency of measurement. If the individuals of a group remain in about the same relative positions or ranks after successive testings, the test is "reliable" for that group. It is unfortunately true that a test will tend to have higher reliability coefficients for groups with a wide spread of scores than for groups with scores bunched more closely together.

The SE_M is less subject to this variation; the formula for computing it takes into account both the reliability coefficient *and* the standard deviation for each group. The formula is simple:

$$SE_M = SD \sqrt{1 - r_{tt}}.$$

Here SD is the standard deviation of the obtained scores of a group and r_{tt} is the reliability coefficient computed for the same group.[1]

TABLE 1. *Standard Errors of Measurement for Given Values of Reliability Coefficient and Standard Deviation*

	Reliability Coefficient					
SD	.95	.90	.85	.80	.75	.70
30	6.7	9.5	11.6	13.4	15.0	16.4
28	6.3	8.9	10.8	12.5	14.0	15.3
26	5.8	8.2	10.1	11.6	13.0	14.2
24	5.4	7.6	9.3	10.7	12.0	13.1
22	4.9	7.0	8.5	9.8	11.0	12.0
20	4.5	6.3	7.7	8.9	10.0	11.0
18	4.0	5.7	7.0	8.0	9.0	9.9
16	3.6	5.1	6.2	7.2	8.0	8.8
14	3.1	4.4	5.4	6.3	7.0	7.7
12	2.7	3.8	4.6	5.4	6.0	6.6
10	2.2	3.2	3.9	4.5	5.0	5.5
8	1.8	2.5	3.1	3.6	4.0	4.4
6	1.3	1.9	2.3	2.7	3.0	3.3
4	.9	1.3	1.5	1.8	2.0	2.2
2	.4	.6	.8	.9	1.0	1.1

This table is based on the formula $SE_M = SD\sqrt{1 - r_{tt}}$. For most purposes the result will be sufficiently accurate if the table is entered with the reliability and standard deviation values nearest those given in the test manual. Be sure the standard deviation and the reliability coefficient are for the same group of people.

[1] We cannot automatically say that the more accurate or reliable of two tests is the one which has the lower value for its SE_M. As may be seen from the computing fromula, the SE_M is tied in with the score units in which the standard deviation is expressed. A test with a standard deviation of 16 points may have the same reliability as a test with a standard deviation of 8 points. However, the SE_M of the first test will be numerically twice that of the second.

Like a true score for an individual, the SE_M for a test should be just one definite number if it is really a characteristic of the test rather than of the people tested. But if we look in a test manual, we may see that there appear to be differences among standard errors of measurement computed for different groups. For example, the SE_M is reported for each of nine groups on the Numerical Test in the *Personnel Tests for Industry* series. The values range from 1.7 to 2.4. The explanation is that we have no way of computing the exact value of the SE_M— the formula merely provides an *estimate* of the SE_M. Estimates of course can be expected to differ. In any situation where we cannot obtain the true value of a statistic it is advisable to have as many estimates of that value as practical. In the case of PTI-Numerical, we can be comfortable with the conclusion that the SE_M is about 2 points.

Many test manuals give both reliability coefficients and standard errors of measurement for the convenience of the user. When the SE_M is not given, it can be estimated readily by use of the reliability coefficient, provided the manual also states the standard deviation of the particular group of people on which the reliability coefficient is based. It is well worth the test user's time to make this computation; Table 1 permits an approximation to be made easily without any figuring.

If, as is too often the case, the manual does not present the standard deviation of the group for which the reliability coefficient is reported, it would be advisable for the user to write a letter to the test author.

NOTE: As textbooks usually point out, it is correct to make a statement of probability (such as "68 per cent of the scores" or "two out of three times") only when the SE_M is applied to the true score. If a test has a standard error of 5.5, it is *not* correct to say of a person who obtains a score of 48 that the chances are two out of three that his true score is between 42.5 and 53.5. This person's true score is a definite number, although we do not know what it is. The statement that his true score lies between 42.5 and 53.5 is either true or false. Intermediate probabilities like "two out of three" or "one out of twenty" cannot properly be attached to it. The "reasonable limits" idea simply helps us to avoid making a mathematical statement of probability which would be technically inaccurate. Precise statements of probability in relation to confidence intervals are possible but lie outside the scope of this article.

10 Tests of the Same Length Do Have the Same Standard Error of Measurement

FREDERIC M. LORD

As noted in the previous article by Doppelt (a suggested prerequisite for this article), one of the two usual ways of reporting reliability information is the standard error of measurement. This term refers to a type of reliability information more helpful for interpreting the scores of individuals than simply the correlation coefficient. To illustrate this interpretation, if the true scores for each of thirty individuals are said to be within a standard error of their observed scores, about twenty of the statements would be expected to be correct.

The standard error is usually computed as a function of the variability and reliability of the scores, but according to Dr. Lord, it tends to be related to the length of the test. Since the usual computation takes more time than many people dealing with tests are willing to spend, the approximation offered by Lord has important practical value. Under certain conditions his approximation formula yields results which are remarkably close to those found using the traditional formula.

At this time it is difficult to say how generally applicable the approximation formula might be, since the effect of violating the assumptions underlying the use of the approximation has not yet been adequately examined. It is therefore recommended that the reader consider the procedure to provide a quick, but perhaps somewhat crude estimate of the desired interval.

Theoretical reasoning implies that among tests for which Kuder-Richardson Formula 20 reliability (r_{20}) is an approximate measure of reliability, the standard error of measurement of a given examinee will be approximately the same for any test of a given length (n). That is, the standard error of measurement does not depend on the subject matter of the test, on the type of items used (provided they are scored 0 or 1), on the item-test correlations, or even on the distribution of item difficulties provided this distribution is within the normal range where r_{20} and r_{21} (Kuder-Richardson Formula 21 reliability) yield similar results. The standard error of measurement ordinarily computed by the formula

$$S_{x \cdot t} = S_x \sqrt{1 - r_{20}}$$

is only an average of the different values for the individual examinees. The individual standard errors of measurement can differ widely from one examinee to another, as is obvious from a consideration of the case of an examinee having a near-perfect true score.

The present article gives empirical evidence showing that in actual practice—

Reprinted and abridged with permission of author and publisher from *Educational and Psychological Measurement*, 1959, Vol. 19, pp. 233–239.

at least for groups where the mean score is between 35 and 65 percent of the maximum possible score—tests of the same length do have about the same standard error of measurement. The procedure followed was to obtain all Test Analyses from the files of the Educational Testing Service for an approximately two-year period. The computation of r_{20} and of $s_{x \cdot t}$ is a standard part of each Test Analysis in all cases where the test score is the number of items answered correctly. All such values of $s_{x \cdot t}$ are presented here except that (a) three tests were excluded from the start because fewer than 14 class intervals were used in the computation and (b) one, and only one form of each test was included.

The data thus obtained consist of 58 values of $s_{x \cdot t}$ for 58 different tests or non-overlapping subtests. Of these, 22 represent actually reported test scores and the remaining 36 represent the fractions into which the remaining tests had been split for purposes of statistical analysis, either because the fractions represented distinct subtests of special interest, or in order to meet the assumption of item homogeneity underlying r_{20}.

Most of the test items were multiple-choice. The 58 tests represented a wide variety of aptitude and achievement areas: Social Studies, Biochemistry, Figure Matrices, English Literature, Algebra, Mechanical Aptitude, Obstetrics and Gynecology, Directed Memory, Spelling, Arithmetic Reasoning, and so forth. Most of the tests were at the college entrance, college, or postgraduate level. The number (n) of items in a test (or subtest) ranged from 19 to 210; the mean score ($\bar{x}$) ranged from 40 percent of n to 78 percent; the Formula 20 reliability ranged from .58 to .945; and the standard deviation of item difficulties varied from $s_p = 0.12$ to 0.28 where p is the proportion of examinees answering the item correctly. All test analyses were based on a sample of 370 examinees except for two tests where only 300 were used.

RESULTS

The main results are shown in Figure 6, where the Formula 20 standard error of measurement is plotted for each of the 58 tests against the number of items in the test, each variable being shown on a logarithmic scale. Except for two unusually easy tests with mean item difficulties greater than 70 percent $\left(\dfrac{\bar{x}}{n}\right)$, it appears that all tests of the same length have nearly identical standard errors of measurement.

It was found further, by plotting $s_{x \cdot t}$ (without logarithmic transformation) against $\sqrt{n}$, that these two quantities show a highly linear relationship. For the 50 tests having mean item difficulties between 35 and 65 (shown in the figure by circles), the correlation between $s_{y \cdot x}$ and $\sqrt{n}$ is .996. Moreover, the line of relationship passes through the origin. The best-fitting regression line through the origin is the line $s_{x \cdot t} = .432 \sqrt{n}$. When plotted on log-log paper, this line appears as the diagonal straight line in Figure 6. The standard error of estimate about the regression line is 0.11, which may be interpreted to mean that for about 95 percent of the tests, the standard error of measurement $s_{x \cdot t}$ deviates less than 0.22 raw-score units from the regression line.

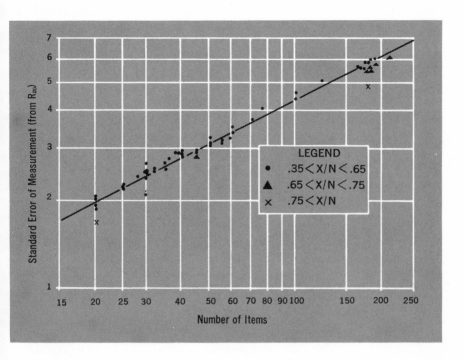

Figure 6.   The Standard Error of Measurement as a Function of the
Number of Items (58 Tests)

Although the result is only incidental to the main purpose of the present article, the equation $s_{x \cdot t} \doteq 3 \sqrt{n}/7$ apparently will, for many purposes, provide an adequate approximation to the average standard error of measurement in the absence of any test data whatsoever, provided only that the test is known not to be excessively easy or difficult for the group to be tested.

Similar results were obtained for the average standard error of measurement computed by Formula 21 reliability coefficient. For these data the correlation between $s_{x \cdot t}$ and $\sqrt{n}$ is .999, the equation of the regression line is $s_{x \cdot t} = .478 \sqrt{n}$, and the standard error of estimate about the regression line is .076.

As might be expected, a plot of the Formula 21 against the Formula 20 standard error of measurement also shows a high linear relationship, the correlation being .996.

The data given here appear to show that in the cognitive area the usual well-constructed tests of medium difficulty, scored on the number of correct answers, have an average standard error of measurement that varies linearly with and correlates extremely highly with the square root of the number of test items.

The empirical results presented are sufficiently startling to justify the incredulity of the reader; hence there is reason to hope that other research workers will carry out similar empirical studies.

IV
DEFINING AND ASSESSING
TEST VALIDITY

Testing experts, although sometimes disagreeing among themselves as to the exact definition of validity, generally concede that it is one of the most important characteristics of a test. In developing a test or in evaluating an instrument for possible use, questions about validity should be central. If only fragmentary evidence on this issue is available, an educator or psychologist will have little confidence in making decisions on the basis of test results.

The number and variety of factors which can influence test scores are legion. Researchers and practitioners are aware of the predictable effects of only a small number of these influences. Consideration of these factors must proceed hand and hand with evaluations of validity. The concept of validity is dynamic and complex, and cannot be adequately treated in a sentence or a paragraph. The reader should more fully appreciate this dynamism and complexity as he reads the papers in this chapter. As he becomes more familiar with some of the ideas advanced in these papers, he should become better able to conceptualize and deal with his own measurement problems.

This chapter and the previous chapter begin in the same way, with excerpts from the 1966 revision of the *Technical Recommendations* (1954, 1955). These *Recommendations* have had a great impact upon current thought and practice through identifying types of validity and reliability, and also in specifying the type of information deemed essential or desirable in a test manual. The revision is similar in style and content to the original set of recommendations with probably the most obvious change being the condensation of predictive and concurrent validity into one type, termed criterion-related validity.

This paper is placed first in the chapter because it provides not only an overview of various types of validity but also a frame of reference for the articles which follow.

A specific type of validity is emphasized in each of the next four articles. Drs. Brogden and Taylor's concern for the criterion is probably most relevant in considering criterion-related validity, although their ideas certainly extend to other types of validity as well. (For illustrations of criterion-related validity studies, the reader is referred especially to Chapter IX.) Often the blame for low validity coefficients is assigned to the criterion. This condemnation is frequently justified because the nature of criteria are seldom discussed or investigated.

Dr. Robert Ebel has provided us with an elaboration of the concept of and a discussion of the problems in assessing content validity. This type of validity frequently seems not only to be misunderstood but also underestimated in importance. While many authors have stated that an achievement test should first be examined for content validity and rejected if this condition is not met, and while Ebel emphasizes the achievement test application, the generality of the content validity topic to the various types of assessment is obvious. It is hoped that the reader's appetite will be whetted sufficiently by this article to consider the articles by Lennon (1956) and Huddleston (1956) in the symposium from which the Ebel article was taken.

The most controversial type of validity—construct validity—was originally specified in the *Technical Recommendations* (1954). Drs. Cronbach and Meehl further explained and extended these ideas in their classic paper. Additional explanation and extension of the concept of construct validity are provided by Campbell and Fiske, using a specific methodological approach as their vehicle.

Finally, an alternative approach to conceptualizing validity is presented. Whether or not the reader prefers the concepts and terminology given by Dr. Raymond Cattell, the reading of this article should assist him in broadening and integrating his ideas on validity.

11   *Three Characteristics of Validity*

NATIONAL COMMITTTEE ON TEST STANDARDS

Of all the questions concerning a test, those related to validity are probably the most important and yet the most difficult to answer. The gathering of reliable evidence bearing on test validity is often expensive and time-consuming. In many instances criteria may be unavailable. This is true primarily because a given test

Reprinted and abridged from *Standards for Educational and Psychological Tests and Manuals*, 1966, pp. 12–24. Copyright 1966 by the American Psychological Association and reproduced by permission.

does not possess singular "validity," but will vary in degree of validity, depending upon the situation and intent of the user. The following discussion highlights three major aspects of validity, as determined by a group of test experts. As will be obvious from reading this discussion and the following articles in this section, defining and assessing validity is a very complex task. What validity characteristic would be most important in the development of a test to measure reading comprehension, mental retardation, attitudes toward minority groups, neuroticism, and typing ability?

Validity information indicates the degree to which the test is capable of achieving certain aims. Tests are used for several types of judgment, and for each type of judgment a different type of investigation is required to establish validity. For purposes of describing the uses for three kinds of validity coefficients we may distinguish three of the rather numerous aims of testing:

1. *The test user wishes to determine how an individual performs at present in a universe of situations that the test situation is claimed to represent.* For example, most achievement tests used in schools measure the student's performance on a sample of questions intended to represent a certain phase of educational achievement or certain educational objectives.

2. *The test user wishes to forecast an individual's future standing or to estimate an individual's present standing on some variable of particular significance that is different from the test.* For example, an academic aptitude test may forecast grades, or a brief adjustment inventory may estimate what the outcome would be of a careful psychological examination.

3. *The test user wishes to infer the degree to which the individual possesses some hypothetical trait or quality (construct) presumed to be reflected in the test performance.* For example, he wants to know whether the individual stands high on some proposed abstract trait such as "intelligence" or "creativity" that cannot be directly observed. This may be done to learn something about the individual, or it may be done to study the test itself, to study its relationship to other tests, or to develop psychological theory.

Different types of tests are often used for each of the different aims, but this is not always the case. There is much overlap in types of tests and the purposes for which they are used. Thus, a vocabulary test might be used (1) simply as a measure of present vocabulary, the universe being all the words in the language, (2) as a screening device to discriminate present or potential schizophrenics from brain-damaged individuals, or (3) as a means of making inferences about "intellectual capacity."

To determine how suitable a test is for each of these uses it is necessary to gather appropriate validity information. The kind of information to be gathered depends on the aim or aims of testing rather than on the type of test. The three aspects of validity corresponding to the three aims of testing may be named content validity, criterion-related validity, and construct validity.

A. Content validity is demonstrated by showing how well the content of the test samples the class of situations or subject matter about which conclusions are to be drawn. Content validity is especially important for achievement and proficiency measures and for measures of adjustment or social behavior based on observation in selected situations. The manual should justify the claim that the test content represents the assumed universe of tasks, conditions, or processes. A useful way of looking at this universe of tasks or items is to consider it to comprise a *definition* of the achievement to be measured by the test. In the case of an educational achievement test, the content of the test may be regarded as a definition of one or more educational objectives. The aptitudes, skills, and knowledges required of the student for successful test performance must be precisely the types of aptitudes, skills, and knowledges that the school wishes to develop in the students and to evaluate in terms of test scores. Thus evaluating the content validity of a test for a particular purpose is the same as subjectively recognizing the adequacy of a definition. This process is actually quite similar to the subjective evaluation of the criterion itself. Unless, however, the aim of an achievement test is specifically to substitute for some criterion, its correlation with a criterion is *not* a useful evaluation of the test.

B. Criterion-related validity is demonstrated by comparing the test scores with one or more external variables considered to provide a direct measure of the characteristic or behavior in question. This comparison may take the form of an expectancy table or, most commonly, a correlation relating the test score to a criterion measure. Predictive uses of tests include long-range forecasts of one or more measures of academic achievement, prediction of vocational success, and prediction of reaction to therapy. For such uses the criterion data are collected at a later date than the test data. If however one wishes to know whether a testing procedure can for example take the place of more elaborate procedures for diagnosing personality disorders test and criterion data are gathered concurrently. A test that is related to one or more concurrent criteria will not necessarily predict status on the same criterion at some later date. Whether the criterion data should be collected concurrently with the testing or at a later time depends on whether the test is recommended for prediction or for assessment of present status.

C. Construct validity is evaluated by investigating what qualities a test measures, i.e., by determining the degree to which certain explanatory concepts or constructs account for performance on the test.[1] To examine construct validity requires a combination of logical and empirical attack. Essentially, studies of construct validity check on the theory underlying the test. The procedure involves three steps. First, the investigator inquires from this theory what hypotheses may we make regarding the behavior of persons with high and low scores? Second he gathers data to test these hypotheses. Third, in light of the evidence he makes

---

[1] See article (#14) by Cronbach and Meehl later in this chapter for more extensive treatment of construct validity.

an inference as to whether the theory is adequate to explain the data collected. If the theory fails to account for the data, he should revise the test interpretation, reformulate the theory, or reject the theory altogether. Fresh evidence would be required to demonstrate construct validity for the revised interpretation.

A simple procedure for investigating what a test measures is to correlate it with other tests. We would expect a valid test of numerical reasoning, for example, to correlate more highly with other numerical tests than with clerical perception tests. Another procedure is experimental. If it is hypothesized, for example, that form perception on a certain projective test indicates probable ability to function well under emotional stress, this inference may be checked by placing individuals in an experimental situation producing emotional stress and observing whether their behavior corresponds to the hypothesis.

Construct validity is ordinarily studied when the tester wishes to increase his understanding of the psychological qualities being measured by the test. A validity coefficient relating test to criterion, unless it is established in the context of some theory, yields no information about *why* the correlation is high or low, or about how one might improve the measurement. Construct validity is relevant when the tester accepts no existing measure as a definitive criterion of the quality with which he is concerned (e.g., in measuring a postulated drive such as *need for achievement*), or when a test will be used in so many diverse decisions that no single criterion applies (e.g., in identifying the ability of Peace Corps trainees to adapt to new cultures). Here the traits or qualities underlying test performance are of central importance. It must be remembered, however, that without a study of criterion-related validity a test developed for diagnosis or prediction can be regarded only as experimental.

These three aspects of validity are only conceptually independent, and rarely is only one of them important in a particular situation. A complete study of a test would normally involve information about all types of validity. A first step in the preparation of a predictive (*criterion-related*) instrument may be to consider what *constructs* are likely to provide a basis for selecting or devising an effective test. Sampling from a *content* universe may also be an early step in producing a test whose use for *prediction* is the ultimate concern. Even after satisfactory *prediction* has been established, information regarding *construct* validity may make the test more useful; it may, for example, provide a basis for identifying situations other than the validating situation where the test is appropriate as a predictor. To analyze *construct* validity all the knowledge regarding validity would be brought to bear.

The three concepts of validity are pertinent to all kinds of tests. It is the intended use of the test rather than its nature that determines what kind of evidence is required.

Intelligence or aptitude tests most often use criterion-related validity to show how well they are able to predict academic success in school or college, but the nature of the aptitudes measured is often judged from the content of the items, and the place of the aptitude within the array of human abilities is deduced from correlations with other tests.

For achievement tests content validity is usually of first importance. For example, a testing agency has a group of subject-matter experts devise and select test items that they judge to cover the topics and mental processes relevant to the field represented by the test. Similarly, a teacher judges whether the final test in his course covers situations about which he has been trying to teach his students an understanding. The teacher also judges content when he uses a published test, but he can appropriately investigate criterion-related validity as well by correlating this test with tests he has prepared or with other direct measures of his chief instructional objectives. When the same published achievement test is used for admissions testing, it may reasonably be checked against a later criterion of performance. In any theoretical discussion of what is being measured by the achievement test a consideration of construct validity is required. Whether the score on a science achievement test, for example, reflects reading ability to a significant degree, and whether it measures understanding of scientific method rather than mere recall of facts are both questions about construct validity.

Development of a personality inventory will usually start with the assembly of items covering content the developer considers meaningful. Such inventories are then likely to be interpreted with the aid of theory; any such interpretation calls for evidence of construct validity. In addition a personality inventory must have criterion-related validity if, for example, it is to be used in screening military recruits who may be maladjusted.

Interest measures usually seek to predict vocational or educational criteria, but many of them are also characterized by logical content and constructs. This makes it more likely that they can provide at least a rough prediction for the very many occupations and activities that exist and for which specific evidence of criterion-related validity has not been obtained.

For projective techniques, construct validity is of most importance, although criterion-related validity using criteria collected either concurrently with the testing or afterwards may be pertinent if the instruments are to be used in making diagnostic classifications.

12 *A Theory and Classification of Criterion Bias*

HUBERT E. BROGDEN AND ERWIN K. TAYLOR

One wonders if test constructors and researchers, especially those primarily concerned with prediction and evaluation, put forth as much time and effort in constructing and assessing the validity of their criteria as they do in analyzing their test instruments. The importance of the criterion problem, particularly in academic prediction studies, has been widely recognized. But this topic, like the "weather," seems to be talked about a great deal, but has lacked a systematic conceptual examination as well as a concerted effort to identify possible solutions. The following cogent discussion highlights some significant factors that a test constructor must be concerned with if he is to produce a valid instrument.

It should also point out some possible areas for interesting research. Assume that you are, in turn, a clinical psychologist concerned with developing a measure of anxiety, a classroom teacher developing a final examination, an industrial psychologist interested in selecting a plant manager. How would each of the four criterion-biasing factors discussed by the author come into play during instrument development and validation? Can you think of any ways that a criterion might be subjected to an empirical validation?

At the outset of this paper, the authors would like to discuss two points important to their general orientation in attacking criterion problems. The essence of the first point may be stated as follows: in seeking to define criterion problems—particularly those of criterion bias—it must be recognized that in general the objective of criterion construction is subsidiary to that of selecting the most efficient battery of predictors. Prediction instruments are validated for the purpose of picking the best selection battery, assigning appropriate weight to each of its several components, and determining the effectiveness of the battery. The criterion achieves its sole function if it makes these objectives of validation possible. In the development of an industrial selection program, for example, the criterion should give an accurate and unbiased measure of the extent to which individuals in the validation population contribute to or detract from the efficiency of the organization. This may be taken as axiomatic. If so, the emphasis in criterion construction must be in terms of the objectives of the prediction problem.

Criteria differ from predictors in that the former must be tested in terms of a concept that we carefully avoid in the latter. In constructing or choosing from among existing predictors an empirical approach can be and often is profitably used. Recourse to previous research results, information based on job analysis, hunches, hypotheses, and intelligent guesses all provide legitimate bases upon

Reprinted and abridged with permission of the first-named author and publisher from *Educational and Psychological Measurement*, 1950, Vol. 10, pp. 159–186.

which to predicate a potential selection battery. Wrong guesses can be costly in terms of wasted research resources, but they are not misleading since they are put to the empirical test of how well each accomplishes the objectives of the prediction task, i.e., how well each correlates with the criterion.

The criterion, by contrast, can be subjected to no wholly satisfactory empirical test of its adequacy. The criterion must consequently *be logically justifiable as valid in its own right.* Invalid and biased criteria, again in contrast to predictors, cannot be eliminated through empirical demonstration of their inadequacy. Thus the faulty criterion not only wastes research efforts, but seriously reduces the effectiveness of the final outcome of the program.

For the purpose of this discussion, a biasing factor may be defined as any variable, except errors of measurement and sampling error, producing a deviation of obtained criterion scores from a hypothetical "true" criterion score. It is apparent that this definition is quite general and leads to the consideration of all factors which bear upon the desirability or undesirability of criterion elements and their combination. Of course the practical consideration which faces the research worker in a "real" situation precludes the complete elimination of all undesirable aspects of criterion construction. Perfection may be approached—it is not likely to be achieved. Nonetheless, to improve his criteria to the point optimal for the conditions under which he is working, the research psychologist must know the importance of different types of bias, the manner in which each will probably affect his results, the proper emphasis to place upon the elimination of those factors producing a distortion of results of indeterminate magnitude, and finally the probable effect of bias that cannot be entirely eliminated. Different types of biasing factors vary widely in their distortive effect, generally as a function of the degree of their correlation with the members of the predictive battery. Some biasing factors influence validity coefficients but have little or no effect on estimates of criterion reliability. Others affect both. Still others may alter the apparent reliability of the criterion without seriously influencing the validity.

CLASSIFICATION OF BIASING FACTORS

Imperfections or bias in the criteria may be classified as:

(1) *Criterion Deficiency*—omission of pertinent elements from the criterion.

(2) *Criterion Contamination*—introducing extraneous elements into the criterion.

(3) *Criterion Scale Unit Bias*—inequality of scale units in the criterion.

(4) *Criterion Distortion*—improper weighting in combining criterion elements.

The above classification of criterion bias is functional in terms of the steps the authors consider essential to adequate criterion construction. These steps may be indicated as follows:

(1) Careful analysis of the total situation in which the criterion behavior

occurs for the purpose of isolating all sub-criterion variables and obtaining preliminary estimates of their relative importance—the determination of what is to be measured.

(2) The construction of procedures and/or scales for the measurement of these elements—determination of how each element is to be measured.

(3) Development of a procedure for combining these elements into the desired single composite—determination of the relative importance of each element to over-all efficiency.

Criterion deficiency is most apt to occur in the process of determining the variables to be included in the criterion. Contamination and criterion scale-unit bias are most likely to appear in the process of constructing scales for the measurement of the sub-criterion elements, while criterion distortion results primarily from faulty methods of combining the criterion elements.

Each of the three steps of criterion construction is necessarily involved, however sketchily, in the development of any criterion. The rationale of our classification of bias is so intimately related to the belief in the need for an explicit plan of construction involving these three steps as to justify further clarification of the implications of each in its relation to bias.

The desirability of establishing the variables important to "success" by observation and job analysis (step 1) before proceeding to scale construction (step 2) and the combination of sub-criterion variables (step 3) deserves special emphasis. From reports of validation studies found in the literature it may be judged that the usual first step in criterion development is the search for available criterion measures. The psychologist employing this procedure very often arrives at a decision as to criterion content that is undesirably influenced by factors of availability. The discovery of several already available or readily obtained measures that are apparently suitable is inclined to lead to neglect of the systematic observation and analysis necessary to insure that all important aspects of on-the-job productivity have been identified. In choosing criteria on the basis of availability, the method of measurement as well as nature of variables is also usually a function of convenience rather than of desirability. Without accomplishing Step 1 before deciding upon the means by which the criterion variables are to be measured, a systematic consideration of alternate methods of scale construction or measurement and choice of the optimal method for each criterion variable is not likely to be made. While it is recognized that in many cases the final decision as to the method of measurement will have to be made in the light of economy and available research resources, it is the firm belief of the authors that there is generally enough freedom of choice within the limitations imposed by even a policy of strict expediency to justify the type of analysis proposed. At least the decision can be made with full and explicit recognition of the basis for making it. It might be added, parenthetically, the careful accomplishment of step 1, in addition to insuring that adequacy of criterion variables, frequently serves the additional function of supplying valuable clues as to possible predictors. Savings realized through this means may in part, if not entirely, offset the extra cost and effort required to make a thorough observation and analysis.

CRITERION BIAS AND PREDICTOR CORRELATION

To this point our classification and discussion of bias have been in terms of the criterion alone. Since effort expended in constructing a bias-free criterion is, as we have stressed before, directed ultimately toward the proper choice and weighting of a battery of predictors, it is essential to consider the effect of criterion bias on the degree to which this objective is realized.

Biasing factors correlating with the predictors will obviously distort the validities and the partial regression weights of the various predictors. They may even result in the inclusion of tests in the battery that predict only bias and have no relationship to the "true" criterion. The introduction of bias having no relation to the predictors is, on the other hand, equivalent in effect to an increase in the error of measurement of the criterion. The relationship of all predictors to the criterion will be attenuated. But this attenuation will be proportional for all predictors. Consequently, the relative magnitude of the validities and the partial regression coefficients will be unaffected. This leads to the highly important conclusion that the "true" validity of the weighted composite resulting from the validation study remains substantially unaffected by test-free bias, even though the exact magnitude of this validity cannot be estimated. With these considerations in mind we may further classify biasing factors into those which are *predictor correlated* and those which are *predictor free.*

The authors do not wish to imply that the attenuating effect of test-free bias is of little import. In addition to the attenuation of the validity coefficients and partial regression weights, two other undesirable results will accrue from the introduction of test-free bias into the criterion: (1) The sampling error of the validity and regression weights will tend to increase, thus rendering these statistics less stable from sample to sample, and (2) biasing factors that are test free may, none the less, distort estimates of the reliability of the criterion in an indeterminate manner.

The first of these faults may be overcome by increasing the size of the experimental population if additional cases are available with, of course, a resulting increase in the cost of the research. The problem of correcting for the unknown effect of test-free bias on criterion reliability is more difficult, and possible solutions are usually less satisfactory. Such possible solutions are, in any event, particular to the nature of the biasing factors.

In spite of these adverse effects of test-free bias, it is believed that effectively it is the presence or absence of test-correlated bias that "makes" or "breaks" the criterion.

13   *Evaluating Content Validity*

ROBERT L. EBEL

Content validity has been regarded by measurement experts as being particularly crucial for achievement tests. In fact, without it further consideration of the test is meaningless. It is less obvious that content validity is an important consideration for any type of instrument. The reader is urged to apply the statements made by the author to the type of instrument in which he has the most interest, and to ask himself questions such as: How can the objectivity of content validity assessment be increased? What is included in the "content" besides the subject matter or topics considered? How may content validity be considered as a part of other validity approaches? Should a test be considered an operational definition of the goals of the constructor or user? At what stage in an instructional sequence should evaluation be employed? What are the sources of evidence for content validity?

THE CONCEPT OF CONTENT VALIDITY

It is often said that an educational achievement test possesses content validity to the degree that it samples adequately some clearly specified universe of educational content. This statement lends itself to a common and rather serious misinterpretation. It suggests that the validity of a test is to be judged in terms of its relevance to the materials of instruction rather than the ultimate objectives of instruction. But the validity of an educational achievement test cannot be judged solely, or even principally, in terms of its sampling of the subject matter of a course. Only when the "content" of education is conceived as a set of goals to be attained, rather than as a set of lessons to be studied or as a set of class activities to be carried out, is it educationally useful to seek content validity in a test.

An educational achievement test is one designed to measure the extent of attainment of the ultimate goals of instruction in a particular area by the individuals in a particular group. In passing judgment on the content validity of an educational achievement test one asks, "To what extent does this test require demonstration by the student of the achievements which constitute the objectives of instruction in this area?" The more directly, completely, and reliably a test measures the attainment of these goals the greater is its content validity.

There is a common and widespread tendency on the part of both teachers and pupils to place primary emphasis on "covering" the subject matter and remembering the materials of instruction, rather than on achieving the objectives of

Reprinted and abridged with permission of author and publisher from an article entitled, "Obtaining and Reporting Evidence on Content Validity," which appeared in *Educational and Psychological Measurement*, 1956, Vol. 16, pp. 269–282.

that instruction, i.e., developing abilities for more effective behavior. No subject has ever been introduced into the curriculum that was not in the first instance designed to enable those who studied it to behave more effectively. But teaching procedures are habit forming. The transmission of learning from teachers to scholars, who in their turn become the teachers of other scholars, tends to shift attention away from the ends of instruction, and to focus it on the means.

OPERATIONAL DEFINITIONS OF GOALS

When tests are derived directly from desired behavioral goals, the tests constitute operational definitions of those goals. Such tests are sometimes called "self-defining" tests. This term seems unfortunate, since it suggests that the contents of the test are immune from criticism. A test does not define itself. It defines an educational achievement, and some definitions of that achievement are likely to be more soundly based or more rational than others.

Three objections have been raised to the statement that achievement tests constitute operational definitions of the goals of achievement. The first is that not all of the ultimate goals of education can be measured effectively in a test situation. This is true, and ought to be recognized frankly. An achievement test provides an operational definition of only those goals whose achievement can be observed in test situations. Operational definitions of other goals of achievement must be sought in non-test procedures appropriate for revealing the extent of their achievement.

A second objection is that, since any achievement test constitutes a sample of items from a much larger potential population of items, it provides a very incomplete definition of the goals of achievement. This also is true, but how serious a limitation it is depends on the complexity of the field to be covered by the test and the adequacy of sampling of items in the test. For measurement purposes the particular sample used does constitute the operational definition of achievement. For instructional purposes it is better to regard the hypothetical population of items, from which this particular sample is presumed to have been selected, as constituting a better operational definition of the goals of achievement.

A third objection is that each test constitutes a different operational definition of achievement. The existence of such a multiplicity of definitions, it is argued, is likely to contribute more to confusion than to clarity in thinking. Again there is some truth in this argument. However it discounts the very considerable areas of agreement in the definitions of the same achievement provided by different tests. Further, it implies that agreement on the goals of instruction can be purchased at the price of clarity in the definitions of those goals. This is certainly true, as many vague statements of educational goals attest, but it is a poor bargain. The use of achievement tests as operational definitions of the goals of achievement does not cause disagreements. It simply brings them to light. There is no better way to define many educational goals concretely than to construct tests of the achievement of them.

With these considerations in mind a more precise description of the concept of educational achievement tests as operational definitions of the goals of achievement may be stated. Any educational achievement test may be regarded as a sample of items from a hypothetical population of items which constitutes one operational definition of the testable goals of instruction in the area.

GOALS, CURRICULA, AND TESTS

It is possible to conceive of a neat division of educational labor in which the educational philosopher defines the goals of education, the curriculum maker devises methods for attaining those goals, and the test constructor devises instruments to measure the extent to which they have been attained. But the problems of education are too complex, and our abilities to construct and communicate ideas too limited to make this neat system workable. Each of the specialists needs not only to have his eye on what the other fellow is doing, but needs also to help him do it. This does not mean that education can do without specialists who are philosophers, curriculum builders, or test constructors. What it does mean is that no one of these specialists can stake a claim to one field of operation and insist that all other specialists keep off.

Emphatic, even angry words have been spoken from time to time concerning the harmful influences of tests on education and the evil influences of test makers on the curriculum. Certainly bad tests, or the improper use of good tests, can affect education adversely. Certainly any intended or accidental enforcement of uniformity in educational procedures through a wide-scale testing program cannot be defended. But it is foolish to disregard, and it would be more foolish to abandon, the powerful forces for educational improvement that are available through proper use of good educational achievement tests. Consider these alternative sequences in the development of an educational program.

FIRST SEQUENCE ■
Step 1. Areas of agreement in desired behavior are identified.
Step 2. Curricula calculated to develop these desired behaviors are designed.
Step 3. Tests are constructed on the basis of the curricula to determine each student's degree of mastery of it.

SECOND SEQUENCE ■
Step 1. Areas of agreement in desired behavior are identified.
Step 2. These behaviors are translated as directly and completely as possible into an extended series of test problems.
Step 3. Curricula are designed to equip students to do as well as possible on problems like those presented in the test.

The first alternative is the one which is commonly followed. The second is equally sound from a logical point of view, and might well in practice prove to be more effective. It is easier to define desirable behavior in terms of test exercises than in terms of curricular procedures. The best of our current educational achievement tests have been derived, not indirectly from curricula, but directly from the ultimately desirable goals of behavior.

QUALITATIVE VS. QUANTITATIVE EVALUATION OF CONTENT VALIDITY

Validity is concerned with the relation between the information the user expects from a test and the information actually supplied by it. There are two bases on which this relationship can be examined, qualitative and quantitative. In using the qualitative basis one asks how closely the behavior apparently called for by the test represents or indicates the desired behavior which constitutes the goal of instruction. At one extreme, a test of competence in shorthand may require behavior identical with the desired behavior. Such a test would be judged highly valid on a qualitative basis. At the other extreme is a test of honesty based on an analysis of handwriting. Since there appears no rational relationship between the behavior called for by the test and the desired behavior, such a test would be judged qualitatively to be low in validity.

Most users of educational achievement tests place considerable faith in the qualitative comparison of the behavior called for by a test with the behavioral goals of instruction. But this process is regarded with considerable mistrust by some specialists in psychological testing. Qualitative examination, they feel, involves personal and highly subjective judgments. Appearances may be deceiving, so that false relationships are accepted as true, and true relationships overlooked. Incidental relationships may be weighted heavily and more fundamental relationships neglected. These specialists discount the importance of content validity, arguing for a more objective, systematic, quantitative approach.

In the quantitative approach the behavior on the test is quantified in the form of a single score. The behavior which the test ought to measure is also quantified, preferably by observing the desired behavior directly and assigning precisely defined scores to various aspects of it. These scores are referred to as criterion scores. A correlation coefficient is then calculated to express the degree of relationship between the test scores and the criterion scores.

On the surface, but on the surface only, this quantitative approach appears to avoid some of the subjective difficulties involved in the qualitative approach. For even in the quantitative approach the selection of acts of behavior to become part of the criterion measure and the assignment of different score values to various manifestations of this behavior involve the exercise of personal, subjective judgment. There are, in fact, added opportunities for error in the quantitative approach, for it involves three steps instead of one. Test behavior must be quantified, desired behavior must be quantified, and the relation between the two must be examined. In the qualitative evaluation of a test, a single, direct comparison is made between test behavior and desired behavior.

The fundamental fact is that one cannot escape from the problem of content validity. If we dodge it in constructing the test, it raises its troublesome head when we seek a criterion. For when one attempts to evaluate the validity of a test indirectly via some quantified criterion measure, he must use the very process he is trying to avoid in order to obtain the criterion measures.

RELATION OF CONTENT VALIDITY TO OTHER TYPES

The nature and importance of content validity may be made clearer by relating it to other types of validity. The degree of *content validity* of a test is a function of the directness, completeness, and reliability with which it measures attainment of the ultimate goals of instruction in a given area. The degree of *concurrent validity* of a test is a function of the correlation between scores on it and scores obtained from an alternative, presumably more valid but less convenient, measurement procedure, *and of the degree of content validity of the alternative procedure*. The degree of *predictive validity* of a test for a given group is a function of the correlation between scores on the test and future measures of the status to be predicted, *and of the content validity of future measures of status*. The degree of *construct validity* of a test is the extent to which a system of hypothetical relationships can be verified on the basis of measures of the construct derived from the test. But this system of relationships always involves measures of observed behavior *which must be defended on the basis of their content validity*. In every case quantitative validation builds on qualitative validation. Statistical validation is not an alternative to subjective validation, but an extension of it. All statistical procedures for validating tests are based ultimately upon common sense agreement concerning what is being measured by a particular measurement process.

OBTAINING EVIDENCE OF CONTENT VALIDITY

The simplest and most direct evidence of content validity is obtained from examination of the test itself by a competent judge. A cursory inspection skimming the test is better than no inspection at all. But if the judge is seriously interested in determining the relationship between what the test asks an examinee to do and what the typical user expects of a test of that sort, he should take the test himself just as a student would do. Only by this means can he give sufficiently close, careful attention to the individual items of the test.

It is true that the judge may not always respond to the items on exactly the same basis as a typical examinee would, and thus may misjudge what a particular item measures. But this does not mean that his judgments of what the test as a whole is measuring are completely untrustworthy. It simply means that he must be competent and work carefully, and that he should if possible check his interpretations against those of other competent judges or typical examinees.

To obtain a summary view of test content it is often helpful to classify the items in broad areas of subject matter and student ability. Areas of content will vary from test to test. In straight subject examinations these areas will ordinarily follow the customary divisions of the subject, as shown in representative textbooks. Even in skills examinations such as reading comprehension the items may be regarded as belonging to different areas of content. Some of the reading passages may be historical, others scientific, others literary prose, and still others poetry.

TYPES OF ABILITY MEASURED

Equally important in judging the content validity of a test is the distribution of items with respect to the types of ability or achievement they require. Many of the items found in educational achievement tests can be classified in one or more of the following broad categories: content detail, vocabulary, fact, generalization, understanding, and application. A content detail item is one of no significance outside the classroom. Its function is to indicate that the examinee has or has not done some particular learning exercises. A vocabulary item is one which requires essential knowledge of the meaning of a particular term for successful response. A factual item is one dealing with an isolated bit of information, frequently a Who? What? When? or Where? type of item. A generalization item is one dealing with a law, principle, general summary, or basic method of procedure. An understanding term is one beginning with the word "Why?", or calling for completions beginning with the word "because." An application item is one which presents a problem to be solved, a decision to be given, or a recommendation to be made in terms of some specifically described situation. Items are classified in these categories, not on the basis of assumed psychological functions involved, but in terms of overt characteristics of the items. While it is seldom possible to classify all of the items in the test with complete confidence that they have been properly classified, the over-all process usually gives a good indication of the emphasis found in the test.

It is sometimes argued that differences in the type of ability called for by a test item are relatively unimportant. A test of factual knowledge was shown in one study to rank pupils in nearly the same order as a test of their problem-solving ability. Other studies have given a contrary indication. Much appears to depend on the character of the previous teaching. If applications are not stressed, pupils may do much better in a test over factual details than on a test involving applications. If applications are stressed, pupils may do equally well on both, since factual knowledge is prerequisite to effective application. Failure to find significant difference in the ranking of a particular group of pupils on different types of test items cannot be accepted as conclusive evidence that the items are measuring identical achievements. In the long run tests which emphasize primarily factual information will tend to direct teaching and learning to the acquisition of factual knowledge. Unless it can be shown, which it has not been and is not likely to be, that pupils who possess factual knowledge can without further emphasis or training achieve desired understanding and make desired applications, emphasis on understanding and applications will be essential in both teaching and testing.

Within both subject-matter and pupil-ability classifications either important or unimportant questions can be asked. The content validity of a test depends on the significance or importance of the questions asked, and on the appropriateness of the balance among various subject-matter and pupil-ability categories. It depends also on the quality of the items themselves. Are they clearly expressed? Is the intended correct answer an adequate answer? Are the distractors plausible, yet not sufficiently defensible to attract many good students? Is the item as a whole of appropriate difficulty?

THE USER AS A JUDGE OF CONTENT VALIDITY

The content validity of a test depends not only on the characteristics of the test itself, but also on the purposes and needs of the user. A test of achievement in first-year high school algebra can be regarded as a generally valid test only to the extent that it measures what good algebra teachers try to teach. It is inevitable that the aims and values of different teachers will differ. It is also obvious that greater weight should be attached to the judgments of certain individuals than to those of others. But it is beyond question that a competent teacher or administrator, clearly aware of appropriate educational goals and familiar with the functions and limitations of various test procedures, can obtain direct evidence concerning the content validity of a test by careful examination of the test itself. Other types of evidence may be useful in judging content validity, but none is more fundamental.

EVIDENCE FROM THE TEST MANUAL

Evidence of content validity may sometimes be obtained by examining the test manual. If the manual presents the test outline, defines the universe of content sampled, summarizes the unique characteristics of the test, and calls attention to the principles guiding the authors and editors of the test in their selection of items, the manual can be extremely helpful in judging the content validity of the test. Since concrete information is more meaningful than abstract, actual items from the test should be used to illustrate the major classifications in the test outline.

In the development of a test, experts are sometimes asked to judge the relationship between the tasks required by the test and the desired behavioral goals. The number of judges used, their competence, and the process they use in evaluating the test help to determine the value of their contributions, and should be reported in the manual. Another factor of great importance, but one which is difficult to assess and report accurately, is the conscientiousness with which they undertook the task of evaluation. In the long run there probably would be greater incentives for the judges to assume responsibility for a careful job if their names were listed on the test booklet or in the manual.

The presentation in test manuals of detailed analyses of the content of a test has sometimes been criticized on the ground that this information tends to encourage teachers to "teach for the test." It cannot be denied that efforts to coach pupils to respond to specific test items is educationally harmful. But it is open to question that a test manual which outlines the contents of the test, or even which indicates the items that fall under each general heading, encourages this practice. Any misguided teacher who regards the final achievement test for her pupils as appropriate lesson material would not be likely to waste time on the manual. As a matter of fact, the manual, in calling attention to the broad categories of items from which the particular items have been drawn, should have the effect of generalizing instruction rather than making it more specific.

VALIDITY AND RELIABILITY

Validity has two aspects, relevance and reliability. What has been said thus far about determining the content validity of a test has been concerned with determining its content relevance. To be valid a test must not only be closely related to the function it is used to measure, but it also must measure that something with reasonable precision. Internal analysis of the data obtained from a single administration of the test under typical conditions to a representative group of examinees can provide adequate evidence concerning the reliability of the test. If item analysis data has been obtained, one of the Kuder-Richardson formulas for reliability is usually most convenient to use. If not, the odds-even coefficient may be more convenient. Either will ordinarily provide quite adequate information on the reliability of the test.

When items are selected empirically on the basis of item analysis data from a particular sample, reliability coefficients should not be computed by rescoring the selected items on the same sample of papers. Nor should the originally obtained indices of discrimination and difficulty be reported as unbiased estimates of these parameters for the selected items. In all cases the reliability coefficient and final item characteristic data should be obtained from a cross-validation sample.

Item analysis data are ordinarily obtained by contrasting the performance of students who scored high on the test with those who scored low. It is possible, and sometimes profitable, to use other sources for the contrasting groups. Two such independently defined groups were used in a recent study which required a test of the grasp of certain concepts in geography. Materials presenting and explaining these concepts were prepared and given to a small group of scholars whose ability to comprehend them was beyond question. The the test was administered to these scholars. The test was also given to a group of students typical of those to be used later in the main experiment. These students had not had an opportunity to study the explanatory materials. Any item which was not answered correctly by all of the informed experts and which was not missed by all except a chance proportion of the uninformed students was rejected.

In the construction of reading interpretation tests it should be more common practice than it is to administer the test questions independent of the background material. Any item which can be answered correctly by a large proportion of students without reference to the background material can hardly be regarded as a valid test of comprehension of that material.

REPORTING EVIDENCE ON CONTENT VALIDITY

What has been said thus far about obtaining evidence on the content validity of educational achievement tests carries with it in most cases obvious implications for reporting that evidence. Such evidence ought to be reported more fully than is the usual practice. The purpose of reporting this evidence is *not* to convince the test user that the test is valid. It is rather to help him judge whether or not the test is valid for his purposes. The validity of a test is relative to the user and his purposes, as well as to the nature of the group on which it is used.

Test developers can aid test users to judge the content validity of their tests by stating the criteria and principles which guided them in choosing item topics and in writing items, by presenting an outline of the achievements covered by the test, and by indicating which items are intended to measure each of the achievements outlined. They can also aid test users by presenting detailed data on the internal analysis of the test, recognizing that these analyses are likely to be somewhat specific to the population tested.

SUMMARY

This article has dealt mainly with eleven points of view:

1. That the content validity of a test is determined by its relevance to the objectives of instruction rather than by its coverage of the materials of instruction.

2. That good tests of educational achievement provide good operational definitions of the goals of instruction.

3. That tests based on educational goals can directly influence teaching procedures constructively.

4. That there is no essential difference between the rational judgments involved in determining the content relevance of a test and those involved in determining the adequacy of criterion scores.

5. That all types of validity are based ultimately on the content validity of some measurement procedures.

6. That the best evidence of content validity is obtained by detailed, systematic, critical inspection of the test itself.

7. That it is possible to analyze the types of achievement required by the items as well as the content covered by the items in judging content validity.

8. That the test user is more competent than anyone else to judge the relevance of the test to his purposes.

9. That presentation of detailed test specifications and outlines in the test manual helps the user judge its relevance to his purposes.

10. That data from internal analysis of test reliability and item-discriminating power are helpful in judging content validity.

11. That evidence of content validity should be reported more fully than is usually true.

14   Construct Validity in Psychological Tests

....

LEE J. CRONBACH AND PAUL E. MEEHL

The following article is a classic discussion of "construct" validity, a concept which has evoked considerable discussion since it was introduced in 1954 in the Technical Recommendations *(APA, 1954). As is true of many carefully conceived and comprehensive statements, the reader can expect to gain greater insight into what the authors are saying with each re-reading. It might be helpful if the reader kept in mind that the demonstration of the construct validity of a test typically requires a series of studies which assess or validate related theory as well as the specific instrument. Because of space limitations the original article has been severely reduced, numerous sections of explanatory material and statements of qualifications having been eliminated. The serious reader is urged to refer to the primary source for clarification and to Bechtoldt (1959) for a different point of view.*

The notion of construct validity is considered by many test authorities as being the essence of what Ebel (1961) has recently labeled the "meaningfulness" of test scores. The overriding intent in applying and evaluating construct validation procedures is an attempt to insure the legitimate interpretability of the scores with respect to the underlying construct purported to be measured. But how does construct validity differ from other types of validity? How is it similar? What are the pros and cons of using specific criteria in test validation? What is the "bootstrap effect"? What are the sources of data that should be drawn upon in

Reprinted and abridged from Lee J. Cronbach and Paul E. Meehl. Construct Validity in Psychological Tests. *Psychological Bulletin*, 1955, Vol. 52, pp. 281–302. Copyright 1955 by the American Psychological Association and reproduced by permission of the first named author and publisher.

evaluating construct validity? What is a "nomological net", and what part does it play in construct validation?

Validation of psychological tests has not yet been adequately conceptualized, as the APA Committee on Psychological Tests learned when it undertook (1950–54) to specify what qualities should be investigated before a test is published. In order to make coherent recommendations the Committee found it necessary to distinguish four types of validity established by different types of research and requiring different interpretations. The chief innovation in the Committee's report was the term "construct validity." The statements agreed upon by the Committee (and by committees of two other associations) were published in the *Technical Recommendations* (American Psychological Association, 1954).

Construct validation is involved whenever a test is to be interpreted as a measure of some attribute or quality which is not "operationally defined." The problem faced by the investigator is, "What constructs account for variance in test performance?" Construct validity does not call for a new scientific approach. Much current research on tests of personality is construct validation.

Construct validity is not to be identified solely by particular investigative procedures, but by the orientation of the investigator. Criterion-oriented validity, as Bechtoldt emphasizes (1951, p. 1245), "involves the acceptance of a set of operations as an adequate definition of whatever is to be measured." When an investigator believes that no criterion available to him is fully valid, he perforce becomes interested in construct validity because this is the only way to avoid the "infinite frustration" of relating every criterion to some ultimate standard. In content validation acceptance of the universe of content as defining the variable to be measured is essential. Construct validity must be investigated whenever no criterion or universe of content is accepted as entirely adequate to define the quality to be measured.

Construct validity would be involved in answering such questions as: To what extent is this test of intelligence culture-free? Does this test of "interpretation of data" measure reading ability, quantitative reasoning, or response sets? How does a person with an "A" rating in Strong Accountant and "B" in Strong CPA differ from a person who has these scores reversed?

EXAMPLE OF CONSTRUCT VALIDATION PROCEDURE

Suppose measure X correlates .50 with Y, the amount of palmar sweating induced when we tell a student that he has failed a Psychology 1 exam. Predictive validity of X for Y is adequately described by the coefficient and a statement of the experimental and sampling conditions. If someone were to ask, "Isn't there perhaps another way to interpret this correlation?" or "What other kinds of evidence can you bring to support your interpretation?," we would hardly understand what he was asking because no interpretation has been made. These questions become relevant when the correlation is advanced as evidence that "test X measures anxiety proneness." Alternative interpretations are possible; e.g., perhaps the test measures "academic aspiration," in which case we will expect different results if we induce palmar sweating by economic threat. It is then reasonable to inquire about other kinds of evidence.

Add these facts from further studies: Test X correlates .45 with fraternity brothers' ratings on "tenseness." Test X correlates .55 with amount of intellectual inefficiency induced by painful electric shock, and .68 with the Taylor Anxiety scale. Mean X score decreases among four diagnosed groups in this order: anxiety state, reactive depression, "normal," and psychopathic personality. And palmar sweat under threat of failure in Psychology 1 correlates .60 with threat of failure in mathematics. Negative results eliminate competing explanations of the X score; thus, findings of negligible correlations between X and social class, vocational aim, and value-orientation make it fairly safe to reject the suggestion that X measures "academic aspiration." We can have substantial confidence that X does measure anxiety proneness if the current theory of anxiety can embrace the variates which yield positive correlations, and does not predict correlations where we found none.

KINDS OF CONSTRUCTS

At this point we should indicate summarily what we mean by a construct, recognizing that much of the remainder of the paper deals with this question. A construct is some postulated attribute of people, assumed to be reflected in test performance. In test validation the attribute about which we make statements in interpreting a test is a construct. We expect a person at any time to possess or not possess a qualitative attribute (amnesia) or structure, or to possess some degree of a quantitative attribute (cheerfulness). A construct has certain associated meanings carried in statements of this general character: Persons who possess this attribute will in situation X act in manner Y (with a stated probability). The logic of construct validation is invoked whether the construct is highly systematized or loose, used in ramified theory or a few simple propositions, used in absolute propositions or probability statements. We seek to specify how one is to defend a proposed interpretation of a test: *we are not recommending any one type of interpretation.*

The constructs in which tests are to be interpreted are certainly not likely to be physiological. Most often they will be traits such as "latent hostility" or "variable in mood," or descriptions in terms of an educational objective, as "ability to plan experiments."

THE RELATION OF CONSTRUCTS TO "CRITERIA"

CRITICAL VIEW OF THE IMPLIED CRITERION ▪ An unquestionable criterion may be found in a practical operation or may be established as a consequence of an operational definition. Typically, however, the psychologist is unwilling to use the directly operational approach because he is interested in building theory about a generalized construct. A theorist trying to relate behavior to "hunger" almost certainly invests that term with meanings other than the operation "elapsed-time-since-feeding." If he is concerned with hunger as a tissue need, he will not accept time lapse as equivalent to his construct because it fails to consider, among other things, energy expediture of the animal.

In some situations the criterion is no more valid than the test. Suppose, for example, that we want to know if counting the dots on Bender-Gestalt figure five indicates "compulsive rigidity," and take psychiatric ratings on this trait as a criterion. Even a conventional report on the resulting correlation will say something about the extent and intensity of the psychiatrist's contacts and should describe his qualifications (e.g., diplomate status? analyzed?). Why report these facts? Because data are needed to indicate whether the criterion is any good.

INADEQUACY OF VALIDATION IN TERMS OF SPECIFIC CRITERIA ▪ The proposal to validate constructual interpretations of tests runs counter to suggestions of some others. Spiker and McCandless (1954) favor an operational approach. Validation is replaced by compiling statements as to how strongly the test predicts other observed variables of interest. To avoid requiring that each new variable be investigated completely by itself, they allow two variables to collapse into one whenever the properties of the operationally defined measures are the same: "If a new test is demonstrated to predict the test scores on an older, well-established test, then an evaluation of the predictive power of the older test may be used for the new one." But accurate inferences are possible only if the two tests correlate so highly that there is negligible reliable variance in either test, independent of the other. Where the correspondence is less close, one must either retain all the separate variables operationally defined or embark on construct validation.

The practical user of tests must rely on constructs of some generality to make predictions about new situations. Test X could be used to predict palmar sweating in the face of failure without invoking any construct, but a counselor is more likely to be asked to forecast behavior in diverse or even unique situations for which the correlation of test X is unknown. Significant predictions rely on knowledge accumulated around a generalized construct.

The present approach to validity appears to conflict with arguments for specific criteria prominent at places in the testing literature. Thus Anastasi (1950) makes many statements of the latter character: "It is only as a measure of a specifically defined criterion that a test can be objectively validated at all. . . . To claim that a test measures anything over and above its criterion is pure speculation." (p. 67) Yet elsewhere her article supports construct validation. Tests can be profitably interpreted if we "know the relationships between the tested behavior . . . and other behavior samples necessarily occupying the preeminent position of a criterion." (p. 75) Factor analysis with several partial criteria might be used to study whether a test measures a postulated "general learning ability." If the data demonstrate specificity of ability instead, such specificity is "useful in its own right in advancing our knowledge of behavior; it should not be construed as a weakness of the tests." (p.75)

We depart from Anastasi at two points. She writes, "The validity of a psychological test should not be confused with an analysis of the factors which determine the behavior under consideration." We, however, regard such analysis as a most important type of validation. Second, she refers to "the will-o'-the wisp of psychological processes which are distinct from performance." (Anastasi, 1950, p. 77) While we agree that psychological processes are elusive, we are sympathetic to attempts to formulate and clarify constructs which are evidenced by performance but distinct from it. Surely an inductive inference based on a pattern of correlations cannot be dismissed as "pure speculation."

SPECIFIC CRITERIA USED TEMPORARILY: THE "BOOTSTRAPS" EFFECT ▪ Even when a test is constructed on the basis of a specific criterion, it may ultimately be judged to have greater construct validity than the criterion. We start with a vague concept which we associate with certain observations. We then discover empirically that these observations co-vary with some other observation which possesses greater reliability or is more intimately correlated with relevant experimental changes than is the original measure, or both. For example, the notion of temperature arises because some objects feel hotter to the touch than others. The expansion of a mercury column does not have face validity as an index of hotness. But it turns out that (a) there is a statistical relation between expansion and sensed temperature; (b) observers employ the mercury method with good interobserver agreement; (c) the regularity of observed relations is increased by using the thermometer (e.g., melting points of samples of the same material vary little on the thermometer; we obtain nearly linear relations between mercury measures and pressure of a gas). Finally, (d) a theoretical structure involving unobservable microevents—the kinetic theory—is worked out which explains the relation of mercury expansion to heat. This whole process of conceptual enrichment begins with what in retrospect we see as an extremely fallible "criterion"— the human temperature sense. That original criterion has now been relegated to a peripheral position. We have lifted ourselves by our bootstraps, but in a legitimate and fruitful way.

EXPERIMENTATION TO INVESTIGATE CONSTRUCT VALIDITY

VALIDATION PROCEDURES ▪ We can use many methods in construct validation. Attention should particularly be drawn to Macfarlane's (1942) survey of these methods as they apply to projective devices.

Group Differences. If our understanding of a construct leads us to expect two groups to differ on the test, this expectation may be tested directly. Thus Thurstone and Chave validated the Scale for Measuring Attitude Toward the Church by showing score differences between church members and non-church-goers. Churchgoing is not the criterion of attitude, for the purpose of the test is to measure something other than the crude sociological fact of church attendance; on the other hand, failure to find a difference would have seriously challenged the test.

Only coarse correspondence between test and group designation is expected. Too great a correspondence between the two would indicate that the test is to some degree invalid, because members of the groups are expected to overlap on the test. Intelligence test items are selected initially on the basis of a correspondence to age, but an item that correlates .95 with age in an elementary school sample would surely be suspect.

Correlation Matrices and Factor Analysis. If two tests are presumed to measure the same construct, a correlation between them is predicted. If the obtained correlation departs from the expectation, however, there is no way to know whether the fault lies in test A, test B, or the formulation of the construct. A matrix of intercorrelations often points out profitable ways of dividing the construct into more meaningful parts, factor analysis being a useful computational method in such studies.

Studies of Internal Structure. For many constructs evidence of homogeneity within the test is relevant in judging validity. If a trait such as "dominance" is hypothesized, and the items inquire about behaviors subsumed under this label, then the hypothesis appears to require that these items be generally intercorrelated. Even low correlations if consistent would support the argument that people may be fruitfully described in terms of a generalized tendency to dominate or not to dominate. The general quality would have power to predict behavior in a variety of situations represented by the specific items. Item-test correlations and certain reliability formulas describe internal consistency.

Study of distinctive subgroups of items within a test may set an upper limit to construct validity by showing that irrelevant elements influence scores. Thus a study of the *Primary Mental Ability* space tests shows that variance can be partially accounted for by a response set tendency to mark many figures as similar (Cronbach, 1950). On the other hand, a study of item groupings in the *Differential Aptitude Test*–Mechanical Comprehension Test permitted rejection of the hypothesis that knowledge about specific topics such as gears made a substantial contribution to scores (Cronbach, 1951).

Studies of Change Over Occasions. The stability of test scores ("retest reliability") may be relevant to construct validation. Whether a high degree of stability is encouraging or discouraging for the proposed interpretation depends upon the theory defining the construct.

More powerful than the retest after uncontrolled intervening experiences is the retest with experimental intervention. If a transient influence swings test scores over a wide range, there are definite limits on the extent to which a test result can be interpreted as reflecting the typical behavior of the individual. These are examples of experiments which have indicated upper limits to test validity: studies of differences associated with the examiner in projective testing, of change of score under alternative directions ("tell the truth" vs. "make yourself look good to an employer"), and of coachability of mental tests. We may recall Gulliksen's (1950b) distinction: When the coaching is of a sort that improves the pupil's intellectual functioning in school, the test which is affected by the coaching has validity as a measure of intellectual functioning; if the coaching improves test-taking but not school performance, the test which responds to the coaching has poor intrinsic validity as a measure of this construct.

Studies of Process. One of the best ways of determining informally what accounts for variability on a test is the observation of the person's process of performance. If it is supposed, for example, that a test measures mathematical competence, and yet observation of students' errors shows that erroneous reading of the questions is common, the implications of a low score are altered. Lucas (1953) in this way showed that the Navy Relative Movement Test, an aptitude test, actually involved two different abilities: spatial visualization and mathematical reasoning.

THE LOGIC OF CONSTRUCT VALIDATION

Construct validation takes place when an investigator believes that his instrument reflects a particular construct, to which are attached certain meanings. The proposed interpretation generates specific testable hypotheses, which are a means of confirming or disconfirming the claim. The philosophy of science which we believe does most justice to actual scientific practice will now be briefly and dogmatically set forth.

THE NOMOLOGICAL NET ▪ The fundamental principles are these:

1. Scientifically speaking, to "make clear what something is" means to set forth the laws in which it occurs. We shall refer to the interlocking system of laws which constitute a theory as a *nomological network*.

2. The laws in a nomological network may relate (a) observable properties or quantities to each other; or (b) theoretical constructs to observables; or (c) different theoretical constructs to one another. These "laws" may be statistical or deterministic.

3. A necessary condition for a construct to be scientifically admissible is that it occur in a nomological net, at least some of whose laws involve observables. Admissible constructs may be remote from observation, i.e., a long derivation may intervene between the nomologicals which implicitly define the construct, and the (derived) nomologicals of type a. These latter propositions permit

predictions about events. The construct is not "reduced" to the observations, but only combined with other constructs in the net to make predictions about observables.

4. "Learning more about" a theoretical construct is a matter of elaborating the nomological network in which it occurs, or of increasing the definiteness of the components. At least in the early history of a construct the network will be limited, and the construct will as yet have few connections.

5. An enrichment of the net such as adding a construct or a relation to theory is justified if it generates nomologicals that are confirmed by observation or if it reduces the number of nomologicals required to predict the same observations. When observations will not fit into the network as it stands, the scientist has a certain freedom in selecting where to modify the network. That is, there may be alternative constructs or ways of organizing the net which for the time being are equally defensible.

6. We can say that "operations" which are qualitatively very different "overlap" or "measure the same thing" if their positions in the nomological net tie them to the same construct variable. Our confidence in this identification depends upon the amount of inductive support we have for the regions of the net involved.

The preceding guide rules should reassure the "tough-minded," who fear that allowing construct validation opens the door to non-confirmable test claims. The answer is that unless the network makes contact with observations and exhibits explicit, public steps of inference, construct validation cannot be claimed. An admissible psychological construct must be behavior-relevant. For most tests intended to measure constructs adequate criteria do not exist. This being the case, many such tests have been left unvalidated, or a finespun network of rationalizations has been offered as if it were validation. Rationalization is not construct validation. One who claims that his test reflects a construct cannot maintain his claim in the face of recurrent negative results because these results show that his construct is too loosely defined to yield verifiable inferences.

When a construct is fairly new, there may be few specifiable associations by which to pin down the concept. As research proceeds, the construct sends out roots in many directions, which attach it to more and more facts or other constructs.

"Acceptance," which was critical in criterion-oriented and content validities, has now appeared in construct validity. Unless substantially the same nomological net is accepted by the several users of the construct, public validation is impossible. The investigator who proposes to establish a test as a measure of a construct must specify his network or theory sufficiently clearly that others can accept or reject it (Macfarlane, 1942, p. 406). A consumer of the test who rejects the author's theory cannot accept the author's validation. He must validate the test for himself, if he wishes to show that it represents the construct as he defines it.

CONCLUSIONS REGARDING THE NETWORK
AFTER EXPERIMENTATION

The proposition that x percent of test variance is accounted for by the construct is inserted into the accepted network. The network then generates a testable prediction about the relation of the test scores to certain other variables, and the investigator gathers data. If prediction and result are in harmony, he can retain his belief that the test measures the construct. The construct is at best adopted, never demonstrated to be "correct."

We do not first "prove" the theory and then validate the test, nor conversely. In any probable inductive type of reference from a pattern of observations we examine the relation between the total network of theory and observations. The system involves propositions relating test to construct, construct to other constructs, and finally relating some of these constructs to observables.

IMPLICATIONS OF NEGATIVE EVIDENCE ∎ The investigator whose prediction and data are discordant must make strategic decisions. His result can be interpreted in three ways:

1. The test does not measure the construct variable.

2. The theoretical network which generated the hypothesis is incorrect.

3. The experimental design failed to test the hypothesis properly. (Strictly speaking we may analyze this as a special case of 2, but in practice the distinction is worth making.)

For Further Research. If a specific fault of procedure makes the third a reasonable possibility, his proper response is to perform an adequate study, meanwhile making no report. When faced with the other two alternatives, he may decide that his test does not measure the construct adequately. Following that decision, he will perhaps prepare and validate a new test. Any rescoring or new interpretative procedure for the original instrument, like a new test, requires validation by means of a fresh body of data.

The investigator may regard interpretation 2 as more likely to lead to eventual advances. It is legitimate for the investigator to call the network defining the construct into question, if he has confidence in the test. Should the investigator decide that some step in the network is unsound, he may be able to invent an alternative network. Perhaps he modifies the network by splitting a concept into two or more portions, e.g., by designating types of anxiety, or perhaps he specifies added conditions under which a generalization holds. When an investigator modifies the theory in such a manner, he is now required to gather a fresh body of data to test the altered hypotheses. This step should normally precede publication of the modified theory. If the new data are consistent with the modified network, he is free from the fear that his nomologicals were gerrymandered to fit the peculiarities of his first sample of observations. He can now trust his test to some extent, because his test results behaved as predicted.

The choice among alternatives, like any strategic decision, is a gamble as to which course of action is the best investment of effort. Is it wise to modify the theory? That depends on how well the system is confirmed by prior data, and how well the modifications fit available observations. Is it worthwhile to modify the test in the hope that it will fit the construct? That depends on how much evidence there is—apart from this abortive experiment— to support the hope, and also on how much it is worth to the investigator's ego to salvage the test. The choice among alternatives is a matter of research planning.

For Practical Use of the Test. The consumer can accept a test as a measure of a construct only when there is a strong positive fit between predictions and subsequent data. When the evidence from a proper investigation of a published test is essentially negative, it should be reported as a stop sign to discourage use of the test pending a reconciliation of test and construct, or final abandonment of the test. If the test has not been published, it should be restricted to research use until some degree of validity is established. The consumer can await the results of the investigator's gamble with confidence that proper application of the scientific method will ultimately tell whether the test has value. Until the evidence is in, he has no justification for employing the test as a basis for terminal decisions. The test may serve at best only as a source of suggestions about individuals to be confirmed by other evidence.

There are two perspectives in test validation. From the viewpoint of the psychological practitioner the burden of proof is on the test. A test should not be used to measure a trait until its proponent establishes that predictions made from such measures are consistent with the best available theory of the trait. In the view of the test developer, however, both the test and the theory are under scrutiny. He is free to say to himself privately, "If my test disagrees with the theory, so much the worse for the theory." This way lies delusion, unless he continues his research using a better theory.

REPORTING OF POSITIVE RESULTS ■ The test developer who finds positive correspondence between his proposed interpretation and data is expected to report the basis for his validity claim. Defending a claim of construct validity is a major task, not to be satisfied by a discourse without data. The *Technical Recommendations* have little to say on reporting of construct validity. Indeed, the only detailed suggestions under that heading refer to correlations of the test with other measures, together with a cross reference to some other sections of the report. The two key principles, however, call for the most comprehensive type of reporting. The manual for any test "should report all available information which will assist the user in determining what psychological attributes account for variance in test scores." (*Technical Recommendations*, 1954, p. 27) And, "The manual for a test which is used primarily to assess postulated attributes of the individual should outline the theory on which the test is based and organize whatever partial validity data there are to show in what way they support the theory." (p. 28)

The proper goals in reporting construct validation are to make clear (a) what interpretation is proposed, (b) how adequately the writer believes this interpretation is substantiated, and (c) what evidence and reasoning lead him to this belief. The test manual cannot always present an exhaustive statement on these points, but it should summarize and indicate where complete statements may be found.

RECAPITULATION

Construct validation was introduced in order to specify types of research required in developing tests for which the conventional views on validation are inappropriate. Personality tests and some tests of ability are interpreted in terms of attributes for which there is no adequate criterion. The following points made in the discussion are particularly significant.

1. A construct is defined implicitly by a network of associations of propositions in which it occurs. Constructs employed at different stages of research vary in definiteness.

2. Construct validation is possible only when some of the statements in the network lead to predicted relations among observables. While some observables may be regarded as "criteria," the construct validity of the criteria themselves is regarded as under investigation.

3. The network defining the construct, and the derivation leading to the predicted observation must be reasonably explicit so that validating evidence may be properly interpreted.

4. Many types of evidence are relevant to construct validity, including content validity, interitem correlations, interest correlations, test "criterion" correlations, studies of stability over time, and stability under experimental intervention. High correlations and high stability may constitute either favorable or unfavorable evidence for the proposed interpretation, depending on the theory surrounding the construct.

5. When a predicted relation fails to occur, the fault may lie in the proposed interpretation of the test or in the network. Altering the network so that it can cope with the new observations is, in effect, redefining the construct. Any such new interpretation of the test must be validated by a fresh body of data before being advanced publicly. Great care is required to avoid substituting *a posteriori* rationalizations for proper validation.

6. Construct validity cannot generally be expressed in the form of a single simple coefficient. The integration of diverse data into a proper interpretation cannot be an entirely quantitative process.

7. Constructs may vary in nature from those very close to "pure description" (involving little more than extrapolation of relations among observation-variables) to highly theoretical constructs involving hypothesized entities and processes, or making identifications with constructs of other sciences.

8. The investigation of a test's construct validity is not essentially different from the general scientific procedures for developing and confirming theories.

15   Convergent and Discriminant Validity

DONALD T. CAMPBELL AND DONALD W. FISKE

Some of the ideas about construct validity found in the preceding article by Cronbach and Meehl are extended in the present article. Campbell and Fiske point out that sometimes we demand high correlations as evidence of construct validity. At other times, however, we wish to discriminate, i.e., to show low correlations where the traits are assumed to be different. Further, we need to assess the importance of the method of measuring traits. The suggested approach for construct validity studies, then, is to measure at least two traits by at least two of the same methods. The various relationships are computed, and are recorded in a table or matrix (multitrait-multimethod matrix). To illustrate, suppose a group was measured by a test battery and also rated by a teacher on verbal reasoning, mathematical ability, and clerical speed and accuracy. What would you expect to be the relationships between verbal reasoning and mathematical ability? What would you expect to be the relationships between verbal reasoning and clerical speed and accuracy? Would you expect that verbal reasoning expressed by a test score would correlate more highly with verbal reasoning expressed by a rating or with clerical speed and accuracy assessed by the same test battery? What four criteria suggested by the authors should be used in evaluating the data included in a multitrait-multimethod matrix?

In the cumulative experience with measures of individual differences over the past 50 years, tests have been accepted as valid or discarded as invalid by research experiences of many sorts. The criteria suggested in this paper are all to be found in such cumulative evaluations as well as in recent discussions of validity. These criteria are clarified and implemented when considered jointly in the context of a multitrait-multimethod matrix. Aspects of the validational process receiving particular emphasis are these:

1. Validation is typically *convergent*, a confirmation by independent measurement procedures. Independence of methods is a common denominator among the major types of validity (excepting content validity) insofar as they are to be distinguished from reliability.

2. For the justification of novel trait measures, for the validation of test interpretation, or for the establishment of construct validity, *discriminant* validation as well as convergent validation is required. Tests can be invalidated by too high correlations with other tests from which they were intended to differ.

3. Each test or task employed for measurement purposes is a *trait-method unit*, a union of a particular trait content with measurement procedures not specific

Reprinted and abridged from Donald T. Campbell and Donald W. Fiske, "Convergent and Discriminant Validation by the Multitrait-Multimethod Matrix," *Psychological Bulletin*, 1959, Vol. 56, pp. 81–105. Copyright 1959 by the American Psychological Association and reproduced by permission of the publisher and first-named author.

to that content. The systematic variance among test scores can be due to responses to the measurement features as well as responses to the trait content.

4. In order to examine discriminant validity, and in order to estimate the relative contributions of trait and method variance, *more than one trait* as well as *more than one method* must be employed in the validation process. In many instances it will be convenient to achieve this through a multitrait-multimethod matrix. Such a matrix presents all of the intercorrelations resulting when each of several traits is measured by each of several methods.

To illustrate the suggested validational process a synthetic example is presented in Table 1. This illustration involves three different traits, each measured by

TABLE 1. *A Synthetic Multitrait-Multimethod Matrix*

| | *Traits* | Method 1 | | | Method 2 | | | Method 3 | | |
		A_1	B_1	C_1	A_2	B_2	C_2	A_3	B_3	C_3
	A_1	(.89)								
Method 1	B_1	.51	(.89)							
	C_1	.38	.37	(.76)						
	A_2	.57	.22	.09	(.93)					
Method 2	B_2	.22	.57	.10	.68	(.94)				
	C_2	.11	.11	.46	.59	.58	(.84)			
	A_3	.56	.22	.11	.67	.42	.33	(.94)		
Method 3	B_3	.23	.58	.12	.43	.66	.34	.67	(.92)	
	C_3	.11	.11	.45	.34	.32	.58	.58	.60	(.85)

Note—The validity diagonals are the three sets of italicized values. The reliability diagonals are the three sets of values in parentheses. Each heterotrait-monomethod triangle is enclosed by a solid line. Each heterotrait-heteromethod triangle is enclosed by a broken line.

three methods, generating nine separate variables. It will be convenient to have labels for various regions of the matrix, and such have been provided in Table 1. The reliabilities will be spoken of in terms of three *reliability diagonals*, one for each method. The reliabilities could also be designated as the monotrait-mono-method values. Adjacent to each reliability diagonal is the heterotrait-mono-method triangle. The reliability diagonal and the adjacent heterotrait-mono-method triangle make up a monomethod block. A *heteromethod block* is made up of a *validity* diagonal (which could also be designated as monotrait-hetero-method values) and the two heterotrait-heteromethod triangles lying on each side of it. Note that these two heterotrait-heteromethod triangles are not identical.[1]

In terms of this diagram four aspects bear upon the question of validity. In the first place, the entries in the validity diagonal should be significantly different

[1] The reader may profit from sketching Table 1 for himself. It is suggested that he consider only Methods 1 and 2, and that for the correlation coefficients he substitute the italicized labels appearing in the above paragraph. (Editors)

from zero and sufficiently large to encourage further examination of validity. This requirement is evidence of convergent validity. Second, a validity diagonal value should be higher than the values lying in its column and row in the heterotrait-heteromethod triangles. That is, a validity value for a variable should be higher than the correlations obtained between that variable and any other variable having neither trait nor method in common. This requirement may seem so minimal and so obvious as to not need stating, yet an inspection of the literature shows that it is frequently not met and may not be met even when the validity coefficients are of substantial size. In Table 1 all of the validity values meet this requirement. A third common-sense desideratum is that a variable correlate higher with an independent effort to measure the same trait than with measures designed to get at difficult traits which happen to employ the same method. For a given variable this involves comparing its values in the validity diagonals with its values in the heterotrait-monomethod triangles. For variables A_1, B_1, and C_1, this requirement is met to some degree. For the other variables A_2, A_3, etc., it is not met and this is probably typical of the usual case in individual differences research, as will be discussed in what follows. A fourth desideratum is that the same pattern of trait interrelationship be shown in all of the heterotrait triangles of both the monomethod and heteromethod blocks. The hypothetical data in Table 1 meet this requirement to a very marked degree, in spite of the different general levels of correlation involved in the several heterotrait triangles.[2] The last three criteria provide evidence for discriminant validity.

Before we examine the multitrait-multimethod matrices available in the literature, some explication and justification of this complex of requirements seems in order.

CONVERGENCE OF INDEPENDENT METHODS: THE DISTINCTION BETWEEN RELIABILITY AND VALIDITY ■ Both reliability and validity concepts require that agreement between measures be demonstrated. A common denominator which most validity concepts share in contradistinction to reliability is that this agreement represents the convergence of independent approaches. The concept of independence is indicated by such phrases as "external variable," "criterion performance," "behavioral criterion" (American Psychological Association, 1954, pp. 13–15) used in connection with concurrent and predictive validity. For construct validity it has been stated thus: "Numerous successful predictions dealing with phenotypically diverse 'criteria' give greater weight to the claim of construct validity than do . . . predictions involving very similar behavior." (Cronbach & Meehl, 1955, p. 295)

Independence is, of course, a matter of degree, and in this sense reliability and validity can be seen as regions on a continuum. Reliability is the agreement between two efforts to measure the same trait through maximally similar methods.

---

[2] For example, the correlation between traits A and B is the highest in each of the triangles. (Editors)

Validity is represented in the agreement between two attempts to measure the same trait through maximally different methods. Some evaluation of validity can take place even if the two methods are not entirely independent. In practice, perhaps all that can be hoped for is evidence for relative validity, that is, for common variance specific to a trait, above and beyond shared method variance.

Discriminant validation. While the usual reason for the judgment of invalidity is low correlations in the validity diagonal, tests have also been invalidated because of too high correlations with other tests purporting to measure different things. Such invalidation occurs when values in the heterotrait-heteromethod triangles are as high as those in the validity diagonal, or even where within a monomethod block the heterotrait values are as high as the reliabilities.

When a dimension of personality is hypothesized, when a construct is proposed, the proponent invariably has in mind distinctions between the new dimension and other constructs already in use. One cannot define without implying distinctions, and the verification of these distinctions is an important part of the validational process. In discussions of construct validity it has been expressed in such terms as "from this point of view, a low correlation with athletic ability may be just as important and encouraging as a high correlation with reading comprehension." (APA, 1954, p. 17)

THE TEST AS A TRAIT-METHOD UNIT ■ In any given psychological measuring device there are certain features or stimuli introduced specifically to represent the trait that it is intended to measure. There are other features which are characteristic of the method being employed, features which could also be present in efforts to measure other quite different traits. The test, rating scale, or other device almost inevitably elicits systematic variance in response due to both groups or features. To the extent that irrelevant method variance contributes to the scores obtained, these scores are invalid.

This source of invalidity was first noted in the "halo effects" found in ratings (E. L. Thorndike, 1920). Studies of individual differences among laboratory animals resulted in the recognition of "apparatus factors," usually more dominant than psychological process factors. For paper-and-pencil tests, methods variance has been noted under such terms as "test-form factors" and "response sets." Cronbach has stated the point particularly clearly: "The assumption is generally made . . . that what the test measures is determined by the content of the items. Yet the final score . . . is a composite of effects resulting from the form of the item used." (Cronbach, 1946, p. 475) "Response sets always lower the logical validity of a test. . . . Response sets interfere with inferences from test data." (p. 484)

While E. L. Thorndike (1920) was willing to allege the presence of halo effects by comparing the obtained high correlations with common sense notions of what they ought to be (e.g., it was unreasonable that a teacher's intelligence and voice quality should correlate .63.), and while much of the evidence of response set variance is of the same order, the clear-cut demonstration of the presence of method variance requires both several traits and several methods. Otherwise, high correlations between tests might be explained as due either to basic trait similarity or to shared method variance. In the multitrait-multimethod matrix the presence of method variance is indicated by the difference in level of correlation between the parallel values of the monomethod block and the heteromethod blocks, assuming comparable reliabilities among all tests. Thus the contribution of method variance in Test A_1 of Table 1 is indicated by the elevation of $r_{A_1B_1}$ above $r_{A_1B_2}$, i.e., the difference between .51 and .22, etc.

The distinction between trait and method is of course relative to the test constructor's intent. What is an unwanted response set for one tester may be a trait for another who wishes to measure acquiescense, willingness to take an extreme stand, or tendency to attribute socially desirable attributes to oneself (Cronbach, 1946, 1950; Edwards, 1957b).

SOME ILLUSTRATIVE MATRICES ▪ Multitrait-multimethod matrices are rare in the test and measurement literature. Most frequent are two types of fragment: two methods and one trait (single isolated values from the validity diagonal, perhaps accompanied by a reliability or two) and heterotrait-monomethod triangles. Either type of fragment is apt to disguise the inadequacy of our present measurement efforts, particularly in failing to call attention to the preponderant strength of method variance. The evidence of test validity to be presented here is probably poorer than most psychologists would have expected.[3]

TABLE 2. *Intercorrelations and Reliabilities of Four Personality Traits of School Children Measured by Two Different Methods* $(N = 311)$[1]

		Peer Ratings				Association Test			
		A_1	B_1	C_1	D_1	A_2	B_2	C_2	D_2
Peer Ratings									
Courtesy	A_1	(.82)							
Honesty	B_1	.74	(.80)						
Poise	C_1	.63	.65	(.74)					
School Drive	D_1	.76	.78	.65	(.89)				
Association Test									
Courtesy	A_2	.13	.14	.10	.14	(.28)			
Honesty	B_2	.06	.12	.16	.08	.27	(.38)		
Poise	C_2	.01	.08	.10	.02	.19	.37	(.42)	
School Drive	D_2	.12	.15	.14	.16	.27	.32	.18	(.36)

[1] Based on data from Kelley and Krey (1934)

[3] Two examples have been selected to illustrate the procedure. (Editors)

One of the earliest matrices of this kind was provided by Kelley and Krey in 1934. Peer judgments by students provided one method, scores on a word-association test the other. Table 2 presents the data for the four most valid traits of the eight employed. The picture is one of strong method factors, particularly among the peer ratings, and almost total invalidity. For only one of the eight measures, school drive, is the value in the validity diagonal (.16) higher than all of the heterotrait-heteromethod values. The absence of discriminant validity is further indicated by the tendency of the values in the monomethod triangles to approximate the reliabilities.

An early illustration from the animal literature comes from Anderson's (1937) study of drives. Table 3 presents a sample of his data. Once again the highest

TABLE 3. *Intercorrelations and Reliabilities of Drive Measures Obtained by Two Different Methods* $(N = 50)$[1]

		Obstruction Box			Activity Wheel		
		A_1	B_1	C_1	A_2	B_2	C_2
Obstruction Box							
Hunger	A_1	(.58)					
Thirst	B_1	.54	( )				
Sex	C_1	.46	.70	( )			
Activity Wheel							
Hunger	A_2	.48	.31	.37	(.83)		
Thirst	B_2	.35	.33	.43	.87	(.92)	
Post Sex	C_2	.31	.37	.44	.69	.78	( )

[1] Based on data presented by Anderson (1937)

Note—Empty parentheses appear where no appropriate reliability estimates are reported in the original paper.

correlations are found among different constructs from the same method showing the dominance of apparatus or method factors so typical of the whole field of individual differences. The validity diagonal for hunger is higher than the heteroconstruct-heteromethod values. The diagonal value for sex has not been *italicized* as a validity coefficient since the obstruction box measure was pre-sex-opportunity, the activity wheel post-opportunity. Note that the high general level of heterotrait-heteromethod values could be due to either correlation of methods variance between the two methods or to correlated trait variance. On *a priori* grounds, however, the methods would seem about as independent as one would be likely to achieve. The predominance of an apparatus factor for the activity wheel is evident from the fact that the correlation between hunger and thirst (.87) is of the same magnitude as their test-retest reliabilities (.83 and .92 respectively).

DISCUSSION

RELATION TO CONSTRUCT VALIDITY ▪ While the validational criteria presented are explicit or implicit in the discussions of construct validity (Cronbach & Meehl, 1955; APA, 1954), this paper is primarily concerned with the adequacy of tests as measures of a construct rather than with the adequacy of a construct as determined by the confirmation of theoretically predicted associations with measures of other constructs. We believe that before one can test the relationships between a specific trait and other traits, one must have some confidence in one's measures of that trait. Such confidence can be supported by evidence of convergent and discriminant validation. Stated in different words, any conceptual formulation of a trait will usually include implicitly, the proposition that this trait is a response tendency which can be observed under more than one experimental condition and that this trait can be meaningfully differentiated from other traits. The testing of these two propositions must be prior to the testing of other propositions to prevent the acceptance of erroneous conclusions. For example, a conceptual framework might postulate a large correlation between Traits A and B and no correlation between Traits A and C. If the experimenter then measures A and B by one method (e.g., questionnaire) and C by another method (such as the measurement of overt behavior in a situation test), his findings may be consistent with his hypotheses solely as a function of method variance common to his measures of A and B but not to C.

The requirements of this paper are intended to be as appropriate to the relatively atheoretical efforts typical of the tests and measurements field as to more theoretical efforts. This emphasis on validational criteria appropriate to our present atheoretical level of test construction is not at all incompatible with a recognition of the desirability of increasing the extent to which all aspects of a test and the testing situation are determined by explicit theoretical considerations, as Jessor and Hammond have advocated (Jessor & Hammond, 1957).

RELATION TO OPERATIONALISM ▪ Underwood (1957, p. 54) in his effective presentation of the operationalist point of view shows a realistic awareness of the amorphous type of theory with which most psychologists work. He contrasts a psychologist's "literacy" conception with the psychologist's operational definition as represented by his test or other measuring instrument. He recognizes the importance of the literary definition in communicating and generating science. He cautions that the operational definition "may not at all measure the process he wishes to measure; it may measure something quite different." (p. 55) He does not, however, indicate how one would know when one was thus mistaken.

The requirements of the present paper may be seen as an extension of the kind of operationalism Underwood has expressed. The test constructor is asked to generate from his literary conception or private construct not one operational embodiment, but two or more, each as different in research vehicle as possible. Furthermore, he is asked to make explicit the distinction between his new variable and other variables, distinctions which are almost certainly implied in his literary definition. In his very first validational efforts, before he ever rushes into print, he is asked to apply the several methods and several traits jointly. His literary definition, his conception is now best represented in what his independent measures of the trait hold *distinctively* in common. The multitrait-multimethod matrix is, we believe, an important practical first step in avoiding "the danger . . . that the investigator will fall into the trap of thinking that because he went from an artistic or literary conception . . . to the construction of items for a scale to measure it, he has validated his artistic conception." (Underwood, 1957, p. 55) In contrast with the *single operationalism* now dominant in psychology, we are advocating a *multiple operationalism*.

Underwood's presentation and that of this paper as a whole imply moving from concept to operation, a sequence that is frequent in science and perhaps typical. The same point can be made however in inspecting a transition from operation to construct. For any body of data taken from a single operation there is a subinfinity of interpretations possible, a subinfinity of concepts, or combinations of concepts that it could represent.

THE EVALUATION OF A MULTITRAIT-MULTIMETHOD MATRIX ▪ The evaluation of the correlation matrix formed by intercorrelating several trait-method units must take into consideration the many factors which are known to affect the magnitude of correlations. A value in the validity diagonal must be assessed in the light of the reliabilities of the two measures involved. Again, the whole approach assumes adequate sampling of individuals: the curtailment of the sample with respect to one or more traits will depress the reliability coefficients and intercorrelations involving these traits. While restrictions of range over all traits produce serious difficulties in the interpretation of a multitrait-multimethod matrix and should be avoided whenever possible, the presence of different degrees of restriction on different traits is the more serious hazard to meaningful interpretation.

Various statistical treatments for multitrait-multimethod matrices might be developed, but we believe that such summary statistics are neither necessary nor appropriate at this time. Psychologists today should be concerned not with evaluating tests as if the tests were fixed and definitive, but rather with developing better tests. We believe that a careful examination of a multitrait-multimethod matrix will indicate to the experimenter what his next steps should be: it will indicate which methods should be discarded or replaced, which concepts need sharper delineation, and which concepts are poorly measured because of excessive or confounding method variance. Validity judgments based on such a matrix must take into account the stage of development of the constructs, the postulated relationships among them, the level of technical refinement of the methods, the relative independence of the methods, and any pertinent characteristics of the sample. We are proposing that the validational process be viewed as an aspect of an ongoing program for improving measuring procedures, and that the "validity coefficients" obtained at any one stage in the process be interpreted in terms of gains over preceding stages and as indicators of where further effort is needed.

THE DESIGN OF A MULTITRAIT-MULTIMETHOD MATRIX ■ The several methods and traits included in a validational matrix should be selected with care. The several methods used to measure each trait should be appropriate to the trait as conceptualized. Although this view will reduce the range of suitable methods, it will rarely restrict the measurement to one operational procedure.

Wherever possible the several methods in one matrix should be completely independent of each other: there should be no prior reason for believing that they share method variance. This requirement is necessary to permit the values in the heteromethod-heterotrait triangles to approach zero. If the nature of the traits rules out such independence of methods, efforts should be made to obtain as much diversity as possible in terms of data sources and classification processes. Thus, the classes of stimuli, the background situations, or the experimental contexts should be different. Again, the persons providing the observations should have different roles *or* the procedures for scoring should be varied.

Plans for a validational matrix should take into account the difference between the interpretations regarding convergence and discrimination. It is sufficient to demonstrate convergence between two clearly distinct methods which show little overlap in the heterotrait-heteromethod triangles. While agreement between several methods is desirable, convergence between two is a satisfactory minimal requirement. Discriminative validation is not so easily achieved. Just as it is impossible to prove the null hypothesis or that some object does not exist, so one can never establish that a trait as measured is differentiated from all other traits. One can only show that this measure of Trait A has little overlap with those measures of B and C, and no dependable generalization beyond B and C can be made. For example, social poise could probably be readily discriminated from aesthetic interests, but it should also be differentiated from leadership.

Insofar as the traits are related and are expected to correlate with each other, the monomethod correlations will be substantial and heteromethod correlations between traits will also be positive. For ease of interpretation it may be best to include in the matrix at least two traits, and preferably two sets of traits, which are postulated to be independent of each other.

In closing, a word of caution is needed. Many multitrait-multimethod matrices will show no convergent validation: no relationship may be found between two methods of measuring a trait. In this common situation the experimenter should examine the evidence in favor of several alternative propositions: (a) Neither method is adequate for measuring the trait; (b) One of the two methods does not really measure the trait; (When the evidence indicates that a method does not measure the postulated trait it may prove to measure some other trait. High correlations in the heterotrait-heteromethod triangles may provide hints to such possibilities.) (c) The trait is not a functional unity, the response tendencies involved being specific to the non-trait attributes of each test. The failure to demonstrate convergence may lead to conceptual developments rather than to the abandonment of a test.

SUMMARY

This paper advocates a validational process utilizing a matrix of intercorrelations among tests representing at least two traits, each measured by at least two methods. Measures of the same trait should correlate higher with each other than they do with measures of different traits involving separate methods. Ideally, these validity values should also be higher than the correlations among different traits measured by the same method.

Illustrations from the literature show that these desirable conditions as a set are rarely met. Method or apparatus factors make very large contributions to psychological measurements.

The notions of convergence between independent measures of the same trait and discrimination between measures of different traits are compared with previously published formulations, such as construct validity and convergent operationalism. Problems in the application of this validational process are considered.

16   Some Suggestions for Reformulating the Validity Concept

RAYMOND B. CATTELL

With the appearance almost weekly of new psychometric devices, the need for a viable set of criteria with which to evaluate such tests becomes increasingly critical. The problem is compounded by the fact that these new devices not only focus on traditional dimensions of human behavior (e.g. intelligence and achievement) but also many purport to assess other complex constructs such as anxiety, motivation, and various types of psychopathology. In the following article Professor Cattell suggests some powerful criticisms of traditional conceptualizations of the validity concept and discusses some possible reformulations.

Reprinted and abridged from Cattell, Raymond B., "Validity and Reliability: A Proposed More Basic Set of Concepts," *Journal of Educational Psychology*, 1964, Vol. 55, pp. 1–22. Copyright 1964 by the American Psychological Association and reproduced by permission of author and publisher.

The reader may find it useful to read this paper with certain questions in mind. In general, how do Cattell's notions about validity differ from more traditional views? According to the author, what are the three major dimensions of validity, and how do these lead logically to definitions of subtypes? What are the advantages and disadvantages of the notion of "concrete" validity? What distinctions does the author make between "concept" and "construct" validity? Why does he believe the reformulation, "concept validity," to be desirable? What is meant by the term "semantic" validity?

Validity in its broadest sense will be defined by a widely accepted but penetrating phrase as the capacity of a test to predict some specified behavioral measure (or set of measures) other than itself. It is contended here that this test property admits always of further analysis along precisely three independent parameters or dimensions as follows.

DEGREE OF ABSTRACTION OF THE REFERENT CRITERION

This dimension extends from *concrete* (or particular) at one pole to *conceptual* at the other. Correlation with a job skill, such as operating a lathe, illustrates the former; and concept validity as a measure of intelligence, anxiety, etc., illustrates the latter. It is particularly to meet the latter case that the expression "a set of measures" is included in the above definition. For a concept can usually only be defined by a whole pattern of measures (taken under defined conditions). This and the remaining two parameters are to be discussed more fully in separate sections below.

DEGREE OF NATURALNESS OF THE CRITERION

This parameter extends from *natural* or *in situ* validity to *artifactual* validity at the other pole, as when correlations are made with some behavior (concrete) or abstraction from behavior (conceptual) which naturally occurs in or derives from our existing culture and environment. Artifactual validity is validity against a criterion which would not naturally exist in our culture, but arises only among the instruments of psychologists, e.g.—in validating an intelligence test against the Binet or some artificial, prescribed laboratory performance. The means of determining such a continuum is discussed below.

DEGREE OF DIRECTNESS OF VALIDATION

This continuum extends from direct to circumstantial or indirect. In the simplest sense the validity of Test x as a good measure of Criterion X might seem sufficiently evidenced by the magnitude of its direct correlation with X. But in a deeper philosophical sense it depends also on x behaving toward "the not-X" universe in the same way as X does. Even at a simple statistical level it is evident that two (or more) tests might show exactly the same correlation with X and yet correlate in very different patterns from each other with the not-X variables. These differences affect the degree and kind of error which will follow when x is allowed to stand for X.

These validity dimensions will be discussed more fully in a moment. Meanwhile, one should note that they are independent as in Figure 7. Thus if considered dichotomous, $2^3 = 8$ varieties or types of validity coefficients are possible.

However, if the following discussion on the nature of the natural-artifactual dimension is correct, it is sufficiently less important (in the sense of being less relevant to most issues and more arbitrary) to justify basing the main classification on the other two. We thus have four main varieties of validity coefficients, for which the following nomenclature and denotation are suggested (see Figure 7).

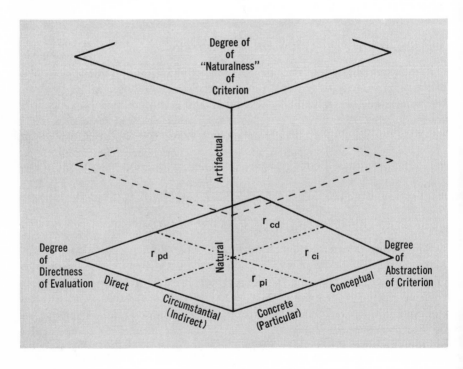

Figure 7.   Eight Validity Coefficients from Three Dichotomous Dimensions of Validation

1. Concrete-direct (or particular-direct) validity coefficient r_{pd}
2. Conceptual-direct validity coefficient r_{cd}
3. Conceptual-circumstantial (or indirect) validity coefficient r_{ci}
4. Concrete-circumstantial validity coefficient r_{pi}

If one wishes to include the natural-artifactual distinction too, an n or an a can be added as the third letter in the above subscripts.

FULLER IMPLICATIONS OF DIMENSIONS

Some further discussion is now necessary to bring out more fully the basic nature of these logical divisions.

CONCRETE VERSUS ABSTRACT OR PARTICULAR VERSUS CONCEPTUAL ■ The concrete-abstract continuum is so well known to philosophy and so readily given operational reality that only minimal illustration is necessary. The correlation of a test with success as a lathe operator, or number of traffic parking offenses, or degree of stuttering, is a concrete (particular) validity. To assert that a test measures intelligence or anxiety, on the other hand, is to claim for it an abstract or conceptual validity.

Concrete validities have perhaps hitherto had greater appeal, especially to practitioners, for two reasons. First, they appear more immediately useful; secondly, they can be calculated with lesser demands on theoretical and statistical sophistication. Despite a serious inferiority in concrete validities, shortly to be mentioned, one can actually sympathize with the educational and industrial psychologists' preference for a concrete or "particular" validity as one contemplates the vague, verbal, and evasive nature of many definitions of conceptual validity. The latter situation has led some psychologists, unfortunately, to conclude that one must abandon operations in accepting concept or construct[1] validity. This is by no means an inevitable conclusion. Indeed any concept worthy of the name in the domain of psychological theory must be reducible to operations. Commonly it will be reducible, however, to a pattern of operations, not to a single measurement operation. Such a pattern is most commonly made available, e.g., as a weighting of battery components in an intelligence or anxiety test.

Indeed, the very popularity of concrete validities is liable to bring confusion in its train, for different psychologists will often use a particular test with an eye to quite different criteria, e.g., the *Rorschach* is preferred by one for diagnosing schizophrenia and by another as an indicator of suicidal tendencies. Most tests correlate significantly with several concrete criteria which are then perhaps better called "referents" until psychologists agree to call one the criterion. Otherwise it does not make sense to talk about the validity of a test as a concrete validity; as a concept validity there is no problem. And it makes sense to talk about a single and concrete criterion only for special purpose and not general purpose tests. (Indeed a special purpose test is defined by its being oriented to one concrete criterion.) But a general purpose test, e.g., an intelligence or personality test, is not intended to correlate exclusively with any one of the millions of possible

---

[1] Concept and construct validity are used interchangeably here. The reasons for ultimately preferring concept validity for the more common "construct" validity are given.

concrete criteria, but strictly with a concept which naturally relates to many concrete expressions. The operational, experimental definition of concept validity is taken up in the following section.

NATURAL VERSUS ARTIFACTUAL ■ This also needs little discussion, except to point out that the cheapness of validating one test against another has made artifactual (and concrete) validation altogether too prevalent. Although we have agreed here, in the interest of comprehensiveness, to admit that "criterion" can be applied to an artificial test or specific laboratory situation performance, let us not forget that psychological testing has as its primary purpose the prediction of real-life behavior! Some may raise the objection to this dimension, as a dimension, that there may be arbitrariness in deciding what is natural and what is artificial. "Ability to adjust in the classroom" or "freedom from automobile accidents" are natural criteria belonging to the natural history of our general culture. Correlation with the AB Inventory of Self-Derogation or the Picayune Intelligence Scale, on the other hand, is an artificial though well-fixed criterion.

Except as an academic gain, or as a preliminary check, or as an unavoidable short cut to avoid the greater labor of going to real-life criteria, concrete artifactual validity against a concept "surrogate" is surely something which the research-minded psychologist will commonly avoid. Furthermore, it has actually tended to bring reverence for a false "apostolic succession," as when a new intelligence test, say, is validated against the *Wechsler Adult Intelligence Scale*, which was validated against the *Stanford-Binet*. One does not validate a modern caesium clock against Big Ben, and Big Ben against a medieval water clock! Concept validity avoids this excessive reverence for the past, demanding in each field an onward movement with the increasing accuracy of the concept per se.

DIRECT VERSUS CIRCUMSTANTIAL ■ Some philosophical reflection will show that there exists a neglected realm of indirect or circumstantial validation which has the virtue of being independent of and supplementary to the familiar realm of direct validation. Circumstantial, incidentally, is probably a better term than indirect, for it connotes the positive aspect of the procedure: the operational relating of the test to many required anchors in the surroundings instead of one. It also reminds us of its generic affiliation to "circumstantial evidence" in the law courts.

NEW ORGANIZATION OF CONCEPTS VIEWED IN RELATION TO CURRENT TERMS

As indicated above, the notion of concept validity is approximately the same as the APA (1954) committee's construct validity. Let us examine what advantages are claimed for reformulating concept validity as a theoretical element both in terms of assumptions and of operations for its measurement.

First, there is an unnecessary limitation and inaptness in the term construct.

Most commonly, in epistemology and logic the latter becomes synonymous with an "empirical construct." As such it dares not have theoretical parentage or be enriched by an ideational content or extra meaning beyond that given by its derivation as a complex of relationships among a set of empirical observations. When a psychologist speaks of intelligence, anxiety, neuroticism, or the self-sentiment, he is generally interested in a whole set of theoretical relations which go therewith, in virtue of which it is properly called a concept. To deny him the right to operate with this concept in the measurement field and to insist that he deal with a mere construct is to perpetuate that divorce of psychological theory from psychometric practice which has so long been unquestionably disastrous to both. On the one hand, it has permitted a rank growth of spurious theory, too vague and overelaborated to be useful as scientific theory and, on the other, it has left us with a purely statistical psychometry too dryly pointless to grip the attention of a psychologist with broad conceptual interests.

If theory and experiment are to get together, we ought to be talking about concept validity, for indeed no theoretical concept worthy of the name need lack translation into measurement operations, if they are sufficiently imaginative. Any concept of course is still a man-made model, not "something in nature," but hopefully it can yield a pretty close fit to something in nature. What has been lacking hitherto has been the discipline and ingenuity to recognize that nearly all concepts (a) can be expressed as measurement derivatives, and (b) cannot be defined by any single operation but require a whole pattern of measurement and control operations.

The argument for an ensuing better integration of psychometrics with personality theory and general psychological theory is the main basis for preferring the concept of concept validity to that of construct validity, proposed as a label by the APA committee.

Now in the APA (1954) committee report and elsewhere a motley list of "validity" terms is in use over and above the basic senses given above. The objection to these is that some of them are not validity at all, while others are better and more accurately conceived as *utility* coefficients rather than validity coefficients. In this list one finds face validity, content validity, predictive versus concurrent validity, fiat validity, semantic validity, and many more.

Face validity would perhaps require nothing but a requiem and a sigh of relief were it not that wishful thinking is too deep in psychologists' reasoning to be so easily eradicated. For example, the belief that by looking at tests you can tell what they measure has recently cropped up again in Campbell and Fiske's (1959) multitrait-multimethod conception and Guttman's "facet analysis." Face validity is part of the callow denial that "there are more things in heaven and earth than are dreamt of in our philosophy." What element of truth exists in this general area really belongs to a logical, distinct, and usable procedure of allocating *semantic* validity (see below). In some trivial sense face or faith validity perhaps still has a role, but in diplomacy rather than psychology, as when an industrial psychologist is pressured to make tests which a chief executive will, from the depths of his ignorance, commend or sanction as measuring what he conceives to be this or that trait. From the standpoint of good test construction, on the other hand, the less face validity one leaves in the items the less fakable the test.

Content validity scarcely deserves a separate term, being a special case of face validity in the achievement or interest field. The idea that an achievement test must be valid if its items have the right content looks at first like an objective foundation, but without other validity criteria one is still on shifting sands. This will be evident if one asks what the content of a history test would be when variously made up by H. G. Wells, Toynbee, Karl Marx, and Henry Ford. A concrete validity against a specific, named textbook or curriculum is perhaps the only firm meaning immediately available for validity here. Fiat valadity, a term more used by test critics than test constructors, is also a form of face validity, but rightly distinguishes the face validity which is self-evident only to the one or two people who made the test. It is exemplified when a psychologist tells us that "need for achievement," or "creativity," etc., is measured by this particular uncorrelated, unfactored, open-ended test which only specially, locally trained people can score correctly.

If by semantic validity we mean that it is appropriate to attach the term "intelligence" or "anxiety" to a clearly defined factor or set of factors found among many behaviors which, according to the dictionary, fall in the general area of intelligent or anxious manifestations, one need take no exception to it. It is purely a matter of suitability of name when the identity of the concept is already fixed by a factor or related real pattern, and is better called semantic appropriateness rather than validity. However, since language shifts, it is always best to tie such a clearly located pattern concept also to an index number in an appropriate series (Cattell, 1957b). This proposal for a universal index to escape semantic contamination and drift is still not taken seriously by as high a proportion of psychologists as chemists and physicists. This is why discussion on theory by the latter succeeds in being brief and to the point, being tied to exact symbols and indexes. Without embarking on the vast sea presented by the philosophy of meaning one can, however, recognize that rating studies, for example, are from the beginning floating on a tide of cultural drift, unless carefully operationalized. This is a second, distinct sense of semantic validity, again perhaps better thought of merely as defining the semantic referent of a behavior.

Still in the service of pruning away unnecessary verbiage in validity terms let us examine the APA proposal for assigning distinct values (and meanings) for what we call the concurrent and predictive validities of any particular test. Information regarding the relative power of tests to give us future prediction is of interest, but it is confused thinking which considers this a property of the test rather than of the trait. It is an unfortunate terminology also because the term "predictive" has long ceased in science to apply specifically to a calculation projected into the future. (Can you predict from the atomic weight of an element its impermeability to X rays?) But even if we are referring to the future, the correlation of a test now with a criterion next year has a host of determinants, among which the properties of the test may well be insignificant. The terms repeat the same mistake of confusing test and trait properties, which is made in the reliability field when a stability coefficient is not distinguished from a dependability coefficient.

Let us suggest that the capacity of a test to help in an estimate of remote future behavior is better conceived under the broader notion of the scientific utility of a test. It is certainly not the test property of validity as such. Future prediction, after all, requires knowledge of the natural history of the trait, the laws of psychology, and (not least!) the changing life situations which will affect the individual in the interim.

SUMMARY

1. A logical and psychological re-examination of the concepts of validity has been made with a view to arriving at more fundamental and practically effective parameters for evaluating tests.

2. Validity appears to have three bipolar (dichotomous or continuous) dimensions: abstract to concrete, or particular; direct to circumstantial; and cultural to artifactual, which yield eight types of coefficients of which four deserve by importance distinguishing titles.

3. Conceptual validity hinges on four ways of operationalizing a theoretical or empirical construct, viz.: as an entity fitting a defined set of conditions (which may yield something real or imaginary), as a correlation cluster, as a natural type difference, and as a simple structure factor across several studies. The last combines measurement precision with unitary character, as well as a meaning enriched beyond that of an empirical construct.

4. It is suggested that several existing popular uses of validity are either unfruitful (the use of "construct" instead of concept validity) or superfluous (face, predictive, concurrent, content, etc. validity).

V
DESIGNING THE TEST

A test constructor must always begin with an outline of the measuring instrument to be developed. A set of specifications similar in intent and function to an architect's blueprint will detail the desired characteristics of the test. It will include indications of the type of reliability considered most important and method of estimating it. This test design blueprint will summarize the type of validity to be established, with special attention being paid to the nature of the criterion. The specifications may also set the number of items, item type to be used (e.g., multiple-choice, rating scale, etc.), nature of administration, and method of scoring. The most important function of the test design, however, is the specification of the behaviors to be measured.

The need to specify these behaviors is as crucial in the development of a classroom achievement test as in any other area of assessment. This is due primarily to the fact that *external* criteria of performance, which might be used for validation purposes, generally do not exist. In one respect an achievement test is self-validating, or more precisely the test constructor "builds in" validity. In developing a classroom achievement test a paramount concern is the specification of the instructional objectives. Ordinarily, the first step a teacher should take in test development is to review instruction up to that point, looking carefully at both the content of instruction and the kinds of student behaviors he has attempted to develop.

Most systematic attempts to identify and classify instructional objectives have fallen far short of expectations. One vital reason being the complexity of the behaviors involved. Dr. Paul L. Dressel in the first article of this chapter points out several ways of looking at instructional objectives. For example, objectives may be viewed in terms of the degree to which they are concrete or abstract.

This particular continuum corresponds to the underlying structure of the *Taxonomy of Educational Objectives* (Bloom, et al., 1956). An instructor might profitably use this Taxonomy in setting up a Table of Specifications for the whole or part of his course.

Table 1 contains an abbreviated sample Table of Specifications for chapters

TABLE 1. *Hypothetical Table of Specifications for Chapters II–V of Payne and McMorris'* Educational and Psychological Measurement

| | DESIRED COGNITIVE OPERATION | | | | |
	Recall of Specifics	Compre-hension	Application	Analysis	Content Total
CONTENT					
Procedures of Test Standardization	5%*				5%
Philosophies of Testing	3%	7%			10%
Types of Reliability	5%	3%	10%	7%	25%
Factors Influencing Reliability	5%		5%		10%
Types of Validity	10%	5%	5%	5%	25%
Nature of the Criterion	6%	4%			10%
Instructional Objectives	5%	10%			15%
Behavior Total	39%	29%	20%	12%	

* Numbers in cells summarize percent of time spent by instructor developing these skills in class relative to the respective content categories and operations.

two through five of the present book of readings. This two-way grid summarizes the instruction for this four-chapter unit. The selection of content and desired cognitive operations to be dealt with will, of course, vary from instructor to instructor, as will the relative emphases indicated by the percentages. The procedure should lead to systematic measurement, as items for the test will be written in proportions dictated by this Table of Specifications. A more balanced and valid test should be the result.

The Taxonomy, according to many experts, still leaves much to be desired due to lack of clarity in defining and sequencing the actual cognitive behaviors involved in instruction. An attempt at a more comprehensive and operational approach to specifying expected test behaviors has been offered by Mager (1962), and Dr. John Flanagan in the second article in this chapter. Whereas Mager's approach is aimed at clarifying and operationalizing the language used to communicate expected behavior, Flanagan's orientation is toward a systematic description and analysis of the *criterion* behavior. Both approaches have merit, but which one of the techniques is selected will depend upon an individual test constructor's purpose.

The advent of any new instructional procedure should invoke a reappraisal of the measurement technique employed to evaluate its effectiveness. Curricular innovations in science, mathematics, and social science have caused educators to re-evaluate expected student behavior. Some of the evaluation problems associated with new curricula and the application of new instructional technologies are discussed by Dr. Robert Glaser in the last article in the present chapter. When objectives change, the measurement techniques employed must of necessity change if we are to insure fair and valid evaluation.

17   *The Measurement and Evaluation of Instructional Objectives*

....

PAUL L. DRESSEL

Systematic definition of what we are attempting to measure is a prerequisite for a valid test. This is particularly true in the assessment of various types of educational outcomes. External criteria against which to evaluate validity are generally unavailable in educational settings. We must of necessity, then, rely on judgments about the test items relative to the instructional objectives. The need to give careful attention to the goals of instruction is obvious. Dr. Dressel's following comments should cause us not only to look critically at how we are evaluating educational objectives, but also to thoughtfully consider what we are trying to accomplish in the classroom.

The reader is urged to relate the content of the present article to the first two steps (Description, and Analysis of Behavior) in the "rationales" approach to test development detailed by Dr. Flanagan in the following paper.

What are some of the major dimensions of educational objectives that need to be examined by a prospective educational evaluator? What contribution, if any, has academic psychology made to the delineation of instructional objectives?

The topic of this paper—the Measurement and Evaluation of Instructional Objectives—presents something of a paradox. Evaluation is a broader concept than measurement in that it is a decision-making, judgmental process in which we continually engage. Furthermore, no one measures or evaluates instructional objectives but rather attempts to measure the progress of individuals with regard to instructional objectives. In fact, there has been all too little evaluation of instructional objectives. A need exists to decide which ones are most important and reasonably attainable. Accordingly, much of this paper is focused on the role and the problems of defining educational objectives.

Reprinted and abridged with permission of author and publisher from *The Seventeenth Yearbook of the National Council on Measurement in Education*, Ames, Iowa: NCME, 1960, pp. 1–6.

THE NATURE OF EDUCATIONAL OBJECTIVES

Educational objectives may be examined relative to several continua. As one example, educational objectives vary from very *simple* to very *complex*. An objective involving the learning of the multiplication tables to 12 times 12 is on the whole relatively simple to grasp. An educational objective which speaks of the cultivation of character is so complex that it provides very little guidance to educational planning. Educational objectives which are excessively simple and specific tend to break education into unrelated bits and pieces. On the other hand, highly complex objectives are usually ignored in instruction.

Objectives also may be *achievable or unachievable*. Learning the multiplication table is certainly an achievable objective. On the other hand, the qualities associated with character education may be unachievable because no one is quite clear as to what they are. Unachievable goals, however, may exist at even such a relatively simple level as that of knowledge in a particular area. It is not possible to acquire complete knowledge of a subject because the knowledge itself is changing and continually increasing. Most objectives of real importance are not completely achievable, but degrees of progress must be identifiable or else the objective must be regarded as unrealistic and unachievable.

A third continuum upon which one may classify objectives is that of *explicit* and *implicit*. Objectives may be stated in great detail for a course, a curriculum, or a school, but unstated objectives implicit in practices often become far more important as guides to learning than do these explicit objectives. For example, factual tests emphasizing memorized materials paint far clearer objectives to the students than stated purposes which emphasize thought, judgment, and values.

Objectives may also be characterized as *intrinsic* or as *transcendental*. Intrinsic objectives are ones which are inherent in the nature of the material or the experience. The same material or experience may be relevant to but quite remote from some transcendental objective. For example, drilling on the multiplication table is clearly indicative of the purpose that students know the multiplication table, but does not immediately indicate the intent that the students develop quantitative reasoning skills. Teachers who feel that the knowledge of the content provides in itself the justification for a course are apparently oriented to intrinsic objectives, whether or not they make these objectives explicit. Objectives specifying thought processes, value judgments, and the like transcend the materials and experiences provided in any particular course, and because they are not intrinsic to what is done in a course on a particular day, require that sustained thought be given to relating the experience therein to the transcendental objectives.

Another way of looking at objectives is to consider whether the objectives represent *goals for the individual or goals for society*. Individuals oriented to the psychological and educational point of view are inclined to state objectives in terms of the development of the individual. Sociologists and social psychologists may state objectives suggestive of the kind of society desired or objectives derived out of the kind of society with which the individual must cope. It is difficult to find objectives clearly representing the extremes of this continuum, inasmuch as individuals who espouse one of the extremes are, in their own view, likely to see the needs of both ends of the continuum as equally satisfied by the same approach.

Yet, on one hand, recent years have been productive of much writing on the pressures for social conformity and the need for more attention to the development of individuality. On the other hand, counseling, clinical psychology, and psychiatry have been criticized as too largely oriented to the individual and not sufficiently to the social order in which the person is imbedded. Some balance is probably desirable, but it should be a balance resulting from awareness that objectives may determine whether education is to perpetuate the current society or produce individuals who will develop a better one.

The *Taxonomy of Educational Objectives*, developed by Bloom and others (1956) uses still another analysis of objectives into *cognitive, affective, and psychomotor*. The treatment of the cognitive domain begins with objectives emphasizing knowledge and then lists a continuum extending through understanding, application, analysis, synthesis, and evaluation. The handbook covering the affective domain has recently become available (Krathwohl et. al, 1964), with the psychomotor domain yet to be published. This classification of cognitive, affective, and psychomotor has considerable utility even though its classes are far from independent. Knowledge and intellectual skills certainly do not proceed without some involvement in the affective domain. Many persons accustomed to working with a pencil in hand would be inclined to say that motor skills are interrelated with the cognitive. It should be noted that the successive objectives in the analysis of the cognitive domain are of increasing complexity in that each one involves those that have preceded. This is an interesting and desirable quality of objectives which will be commented upon later.

Another way to make distinctions among educational objectives is by noting whether they deal with *characteristics of the experience* or with *characteristics to be developed by experience*. Research projects often are set up in an attempt to evaluate the effectiveness of a program in producing certain qualities in individuals without giving any great amount of thought to determining whether the qualities desired are actually involved in or required by the experience. An educational objective that the individual should increasingly "be able to think critically about problems" is irrelevant unless the educational experiences provide repeated opportunity for such critical thinking. The same point might be made by reference to an earlier classification by noting that unless the characteristics are intrinsic to an experience, they are hardly likely to be developed by it.

PSYCHOLOGICAL AND PHILOSOPHICAL BASES FOR OBJECTIVES

The *statement* of objectives for an educational program is sound psychologically in that learning must be directed or guided. However, educational objectives seem not to have much relationship to psychological studies of learning. On the contrary, educational objectives seem to be largely rational formulations varying considerably with the philosophical and religious positions taken by those who state them. Psychological trait models, factor analytic studies, and the hypotheses developed out of them as to how the mind functions have so far little effect on education.

Psychologists, on the whole, seem to have been interested in defining traits which are reasonably independent and reasonably stable. This would seem to mean that such traits will not be greatly modified by educational experience. Research in education, however, is concerned with objectives which define modifiable qualities of human beings. Here research on objectives is needed, for some of our stated objectives may not be particularly modifiable and, if so, these should be dropped in preference to more realistic ones. In other cases we may have stated objectives which are primarily modified, if at all, by experiences outside of the usual school program. Probably no school today has stated as an objective the development of a high level of extrasensory perception, but some of the frequently stated objectives are quite as meaningless because the experiences whereby they are achieved are not known. More research is needed to determine *objectives* which are psychologically sound and to determine experiences which are likewise psychologically sound for the achievement of those objectives. This does not rule out philosophical considerations which will still be paramount in choosing among attainable objectives.

THE ROLE OF OBJECTIVES IN EDUCATION

The purpose of objectives is to give direction both to the development of the student and to the planning of the educational program. This means that the materials, the assignments, the instructional methods, and indeed all aspects of the educational experience must be chosen in relationship to the objectives. The wide range of possibilities involved and the span of time to be covered require that the experiences be organized in such a way as to provide for continuity, sequence, and integration. The objectives also provide a basis for evaluation; that is, a judgment of the effectiveness of education. Objectives are often regarded as definitive only in describing outcomes, abilities, or qualities expected of the individual. The examination of the relation of these objectives to classroom experiences is not commonly made. In a few cases, such as in the studies by Bloom and some of his associates at the University of Chicago, it has been demonstrated that overt participation in a class is not necessary for high-level thought about the issues discussed. Since covert and overt experiences seem not too closely related, it follows that the incidence of classroom experience relative to objectives is at best uncertain.

Apparently then there is much research to be done on the meaning of objectives or the implications of objectives with regard to qualities of the educational experience itself. Content-oriented teachers have been criticized by the objective-oriented as too much obsessed with the importance of the particular facts and with day-to-day activity, with a resulting lack of a sense of direction. Individuals concentrating on broad, long-term objectives may sometimes forget that a compass does not relieve the traveler from the necessity of choosing routes and means of transportation.

EVALUATION OF THE OBJECTIVES

Objectives are sometimes regarded as external to the evaluation process even when they are accepted as starting points of it. The teacher or administrator states the objectives and *then* the evaluator helps to determine the progress made by students with regard to them. It is a common experience of evaluators that the stated objectives need clarification, and one of the common ways of doing this has, of course, been to ask for statements as to the behavior desired. This is usually regarded not as a change in the objective, but simply a rephrasing or another approach to it. Not uncommonly this clarification results in actual modification of the objectives. It may not, therefore, be too radical to suggest that elimination or replacement of objectives may follow from the attempt to evaluate them. Those teachers who see their objectives as absolutes will object to uses of an analytical basis for the discard of objectives, but those who view the educational process as an extremely complicated phenomenon and regard objectives as hypotheses regarding the significant changes which it is possible to induce in individuals through the educational process, might readily admit that some objectives may be unrealistic, idealistic, or at least incapable of attainment under the circumstances in which the formal educational program operates. In stating objectives, as in traveling, one has choice as to where he shall go only if he chooses to go where he can go. Clinging to ethereal, meaningless objectives only confuses our thinking about the nature of education. It has been wisely said that a man's reach should exceed his grasp, but the man who futilely reaches for something so unattainable that he cannot even make significant progress toward the goal must be considered a failure.

18   *The Use of Comprehensive Rationales in Test Development*

JOHN C. FLANAGAN

Is there any method a test constructor may use in the initial stages of development, to insure that his test will be valid? Obviously and unfortunately no technique or procedure will guarantee the production of a valid test. The better able we are to define what it is we are trying to measure and the closer we can tie our

Reprinted and abridged with permission of author and publisher from *Educational and Psychological Measurement*, 1951, Vol. 11, pp. 151–155.

instrument to these definitions, however, the higher the likelihood that we will obtain a viable measure.

If test development is to proceed systematically, we must achieve clear and precise descriptions of what we are attempting to assess. Dr. John Flanagan here presents a method referred to as "rationales", as a reasonable approach to the problem of operationalizing measurement objectives. What are the major components of the "rationales" method? The student might find it interesting and instructional to select a trait he might wish to measure and follow the proposed three-step process in determining the test specifications.

The method of rationales begins with a list of behaviors to be sampled or predicted. The objective of the procedure is to develop a series of sets of specifications for writing items which will provide valid estimates of each of the behaviors on the list. If the behavior is of a type which can be tested directly, such as adding or multiplying, the problem is to define a standard sample of this behavior which will represent as validly as possible the behavior defined on the list. If the behavior cannot be tested directly but is something like succeeding or failing as a clinical psychologist or adjusting or not adjusting to a difficult social situation, the problem is one of specifying test items which will predict as accurately as possible this behavior.

Since most of the lists of behaviors for which tests are desired refer to specific practical situations, and since tests usually tend to be abstract and artificial in order to be efficient and precise, the problem referred to the test developer is most often one of prediction. It is very important that the list of behaviors to be predicted be a valid one. This is primarily a matter of job analysis, job definition, and specifying the criterion, and these factors will not be discussed here. However, it should be emphasized that a valid list of behaviors is not easily obtained and can only be expected to result from a systematic and comprehensive set of records of observations by competent personnel.

Assuming that a valid list of the behaviors to be sampled or predicted is available, the development of rationales regarding the measurement of these behaviors consists of three parts. These are: (1) Description of the Behavior, (2) Analysis of the Behavior, and (3) Formulation of Item Specifications.

1. Description of the Behavior involves the definition, delimitation, and illustration of the variety and scope of the actions included. An illustration is presented below.

The behavior is "Perform a series of simple computations without error." The Description of Behavior is as follows:

This behavior consists of doing a series of simple arithmetic problems with no errors. Calculations may be done either entirely "in one's head" or with the aid of paper and pencil. By "simple arithmetic" is meant addition, subtraction, multiplication, division, percentage, and fractions. Speed is of little concern here—accuracy throughout an extended series of calculations is the important factor. In many instances the individual has plenty of time to perform the necessary arithmetic computations which are a part of his job. In spite of this, however, some individuals make errors even though they are trying to be very careful. A flight engineer would be considered ineffective if his computation on gas consumption was erroneous because he said $43 - 11 = 22$. Effective behavior, on the other hand, would be illustrated by a navigator whose computations while making a round-the-world training flight were found both by himself and by others who checked his work periodically to contain not a single error.

2. Analysis of the Behavior includes classifying it with respect to other behaviors and making inferences about its nature, culminating in the formulation of one or more hypotheses regarding its generality and predictability.

An example of this step given for the same behavior included in the Description of Behavior is presented below:

The performing of simple computations is probably influenced by both basic aptitude and long-established training or habits. Individuals effective in this regard do not have to make a conscious effort to avoid errors; their computations are "just naturally" correct. Individuals lacking the fundamental characteristics may also turn in errorless work, but their effectiveness is due to the fact that they very carefully checked and rechecked their work so that all errors were eliminated. Actually, it may be that the person who is given credit for possessing the fundamental ability has an "automatic" checking system of which he is not consciously aware and which operates simultaneously during the making of the actual computations. In any event his computations come out accurately the first time without undue effort or concern on his part.

3. Formulation of Item Specifications carries the procedure on to describe a specific type of item which it appears should provide a valid estimation of the specified behavior. It consists mainly of deductions and practical suggestions. The examples of this step for the same behavior are given below:

For measuring computational behavior the test should consist of a large number of relatively simple problems involving addition, subtraction, multiplication, division, fractions, and percentages. They should not include any particularly difficult or any "trick" problems. The examinee would be instructed to work at his own rate but not to spend more time on any problem than is necessary to get an answer.

The primary advantages to be gained by this method of explicit rationales are a more systematic consideration of the available information by the test constructor; the easy and efficient checking of his descriptions, analyses, inferences, and item specifications by editors and critics before the test items are prepared; and the availability of detailed hypotheses for testing against the findings obtained from the test items as prepared.

The use of comprehensive rationales based on systematic, empirically developed definitions in terms of *actual behavior* of the functions to be measured, and consisting of carefully formulated hypotheses regarding the specifications for items which can be expected to provide valid measures or predictions of the behaviors involved rather than merely test knowledge about the topics involved, should significantly improve the quality of many examinations.

19   *Instructional Technology and the Measurement of Learning Outcomes*

....

ROBERT GLASER

According to Dr. Glaser, achievement tests and criterion measures suffer from the appropriated strategies of aptitude test construction; procedures used when devising an instrument to describe present competence reflect those procedures used when seeking to estimate future behavior. In deciding how to select test items, he suggests differentiating between comparisons with an acceptable standard of performance and comparisons with other individuals, i.e., differentiating between absolute and relative standards. Further, he would differentiate between the comparison of individuals and the comparison of treatments.

The importance of these differentiations may be illustrated by referring to the context of programmed instruction referred to in this article. For the development of materials for programmed instruction what kinds of comparisons and hence, what kinds of items would be indicated? Similarly for an intact group, if performance using programmed instruction is to be compared with that using a textbook, what are the categories which should be considered and the types of items which are desired? How would the items differ if it were proposed that some individuals might learn more with programmed instruction while others learn more with a traditional text?

Evaluation of the effectiveness of teaching machines and programed learning and of broadly conceived instructional systems has raised into prominence a number of questions concerning the nature and properties of measures of student achievement. In the evaluation of instructional systems the attainment of subject matter knowledge and skill as well as other behavioral outcomes must, of course, be considered, but the remarks in this paper will be restricted primarily to the measurement of subject matter proficiency, as it may be defined by recognized subject matter scholars.

From Robert Glaser, "Instructional Technology and the Measurement of Learning Outcomes," *American Psychologist*, 1963, Vol. 18, pp. 519–521. Copyright 1963 by the American Psychological Assn. and reproduced by permission of the author and publisher.

Achievement measurement can be defined as the assessment of terminal or criterion behavior. This involves the determination of the characteristics of student performance with respect to specified standards. Achievement measurement is distinguished from aptitude measurement in that the instruments used to assess achievement are specifically concerned with the characteristics and properties of present performance, with emphasis on the meaningfulness of its content. In contrast, aptitude measures derive their meaning from a demonstrated relationship between present performance and the future attainment of specified knowledge and skill. In certain circumstances of course this contrast is not quite so clear, for example, when achievement measures are used as predictor variables.

The scores obtained from an achievement test provide primarily two kinds of information. One is the degree to which the student has attained criterion performance, for example, whether he can satisfactorily prepare an experimental report, or solve certain kinds of word problems in arithmetic. The second type of information that an achievement test score provides is the relative ordering of individuals with respect to their test performance, for example, whether Student A can solve his problems more quickly than Student B. The principal difference between these two kinds of information lies in the standard used as a reference. What I shall call criterion-referenced measures depend upon an absolute standard of quality, while what I term norm-referenced measures depend upon a relative standard.

CRITERION-REFERENCED MEASURES

Underlying the concept of achievement measurement is the notion of a continuum of knowledge acquisition ranging from no proficiency at all to perfect performance. An individual's achievement level falls at some point on this continuum as indicated by the behaviors he displays during testing. The degree to which his achievement resembles desired performance at any specified level is assessed by criterion-referenced measures of achievement or proficiency. The standard against which a student's performance is compared when measured in this manner is the behavior which defines each point along the achievement continuum. The term "criterion," when used in this way, does not necessarily refer to final end-of-course behavior. Criterion levels can be established at any point in instruction where it is necessary to obtain information as to the adequacy of an individual's performance. The point is that the specific behaviors implied at each level of proficiency can be identified and used to describe the specific tasks a student must be capable of performing before he achieves one of these knowledge levels. It is in this sense that measures of proficiency can be criterion-referenced.

Along such a continuum of attainment, a student's score on a criterion-referenced measure provides explicit information as to what the individual can or cannot do. Criterion-referenced measures indicate the content of the behavioral repertory, and the correspondence between what an individual does and the underlying continuum of achievement. Measures which assess student achievement in terms of a criterion standard thus provide information as to the degree of competence attained by a particular student which is independent of reference to the performance of others.

NORM-REFERENCED MEASURES

On the other hand, achievement measures also convey information about the capability of a student compared with the capability of other students. In instances where a student's *relative* standing along the continuum of attainment is the primary purpose of measurement, reference need not be made to criterion behavior. Educational achievement examinations, for example, are administered frequently for the purpose of ordering students in a class or school, rather than for assessing their attainment of specified curriculum objectives. When such norm-referenced measures are used, a particular student's achievement is evaluated in terms of a comparison between his performance and the performance of other members of the group. Such measures need provide little or no information about the degree of proficiency exhibited by the tested behaviors in terms of what the individual can do. They tell that one student is more or less proficient than another, but do not tell how proficient either of them is with respect to the subject matter tasks involved.

In large part achievement measures currently employed in education are norm-referenced. This emphasis upon norm-referenced measures has been brought about by the preoccupation of test theory with aptitude, and with selection and prediction problems; norm-referenced measures are useful for this kind of work in correlational analysis. However, the imposition of this kind of thinking on the purposes of achievement measurement raises some question, and concern with instructional technology is forcing us toward the kind of information made available by the use of criterion-referenced measures. We need to behaviorally specify minimum levels of performance that describe the least amount of end-of-course competence the student is expected to attain, or that he needs in order to go on to the next course in a sequence. The specification of the characteristics of maximum or optimum achievement after a student has been exposed to the course of instruction poses more difficult problems of criterion delineation.

THE USES OF ACHIEVEMENT MEASUREMENT

Consider a further point. In the context of the evaluation of instructional systems achievement tests can be used for two principal purposes. First, performance can be assessed to provide information about the characteristics of an individual's present behavior. Second, achievement can be assessed to provide information about the conditions or instructional treatments which produce that behavior. The primary emphasis of the first use is to discriminate among *individuals*.

Used in the second way, achievement tests are employed to discriminate among treatments, that is, among different instructional procedures by an analysis of *group* differences.

Achievement tests used to provide information about *individual* differences are constructed so as to maximize the discriminations made among people having specified backgrounds and experience. Such tests include items which maximize the likelihood of observing individual differences in performance along various task dimensions; this maximizes the variability of the distribution of scores that are obtained. In practical test construction the variability of test scores is increased by manipulating the difficulty levels and content of the test items.

On the other hand, achievement tests used primarily to provide information about differences in treatments need to be constructed so as to maximize the discriminations made between *groups* treated differently and to minimize the differences between the individuals in any one group. Such a test will be sensitive to the differences produced by instructional conditions. For example, a test designed to demonstrate the effectiveness of instruction would be constructed so that it was generally difficult for those taking it before training and generally easy after training. The content of the test used to differentiate treatments should be maximally sensitive to the performance changes anticipated from the instructional treatments. In essence, the distinction between achievement tests used to maximize individual differences and tests used to maximize treatment or group differences is established during the selection of test items.

In constructing an achievement test to differentiate among *individuals* at the end of training, it would be possible to begin by obtaining data on a large sample of items relating to curriculum objectives. Item analysis would indicate that some test items were responded to correctly only by some of the individuals in the group, while other items were answered correctly by all members of the group. These latter 100% difficulty level items, since they failed to differentiate among individuals, would be eliminated because their only effect would be to add a constant to every score. The items remaining would serve to discriminate among individuals and thus yield a distribution of scores that was as large as possible, considering the number and type of items used.

On the other hand, if this test were constructed for the purpose of observing *group* instead of individual differences, the selection of items would follow a different course. For example, where instruction was the treatment variable involved, it would be desirable to retain test items which were responded to correctly by all members of the post-training group, but which were answered incorrectly by students who had not yet been trained. In a test constructed for the purpose of differentiating groups, items which indicated substantial variability within either the pre- or post-training group would be undesirable because of the likelihood that they would cloud the effects which might be attributable to the treatment variable.

In brief, items most suitable for measuring individual differences in achievement are those which will differentiate among all individuals exposed to the same treatment variable, while items most suitable for distinguishing between groups are those which are most likely to indicate that a given amount or kind of some instructional treatment was effective. In either case, samples of test items are drawn from a population of items indicating the content of performance; the particular item samples that are drawn, however, are those most useful for the purpose of the kind of measurement being carried out.

The points indicated above reflect the achievement measurement concerns that have arisen in my own work with instructional technology. There is one further point which must be mentioned, and that is the use of diagnostic achievement tests prior to an instructional course. It appears that with the necessity for specifying the entering behavior that is required by a student prior to a programmed instructional sequence, diagnostic assessment of subject matter competence must take on a more precise function. This raises the problem of developing an improved methodology for diagnostic achievement testing. In this regard researchers using programmed instructional sequences to study learning variables point out that prior testing influences learning, and that this effect must be controlled for in determining the specific contribution of programming variables. In an instructional sense, however, the influence and use of pretesting is an important variable for study since it is not the terminal criterion behavior alone which dictates required instructional manipulations, but the differences between entering and terminal behavior. Furthermore, pretesting of a special kind may contribute to "motivation" by enhancing the value of future responses. There is some indication that this may be brought about by prior familiarity with future response items or by permitting some early aided performance of the terminal behavior.

In conclusion, the general point is this: Test development has been dominated by the particular requirements of predictive, correlational aptitude test "theory." Achievement and criterion measurement has attempted frequently to cast itself in this framework. However, many of us are beginning to recognize that the problems of assessing existing levels of competence and achievement and the conditions that produce them require some additional consideration.

VI
ITEM CONSTRUCTION
AND EVALUATION

Up to this point the papers in this volume have progressed from a discussion of the purposes of measurement through both theoretical and practical considerations of reliability and validity to consideration of test design. At this point we turn our attention to the difficult task of item writing and evaluation. The word "difficult" is used intentionally, as even the most experienced item writer may produce only a few relatively flawless items in a full day's work. In addition to possession of considerable knowledge and skill in the technical aspects of item writing, the test constructor must be thoroughly grounded in the subject matter or behavior to be measured.

The first article in this chapter, by Dr. Max D. Engelhart, provides some valuable guidelines for writing, administering, and evaluating various types of objective paper-and-pencil achievement test questions. He not only considers the traditional item types such as true-false, multiple-choice, and matching exercises, but also presents some interesting variations. Item forms that can be useful in getting at cause-and-effect reasoning and other higher order cognitive skills as application, extrapolation, and interpolation are illustrated.

If the suggestsions for writing test items as outlined by the experts are followed, will these insure that we measure what we wish to measure? Obviously not, for the structural characteristics of a set of test items are only one of many factors which may influence test performance. Does following the suggestions for writing items really make a difference with regard to such relevant test parameters as reliability, validity, and difficulty? Perhaps not for reliability and validity, say Drs. Dunn and Goldstein—an answer based on their experimental study involved with selected multiple-choice item construction principles. Although these investigators did not observe significant changes in all relevant test parameters in their study, the fact that the test performances of a relatively few examinees were influenced is justification enough for "followings the rules." One might argue that there are some known sources of error that we can control, and since there are so many sources that cannot be controlled, it would seem unwise to allow the test performance of even one examinee to be spuriously affected. Structural defects may serve to either artificially inflate a score or depress it. In either case the purpose of measurement has been subrogated.

The final two articles in the present chapter deal with the general topic of test and item analysis. The case study presented in the third article of the chapter speaks eloquently for the careful analysis of a test by a classroom teacher. Dr. Foreman demonstrates how the application of common sense, logical and elementary test analysis procedures can significantly improve the quality of a measuring instrument. Considering the kinds of decisions that are made about students every day on the basis of classroom tests, one should take the moral of Foreman's paper to heart (and head).

The final article by Dr. Richard C. Cox contains experimental evidence bearing on sources of test item bias. When statistics alone become the criterion of item inclusion or exclusion from a test, a type of constant, invalidating error is introduced. This research also demonstrates the influence of the sex make-up of the group on the resulting test.

20   Suggestions for Writing Achievement Test Exercises

MAX D. ENGELHART

The production of a valid test item is both an art and a science. The scientific aspects involve technical knowledge and skills regarding item structure and format, discrimination, difficulty, and reliability. Art comes into play in integrating the scientific, the verbal, and practical aspects of the total operation.

The largest single population of test makers is teachers. They obviously should be well versed in both the art and science of test construction. Unfortunately, many are deficient in both. The guidelines for writing "objective" type test items presented by Dr. Engelhart in the following paper should and hopefully will find wide audience among educators at all levels.

Reprinted and abridged with permission of author and publisher from an article entitled, "Suggestions for Writing Achievement Test Exercises to Be Used in Tests Scored on the Electric Scoring Machine," which appeared in *Educational and Psychological Measurement*, 1947, Vol. 7, pp. 357–374.

Attempting to write a sample item illustrating each of the exercise types discussed by the author would be an aid to the comprehension of the material of the following article.

Extended discussions of item writing may be found in any number of basic texts on educational and psychological measurement (Ahmann & Glock, 1960 & 1963; Allen, 1958; Adams, 1964; Ebel, 1965; Noll, 1965; Thorndike & Hagen, 1961; Dressel, et. al, 1961; Davis, 1964; and Stanley, 1964).

The production of locally constructed achievement tests can be greatly facilitated by making available to the participating teachers directions for the writing of test exercises. Unless the instructions are quite explicit, teachers tend to produce exercises which are faulty. Many teachers have difficulty in phrasing adequate directions for a series of exercises. Some teachers are likely to forget that the standard answer sheet limits the number of answers to a given exercise to no more than five. Few teachers realize that it is possible to use a variety of forms. Hence it is desirable to provide teachers with samples of various forms, along with the directions necessary for the writing of exercises of these types. The rest of this article describes the kind of material which may be given to teachers as a means of directing and stimulating the production of achievement test exercises.

GENERAL DIRECTIONS FOR WRITING ACHIEVEMENT EXERCISES

The exercises used in tests must conform to certain patterns so that the students will have no difficulty in recording their answers. Generally, no exercise or test item should have more than five answers including correct and incorrect ones. Each exercise number on the answer sheet is followed by lettered spaces for only five answers. It is possible to write exercises having more than one answer of the five correct, but this practice is not recommended. Where certain series of exercises call for more than one correct answer to each exercise, students are stimulated to mark in the same way in other series of exercises where only one answer per exercise is expected. The practice of asking for more than one answer complicates scoring whether the score is simply to be the number right or the number right minus some fraction of the number wrong. While it is desirable to prepare exercises similar to the types described in later paragraphs, this does not mean that measurement is restricted to the recall of isolated facts. The content of achievement exercises has more influence than their form on the nature of the responses made by the students. Abilities other than mere memory are tested when the content is to some extent novel and when the selection of the correct answer requires discrimination. On the other hand, measurement of memory abilities is justified when the content relates to important facts, concepts, or principles.

In the production of objective exercises serious thought should be given to the planning of the distribution of exercises of various types in order to secure both representative sampling of the subject matter of the course and of a variety of abilities. While it is possible to weight different series of exercises differently in machine scoring, it is much easier to secure appropriate weighting by having the numbers of items or exercises pertaining to each division of subject matter proportional to the importance of the subject matter division. If the general organization of the test as a whole is to follow that of the course, a variety of abilities may be tested within each series of exercises. For example, certain exercises of a series of multiple-answer exercises may require no more than the ability to remember the term defined by the introductory part of each exercise. Other exercises in the same series may require the functioning of abilities transcending memory, if the content of the exercises is to some extent novel. While the introduction of novel content is essential if more than the memory of facts is to be tested, the novel content should be such that the student is able to determine the correct answer by means of thinking about facts he has had an opportunity to learn. This may be illustrated by an example from the field of physics. Suppose that the students have studied Archimedes' Principle that a body is buoyed up by a force equal to the weight of the fluid displaced. Suppose further that the applications of this principle have largely or exclusively been with respect to bodies floating or immersed in liquids. Presume also that the students have learned at some time during the course that both liquids and gases are fluids and that gases, particularly, become less dense as they become warmer. Then the students have had the opportunity to acquire the facts needed in answering a novel and thought-provoking multiple-choice exercise based on the question: "Assuming that the temperature of the gas in a dirigible balloon remains constant, will the balloon go up more rapidly in warm air or in cold air?"

Discriminative thinking is promoted by presenting the student with plausible and somewhat related incorrect answers as well as by the use of novel content or by the presenting of more or less familiar content in unanticipated ways. Discriminative thinking is also promoted by preparing a series of related exercises.

SUGGESTIONS FOR WRITING OBJECTIVE TEST EXERCISES

TRUE-FALSE ITEMS ■ When constructing true-false exercises, avoid writing obviously trivial or meaningless ones. Avoid making broad generalizations which are obviously true or false, i.e., avoid writing statements involving such terms as "always," "never," "none," "only," "all," and "every." Such terms are permissible, however, in intrinsically difficult statements, for example, "All persons born in the United States are citizens of the United States" and "All amphibia live in fresh water." Avoid items that are partly true and partly false, for example, "Cases in equity are sometimes tried by a judge and sometimes by a jury." Avoid items which express opinionated views, unless the purpose is to test the knowledge of the source of an option, as for example, "According to Keynes, government spending is an excellent means of combating depressions." In items designed to measure the knowledge of an important concept or principle, avoid unnecessary technical terms or obscure minutiae. Avoid the writing of unusually long and involved statements. Such statements are more often true than false and test-wise students realize that this is the case. The principles just mentioned also apply to other types of objective exercises. Directions similar to the following should precede each series of true-false statements in the completed test:

After each item number on the answer sheet, blacken *one* lettered space to indicate that the statement is

> A. true.
> B. false.

True-false exercises may be written on cards, one exercise to a card. The truth or falsity of the exercise should be indicated. Writing exercises on separate cards facilitates the rejection of poor exercises. It is also the best way to proceed if it is the intent to accumulate a file of exercises for future use. If the exercises pertain to a particular chapter of a text or a unit of a syllabus, it is desirable to specify on the card the chapter or unit to which the exercise pertains in order to facilitate checking the accuracy of the phraseology of the exercise and the correctness of the key. The method also facilitates representative sampling of the content of the course.

MULTIPLE-CHOICE ITEMS ▪ To reduce the influence of guessing, four or five alternatives should be given. One of the answers should be definitely correct and the others *should be plausible* although incorrect. Avoid consistently writing correct answers which are longer than incorrect ones. The incorrect answers may be similar in form to the correct answers, opposite in meaning to the correct answers, or slightly less precise or complete than the correct answers. (In the latter cases students may be asked to mark the "best" answer.) The exercises should not be unusually long or complex. The answers may be single words or brief phrases, but unless the exercise begins with a question, *each answer must complete the introductory sentence grammatically.*

Where the answers to a multiple-choice exercise are longer than single words or very brief phrases, it is desirable to list the answers. Note that each answer of the first exercise grammatically completes the sentence with which the exercise began. In the following examples note also the difference in style where the "item stem" is a question. Both methods of writing are equally desirable.

1. The fatigue of muscle is due primarily to
   A. the overuse of the individual muscle fibers.
   B. the production of lactic acid within the muscle cells.
   C. excessive carbon dioxide production.
   D. a limitation of the oxygen supply.
   E. a limitation of the food supply.

2. The United States Government under the Articles of Confederation was most successful in meeting which of the following problems?
A. The raising of money to pay our debts to France and Holland.
B. The regulation of trade between the states.
C. The organization of the Northwest Territory.
D. The alleviation of social discontent.
E. The making of commercial treaties with foreign nations.

Where multiple-choice exercises are problems in mathematics, or are exercises with numerical answers as in chemistry and in physics, it is an effective device to use the phrase "None of the above answers" as answer E. Occasionally this phrase should represent the correct answer. It should not be used as an incorrect answer, however, if the correct answer listed as an A, B, C, or D answer is an approximation. In this case a student could argue that the exercise has two correct answers.

The following directions might precede each series of multiple-choice exercises in the completed test:

After each item number on the answer sheet, blacken *one* lettered space to indicate the *best* answer.

(If the exercises can be given a "correct" answer, substitute the word "correct" for "best" in the directions above.)

MATCHING ITEMS ■ If using a standard IBM answer sheet, each exercise may consist of three definitions to be matched with three terms included in a list of five. The definitions should concern terms that are likely to be confused by the student whose knowledge is not precise. Furthermore, the two extra terms should be good distracters. Similar exercises may pertain to content other than definitions and the terms may be names of places, personages, formulas, or other brief answers. To promote discriminative thinking all of the items in each group of three should pertain to related concepts. Usually the items of a given group should be drawn from the same chapter or unit of subject matter. If these suggestions are followed, repeated use of the exercises is facilitated. An example is given below:

	Outcome	*Battle*
3.	This victory ended an attempt to cut off New England from the rest of the colonies and was a major factor in the obtaining of the alliance with France.	A. Bunker Hill B. Yorktown C. Saratoga D. Monmouth E. Trenton
4.	After Washington's retreat from New York, hope was renewed in the American cause by this victory.	
5.	This victory involved a feint toward New York followed by strategy which resulted in a large body of enemy troops being cut off from help by either land or sea.	

Each group of three numbered items should be set off as indicated above. The entire series should be preceded by directions like the following:

After each number on the answer sheet, blacken *one* lettered space to indicate the term at the right to which the item refers.

KEY-LIST ITEMS ▪ There must be not more than five categories in an exercise, but the number of items may vary. The categories should be in some way related to each other, for if one category is unrelated to the others, the items which pertain to it are too easily identified. The numbered items may be phrases or complete sentences. In a given series all of the items should be similar in construction. To facilitate repeated use, all of the items should pertain to the same chapter in a text, to related chapters, or in general to related subject matter. Several examples of key-list exercises are given below. In each case only a few samples of items are listed below each set of directions. All of the types of categories are applicable to a variety of subject-matter fields.

For each of the items 6 through 9, blacken *one* lettered space to indicate that the item is true of
    A. the Monroe Doctrine.
    B. the Open Door Policy.
    C. both the Monroe Doctrine and the Open Door Policy.
    D. neither the Monroe Doctrine nor the Open Door Policy.
  6. By adopting this policy the United States sought to safeguard important interests of the American people.
  7. According to this policy the interests of the United States take precedence over those of any European country.
  8. Violation of this policy occasioned the enunciation of the "Stimson Doctrine."
  9. Our traditional policy of freedom of the seas is basic to this policy.

For each of the items 10 through 12, blacken *one* lettered space to indicate that the statement is
    A. true, and is supported by the reason given.
    B. true, but not because of the reason given.
    C. false.
10. *Everyman* is classified as a morality play, because it deals with material drawn from the *Bible*.
11. The play is essentially an allegory concerning the way to salvation, because the characters are chiefly personifications of human qualities and the plot is an account of how Everyman makes his peace with God.
12. The author describes a systematized and predictable arrangement of the ways of God, because the steps necessary for the salvation of Everyman are clearly defined and commonly accepted.

For each of the following paired items (13–15), blacken *one* lettered space to indicate that the *first* item is
    A. greater than the second.
    B. less than the second.
    C. equal to the second.

13. Amount of energy released in external respiration.	.... Amount of energy released in internal respiration.
14. Amount of time the ventricles of the heart are contracted.	.... Amount of time the auricles of the heart are contracted.
15. The rate at which blood pressure falls as the blood passes through the capillaries.	.... The rate at which blood pressure falls as the blood passes through the veins.

Exercises of the type illustrated below are useful in measuring how well students handle correlated or cause-and-effect relationships. In writing such items where the relationship is definitely cause and effect, the cause should be given first.

For each of the following paired items (16–18), blacken *one* lettered space to indicate that an increase in the first thing is normally associated with
  A. an increase in the second.
  B. a decrease in the second.
  C. no related change in the second.
16. Amount of carbonates dissolved in the water of a river.
     Number of clams in the river.
17. Temperature of the environment of a mammal.
     Body temperature of the mammal.
18. Number of lemming in an arctic area.
     Number of caribou in the same area.
One means of presenting students with exercises which require reflective thinking rather than memory alone is to set up hypothetical situations which differ from the situations encountered during instruction. The exercises given below illustrate such a series. The facts required in answering these exercises correctly were a part of the regular instruction in physical science.

You have acquired some knowledge of the earth and its motions as they really exist. In this exercise you are to identify the effects of some wholly imaginary conditions. For each of the items 19–22, blacken *one* lettered space to indicate that the item would be true *if* the
  A. orbit of the earth were a circle rather than an ellipse.
  B. orbit of the moon were exactly in the same plane as the orbit of the earth.
  C. axis of the earth were not inclined.
  D. earth had half its present diameter, but retained its present mass.
  E. earth were a perfect sphere.
  (Assume only one of the above imaginary conditions occurs at a time.)
19. All the solar days would be of equal length.
20. Objects would weigh four times as much as they do now.
21. The celestial equator and the ecliptic would be identical.
22. An eclipse of the sun would occur each month.

EXERCISES PERTAINING TO QUOTED MATERIAL ■ The following directions are useful in writing key-list exercises which pertain to quoted material (a paragraph or two, or even a table or a graph).

Basing your judgments solely on the data summarized above, blacken *one* lettered space to indicate that the item is
A. definitely true.
B. probably true.
C. impossible to prove or disprove from the data given.
D. probably false.
E. definitely false.

Probably-true statements are justifiable interpolations, extrapolations, or predictions from the information or data given. They may represent legitimate generalizations from information describing a sample, or deductions with respect to a sample where the information pertains to things in general. For example, if the selection pertains to industrial conditions characteristic of the war years, a statement to be marked "B" may describe a trend or condition in a single industry analogous to the general trend or condition, although the particular industry is not mentioned in the selection. Similarly, a statement to be marked "D" may describe a trend for a particular industry opposite to that of the general trend described in the selection. Such exercises may be scored not only to determine the general accuracy of the students in interpreting data, but also to identify students who have tendencies to be overcautious, to go beyond the data, or to make crude errors of judgment. For example, the overcautious student marks A items B or C, and E items D or C. Conversely, the student who tends to go beyond the data, or overgeneralize marks B items A, D items E, and C items by some letter other than C.

Exercises of this type are very appropriate in achievement tests. Since the facts needed in thinking are presented in the quoted material, it seems legitimate to attribute differences in the scores of the students to differences in their ability to think in the subject-matter field. Where the quoted material is novel, or is on a level above that encountered in the course, the scores may be useful as predictions of future success in advanced courses in the same field. Since course marks should be predictions of future success rather than rewards for time spent in class, achievement tests used in determining final marks may well contain a considerable proportion of such exercises.

EXERCISES INVOLVING DIAGRAMS OR PICTURES ■ If there are no more than five pictures or things to be labeled in a diagram, the pictures or parts may be labeled A, B, C, D, and E, and the directions preceding the items may be written: "After each item number on the answer sheet, blacken the *one* lettered space which designates the part of the diagram (or the picture) to which the items correctly refers." Since the categories are inherent in the diagram or pictures, no further directions are needed. The directions, the diagram or pictures, and the statements which constitute the test items should all be on the same page of the test booklet or on a facing page.

The following directions are useful where comparisons are to be made between two diagrams or pictures, for example, reproductions of paintings representing different styles of art. In this instance the pictures may be labeled with Roman numerals.

After each item number on the answer sheet, blacken *one* lettered space to indicate that the item is true of
A. picture I.
B. picture II.
C. both pictures.
D. neither picture.

Where more than five parts of a diagram or locations on a map need to be identified, it is usually preferable to write exercises of the multiple-choice rather than the key-list type. Each exercise may begin with a reference to one of the diagram symbols, for example, "The symbol 'I' refers to (A......, B......, C......, etc.)." In this case the order of the exercises should be the order of the symbols in the diagram. In some cases one can use the answer sheet or exercise numbers as diagram or map symbols. For example, suppose that a map exercise involves locations of battlefields of the Civil War. Number 23 on the map may be in the location of Gettysburg. The corresponding exercise, given on the same page or on a facing page, and in a series of similar exercises may simply be:

23. A. Antietam, B. Gettysburg, C. Chancellorsville, D. Bull Run, E. Petersburg.

The directions for such a series of exercises may be phrased: "After the number on the answer sheet which corresponds to each map or exercise number, blacken the *one* lettered space which designates the correct answer."

In certain fields it is effective to use small diagrams labeled A, B, C, D, and E as answers to ordinary multiple-choice exercises. For example: "Which of the following curves best represents the distribution of intelligence test scores of a large group of 12-year-old children?" "Which of the following symbols represents a cold front on a weather map?" "Which of the following tools should be used to......?" An effective E answer is "None of the above......" which, if used in several of such exercises, should be the correct answer at least once.

CRITICAL EXAMINATION OF THE ITEMS

After exercises have been written they should be carefully checked for accuracy of phraseology and correctness of the key. It is very desirable to have other teachers of the subject evaluate the exercises with respect to fairness, freedom from ambiguities, and elimination of the too obviously incorrect answers. It is an excellent practice in seeking helpful criticism to have other teachers attempt to key the exercises. When teachers respond differently to an exercise, faults may be encountered of which the writer of the exercise was unaware.

The suggestions contained in this paper should assist teachers in becoming more expert in the art of writing exercises for achievement tests. Critical evaluation of exercises by teachers is suggested above. An examination staff can promote such evaluation by undertaking informal and formal analyses, i.e., by scrutinizing both content and statistical item analysis data. (See the articles by Foreman and Cox later in this chapter for expanded discussion of item analysis techniques.)

The item analysis data pertaining to individual exercises may be recorded on the original cards containing the test items, or they may be recorded adjacent to each item in a keyed test booklet. The percents of correct response are particularly useful to teachers in evaluating attainment of objectives. Both the percents of correct response and the item discrimination indices are useful in identifying faulty exercises. A combination of scholarly writing of exercises, painstaking criticism and editing prior to first use, and thoughtful interpretation of item analysis data cannot help but result in the production of superior achievement tests.

21 An Experimental Evaluation of Selected Multiple-Choice Item Construction Principles

THEODORE F. DUNN AND LEON G. GOLDSTEIN

While textbooks dealing with instrument construction present many suggestions for item writing, the empirical evidence demonstrating the worth of such apparently sound rules is meager. In the following experimental study, test items were systematically modified, and the difficulty, validity, and reliability of the resulting tests were compared. What effect did the introduction of "faults" have upon these three characteristics? How might you design another study to help verify these conclusions?

Four item-writing principles suggested by a survey of the literature were selected for investigation. The specific purpose was to determine whether these authority-preferred multiple-choice item construction principles affect the difficulty, validity, or reliability of achievement tests. The item characteristics or construction principles selected for study were as follows:

1. Inclusion vs. exclusion of irrelevant cues or specific determiners.
2. Question lead vs. incomplete statement as lead.
3. Equal-length alternatives vs. extra-long alternatives.
4. Consistency vs. inconsistency of grammar between lead and alternatives.

Reprinted and abridged with permission of the first-named author and publisher from an article entitled, "Test Difficulty, Validity, and Reliability as Functions of Selected Multiple-Choice Item Construction Principles," appearing in *Educational and Psychological Measurement*, 1959, Vol. 19, 171–179.

PROCEDURE

The over-all design consisted of two experiments. The first experiment, designated as Series A, tested the effects of the first two principles listed above. The second experiment, Series E, tested the effects of the second two principles.

DEVELOPMENT OF PREDICTOR VARIABLE ▪ The procedure for developing the experimental instruments was to rewrite an acceptably constructed item in order to violate an item-writing rule or set of rules. The items were obtained from the Army Basic Military Subjects Tests. Four-choice items were used with the instruction to choose the best answer and to guess if the correct answer was unknown. Four 100 item Basic Military Subjects Tests (A. B, C and D) were constructed for what is called the Series A experiment. Each test was composed of the following four 25-item content areas or item-blocks: weapons; care of self in combat; combat training; and non-combat. The items in the tests were identical except that they varied in their degree of conformance to the first two item construction principles mentioned above. Each item was written according to one of the following four writing techniques:

1. An open-ended lead with no cue to the correct alternative
   (open lead—no cue)
2. A question lead with no cue to the correct alternative
   (question lead—no cue)
3. A question lead with a cue to the correct alternative
   (question lead—cue)
4. An open-ended lead with a cue to the correct alternative
   (open lead—cue)

In order to test the second two-item construction principles, another set of four Basic Military Subject Tests, E, F, G, and H, covering the same four content areas were written from 100 different basic military subject four-choice items. This test comprised the Series E experiment. Each item in the Series E tests were written according to the following four item-writing techniques:

1. Equally long alternatives with no grammatical inconsistencies between the lead and the incorrect alternatives (equal choices–good grammar).
2. An extra-long correct alternative with no grammatical inconsistencies between the lead and the incorrect alternatives (unequal choices–good grammar).
3. An extra-long correct alternative with grammatical inconsistencies between the lead and the incorrect alternatives (unequal choices–poor grammar).
4. Equally long alternatives with grammatical inconsistencies between the lead and the incorrect alternatives (equal choices–poor grammar).

CRITERION AND REFERENCE VARIABLES ▪ The basic method in the study involved the comparison of the difficulties, validities, and reliabilities of item-blocks written in different degrees of conformance to the item construction principles as indicated above. Total raw scores on a Performance Test of Basic Military Subjects served as the primary criterion. As a second criterion ratings were used; approximately three superiors and two associates rated each examinee on his over-all achievement during basic military training. The Army's measure of over-all mental ability, Army Aptitude Area I, was used as a reference variable.

SAMPLE ■ The subjects used in the study were 832 enlisted Army trainees completing their eighth week of basic military training; this group was randomly divided into four subgroups of approximately 200 each. Each subgroup was administered one test form of each series. In short, every subject in the study received two tests: one of Series A and one of Series E.

RESULTS

EFFECT OF ITEM CONSTRUCTION PRINCIPLES ON DIFFICULTY ■ On an *a priori* basis, item-sets containing "faulty" items in which the answers are "given away" would be expected to be easier than item-blocks, identical in concept but written in conformity with traditional rules of good item construction. That such was the case is clearly demonstrated in Table 1.

TABLE 1. *Mean Scores on Sets of Items of Varying Content and Item Characteristics*

	CONTENT			
	I	II	III	IV
Combinations of Item-Writing Rules	*Weapons*	*Care of Self in Combat*	*Combat Training*	*Non-Combat Areas*
SERIES A (N = 204/cell)				
Open Lead No Cue	11.28	12.72	10.31	16.86
Question Lead Cue	12.53	13.33	11.31	17.43
Open Lead Cue	12.53	13.11	11.38	16.91
Question Lead No Cue	11.56	12.57	10.74	16.68
SERIES E (N = 208/cell)				
Equal Choices Good Grammar	11.35	12.25	11.97	16.73
Unequal Choices Poor Grammar	14.24	15.03	13.79	18.13
Equal Choices Poor Grammar	12.22	12.67	12.98	17.18
Unequal Choices Good Grammar	13.43	14.15	13.63	17.93

For Series A tests, the presence of cues is associated with the higher mean scores and the absence of cues with the lower mean scores. Apparently the form of lead (question vs. open) did not have a differential effect on mean item-block scores. Actually it was only for purposes of convenience that open lead was designated as the "rule." For Series E tests, the highest mean scores were invariably obtained when both rules were broken. On the other hand, following both rules resulted in the lowest mean score. Item-sets in which the items adhere to one rule and break the other yielded intermediate means.

The homogeneities of these means within contents were checked by analyses of variance for each series of tests. The analysis in the Series A tests indicated that item-block means within Content I (Weapons) and III (Combat Training) were not homogeneous, whereas within Content II (Care of Self in Combat) and Content IV (Non-Combat Areas) they were homogeneous. In the Series E experiment, the over-all differences between the means within each content were statistically stable. (The probability that such results could occur by chance was less than 1 percent.)

By way of consolidation of results here, a clear-cut hierarchy of means within the Series E tests has been shown, which reflects the manner of writing the item-blocks. Within the Series A tests this hierarchy has not been clearly demonstrated. The situation may be easily understood if it is recalled that one of the rules in Series A (namely, whether the lead is written in an incomplete statement or a question form) was not expected to be reacted to differentially by the examinees. Further analyses of these same data revealed that for the Series A tests only the presence of cues increased the means, while form of lead had no effect.

EFFECT OF ITEM CONSTRUCTION PRINCIPLES ON VALIDITY ▪ The ranges of validity coefficients of item-sets against performance test criterion across item-writing techniques within each content area is shown in Table 2. The homogeneity of

TABLE 2. *Ranges of Selected Validity and Reliability Coefficients across Different Item-Writing Techniques within Content Areas*

Content Area	Validity Coefficients	Reliability Coefficients	r's Between Item-Sets and Apt. Area I
	SERIES A ($N = 204/cell$)		
I	.35 – .40	.56 – .65	.55 – .66
II	.28 – .42	.49 – .64	.54 – .65
III	.32 – .42	.40 – .57	.56 – .72
IV	.35 – .48	.67 – .70	.60 – .66
	SERIES E ($N = 208/cell$)		
I	.34 – .42	.50 – .72	.52 – .58
II	.31 – .44	.57 – .71	.56 – .67
III	.24 – .40	.51 – .63	.56 – .69
IV	.35 – .43	.73 – .80	.57 – .69

these correlation coefficients was checked separately for each content. There is no evidence here that item-writing rules had a significant effect on validity. In addition, an inspection of the complete set of validities revealed no pattern of validities with respect to item construction rules.

Similar analyses by the authors of the validities of differently written item-blocks were made using both rating scales as the criterion and a combined criterion of performance tests and rating scales. In all cases the conclusion was supported that validities of tests of the type used in this study are not significantly influenced by adherence to the item-writing rules investigated.

EFFECT OF ITEM CONSTRUCTION PRINCIPLES ON RELIABILITY ▪ Kuder-Richardson reliabilities, Formula 20, were computed for each set of items. The effects of item-writing rules on these reliabilities were evaluated by testing their homogeneity within each content for both series of experiments. The range of reliabilities across item-writing techniques within content areas are presented in Table 2.

In the Series A tests the hypothesis that the reliabilities within any content are homogeneous cannot be rejected. In the Series E tests a significant clue appeared only in the weapons content; in this case the "poorly" written item-blocks were more reliable than the "well" written item-block. There seems to be a slight tendency in this direction in the Series E tests. Since the presence of cues should reduce random guessing, this tendency is in the expected direction. From the data as a whole, however, it cannot be said that the Kuder-Richardson reliabilities are differentially influenced by the rules studied.

RELATION OF "INTELLIGENCE" TO TEST-WISENESS ▪ If general mental ability were related to the ability to detect clues to the correct answer in multiple-choice items, then it could be hypothesized that the correlation of intelligence test scores with item-sets having construction "errors" in them would be higher than with item-sets which adhered to accepted principles. To obtain some indication of the relation between intelligence and test-wiseness, correlation coefficients were computed between scores on the Army's measure of general mental ability, Aptitude Area I, and item-set scores in each series. Tests of the homogeneity of these coefficients were made for each content area in each series. The range of these coefficients across item-writing techniques within content areas is presented in Table 2. The correlations were homogeneous across item-writing rules within each content in both series, except for Content III in the Series A tests. Even in this case differences in the magnitude of the coefficients were not in the expected direction—considering the previous findings that nature of lead is irrelevant, the two item-sets involving cues should both have the highest correlation coefficients instead of the highest (.72) and the lowest (.56). These general results suggest that the ability to pick up cues on the type of material tested may be found at all levels of intelligence.

The results of this study are not to be interpreted as a sweeping repudiation of the usefulness of item construction principles. In addition to the restrictions placed upon interpretation by the limited number of principles tested, the unique subject matter, and the nature of the sample examinees, it is entirely possible that certain variables operated in a compensating manner to offset the effect of breaking the rules. For example, assuming the same motivation which led to doing well on the criterion measure also led some subjects to pick up the cues on the badly written tests, the resulting increase in validity could completely cancel out a decrease in validity caused by giving away the cues to examinees in general. Nevertheless, the results have occurred in an operational situation. It seems reasonable to assume that the same results may occur under other conditions. Clearly, more research into the utility of item construction rules and their interaction with other variables is warranted before final conclusions are drawn.

22   Improving a Teacher-Made Test: A Case Study

EARL FOREMAN

The following article presents in a rather nontechnical manner the logical sequence of procedures used in developing a test. A common-sense approach to test development is indicated throughout the study. Obviously a considerable amount of time went into constructing and refining the instrument described in this paper. Considering the kinds and significance of the evaluations that are likely to be made on the basis of a classroom test, the effort would seem to be justified. What effect did the revision of the directions for taking the test have on reliability? How did the item response data lead to test revisions? What effect did the item analysis have on reliability?

The writer desired to construct a test in the area of literature comprehension at the seventh-grade level. After careful consideration, certain objectives were selected for measurement. Table 1 shows these objectives and the number of times each objective was included among the test items.

The purpose was to measure the skills named as many times and through as wide a variety of devices as was possible in a reasonably timed test. Literary selections were chosen from various sources, and in certain cases the writer composed selections to test specific abilities. The items were arranged roughly in progressive order from simple to difficult. Since the object was to measure

Reprinted and abridged with permission of the publisher (the University of Chicago Press) from an article entitled, "Improving the Reliability of a Teacher-Made Test", which appeared in the *School Review*, 1950 (May), Vol. 58, pp. 285–290.

TABLE 1. *Objectives Selected to Be Measured in a Literature-Comprehension Test*

Objective	Number of Times Included
1. Understanding of the situation portrayed	6
2. Understanding of the underlying cause and result of the situation	3
3. Understanding of the author's intent	6
4. Understanding of the moral or lesson, if any	4
5. Understanding of the meaning of specific lines	4
6. Understanding of the meaning of specific words	16
7. Understanding of the meaning of words or phrases used differently in separate contexts	7
8. Critical determination of good and lesser literature	2
9. Ability to compare and analyze central thoughts	2
10. Ability to discover in selections accepted life values or criteria and to distinguish them from values not generally accepted	2

depth of comprehension without regard to rate, no time limit was set for the test. As a "dry-run" trial the test was administered individually to children at various levels and to adults, one of whom was an English instructor. Through this device surface defects, such as ambiguities in language and structural obscurities, were discovered and eliminated before the actual administration of the test.

The test in final form consisted of ten sections. Each part contained one literary selection followed by certain statements concerning the selection. By restricting the number of selections, the writer was able to measure, within samples of broader continuity, a factor which seemed of considerable importance in the evaluation of most of the skills listed.

For various statistical purposes the first edition of the test was administered to both seventh- and eighth-grade pupils. A total population of ninety pupils took the test—forty-four in Grade VII and forty-six in Grade VIII. As was to be expected, this first administration revealed obvious faults. Among these perhaps the most serious was a low reliability coefficient of .52 as calculated by the Kuder-Richardson Method.

REVISING THE TEST

REVISION OF THE DIRECTIONS ■ The decision was made to revise the test in an effort to increase the reliability. One of the more commonly known devices, that of lengthening the test, was rejected as being impractical in this case and, furthermore, as being a statistical rather than an evidential technique. Instead, attention was directed toward adjustment and revision within the test as it was then constructed.

Upon careful consideration the question arose regarding the pupil's ability to understand the directions given in the test and the difficulty he might experience in indicating his response choices on the test form. It was decided to revise the directions only and to determine what effect this would have on the reliability of the test.

One fault appeared to lie in the method by which the pupil was asked to indicate his answers. In the first edition each literary selection was followed by groups of statements about the selection. One statement in each group was true. The statements were lettered, and corresponding letters were printed at the right margin of the form. The pupil was directed to cross out the letter at the right which corresponded to the letter in front of the true statement. An example taken from the test is given below.

Item 1. In this poem the author is:
  a) Telling a story
  b) Talking nonsense
  c) Describing a scene
  d) Pointing out a moral   a b c d

It seemed unsound psychologically to ask the pupils to cross out a correct-response indication. In addition, he was asked to transfer his attention from the statements to groups of letters placed elsewhere. It should be remembered that this test was constructed for seventh-grade children who, for the greater part, were not "test-wise" in such matters as the use of separate answer sheets. The new directions simplified the answering procedure by asking the pupil to encircle the letter in front of the true statement in each group. This eliminated the attention split and called for a positive response.

In the original administration of the test no introduction was given either by the administrator or within the test form. The pupil was presented immediately with the first selection. In an effort to make clear exactly what the pupil was to do, the revised form included a preface, which presented explanatory samples similar to the material in the test. Directions, marking procedures, and format exactly duplicated the test content. Three groups of statements were presented with each sample selection. In the first group the correct response was indicated. In the second group the pupil was told which was the true statement and was directed to encircle the letter in front of it. In the third group the pupil was asked to determine the correct statement and to indicate it in the proper manner. During the administration of the test the pupils and the administrator read the preface together, and the administrator made sure the pupils understood the directions before proceeding with the test.

Other directions were modified in the attempt to clarify for the child what was to be done. In one section of the test, for example, two literary selections were used instead of one. A short paragraph was introduced in the revised form to indicate to the pupil the departure from the usual form. The mortality on one of the last sections of the test had been high in the first administration. While some of this difficulty was acceptable and was probably due to the complexities presented in the section, it was thought that confusion might be partially due to obscure directions. The directions were, therefore, reworded, and a longer example was included which closely approximated the material in the section. In the original edition the last section had required two answers. The directions were revised so that only one answer needed to be indicated. This revision was accomplished without diminishing in any way the measuring value of the item.

No changes were made in the actual test material. Literary selections, statements, wording of items, and arrangements of items were reprinted exactly as they had appeared in the previous edition. Although certain items obviously needed revision or deletion, the object on this particular administration was to determine the effect of the revision of directions on the reliability. The Kuder-Richardson technique was applied to the scores of the second administration, and the calculations yielded a reliability coefficient of .78. Since no changes had been made other than in directions, the conclusion was reached that for this population the revision of directions was probably responsible for the increased reliability.

REVISION OF THE TEST ITEMS ▪ The second attempt to increase the reliability was made through revising the test items. Item analyses had been made on both administrations of the test. An examination revealed that several items should be altered or discarded completely. The difficulty of determining in advance what sorts of changes in items will bring about desired results is illustrated in the following example, of which the results of revision were not significantly successful. One of the first selections presented the story of the fox, the crow, and the piece of cheese. An item concerning the fable follows.

Item 2. The moral in this story is:
   a) Beware of foxes
   b) Use any method you can to get food when you are hungry
   c) Beware of flattery
   d) Don't try to sing if you know you can't

The statement identified by the letter c is, of course, the correct response. However, 29 percent of the pupils in the first administration and 22 percent of the pupils in the second administration had indicated statement d as their choice. It was possible either that the word "flattery" was unfamiliar to many children at the seventh-grade level or that statement d too nearly approached a reasonable solution for the child. An effort to discriminate more closely was made by changing both statements. Statement c in the new form read, "Beware of too much praise." Statement d read, "If you sing, you may lose your food." The results on this item in three administrations of the test are given in Table 2. For this small population the revision of the item had no significant effect.

The revision of a second item was more successful. This selection was a poem in five stanzas. The fourth verse of each stanza indicated that the reader was to complete the thought of the stanza in any manner he chose. This is to say, the poet had written what was actually nonsense verse, concluding each stanza with such a remark as, "Anything you choose to say!" An item following the selection appears below.

Item 3. The poet who wrote this selection:
   a) Is telling a story
   b) Thinks that your ideas are better than his
   c) Is getting you to imagine the story yourself

On the first administration 45 percent of the pupils indicated the correct answer, *c*. However, 47 percent indicated statement *a* as the correct response. On the second administration 30 percent of the pupils indicated statement *a* as their choice. Examination of the selection revealed the fact that statement *a* might be considered correct, since the poem actually was a little story although it was incomplete. Statement *a* was changed to read "The poet . . . has no idea of how to write a poem." Results of the three administrations on this item are also shown in Table 2.

For this population, revision of the statement eliminated the persistent indication of what had been previously considered a false response. The overbalance

TABLE 2. *Pupil Responses to Two Statements Appearing in Three Editions of a Literature-Comprehension Test*

Statement and Edition of Test	Number of Pupils	Percent of Pupils Indicating Each Choice as Correct			
		a)	b)	c)	d)
Item 2:					
Edition I	44	9	9	53	29
Edition II	46	7	14	57	22
Edition III	54	12	12	54	22
Item 3:					
Edition I	44	47	6	45	. .
Edition II	46	30	4	60	. .
Edition III	54	4	4	92	. .

of correct responses on the last edition, although this selection is near the less difficult end of the scale, probably calls for some consideration of an increase in the over-all difficulty of the particular group of statements.

Various other item revisions were made. One group of statements concerning a selection in the middle range of difficulty showed a correct response of only 17 percent on the first administration and 9 percent on the second administration. The other two groups of statements concerning the same selection yielded correct responses ranging from 55 percent to 67 percent in the two administrations. While it was expected and entirely acceptable that considerable variation would occur within the groups in any one section, such a wide differential was felt to be a violation of the consistency of the instrument. The entire group of statements under question was discarded, and a new set on a simpler level was devised. The third administration resulted in a correct response of 72 percent.

One of the literary selections was an excerpt from an essay by Emerson. Certain words were incorrectly substituted, other words were misspelled, and various errors were introduced. The pupils were to indicate the errors. Results on the first two administrations were so poor that it appeared that this section of the test was too difficult for any of the seventh-grade pupils tested. The extreme difficulty was traced in part to the original article, which, it was decided, was probably too abstract for Grade VII even in its correct form. A simpler article was written which retained the same number and types of errors. The results of the administration of this item were more satisfactory. While still difficult enough to discriminate, the scoring results were evened out so as to approach more closely the curve of the entire test.

Statistical treatment of the results of the third edition of the entire test yielded a reliability coefficient by the Kuder- Richardson method of .82. While this figure is still not high, the various revisions had resulted in an overall increase of .30 in reliability. Further revision is indicated, and of course administration of the test to larger populations will yield more reliable data.

23   *Item Selection Techniques and the Evaluation of Instructional Objectives*

RICHARD C. COX

Test experts agree that for a classroom test to be considered valid there must exist a high degree of correspondence between the instructional objectives and the test items. Evaluation of the items must involve both thoughtful and subjective evaluation by a subject-matter expert, as well as statistical data bearing on item difficulty (how many examinees respond correctly) and discrimination (does the item correlate with a logical criterion, usually total test score). A tremendous variety of item analysis techniques have been devised (see, for example, Davis, 1951 and 1952). The following procedures described by Cox are representative of the usual methods employed by classroom teachers and commercial test publishers.

If we rely solely on statistical data in the selection of items, what kinds of biases might be introduced into the final test? How does the type of behavior

Reprinted and abridged with permission of author and publisher from the *Journal of Educational Measurement*, 1965, Vol. 2, pp. 181–185.

measured with the test item (Taxonomy classification) interact with difficulty and discrimination?

The initial planning of an educational achievement test involves the identification of the subject-matter content and the instructional objectives to be tested. A two-way table of specifications is often utilized at this stage of test construction to insure that these two aspects of test construction are represented.

The *Taxonomy of Educational Objectives* (Bloom, 1956) can be used to classify test items. To accurately classify a test item it is necessary to know or assume the learning experiences which have preceded the administration of the test. It has been demonstrated that such a classification of test items into the major categories of the Taxonomy can be accomplished with a considerable degree of reliability.

The usual procedure in objective test construction is to prepare a larger pool of test items than will be used in the final form of the instrument. This large pool of items is administered to a tryout group to obtain statistical information to aid in the selection of items for the final test form. When the test is designed to rank subjects on some specified characteristics, item-discriminating power is often used as the criterion for selection of items.

Using the Taxonomy it is possible to classify the items in the original item pool according to the instructional objectives they are designed to measure. If the final form of the evaluation instrument is to validly measure the objectives identified in the original item pool, the method of item selection should not appreciably alter the taxonomical structure of the original item pool. If the item selection procedure biases the final test form by disproportionate selection of items measuring certain instructional objectives, the final form of the test will not validly evaluate the objectives measured by the total test pool. It is the purpose of this study to evaluate the effect of statistical item selection on the structure of the final evaluation instrument as compared with the structure of the original item pool.

PROCEDURE

The item pool used in this study was comprised of 379 four- and five-option multiple-choice items used in an introductory college-level natural science course. The 379 items were classified using the categories of the Taxonomy. Three judges worked independently on this classification using the examples presented in the Taxonomy and in Nelson (1961). There was agreement on the classification of approximately 85 percent of the items. The classification of the remaining items was established after consultation with the subject-matter expert. The total pool of 379 items was classified as follows: Knowledge 108 (27%), Comprehension 110 (29%), Application 91 (24%), and Analysis 76 (20%). None of the items were classified in the Synthesis and Evaluation categories.

Samples of 1,000 males and 1,000 females were selected at random from the 3,150 students who had taken the natural science examinations. The mean score was 235.86 for males and 233.70 for females.

The upper and lower 270 subjects (27 percent) in each distribution were used to compute indices of item difficulty and discrimination. The index of difficulty for a particular item was determined by the percentage of subjects in the upper and lower 27 percent of the total test scores who passed the item. No correction for guessing was employed. The difference and Davis indices were used as item discrimination coefficients.

The average difficulty level of items for males was 62.10 and for females 61.79. The test items were, on the average, slightly easier for males as reflected previously in the mean test scores. The average Difference index for males was 20.28 and for females 21.34. The average Davis index for males was 15.66 and for females 17.04. The difference indices are higher on the average than the Davis indices since the Difference index tends to assign higher values to middle difficulty items than does the Davis index. The higher average values for females also reflects difficulty levels.

To simulate the assembly of a final test form the 100 items with the highest Davis indices were selected from the total item pool. The procedure was repeated using the difference indices as the criteria for item selection. The procedures were followed for both male and female groups. There was approximately 80 percent overlap of common items selected by the two techniques.

RESULTS

Table 1 presents the average difficulty and discrimination indices computed on

TABLE 1. *Average Difficulty and Discrimination Indices by Taxonomical Category for Total Item Pool*

Taxonomical Category	Difficulty Index		Davis Index		Difference Index	
	Male	Female	Male	Female	Male	Female
Knowledge	65.98	66.39	15.25	16.83	19.28	20.18
Comprehension	63.74	63.45	17.16	18.08	22.32	23.22
Application	59.18	58.37	15.24	17.08	19.98	21.31
Analysis	58.04	57.29	14.54	15.79	19.01	20.21

the total item pool for the male and female groups.

The values of the average difficulty and discrimination indices differ with taxonomical category. The average difficulty levels increase with increasing complexity of taxonomical category. Knowledge items are easiest while Analysis items are the most difficult for both males and females.

The average discrimination indices also follow a similar pattern for males and females. In general, Comprehension items are the most discriminating while Analysis items are least discriminating.

After the 100 item tests were selected, the percentage of items classified in each taxonomical category was compiled. These values are presented in Table 2 along

TABLE 2. *Percentage of Most Discriminating Items Classified in Taxonomical Categories by Sex*

	Males		Females		
	Items Selected by:		*Items Selected by:*		
Taxonomical Categories	Davis Index	Difference Index	Davis Index	Difference Index	Total Item Pool
Knowledge	24	22	24	20	27
Comprehension	38	40	29	36	29
Application	18	21	31	27	24
Analysis	20	17	16	17	20
Total	100	100	100	100	100

with the comparable percentages for the total item pool. Chi-square tests for the comparison of observed and theoretical frequencies were computed for each of the first four columns in Table 2 against the percentages in the total item pool. All chi-square values were significant at the .01 level.

The tests composed of the most discriminating items are not representative of the total item pool from which they were selected. These tests would not adequately measure the instructional objectives measured by the total item pool. In general, less emphasis is given to Knowledge and Analysis items and more emphasis to Comprehension items than is the case in the original item pool.

The chi-square test was also used to compare the percentage of items in each category for the male versus female groups. This was done separately for the Davis and Difference indices. Again, chi-square values were significant at the .01 level. These results are especially interesting since approximately 70 percent of the items selected were the same for the male and female groups.

CONCLUSIONS

The major conclusions of this study are as follows:

1. Statistical selection of items from the total item pool has a biasing effect on the selected tests. The proportion of items in the selected tests which measure certain instructional objectives is unlike the proportion of items in the total item pool which measures the same objectives. The selected tests are not representative of the total item pool in this respect.

2. Statistical selection of items from the total item pool operates differentially for male and female groups. When the statistical data obtained from the female

tryout group is used to select tests from the total item pool, the results differ from those obtained using the male tryout group. The structure of the selected tests as indicated by the taxonomical structure of the items differs for the male and female groups.

IMPLICATIONS

The practice of statistical selection of items for the final form of an evaluation instrument is seriously questioned by the results of this study. Statistical item selection alone is not sufficient; other variables should be considered.

It has been shown that in the test pool the average discrimination values differ for the four major categories of items classified according to the instructional objective being measured. This should indicate to the test constructor that selection of items from the item pool on the basis of these discrimination indices will be biased in favor of the group of items which contains the highest average discrimination values. This suggests the possibility of selecting the most discriminating items within a particular taxonomical category rather than selecting the most discriminating items from the total item pool. The discrimination index would be computed using only those items in that particular category to obtain items which correlate well with other items in that category. In the planning stages the test constructor should specify the number of items measuring each instructional objective to be included in the final form of the test. The items for the item pool would be written accordingly. Then, within each category a specified number of items would be selected for inclusion in the final form of the test.

This study has also indicated that the sex make-up of the tryout groups has an effect on the statistical item selection. It is a well-known principle that the tryout groups should be essentially similar to the groups for which the test is to be used. The results of this study clearly indicate that the sex make-up of the tryout group makes a difference in the selection of certain types of items for inclusion in the final test form. If, for example, Application items discriminate better for females than for males, then a test constructed using discrimination indices based on a female tryout group will include more Application items than will a test constructed using data for a male tryout group. If the proportion of males and females in the group or groups for which the test is intended is not similar to the proportion of males and females in the tryout group, the test would not validly measure the instructional objectives specified in the planning stage. This could be a critical consideration in the construction or use of a test with an all-male or female group. The test constructor might consider the possibility of computing item discrimination indices separately by sex as well as by taxonomical category and selecting items for the final form of the test accordingly.

VII

SELECTED PSYCHOLOGICAL
FACTORS INFLUENCING
TEST SCORES

So many factors influence test scores that tests do not always measure what their titles imply. Many of these factors were identified and discussed in the previous chapters dealing with reliability and validity. It is the purpose of the present chapter to illustrate and in some cases summarize research which has been aimed at identifying and describing selected factors which may distort test scores.

It would be almost impossible to attempt a listing of all the sources of error which can modify test scores. One reasonable classification scheme may emphasize the source of error; e.g., examinee, examiner, instrument, and environmental-centered sources of error. Such a scheme has the appeal of parsimony, but could be quite misleading, to the degree that it may mask significant interactive effects. For example, let us assume that the personnel director of a large industrial concern has decided to use a personality inventory to make decisions regarding the promotion of managerial-level personnel. Without much notice to the employees he schedules a group examination at the end of a week and work day. Some employees are very much interested in the several positions that will soon be available; others are not. We can already see many factors which exist as potential sources of distortion in the personality inventory scores. The testing situation itself, being a group activity late in the day and at the end of the week, and the administration itself, being almost unannounced, might be considered environmental-centered factors. Differences among individuals with respect to motivation for the position and their willingness to "reveal themselves" on a personality inventory would be considered examinee-centered sources of error. Both categories of error would influence the reliability and validity of the instrument, thereby serving as a source of instrument-centered error. Admittedly the above hypothetical situation would not be considered common or accepted practice, but it nevertheless points out possible significant interactive effects that may influence test scores.

The "interactive" theme presented in the opening paragraph above is developed by Dr. Edwin E. Ghiselli in the first article in this chapter. His data and presentation are important from two standpoints. First, his discussion helps explain some low reliability and validity coefficients by taking into account moderator variables. Second, he demonstrates how the notions of moderator variables and intra-individual variability can be made to work for, not against the purpose of measurement.

A somewhat less theoretical view of interaction is taken by Dr. Lawrence Wrightsman in the next article. In his experiment the author was able to induce conditions in his examinees which differentially influenced test performance. He was able to show how a stressful situation can inhibit performance on a complex intellectual task, if the examinees are initially pre-disposed to anxiety. This study underscores the importance of standardized procedures in test administration. It is also interesting to note that the experimental effects most outstanding in this study were the interactive ones.

Although the interactive effects in testing are probably the most significant, distortion in test scores may be due to other sources. In the third article of the chapter Dr. Charles Dicken presents evidence that with conscious effort the scores, patterns, and profiles of a personality inventory can be significantly distorted. The study is interesting because it involves the *Edwards Personal Preference Schedule* (1957a), a widely used standardized self-report inventory, and because of the marked "faking" effect discovered. The information provided by the type of study reported by Dicken in the third paper of this chapter is invaluable. It points out the importance of validational studies, particularly where personality inventories are concerned. Although the sample sizes were small and the experimental situation somewhat contrived, the implication of Dicken's study cannot be denied.

In the next paper Dr. Gerald Wiener argues that examiner factors must also be considered in evaluating the scores derived from a test, particularly an individually administered test. His data support such a contention. Although the experimental effect was not nearly as marked as in the previous study by Dicken, the influence of the examiner's attitude on the examinee was evident.

In the final article of the chapter Dr. Lee J. Cronbach presents a summary of research relating to essentially instrument-centered sources of error. After extensively reviewing the literature, the author concludes that the item format of a test can significantly influence the resulting scores by reducing validity. His recommendations for changes in test construction practice, particularly those relating to the development of correction keys, have constituted a major contribution to psychometrics.

24   *Moderating Effects and Differential Reliability and Validity*

EDWIN E. GHISELLI

The search for methods yielding accurate measurements and predictions seldom results in the development of unique, yet relatively simple and comprehensive procedures. A notable exception is described in the following article. Here it is recognized that the extent of the relationship between two variables may be related to scores on a third or moderating variable. To illustrate, Fredericksen and Melville (1954) concluded that interests were a good predictor of grades for the non-compulsive students, but not for the compulsive students. Compulsivity "moderated" the relationship between interests and grades. When evaluating studies involving moderators the critical student will ask: Do the resulting more homogeneous groups, or at least the techniques used to establish them, appear reasonable? How can this differentiation of groups contribute to construct as well as criterion-related validity? Is the additional predictability worth the addition complexity involved when employing a moderator? How might the scores on the variables be represented in three dimensions?

OVERVIEW OF CLASSICAL MEASUREMENT THEORY

For more than half a century the notions of Yule and Spearman have dominated theoretical formulations in psychometrics. Pursuant to these classical notions errors are taken to be random and scores are combined additively. The possibility of interactive effects among variables is not recognized. Because in the linear combination of variables their weights are the same for all individuals, it is presumed that the psychological structure of all individuals is precisely the same.

On any one administration of a test, error scores are taken to vary from individual to individual. Hence for some individuals the error of measurement is smaller and for others it is larger. However, over many parallel tests the standard deviation of the errors is taken to be the same for all individuals. More correctly it should be said that as the number of parallel tests increases without limit the

Reprinted and abridged from Edwin E. Ghiselli, "Moderating Effects and Differential Reliability and Validity", *Journal of Applied Psychology*, 1963, Vol. 47, pp. 81–86. Copyright 1963 by the American Psychological Association and reproduced by permission of author and publisher.

standard error of measurement approaches the same value for all individuals. Hence it is concluded that for a given test all individuals are measured with the same degree of reliability.

Similarly, for any one administration of a given criterion and a test the error with which the test predicts the criterion is taken to vary from individual to individual. Hence for some individuals the error of prediction is smaller and for others it is larger. However, over many parallel criteria and tests the standard deviation of the errors is taken to be the same for all individuals. Again, more correctly it should be said that as the number of parallel criteria and tests increases without limit the standard error of prediction approaches the same value for all individuals. Hence it is concluded that for a given criterion and test all individuals are measured with the same degree of validity.

Because it is held that errors are random and equal for all individuals, and scores are additive with no interactive effects, it follows that neither reliability nor validity can be improved by selecting out from the total group those individuals for whom error is smaller. Reliability can be improved only by increasing the number of measurements, elimination of elements of lesser reliability, or better "housekeeping" procedures designed to reduce random error. Validity can be improved only by increasing the reliability of the criterion and predictor, or adding other predictors which cover aspects of the criterion not measured by the original predictor or aspects of the original predictor which are independent of the criterion.

THE RATIONALE FOR MODERATOR VARIABLES

Classic psychometric theory deals with a large number of sets of measurements, but let us concern ourselves only with two as we ordinarily do in the practical situation. Consider the bivariate distribution of scores on two variables where the relationship is less than unity. The two variables can be either two parallel tests or a criterion and a predictor. Running from the upper right hand to the lower left hand of the bivariate distribution chart is a group of individuals for whom scores are highly related. For this group the differences, regardless of sign, between standard scores on the two variables and the error of measurement or of prediction are small. For the remainder of the individuals the differences between the two standard scores are greater and hence the error is greater. If it could be demonstrated that these differences, or some other measure of error such as the standard error or the correlation coefficient, were related to another variable, then some modification of classic psychometric theory would appear to be in order. Ghiselli (1960b) has called this other variable a predictability variable, but Saunders (1956) has better termed it a moderator, thus drawing attention to the interactive effects.

EVIDENCE FOR THE EXISTENCE AND USEFULNESS
OF MODERATOR VARIABLES

Fisk and Rice (1955) and Berdie (1961) have summarized early evidence indicating that individual error of measurement may be predicted by a moderator. Other investigators have shown that the error of prediction itself may be predicted by a moderator.

Using the procedure he employed to study moderating effects on validity, the present author has examined moderating effects in reliability of measurement. Two parallel forms of a complex reactions test were administered to 775 semi-skilled workers, 517 of whom were used as an experimental group and 258 as a cross-validation group. Each person took both forms of the test on the same occasion. For each member of the experimental group the difference, regardless of sign, between standard scores on the two forms was determined. It was found that age, education, and scores on a tapping and dotting test were related to these differences. A combination of scores on these variables was taken to form a moderator. The reliability coefficient, the correlation between the two parellel forms, was .92 for the entire group, whereas for the 9 percent of subjects earning the lowest moderator scores it was only .82 and for the 15 percent earning the highest moderator scores it was .97.

Another instance of moderating effects in validity also may be described. A 64-item forced-choice inventory was administered to 96 factory workers on whom criterion scores in the form of supervisors' ratings were available. Seventeen of the items were used in a scale designed to measure "Sociometric Popularity." Half of the workers were used as an experimental group and half as a cross-validation group. For the experimental group the differences, regardless of sign, were determined for each individual between standard criterion and standard test scores. For the 47 items not used in the predictor scale an item analysis was performed against these differences. Responses to 15 of these items were found to be significantly related to the differences and were formed into a moderator to be applied to the cross-validation group. For the entire cross-validation group the validity of the scale, as given by the Pearsonian correlation coefficient, was —.01, whereas for the 19 percent earning the lowest moderator scores the validity was —.47 and for the 32 percent earning the highest it was .39.

There is, then, a substantial body of evidence indicating that it is possible to predict individual error of measurement and error of prediction. Clearly those individuals for whom a test has a greater degree of reliability or validity can be systematically differentiated from those for whom it has a lesser degree. The higher the cutting score on the moderator is set, the higher is the reliability or validity of the test for those individuals who fall above it. The choice of a cutting score is a matter of how many individuals one is willing to eliminate in order to achieve a higher degree of reliability or validity.

THE PRACTICAL UTILITY OF MODERATOR VARIABLES

Even recognizing that it is possible to differentiate within a group those individuals whose scores are more reliable from those whose scores are less reliable, we might well question the practical value of such a differentiation. However, purely for descriptive purposes it might be desirable to know how reliably an individual is measured. Thus if administrative decisions are to be made on the basis of some test or other measuring device, it would be very helpful in borderline cases to have some indication of whether a given individual is measured with a small or large error. Furthermore, with a lower error of measurement, validity should be enhanced. Classic psychometric theory itself teaches this, and Berdie (1961) has given an empirical demonstration. Finally, in some situations it might be highly desirable to be able to predict the extent of intra-individual variability in performance. In personnel selection ordinarily the aim is to pick out those individuals whose performance is high. But for planning purposes or to insure the smooth flow of work it might be equally important to select individuals whose rate of work does not vary greatly from one period to another, that is, has a high degree of self-consistency or reliability.

The case for validity is much clearer, since a reduction in error means more accurate prediction and hence the selection of higher performing individuals. But even here the use of moderators might be criticized on the grounds that it necessitates the elimination of a substantial proportion of cases from the appraisal procedures which in turn eliminates even more. However, this is not necessarily the case. Ghiselli (1956) has shown that if a given percentage of individuals is to be selected and the rest eliminated, selecting that given percentage on the combined basis of their moderator and test scores yields a substantially superior group of individuals than those selected on the basis of test scores alone.

Furthermore, in some instances, especially those where the validity for the total group is low or zero, for those individuals who earn low scores on the moderator and who might therefore be eliminated from the appraisal, the validity coefficient may be of respectable magnitude and negative. For example, with the factory workers mentioned earlier the validity of the predictor for the 32 percent earning the highest moderator scores was .39. But in addition for the 19 percent who earned the lowest moderator scores the validity coefficient was —.47. So for these latter individuals high predictor scores were associated with low criterion scores. Consequently for half of the total group, the 32 percent earning high moderator scores and 19 percent earning low moderators scores, the validity of the predictor is of the order of .40. It may seem peculiar, but a given score on a test may indicate the promise of success for some individuals, whereas for others it may indicate the likelihood of failure.

Another way to use a moderator, and a way which permits an assessment of all individuals, is to determine which of two predictors to use in selection. Ghiselli (1960a) accomplished this by determining for each individual the difference between his standard criterion score and his standard score on Predictor 2. These differences were taken regardless of sign. Thus for each individual the difference between the two differences was determined. For a given individual a positive difference indicates that the one test gives the better prediction and a negative difference indicates that the other is better. Moderators were then developed which were related to these differences and could be applied to cross-validation groups. For some individuals the moderator selects Predictor 1 and for the others it selects Predictor 2, but the standard scores for all individuals are thrown together regardless of predictor.

Ghiselli presents three instances where this proved to be an effective procedure. In one the validity coefficients for two predictors for a particular criterion were .02 and .20, and using predictors selected by the moderator the coefficient was .33. In another instance the validity coefficients of the two predictors were .55 and .61, with predictors selected by the moderator having a validity of .73. Finally, in an instance where the two validity coefficients were .17 and .51, using a moderator to select the better predictor for each individual gave a coefficient of .73.

IDENTIFYING MODERATORS

Obviously the nature of the traits which function as moderators is a matter of considerable importance. Clearly it would be most helpful if all moderators had characteristics in common. Some of the research does suggest that "undesirable" traits such as a lack of personality integration and low motivation are associated with larger error. But certainly many of the traits which have been found to be effective as moderators are of quite a different sort, such as age, education, type of interest, and manual dexterity. In a number of Ghiselli's studies moderators were developed through item analyses of the same inventory, so that similarity of items which form different moderators can be examined. His results indicate that there is a high degree of specificity. With two different tests predicting the same criterion for a given group, and with the same test predicting different though similar criteria for two different groups, the items which form the moderators are quite different. While moderator variables are by no means as elusive as suppressor variables, since so many investigators have been able to find or develop them, they do seem to be just as specific. It would therefore appear to be impossible to state any general principles about the nature of the traits which act as moderators.. Of course when the bivariate distribution of criterion and test scores is heteroscedastic, then test scores themselves serve as a moderator because they are related to error of prediction.

Some of the findings indicate that the relationship between moderator scores and scores both on criteria and predictors are quite low. Therefore, they do not add to prediction in a multiple correlation sense. The contribution of moderators is of an entirely different order, differentiating those individuals for whom error is smaller from those for whom it is larger. Their contribution, then, is unique.

CLASSICAL MEASUREMENT THEORY AND MODERATING VARIABLES

As has been seen, there is a substantial body of empirical evidence indicating that moderator effects do occur. Convincing though these findings may be, one would be much more persuaded of moderating effects if some theoretical foundation of them were provided. It could be, as Saunders (1956) and Berdie (1961) have suggested, that moderators operate by sorting a heterogeneous aggregation of individuals into homogeneous groups. The magnitude and pattern of intercorrelations among variables, and hence reliability and validity, vary from group to group. Heterogeneity would be indicated by systematic variation of error from individual to individual whereas homogeneity would be indicated by all individuals having the same error. This notion permits retention of the classic psychometric concepts of randomness of errors and the linear combination of variables. What it adds is the admission that the magnitude of error and the differential weights carried by the components in a composite, the psychological structure, may vary from group to group. However, within a group the error of measurement and of prediction and the relative weights carried by a set of tests in predicting a criterion are the same for all individuals.

Thus, women might be less distracted than men by environmental changes during a testing session and hence be more reliably measured. In this case sex would moderate error of measurement. Intelligence might be more related to grades in engineering school for those students who have substantial interest in engineering than for those whose interest is low. Engineering interest, then, moderates error of prediction. For younger factory workers finger dexterity might be more important than spatial ability in predicting rate of production on the job, and the reverse might be true for older workers. So age would function to moderate the relative weights finger dexterity and spatial ability have in predicting rate of production.

This notion that moderators sort heterogeneous aggregations of individuals into homogeneous groups is a very useful way of conceptualizing moderator effects. It focuses attention on the kinds of differences which exist among individuals who in some given respect are homogeneous, thereby suggesting types of moderators. Furthermore, it does little violence to classic psychometric theory. However, it presumes individuals can be divided into clear and distinct classes. Yet in actual practice moderators distribute individuals along a continuum. Individuals are not sorted into separate classes and a "group" is merely those individuals who fall at the same point on the continuum.

Another possible explanation of moderator effects is that the common elements which account for the correlation between two variables differ from individual to individual rather than just from group to group. What in the first point of view were considered as classes are now thought of as class intervals.

Error of measurement would be taken as varying from being quite small for some individuals to being quite large for others. Consequently error scores would carry less weight in determining fallible scores for some individuals than for others. Obviously a necessary condition is that individual differences in error scores possess some consistency or reliability over parallel tests. Evidence supporting this is provided by Fisk and Rice (1955) and Berdie (1961). Such a position would not require that all variation commonly termed error of measurement is predictable by the moderator, but only a portion of it. The remainder would still be thought of as being random error. The reliability coefficient, then, would be an average description of precision of measurement.

The importance of a given trait in determining performance on some criterion is taken to differ among individuals. The trait varies from being of prime importance in determining criterion performance for some individuals to being of little or no importance for others. At the one extreme, then, error of prediction is smaller and test validity higher and at the other, error is larger and test validity lower. Consequently the weight a test carries in prediction varies from individual to individual. Ghiselli's demonstration that two tests can be differentiated in terms of the accuracy with which they predict a criterion for a given individual is evidence of this effect. In effect Ghiselli weighted one test 1 and the other 0 for some individuals and the reverse for the remaining. Applying the optimally predicted pattern of weights for each individual accounted for a greater proportion of criterion variance. Pursuant to this position validity coefficients are average descriptions of predictive accuracy, and multiple-regression weights are indicators of the average relative importance of the different predictors.

With respect to validity, the function of the moderator is to predict for a given individual the weight a test carries in determining criterion performance. It is not necessary that the moderator account for all criterion variance unpredicted by the tests, since some of this variance can be due to unreliability and the rest to unmeasured but important traits. The individuals' weights might be unrelated both to their criterion and test scores, or related to one or both. But nothing in this concept indicates what such correlations should be. Perhaps the correlations between the weights and the criterion and test differ from situation to situation.

Moderators are most attractive since they promise significant improvements in reliability and especially in predictive validity. However, that other subtle variable, the suppressor, also promises much in adding to prediction but in practice seldom makes much of a contribution nor holds up well from sample to sample. Hence some counsel of caution might be in order. It is quite possible that the time and effort required to develop moderators might be more fruitfully spent in seeking improvements in reliability and validity of the sort that follow from classic psychometric theory. Furthermore, since the indications are that moderators are rather specific, it might be that they, like suppressors, do not hold up well from sample to sample.

25 The Effects of Anxiety, Achievement Motivation, and Task Importance on Intelligence Test Performance

LAWRENCE S. WRIGHTSMAN, JR.

It would be virtually impossible to specify all the possible examinee-centered variables that influence test performance. Some variables have been alluded to in earlier sections, particularly in Symonds' article found in the chapter on reliability. Dr. Wrightsman, in the following article, identifies three possible significant sources of influence on intelligence test scores. What are these influences and how did they affect results of the intelligence test administration? How could some of these influences be controlled? In addition to the reasons discussed by the author, how can you account for the lowered intelligence test performance of the low-motivated individuals under the test-important condition?

In the present study it was hypothesized that when the intelligence test was seen as unimportant there would be no relationship between level of anxiety and score on the intelligence test, but that when the test was seen as important the relationship would be a negative one. In addition, it was hypothesized that the purported importance of the task would not influence performance of subjects high in internalized achievement motivation, but would influence the performance of subjects lower in internalized achievement motivation.

METHOD

Normally all freshmen at George Peabody College for Teachers are administered the *American Council on Education Psychological Examination* (ACE) and the *Cooperative English Tests* as a part of the freshman orientation program. After responding to these instruments, the 234 freshmen (59 males and 175 females) entering in the fall of 1959 were administered three additional tests. These were the MA scale, a measure of manifest anxiety (Taylor, 1953); the Test of Insight, a projective measure of achievement motivation devised by French (1958); and the Adaptability Test (Tiffin & Lawshe, 1954), a timed measure of intelligence. Before taking this last test, 122 subjects were led to believe that the results of this intelligence test would be very important to them, in that the results would follow the student throughout his college career (Important Test condition). The other 112 subjects, members of the Unimportant Test condition, were

Reprinted and abridged from Lawrence S. Wrightsman, Jr., "The Effects of Anxiety, Achievement Motivation, and Task Importance on Intelligence Test Performance," *Journal of Educational Psychology*, 1962, Vol. 53, pp. 150–156. Copyright 1962 by the American Psychological Association and reproduced by permission of author and publisher.

led to believe that their responses to the intelligence test were being collected for normative purposes only. Subjects in the two conditions were tested at the same time, as the manipulation of the importance of the test was done entirely through the use of printed instructions on the front of the test. After completing the intelligence test, subjects were asked to indicate how important they thought it was for them to do well on the test by placing a number from 1 through 10 under their name on the test booklet. An analysis indicated that the manipulation was successful in that subjects in the Important Test condition placed significantly greater importance to doing well.

No significant between-condition differences were found on the ACE, the MA scale, or the achievement motivation measure. An estimate of the interscorer reliability of the achievement motivation measure was determined by comparing the experimenter's scoring of the responses of 30 subjects with the scoring done by another person trained in the scoring procedures. The resultant reliability estimate was .83.

There were no significant sex differences on any of the measures. Despite the absence of sex differences in mean score, the relationships between MA scores and measures of aptitude such as the ACE and Adaptability Test were more negative for females than for males. Henceforth, findings for each sex will be reported.

Correlation between the MA scale and the achievement motivation measure was −.14. Despite its being significant, the relationship is of such small magnitude that it may be said with confidence that the two scales are measuring essentially different variables.

In both conditions performance on the MA scale was significantly negatively correlated with ACE-L and ACE-Q scores (−.19 and −.14 in the Unimportant Test condition and −.28 and −.25 in the Important Test condition). This confirms previous findings that in college samples there is sometimes a slight, but significant negative relationship between level of anxiety and performance on measures of scholastic aptitude (Spielberger, 1958). Those subjects who were to be in the Important Test condition had higher ACE-MA correlations than did those who were to be in the Unimportant Test condition. These differences (−.19 vs. −.28 and −.14 vs. −.25) approach but do not reach the .05 level of significance, and there is no clear-cut reason other than a coincidental one for the differences. However, the differences should be borne in mind, and the effect of the manipulation should be seen as possibly increasing an already existing near-difference. In an effort to eliminate these differences partial correlation coefficients were computed in addition to the first-order coefficients.

RESULTS

As is indicated in Table 1, the correlation coefficient between MA scores and the Adaptability Test scores in the Unimportant Test condition was nonsignificant (−.06); but in the Important Test condition the comparable correlation was −.37.

TABLE 1. *Correlations between MA Score, Adaptability Test Score, and ACE Scores*

Correlation	Unimportant Test condition			Important Test condition		
	Males (N=32)	Females (N=80)	Total (N=112)	Males (N=27)	Females (N=95)	Total (N=122)
MA and Adaptability	.09	−.12	−.06	−.30	−.40**	−.37**
MA and Adaptability, with ACE-L partialed out	.24	.00	.07	−.30	−.24**	−.25**
MA and Adaptability, with ACE-Q partialed out	−.04	.12	.05	−.31**	−.28**	−.28**
MA and ACE-L	−.22	−.18	−.19	−.13	−.32**	−.28**
MA and ACE-Q	.17	−.28**	−.14	−.06	−.31**	−.25**
Adaptability and ACE-L	.50**	.68**	.63**	.71**	.71**	.71**
Adaptability and ACE-Q	.71**	.71**	.71**	.52**	.61**	.59**

** Significantly different from zero at the .01 level.

significant at the .01 level. The correlations for the two conditions differed significantly at the .01 level using a one-tailed test. The relationship was greater in the case of the females than the males, although the difference was not statistically significant.

A similar result occurs when the effects of ACE scores are partialed out; performance on the Adaptability Test is related to MA score only under the condition that the test performance is important. It thus appears that when performance on the intelligence test carries little importance, a person's level of anxiety is unrelated to his performance, but when the task is seen as important, persons high in anxiety suffer impaired performance. Sex differences in the Important Test condition are reduced after partialing out the effects of the ACE test.

Further confirmation is found in a comparison of the MA-Adaptibility correlations in the upper part of Table 1 with the MA-ACE correlations in the lower part. Since the ACE was administered to the subjects as a part of the standard freshman testing battery, it may be assumed that to the Unimportant Test subjects it bore a level of importance greater than that attached to the Adaptability Test, and to the Important Test subjects, a level of importance less than that attached to the Adaptability Test. If this assumption is correct and if anxiety has a debilitating effect on test performance only when the test is considered important, differential effects would be expected in the two conditions. In the Important Test condition the MA-Adaptability correlation should be more negative than the MA-ACE correlations, to reflect the greater perceived importance of the Adaptability Test and the consequent deterioration of performance by anxious subjects. For Unimportant Tests subjects the MA-Adaptability correlation should be less negative than the MA-ACE correlations, as here performance on the test is presented as unimportant. This differential finding does hold, as is indicated in Table 1, although the differences between the MA-Adaptability and MA-ACE correlations do not reach a level of statistical significance.

To study the effects of level of achievement motivation, subjects were divided into high, medium, and low groups on the basis of achievement motivation score. The prediction that the importance of the task would influence performance of low achievement motivation subjects but not influence that of high achievement motivation subjects would imply the presence of a significant interaction between treatments and levels of achievement motivation. A significant interaction was found. However, neither the importance of the tasks nor the internalized level of achievement motivation in the subjects had any effect upon their scores on the intelligence test.

In addition, it was found that the importance manipulation was successful in influencing Adaptability scores, but only for the low achievement motivation subjects, who did poorer when the test was important than when it was unimportant. This finding occurred in the case of subjects of each sex.

DISCUSSION

The findings regarding the effects of anxiety confirm the presence of "cautiousness" and "emotional reactivity", and indicate that a stressful situation interferes with the successful performance of highly anxious subjects on a complex task. The contribution of this study may lie in the type of complex task used, for the effects upon performance in an intelligence test demonstrated in this study are quite similar to the effects of anxiety arousal on maze learning performance and on the learning of paired associates.

If the findings may be generalized to other testing situations, it would seem that the actual test performance of extremely anxious persons is an underestimate of what they can do under more relaxed conditions. The performance of extremely anxious subjects in this study was reduced by almost one standard deviation by the stress of the instructions. The test performance of less anxious subjects seems unaltered by the stress of the situation.

The findings regarding achievement motivation indicate that subjects with a high drive to do well try equally hard regardless of the task's importance, and corroboration is found for past research indicating that college students perform equally well on an intelligence test whether the test is seen as important or not. The attempt to increase level of performance through experimental arousal of motivation was apparently not successful.

The worsened performance of low achievement motivation subjects when the task is important perhaps indicates an almost deliberate failure to exert full effort under the challenge of an important situation. Atkinson (1958, p. 332) states that there seems to be good presumptive evidence that fear of failure is greater in low achievement motivation groups. In the earlier scoring of the Test of Insight responses indicating both positive and negative aspects of achievement motivation were scored together. The two items of the Test of Insight most likely to elicit responses of fear of failure in achievement were rescored for this type of response alone. (These items, on the female form, were Number 5, "Mary Ann worries a lot about how she has done on tests and examinations" and Number 8, "Janet works harder than most people.") Though much more evidence is necessary, there was very little indication that the low achievement motivation subjects shield themselves from full output on an important task because they fear the outcome.

26   Faking on a Personality Inventory

CHARLES F. DICKEN

Both professional and amateur testers are aware that most personality and interest inventories can be "faked," i.e., an examinee can consciously control the kind of picture that he wants to present of himself. As the author of the following article has noted, an examinee may deliberately and overtly attempt to deceive the examiner. He may also respond to the items as he thinks other people expect him to or actually respond honestly but without actually being aware of what he is doing. The data of the present study aptly demonstrate how with a little effort on the part of the examinee a self-report instrument may be "forced" to yield scores which do not accurately represent—indeed may misrepresent—the true characteristics or interests of that individual. How did the forced-choice format of the Edwards Personal Preference Schedule *(EPPS) influence the score changes? How effective was the Consistency score? Were the examinees able to take on different test-taking roles? Has the social desirability variable been adequately controlled on the EPPS?*

The Edwards Personal Preference Schedule (EPPS) (Edwards, 1957a) was constructed to measure a set of personality variables drawn from Murray's (1938) list of manifest needs.[1] The unique feature of the Schedule is an attempt to control the social desirability (SD) factor by means of a forced-choice format in which paired items scored for different variables are equated for independently judged SD. Control of SD would presumably eliminate one means by which an examinee

Reprinted and abridged from Charles F. Dicken, Simulated patterns on the *Edwards Personal Preference Schedule, Journal of Applied Psychology,* 1959, Vol. 43, pp. 372–378. Copyright 1959 by the American Psychological Association and reprinted with permission of author and publisher.

[1] The names of the EPPS variables are as follows: Achievement (ach), Deference (def), Order (ord), Exhibition (exh), Autonomy (aut), Affiliation (aff), Intraception (int), Succorance (suc), Dominance(dom), Abasement (aba), Nurturance(nur), Change (chg), Endurance (end), Heterosexuality (het), Aggression (agg). A consistency score (con) is also computed, based on the number of identical choices made in two sets of the same 15 items.

can obtain scores which are not truly characteristic of him, that of responding in the socially desirable direction.

Recent evidence on the EPPS casts doubt on the success of the control of SD and on the resistance of the Schedule to simulation.

The present study investigated the qualitative properties of EPPS score changes under four different role-playing instructions. The hypotheses were: (a) Subjects motivated to simulate a personality trait are capable of inducing substantial changes in their EPPS scores. (b) Substantial score changes will occur under the role playing of a "good impression," in spite of the attempted control of the SD factor (c) Subject groups that role play different personality variables will obtain different simulated patterns. (d) The consistency score is not an effective index of simulation.

METHOD

The EPPS was administered with standard instructions to 75 students in five introductory psychology classes at the City College of San Francisco. The Ss for the experiment ranged in age from 18 to 30. They were permitted to identify their records by code numbers to preserve anonymity.

The sample was then divided into four role-playing groups: need order (ORD), 8 males, 9 females; need dominance (DOM), 8 males, 11 females; need change (CHG), 13 males, 7 females; and good impression (GI), 8 males, 11 females. The first three roles were chosen to represent a variety of the EPPS variables. The fourth role relates to Hypothesis b.

Each group was retested separately with instructions to simulate for the purpose of winning an imaginary but highly desirable college scholarship. Subjects in each of the first three groups were told to suppose a hypothetical "scholarship committee" used the EPPS to select individuals with a particular kind of personality trait. The name of the need variable for the ORD, DOM, and CHG groups and a three- or four-sentence description based on Murray (1938) were read to the group and printed on a blackboard visible throughout the session.

The GI group was told to respond so as to give the most favorable possible impression of themselves to the scholarship committee, without further specification of role. One week elapsed between the first and second test administrations for all groups.

RESULTS

Table 1 shows the means and standard deviations of the EPPS scores of the role-playing group for standard and simulation conditions.[2] The mean difference

---

[2] Editorial Note: For the sake of brevity only data under the GI condition is tabled here. Comparable results were obtained under the other conditions.

scores (simulation condition minus standard condition) are also shown.[3] The means for the standard condition are comparable for the four samples and are, in the main, reasonably close to those of Edwards' normative sample.

TABLE 1. *Means, Standard Deviations, and Mean Differences of EPPS Scores under Standard (Std) and Simulated Good Impression (GI) Conditions* (N = 19)

Scale	Std.		GI		D
	M	SD	M	SD	
ach	52.0	8.1	63.0	8.0	11.0**
def	47.8	8.4	68.6	7.2	20.8**
ord	54.5	12.5	71.8	8.7	17.3**
exh	52.4	14.4	44.7	10.0	−7.7**
aut	50.3	9.7	38.3	10.7	−12.0**
aff	47.0	6.6	42.9	7.1	−4.1*
int	47.0	10.0	50.4	6.7	2.5
suc	50.4	10.0	42.5	7.3	−8.0**
dom	51.2	10.3	52.4	9.8	1.2
aba	48.2	9.7	46.9	7.4	−1.2
nur	48.5	8.4	45.9	10.1	−2.5
chg	50.4	11.5	42.2	8.9	−8.2**
end	51.7	11.5	67.8	7.8	16.1**
het	46.5	11.7	34.6	8.5	−11.8**
agg	51.0	7.8	41.6	9.1	−9.4**
con	47.8	11.5	47.5	11.9	−.3

* Differs from zero at .05 level.
** Differs from zero at .01 level.

The *t*-test for correlated measures was used to compare the mean differences with a null hypotheses of zero difference. The effect of the forced-choice format of the EPPS on score changes in simulation should be noted in interpreting the outcomes of the significance tests for individual scales. An altered item response which increases an S's score on one variable also decreases his score on some other variable. Thus while the increases in any sample are independent of each other, and while the set of decreases is similarly internally independent, the increases and the decreases are not independent. A conservative interpretation would consider the significance of the changes for a single direction only (increases being probably of greater interest here), and would treat the remaining changes (e.g., decreases) in terms of relative magnitude only.

The effect of the role instructions on the similarity of individual EPPS profiles within each sample is shown in Table 2. Score patterns of individuals show little

---

[3] The raw scores were converted to T-score values appropriate to the sex of the S. Preliminary analysis of the four samples indicated no substantial sex differences in either standard or simulation conditions. There were no male-female reversals of the direction of mean change scores where both change-score means differed significantly from zero. Data for male and female Ss were combined for the main analyses.

TABLE 2. *Kendall Coefficients of Concordance (W) of EPPS Profiles in Standard (Std) and Simulation (S) Conditions for Four Role-Playing Samples and for Borislow's SD and PD Samples*

Sample	Std	S
ORD	.11*	.64**
DOM	.04	.43**
CHG	.08	.30**
GI	.04	.61**
Borislow PD		.26**
Borislow SD		.38**

    * *W* significant at .05 level.
   ** *W* significant at .01 level.

concordance in the standard conditions, but have a highly significant level of concordance in every simulation condition. This indicates a shift from an "individual" pattern of responses to a "role-characteristic" pattern when the *S* simulates. Borislow's (1958) concordance values for his simulated social desirability (SD) and personal desirability (PD) groups are included in the table for comparison. The present good impression group appears to have simulated in a more homogeneous fashion than the earlier SD group.

The large and statistically reliable mean changes in all samples and the consistent concordance shifts confirm Hypotheses *a* and *b*. The differences in the mean simulated patterns and the between-condition correlations of mean changes (Table 3) confirm Hypothesis *c* with one exception. The three trait-simulation

TABLE 3. *Between-Condition Spearman Correlations of Ranks of Mean Change Scores for Fifteen Need Variables*

Condition			
DOM	−.02		
CHG	−.67	−.22	
GI	.90*	−.02	−.48
	ORD	DOM	CHG

  * Rho differs from zero at .01 level (no values significant at .05 level).

conditions induced mean changes in the 15 variables which are either essentially uncorrelated or negatively correlated. In each case the pattern of prominently elevated scores is different, and the peak score is on the relevant variable. However, conditions ORD and GI yielded changes which are highly correlated, and mean simulated profiles which are for practical purposes indistinguishable.

Edwards found relatively low intercorrelations of the EPPS variables in the normative sample. However, the simulation instructions in the present experiment induced significant changes in scales other than the "primary" scale for which the instructions were written. One hypothesis which might account for the changes in the "nonprimary" scales is that these changes relate to the size of the correlations of the nonprimary scales with the primary scale, even though the correlations are of a generally low order. The rank difference correlations between the amount of change in nonprimary scales and the magnitude of the normative sample correlations of these scales with the primary scale are positive and significant in conditions ORD (rho = .85) and DOM (rho = .55), but there is no association in condition CHG (rho = .03). There is no immediate explanation for the failure of the hypothesis in the CHG condition, although it may be noted that the score changes and the concordance shift are least in this condition.

Hypothesis d is confirmed by the data from all four conditions. Although the mean *con* score decreased in all conditions, the decreases are not significant in two groups, and the overlap of *con* scores for simulation and standard conditions is large in all groups. Even if a liberal cutting score of 10 or less raw score points on *con* is used as a simulation index (which would identify as "simulated" 15 percent of the records in the normative sample), only the following relatively small proportions of the simulated records would be detected: ORD, 5/17; DOM, 6/19; CHG, 8/20; and GI, 5/17. Unsimulated records from these samples misidentified by this cutting score would be seven, two, seven, and four cases respectively.

DISCUSSION

One of the most important findings is the failure of the social desirability pairings of items to control the distorting effect of test-taking attitudes. The changes in the GI condition tend to support the conclusion that SD is not equated in some of the pairs. Even if the item format partly controls social desirability bias, which seems likely, the role-playing data suggest that distortion of the EPPS by simulation of characteristics other than SD remains a distinct possibility.

Since the Ss in the three trait-simulation conditions were given descriptions of the variables they were to simulate, the question arises whether these experimental distortion sets are meaningfully related to conscious or unconscious role-taking in a normal testing situation. The reader may verify the degree of similarity of the role instructions to the content of the EPPS items by reference to the scoring keys. Some correspondence was unavoidable because of the "obvious" character of the items. In general, however, the role instructions make a broader and more abstract reference to the need variables than do the items, suggesting that to some degree true role taking rather than information on specific item content determined the changes. The success of the essentially uninstructed "scholarship applicants" in condition GI in simulating traits (order, achievement, endurance, and deference) which are both relevant and "desirable" with respect to the goal they sought argues rather cogently against assuming that simulation could not occur except in Ss with specific information about the instrument.

The evidence for susceptibility to distortion gives cause for question of the feasibility of constructing an instrument for variables of this type without a systematic procedure for determining item and scale validities. The Manual makes no reference to item selection other than for social desirability values. The nature and arrangement of the items suggests that the questions of subtlety and of comprehensiveness of content were similarly neglected. Scores for each scale are determined by endorsement of a very small number of statements (nine), because statements are repeated in identical form in the sets of 28-item pairs scored for each scale. The statements for each variable appear highly "face valid" and are strikingly similar in content. The effect of face validity and content homogeneity in facilitating selective endorsement of a particular kind of item is probably augmented by the arrangement of the test booklet. More than half the statements scored for each scale appear in "runs" of five consecutive item pairs.

The effect of conscious distortion, the limitations in content and subtlety of the items, and the inadequacy of validity data suggest there is relatively little basis at present for regarding EPPS scores as measures with properties other than those of a self-report. If this conclusion is correct, interpretation of a score as a measure of an examinee's actual characteristics rests on the assumption that he is both (a) able to perceive his own characteristics accurately and (b) willing to report these perceptions candidly. Meehl's rationale for empirically constructed scales, "the scoring does not assume a valid self-rating to have been given" (1945, p. 299), cannot be used. In selection problems (a) is usually unknown and (b) often false. In counseling (b) may often be assumed, but if (a) is correct the need for a personality inventory may be vitiated.

A final and important practical implication of the findings is that the lack of effective validity indices for detecting distorting attitudes is one of the most crucial weaknesses of the EPPS in its present form.

27   *The Effect of Distrust on Some Aspects of Intelligence Test Behavior*

GERALD WIENER

As has been noted at various points thus far, in articles of this book, test scores are subject to many sources of error. The errors may be examinee-centered or instrument-centered. The test administrator or examiner may also significantly influence the magnitude and meaning of a test score. In the following study by

Reprinted and abridged from Gerald Wiener, "The Effect of Distrust on Some Aspects of Intelligence Test Behavior," *Journal of Consulting Psychology*, 1957, Vol. 21, pp. 127–130. Copyright 1957 by the American Psychological Association and reproduced by permission of author and publisher.

Dr. Wiener it should be noted that the examiner-centered influences demonstrated might be considered unstable due to the small sample size, but they are, nevertheless, suggestive of the type of impact the examiner may have in a testing situation. Much more research like that reported here needs to be undertaken.

The reader may wish to consider how such potentially harmful factors as low self-confidence, anxiety, fear of embarrassment, and distrust may be controlled in group and individual testing situations. Would such factors be equally important if one were interested in measures of maximum as well as typical performance?

This experiment is concerned with the effect of trustful compared to distrustful attitudes upon the Picture Completion (*PC*) and the Similarities (*Sim*) subtests of the *Wechsler Adult Intelligence Scale* (WAIS) (Wechsler, 1955). The hypotheses tested were:

1. Those *Ss* who are distrustful respond to the instructions of the *PC* and *Sim* subtests with a task-inappropriate distrustful attitude. They tend to think, "There is nothing missing in that picture," or "There is no similarity between those things." Such inappropriate responses impair performances on these tests and are reflected in comments made during the test.

2. Instructions given to *Ss* designed to make them distrustful of the experimental situation have a similar impairing effect on *PC* and *Sim* performances because of the task-interfering attitudes aroused. Comments indicating distrust are increased by such instructions.

3. No predictions are made concerning the interaction of *Ss'* predisposition and the experimental instructions. Those *Ss* who are inclined to be distrustful may be made more so if the situation conforms to their expectations. Trustful *Ss* may be made distrustful. On the other hand, it is possible they will not perceive the experimental situation as distrustful and will not react to it as such.

PROCEDURE

Four groups of 10 *Ss* each were used. Two groups were chosen from *Ss* rated as highly distrustful (*HD* groups). The remaining two groups were rated low in distrust (*LD* groups). One *HD* and one *LD* group were given experimental instructions designed to engender a distrustful attitude (*IN* groups). One *HD* and one *LD* group were not given distrust-producing instructions (*NIN* groups).

The *Ss* were rated for distrust according to their responses to a 24-item inventory which was administered to 148 female student nurses. Eleven of the items were culled from the *Minnesota Multiphasic Personality Inventory* (MMPI) scale for paranoia. These items were changed slightly in order to conform to the *Ss'* background. The remaining 13 filler items were from the L scale of the MMPI. The L score variable was controlled so that the four groups did not differ with respect to this variable. The items were worded so that they permitted a five-category response ranging from entirely trustful to entirely distrustful. Each critical item was then scored from 1 to 5 and the scores totaled. The highest score was taken to be indicative of the most distrustful attitude. The scores ranged from 14 to 45. The mean score was 27.0 and the standard deviation was 4.6. *LD Ss* had scores of 21 or less; *HD Ss* had scores of 33 or higher. All *Ss* used were within the upper or lower 15 percent of the distribution. The inventory was administered independently of the experiment and two weeks prior to it. Two of the 40 *Ss* asked if a relationship existed between the experiment and the questionnaire.

The 20 *NIN Ss* were given the WAIS Vocabulary (*V*), *PC*, and *Sim* subtests in that order. At the start of the experiment they were told that the examiner was comparing student nurses with other groups. The 20 *IN Ss* were given instructions designed to induce a distrustful attitude. They were presented with the *V* subtest in the same way that the *NIN* groups were. However, at the conclusion of the *V* subtest the examiner announced that he had lied and that he was conducting the experiment for other purposes about which he would later inform the *Ss*. An impossible-to-solve block design problem was then presented. After 90 seconds of coping with this problem, each *S* was told that she was once again deceived and that the problem could not be solved. The *PC* and *Sim* subtests were then administered. All tests were presented in accordance with the WAIS manual instructions. Verbatim responses and spontaneous comments were recorded.

The dependent variables consisted of the discrepancy of the scaled *PC—V* and *Sim—V* scores appropriate to each *S's* age. Since the scaled scores are *z* scores and are based on each *S's* age group, age and general level of intelligence (as is judged by the V test) were controlled. If a 20-year-old *S* had raw scores of 55, 13, and 16 on the *V*, *PC*, and *Sim* subtests, her weighted score on each of these subtests were 12, 9, and 11 respectively. Her *PC—V* discrepancy score would have been —3 and the *Sim—V* discrepancy would have been —1. The *V* scale was chosen as a base for measuring impairment, because it is highly correlated with the total WAIS score. *A priori* the *V* subtest would not seem to be sensitive to a distrustful attitude. *PC* and *SIM* subtests were chosen as dependent variables, because they were thought to be more sensitive to distrustful attitudes. The instructions used in administering these tests would allow for disbelief.

The responses and spontaneous comments were also examined for expressions of disbelief. For the *PC* these included expressions such as "Nothing is missing from this picture," "Is there always something missing?", and "Nothing that I can see . . .", etc. Expressions of disbelief on the *Sim* included: "They are not alike," ". . . Opposite . . .," "Praise and punishment . . . alike did you say?", etc. The number of disbelief statements for each *S* for the *PC* and *Sim* subtests was tabulated.

RESULTS

Data concerning impairment as a function of *Ss'* distrustful attitudes and experimental conditions appear in Table 1. *HD Ss* compared to *LD Ss* are significantly impaired on the *PC*. Impairment on the Sim was also significantly

TABLE 1. *Mean Impairment Scores of Groups*

| | Group | | | |
| | LD | LD | HD | HD |
Tests compared	NIN	IN	NIN	IN
PC—V	−2.2	−1.5	−3.2	−3.1
Sim—V	+ .2	− .5	−1.2	−1.3
(PC—V)+(Sim—V)	−2.0	−2.0	−4.4	−4.4

greater for *HD* than *LD Ss*. When impairment on both the *PC* and *Sim* is combined, it is seen that *HD Ss* compared to *LD Ss* are more significantly impaired. Instructions designed to create a distrustful attitude apparently do not produce a significant impairment for either *HD* or *LD* groups or for both combined. Nor do instructions interact significantly with *Ss'* predispositions to affect performance.

Table 2 contains data relevant to comments indicating distrust. When the PC

TABLE 2. *Mean Number of Comments Indicating Distrust*

| | Group | | | |
| | LD | LD | HD | HD |
Test	NIN	IN	NIN	IN
PC	.5	1.8	1.1	2.1
Sim	.4	.9	1.2	.9
PC + Sim	.9	2.7	2.3	3.0

alone is considered, *HD Ss* compared to *LD Ss* do not tend to make more remarks indicative of distrust. The *IN* groups make more comments indicative of a distrustful attitude. The interaction between experimental conditions and *Ss'* predispositions was not significant. Considering the *Sim*, the only finding attaining a significant level was that *HD Ss* compared to *LD Ss* produce more spontaneous distrustful comments. Combining the *PC* and *Sim* comments, it was found that *HD Ss* verbalize more distrustful comments than *LD Ss*. The *IN Ss* compared to *NIN Ss* respond with more comments indicating distrust. The interaction between instructions and predispositions was not significant with the *PC* and *Sim* combined.

In summary, evidence was provided to show that comments associated with distrust tend to occur as a function of *Ss'* predispositions as well as experimentally induced attitudes. Intellectual impairment is more significantly manifested by *Ss* who tend to be distrustful. Experimental conditions are not associated with intellectual impairment, although they lead to comments which indicate distrust.

It was hypothesized that a distrustful attitude stimulates an interfering response because it prevents the task-appropriate response from being made. People who say, "There is nothing missing in that picture!" are responding to internal needs rather than to the testing situation. If this is the case, there should be a positive correlation between interfering verbal responses and impaired scores. Of 40 *Ss* tested, nine *Ss* made five or more remarks classified as distrustful on both the *PC* and *Sim*. Their combined *PC* and *Sim* impairment was 4.4 units. Sixteen *Ss* produced none or only one interfering comment on both the *PC* and *Sim*. These *Ss* were impaired by 2.7 units. The mean difference between these *Ss* was 1.75. Thus there is some indication that interfering responses, as indicated by the emergence of verbal comments, are followed by an impaired intellectual performance.

DISCUSSION

The results indicate that *Ss'* distrustful predispositions are correlated with impaired performances on the WAIS *PC* and *Sim* subtests. Distrustful *Ss* will verbalize their attitude of not accepting the test instructions as true. Suggestive evidence was obtained to show that a distrustful attitude stimulates responses which interfere with task-appropriate behavior. In turn, intellectual impairment is in part a function of such task-inappropriate responses.

Experimental instructions designed to induce a distrustful attitude were not effective in inducing impaired performances, but were associated with spontaneous comments indicative of distrust. This datum indicates that the test instructions were in some measure effective in inducing the desired attitude. It is unclear why experimental instructions produce task-interfering responses but do not impair intellectual performance. There are gradations in the strength of a distrustful attitude. Verbal comments might emerge rapidly as a result of instructions. However, *Ss* may retain their ability to recover and assert a task-appropriate attitude. Possibly the instructions produced some distrust, but not enough to hinder intellectual functioning.

The experiment generally indicates that character traits may affect WAIS performance. It is possible that paranoid conditions which generally are highly associated with a distrustful attitude would be revealed by lowered WAIS *PC* and *Sim* scores and that such scatter would constitute a diagnostic sign. Numerous personality characteristics make up a paranoid state. Some of these traits may end to enhance rather than detract from a given intellectual skill. For example, the perceptual alertness of a paranoid may make him very sensitive to missing details within pictures so as to neutralize the impairing effect of his distrustful attitude.

SUMMARY

It was hypothesized that distrustful attitudes are reflected in intellectual behavior as measured by impaired *Wechsler Adult Intelligence Scale* Picture Completion and Similarities subtest scores. A distrustful attitude is hypothesized to be a stimulus for an interfering response which prevents task-appropriate responses from being made.

Four groups of 10 *Ss* each were tested. Two groups were considered highly distrustful and two groups low in distrust. Distrustful attitudes were measured by a questionnaire. One high and one low distrustful group were given experimental instructions designed to induce a feeling of distrust toward the experimental situation. The remaining groups were given neutral instructions.

The *Ss* prone to be distrustful are significantly more impaired in their intellectual behavior. These *Ss* also tend to make more spontaneous comments indicative of a distrustful attitude. Experimental conditions designed to encourage distrust were not effective in impairing performance but were associated with spontaneous comments indicative of distrust.

28   *Response Sets and Test Design*

LEE J. CRONBACH

Cronbach (1946, p. 476) has defined response set as the "tendency causing a person to give different responses to items than he would when the same content is presented in a different form." To illustrate, suppose two individuals who scored the same on a multiple-choice achievement test scored quite differently on a true-false test based on the same content. Similarly, they might have scored identically on a multiple-choice personality test but quite differently when the same items appeared in a checklist form. Assuming these differences were not due to lack of reliability, they may have been due to response sets operating more for one individual than for another. For example, one of the individuals might tend to select "true" when in doubt, and also one might tend to check many items on a checklist.

Professor Cronbach forcefully demonstrates in the following article how the presence of response sets can invalidate or at least sufficiently mask test scores so as to leave them ambiguous or uninterpretable. (See an article by Rorer (1965) for expanded discussion of this topic.) What are some of the major types of response sets? Under what conditions are they likely to occur? How can we minimize, control, or utilize their influence?

When a person takes an objective test, he may bring to the test a number of test-taking habits which affect his score. Personal ways of responding to test items of a given form (e.g., the tendency to say "agree" when given the alterna-

Reprinted and abridged with permission of author and publisher from an article entitled "Further Evidence on Response Sets and Test Design," which appeared in *Educational and Psychological Measurement*, 1950, Vol. 10, pp. 3–31.

tives "agree"—"uncertain"—"disagree") are frequently a source of invalidity. In 1946 the writer assembled evidence demonstrating that these "response sets" are present in a wide variety of tests. Since that time much new evidence has come to light, and it is now possible to examine more completely the nature of response sets.

As our earlier report demonstrated, response sets have been identified in tests of ability, attitude, personality, and interest, and in rating scales. Among the most widely found sets are acquiescence (tendency to say "True," "Yes," "Agree," etc.), evasiveness (tendency to say "?," "Indifferent," "Uncertain," etc.), and similar biases in favor of a particular response when certain fixed alternatives are offered. Other sets include the tendency to work for speed rather than accuracy, the tendency to guess when uncertain, the tendency to check many items in a checklist, etc. Response sets become most influential as items become difficult or ambiguous. Individual differences in response sets are consistent throughout a given test, as shown by split-half coefficients. Response sets dilute a test with factors not intended to form part of the test content, and so reduce its logical validity. Response sets tend to reduce the range of individual differences in score.

EVIDENCE THAT RESPONSE SETS EXIST

It is scarcely necessary to marshal further evidence that reliable individual differences in response sets exist. Yet the widespread use of test forms which permit response sets indicates that their existence is not adequately appreciated. It is not only the old tests—Seashore, Bernreuter, Thurstone attitude, Strong— that suffer from response sets. New tests appear continually, especially tests of attitude and personality, whose forms invite response sets. The writer has routinely requested graduate students to analyze their data for response sets whenever their research employed tests with fixed response categories (A-U-D, Yes-No-?, etc.). *Never has such an analysis failed to disclose individual patterns of response, statistically consistent from item to item.*

The most effective simple design to demonstrate response sets is to obtain a score for each person on the suspected response set. Thus, Lorge (1937) tested the existence of "gen-like," or acquiescense on the Strong test, by counting how many items each person marked "Like." The split-half or Kuder-Richardson reliability of the response-set score can then be computed. Table 1 condenses the evidence obtained by this and other techniques, evidence which, together with that previously assembled, shows conclusively that response sets are to be found in a great many tests.

RESPONSE SETS IN MULTIPLE-CHOICE TESTS ▪ The only major form of fixed-alternative test which has so far been found relatively free from response sets is the multiple-choice item. In order to determine whether response sets can be extracted from a typical test of this type, the writer has studied the *Henmon-*

TABLE 1. *Sample Studies Reporting Response Sets*

Investigator and references	Name and nature of test	Response called for	Response set	Finding
Bennett, Seashore, Wesman (1947)	Differential Aptitudes, Clerical	Checking errors	Speed vs. carefulness	Good students may earn falsel low scores due to set to work accurately at slow speed.
Brotherton, Read. Pratt (1948)	Questionnaire on word meanings	Checking fixed categories on six-point scale	Definition of terms	Substantial differences in mear ing are found from person to person and group to group. Questionnaires involving many few, several, etc. "are invalid and unreliable."
Guilford (1947)	Tests of plotting, scale reading, etc.	Solving many items, with time limit	Speed vs. carefulness	In one test, reliability of Rights .76, Wrongs .56. But intercorrelation only —.48. Factor analysis shows "carefulness" often the most prominent factor in Wrongs scores.
Lorge (1937)	Strong Vocational Interest Blank	Like, Indifferent, Dislike	Acquiescence, evasiveness	Reliability for number of L's in two testings is .8; for number of I's, .84.
Mathews (1929)	Interests	L-l-i-d-D	Acquiescence	Reliability of tendency to "like many items is .75–.79. Respons are altered when choices are in order D-d-i-l-L. Responses at extreme left and fourth from left tend to be used. Shift is greatest on items where studen have least pronounced views.
Philip (1947)	Judgment of proportion in color mixtures	Absolute judgment on 11-point scale	Tendency to use certain portions of scale	Some individuals scatter their judgments more broadly over the scale than others. Each ind vidual uses certain "foci" along the scale more often than other responses. Stimuli at the foci and ends of the scale are more often judged correctly than others. "Subsidiary cues" have greatest influence when discrimination is difficult.
Wesman (1947 b)	Spelling	Check all misspelled words	Acquiescence	Incorrect spellings correlate higher with total test than correctly spelled items.

Nelson Test of Mental Ability, Form A, for Grades 3–8. (The data for this study were supplied by Kenneth Eells.) Thousands of test papers were available, since every child in several grades in a mid-western city had been tested. The sample for this study was chosen indiscriminately from papers of upper-lower and lower-middle-class children. In administering the test experimentally Eells allowed an extended time of 20 minutes beyond the standard time of 30 minutes. Papers not completed even in the extended time were discarded in the present analysis.

The *Henmon-Nelson* is a suitable test for investigating response sets because items were prepared with care, are fairly well arranged as to difficulty, and are designed so that the correct answer appears about equally often in each of the five response-positions. The hypothesis is that some students may persistently tend to select choices early in the group of five. This would raise their scores on items where the correct answer is choice "1" or "2," but lower them on items keyed "4" or "5." The psychological basis for the hypothesis is the possibility that some students read every alternative and discriminate carefully, where some merely read through the item to find a plausible answer, mark it, and go on to the next item.

The procedure was the usual one: to obtain a "bias" score for each individual and determine its reliability. If the score is reliable, the response set is proved to exist. The response-set score for the present hypothesis consists of "number of errors appearing to the left of the correct answer" minus "number of errors to the right of the correct answer." Before rescoring papers for bias, papers of high-scoring pupils (those having a score above 60 out of 90 items correct) were discarded. This was done to increase the likelihood of finding a response set, since response sets have no opportunity to show themselves when the pupil gets most items correct. For a group of 66 papers bias scores ranged from 24 to −12. The person with the bias score 24 had made 39 errors to the left of the true answer, and only 15 errors to the right of the true answer. Such a preponderance is hard to explain as other than a habit of marking items. For the cases studied, however, the split-half reliability of the bias score was only .095, corrected. Such a low correlation indicates that the postulated response set is of no consequence for this group. A second sample of 84 cases having raw scores of 40 or below in extended time (these pupils had IQ's near or below 80) were studied separately, in order to increase the probability of finding a response set. For these pupils the reliability of the bias score was .42, corrected. Evidently for a group of pupils taking a difficult multiple-choice test, reliable response sets can be found. Bias has a slight relation to raw score; the mean raw score for these poor pupils was 24.5 for those with negative bias, and 29 for those with positive bias. For some reason very poor students tended to mark alternatives to the right of the correct answer proportionately more often than slightly better pupils.

An attempt was made to demonstrate such biases as "preference for position 1." No statistical evidence for such sets could be obtained, although an occasional case does suggest that such biases may occur. One boy, for example, in 90 items never marks the fifth choice as correct, and another student places 30 of his marks on position "1."

A second study was made with a modified version of the *Ohio State University Psychological Examination*, using data made available by N. L. Gage and Dora

Damrin. The shortened test they used consists of 90 five-choice vocabulary items, unspeeded. This test was administered to unselected juniors and seniors in several high schools. When papers for all 171 pupils were scored for tendency to place answers before rather than after the correct position, the odd-even reliability of the bias score was found to be .20. When only the lowest 65 students (as judged by the total number right on the test) were used as a sample to determine the reliability of the bias score, the reliability rose to .29. This was a group of students for whom the test was extremely difficult; the highest score for the group was 22 right out of 90. It should be noted that this test is normally used for predicting college success among superior high-school students; the highest score in this limited subdivision of our sample is only chance expectation. When an even more restricted sample was used—the lowest 26 cases, all of whom fell below a raw score of 15 items correct—the reliability of the bias score rose to .54. The mean bias score changed as the quality of students became poorer. For the total group the mean bias score was −6.5; for the second group, −7.7; and for the very lowest group, −9.7. Here, also, the poorest students apparently tended particularly often to mark errors to the right of the correct answer.

Both of these studies demonstrate that response sets are a minor factor, since so great a selection of cases was required in order to demonstrate any evidence of bias. Probably other multiple-choice tests where all subjects mark all items suffer little from response sets. Confirming studies on other multiple-choice tests are desirable, but the generally satisfactory experience with forced-choice tests should encourage their continued widespread use.

STABILITY OF RESPONSE SETS

While there is ample evidence that response sets are consistent throughout a single test, it is important to determine whether they are characteristics of the individual stable from time to time, or are transient sets which can only be regarded as errors in testing rather than personality characteristics.

Some evidence that response sets are stable appears in scattered studies. R. L. Thorndike (1938) reports that on a speeded Air Force test scores obtained at the same sitting correlate no more than scores obtained several hours apart. If a speed-accuracy set is operating, it is not a set which shifts from hour to hour. Singer and Young (1941) found that a tendency to rate varied stimuli as "pleasant" was highly stable, correlations as high as .90 being found under certain conditions over time intervals of two weeks.

Whereas these and similar studies tend to stress the stability in response sets, we ordinarily think of mental sets as easily changed by suitable directions. If the response set is viewed as a way of interpreting an ambiguous situation, as when the word "like" is left for the subject to define, any change in directions should redefine the stimulus elements and alter individual response sets. Several studies show that this can be done.

Rubin (1940) several years ago demonstrated the existence of bias in the Seashore Pitch Test. He gave the Revised Test B twice to 245 college students, and found that the group as a whole used 13958 "High" responses and only 10542 "Low" responses, in judging whether the second tone was higher or lower. According to the key, there were actually an equal number of differences in each direction.

In two ingenious studies Rubin then established that temporary sets are a major element in bias. First he gave a "guessing" test, in which subjects imagined a tossed coin, and wrote down the way they imagined it would fall. One group was given directions as follows: "Imagine a coin which has an H for high on one side, and an L for Low on the other side." In the other group this was reversed: "Imagine a coin which has an L for Low on one side, and an H for High on the other side." There was a significant preponderance of the first-mentioned response on the first-guessed item (i.e., the former group tended to say "H"; the second group to say "L"). There was a significant preponderance of the second-named response on the third guess of the series. Rubin then applied the same reversal to the Seashore test directions. Two hundred and seventy-two students were told, "If the second tone is lower than the first tone, print L; if higher, print H." Only 56.8 percent of the errors were lows marked "H," compared to 60.0 percent when much the same group was given the original directions (but note that some bias remained).

A report that altering directions affect response sets is made by Goodfellow (1940). He finds that in psychophysical judgments the predisposition to report a stimulus as absent was reversed when the directions were worded: "Remember that in approximately one-half of the trials the correct answer will be yes."

GENERALITY OF RESPONSE SETS

To some degree, a person shows consistent response sets from situation to situation. When similar situations are presented, response set scores are significantly correlated. But there is no evidence that response sets are consistent over widely different situations, and Singer and Young's evidence indicates that this is not true. But one does not measure response sets alone. Response sets show only when the response to a situation is in some way unclear. Singer and Young point out that habits of using their rating scale are operative only when "affective arousal is weak or absent." Perhaps affective arousal is weak for one person on tones, for another on odors. This would reduce the response-set correlations.

Response sets might be mere incidental sources of error in measurement, or they might reflect deeper personality traits. Evidence from many sources now combines to show that response sets reflect "real" variables.

Johnston (1948) gave the *Bernreuter Inventory* and the *Hunter Attitude Scale* to two groups of teachers. These groups were chosen on the basis of ratings by their principals, so that one group consisted of "autocratic" teachers, and one consisted of teachers who were markedly "democratic" in classroom practice. Johnston found that these groups differed significantly in response sets. On the Bernreuter, the autocratic group gave an average of 52.6 "Yes," 62.3 "No," and 10.8 "?" responses. The three totals for the democratic group were 55.9, 66.8, and 4.7 respectively. There were 42 teachers in the former group, and 43 in the latter. The difference in "tendency to use question marks" (evasion?) was significant. There was a similar difference on the Hunter scale. The mean number of statements marked "Undecided" rather than "Agree" or "Disagree" was 15 in the autocratic group and 10 in the democratic group.

Possible significance of response sets for empirical prediction is suggested by a study which finds that tendency to respond "?" is correlated negatively with success in selling life insurance (Kahn & Hadley, 1949). While the relationship found was not statistically significant, the difference between the mean number of question marks in the good and poor groups (8.4 vs. 12.8) is large enough to suggest further investigation along this line.

IMPROVEMENT OF TEST DESIGN

The heterogeneous bits of evidence pieced together here and in our previous report have established several generalizations.

1. Any objective test form in which the subject marks fixed-response alternatives ("Yes"-"No," "True-False," "a"-"b"-"c," etc.) permits the operation of individual differences in response sets. The influence of response sets in the multiple-choice test is, however, of minor importance.

2. Response sets have the greatest variance in tests which are difficult for the subjects tested, or where the subject is uncertain how to respond.

3. Items having the same ostensible content actually measure more than one trait, if response sets operate in the test. This is true even for tests which, scored as a whole, are "factorially pure."

4. Slight alterations in directions or training in test-taking alter markedly the influence of response sets. But if the situation is not re-structured by the tester, individual differences in response set remain somewhat stable when similar tests are given at different times.

5. Response sets are to a small degree correlated with external variables such as attitudes, interests, and personality. This shows that they are in part a reflection of "real" and stable traits. To this degree, response-set variance may be valid variance in some investigations.

6. Tests are usually constructed to measure a trait defined by the content of the test items. If the form of the items permits response sets, two persons having equal true scores on the content factor will often receive different scores on the test. Response sets therefore ordinarily dilute the test and lower its validity.

Generalizations (5) and (6) crystallize the paradox response sets present. Some of the response-set variance is potentially useful, some of it is an interference with measurement. The problem for the tester is to capitalize on the effect of response sets where they are helpful to validity, and to eliminate their influence where it is undesirable. It is therefore important to decide which view is to be taken in any given situation.

METHODS OF ELIMINATING RESPONSE-SET VARIANCE ■ The writer concludes that as a general principle the tester should consider response sets an enemy to validity. Therefore, in most tests and certainly in those not intended to measure personality, we should keep response sets from affecting the test score by one of the following methods: designing test items which prevent response sets, altering directions to reduce response sets, or correcting for response sets.

(a) *Test design.* Since response sets are a nuisance, test designers should avoid forms of items which response sets infest. This means that any form of measurement where the subject is allowed to define the situation for himself in any way is to be avoided. (We must make an exception for tests where his way of interpreting the test is treated as a significant variable. But even so, the above analysis suggests limits to the possible validity of tests like the Rorschach which capitalize on ambiguity.)

Item forms using fixed-response categories are particularly open to criticism. The attitude-test pattern, where the subject marks a statement A, a, U, d, or D, according to his degree of agreement, is open to the following response sets: Acquiescence, or tendency to mark "A" and "a" more than "d" and "D"; evasiveness, tendency to mark "U"; and tendency to go to extremes, to mark "A" and "D" more than "a" and "d". Probably not all three of these sets will operate to a significant degree in any given test, but it is better to eliminate the sets at the outset than to spend effort later trying to measure the effect of the sets and root them out. Test designers generally have argued for retaining the five-point scale of judgment, or the more indefinite seven-point, ten-point, or even continuous scales. Such scales are open to marked individual differences in definition of the reference positions, with the more complex scale offering more chance for personal interpretation. The usual argument for the more finely divided scale of judgment on each attitude item is that it is more reliable and that subjects prefer it. If the latter advantage is significant, the finer scale may be retained and scored dichotomously. The argument that the finer scale gives more reliability is not a sound one, since this is precisely what we would expect if all of the added reliable variance were response-set variance and had no relation to beliefs about the attitude-object in question. There is no merit in enhancing test reliability unless validity is enhanced at least proportionately. It is an open question whether a finer scale of judgment gives either a more valid ranking of subjects according to belief, or (what we are beginning to recognize as even more important) scores more saturated with valid variance. With raters trained to interpret the scale uniformly so that response-set variance is removed, the finer scale may be advantageous.

The writer therefore renews his earlier recommendation that the following forms of item be avoided in tests where high validity is more important than speed-of-test construction: true-false, like-indifferent-dislike, same-different, yes-?-no, agree-uncertain-disagree, and mark all correct answers. What does this leave? Foremost, it leaves the forced-choice or best-answer test. Our attempt to find a response set in the multiple-choice test was almost completely unsuccessful. A set was extracted, and with little reliability, when the test was applied to subjects for whom it was unreasonably difficult. Further studies of multiple-choice tests are still in order, but experience to date justifies the assumption that they are generally free from response sets. One confirmation of the argument that forced choices should be used comes from a study by Owens (1947). He found that substituting forced-choice for the "yes-no" response of the conventional neurotic inventory significantly reduced the number of false positives, i.e., it increased empirical validity. The forced choice has long been used successfully in many fields. Tests of mental ability now use it almost to the exclusion of other forms. Spelling, arithmetic, and grammar tests can certainly be cast in "recognize the right (or wrong) choice" form, rather than checklist forms and others open to response sets. Thurstone used it successfully in his paired-comparison approach to attitudes.

Another important consideration is test difficulty, regardless of item form. The influence of response sets rises with difficulty, and therefore measurement of differences between students who find the test difficult is particularly invalid. This is, first, a reason for not using a test on subjects for whom it is quite difficult. Second, however, it suggests basing measurement on scales of adaptable difficulty. Thus, with the Kuhlmann-Anderson mental-test series, one selects the scales which have a difficulty appropriate for the subject, and if the first tests tried prove to be too difficult, the tester can move to an easier set of items to obtain more accurate measurement. Tests of this type, which are common in psychophysics, would be hard to use in group measurement; but experimental trial of such test designs is worth considering.

(b) *Modification of directions.* If in any test we expect a particular response set to arise, we can revise the directions to reduce the ambiguity of the situation. Another way of accomplishing the same end is to give students general training in test-wiseness. For example, if they know that in most true-false tests about half the items are false, they will tend to avoid excessive acquiescence. If they know that the correction formula is based on chance, they will know that the odds are in their favor when they respond to items where they are uncertain.

It appears to the writer that in most tests subjects should be directed to answer all items, even though this tends to increase the random error variance. In many situations this source of error is less damaging than the constant errors introduced by differences in tendency to guess, checking threshold, or diligence in searching for correct answers. Wesman (1947a) reports partial evidence that grammar items, where the subject marks each error he notices in given sentences, becomes more reliable when the subject is directed to mark every sentence-part "correct" or "incorrect," rather than just checking the "incorrects" (but evidence on validity is lacking).

Whisler (1938) raised the question of response-habits in Thurstone-type attitude scales. He found that some subjects marked six or more items in a 22-item scale, and for them the reliability (parallel-test) of the attitude score was .89. But for the subjects who marked five or fewer items that they agreed with, the reliability was .62. Whisler thought that the subjects who checked more items were more careful in using the scale or that their attitudes were more integrated. Hancock (1938) followed Whisler with an experimental alteration of directions. First, he directed subjects to mark all the statements they accepted, then the five with which they most agreed, and finally the three of that five which they most strongly accepted. The shift of directions produced some alteration in scores. Generally, the standard deviation (in scale value) of scores increased when fewer items were counted. For those with attitudes favorable to an occupation, the more items they checked, the closer their score was to the indifference position. Unfortunately, there is not enough evidence in the Hancock report to give a basis for selecting any particular number of checks as preferable. If the number of items checked affects the mean, standard deviation, and reliability, there can be little justification for permitting the number to vary. It appears desirable to require every subject to mark a fixed number of alternatives, selecting the statements with which he most agrees. Limited experience with this procedure suggests that the subject should check around one-fourth of the statements.

(c) *Correction for response sets.* When response sets are entering scores on a test, we may control or correct for the effect by special scoring keys. One widely used method is the control score. If a "response-set score" can be obtained, we may identify all cases with extreme response sets and drop such cases from the sample, admitting that measurement for them is invalid. The most familiar examples appear in the control scores of the *Minnesota Multiphasic Personality Inventory.* Many other tests also permit us to derive such scores as bias or acquiescence, or number of items marked. In some tests it may be acceptable to report two scores for every subject; all the essential data in the hypothetical spelling test discussed earlier could be reported in one score "number right" and a second "number marked as incorrect." But simultaneous consideration of patterns of scores is awkward.

CAPITALIZING ON RESPONSE-SET VARIANCE ■ If response sets are thought of as possibly contributing to validity, one may weight the response sets in a way that maximizes their contribution. Cook and Leeds (1947) correlate each possible response on an attitude scale for teachers with a criterion, and assign positive or negative scoring weights accordingly. One item is as follows, where the numbers in parentheses are weights:

	1	2	3	4	5
It is sometimes necessary to break promises to children.	Strongly agree	Agree	Undecided	Disagree	Strongly disagree
	(0)	(4)	(−1)	(4)	(−1)

The criterion used was a dependable estimate of the ability of teachers to establish rapport with children, which the scale was supposed to predict. It will be noted that the scoring weights are "illogical," since there can be no stronger response to "It is sometimes necessary. . . ." than to disagree (response 4), which amounts to saying "It is never necessary." The weights for responses 4 and 5 reflect the difference in response set (not in logically considered opinion) between teachers in the superior and inferior criterion groups. The defense of the Cook-Leeds procedure, and the comparable method used in Strong's Interest Blank, is that it yields considerable validity. The limitation is that invalid variance is weighted just like valid variance. A particular "good" teacher who has a set to respond very emphatically will be penalized by the weights. The majority of "good" teachers, who avoid extreme responses, will be reliably discriminated by the key. One difficulty with the sheer empiricism represented here is that the weights serve their practical purpose but give little insight into the nature of the variables tested. The only basis for extending or improving the test is trial-and-error, developing many more items of all sorts, and trying them to see how the weights come out.

SUMMARY

This paper summarizes extensive evidence demonstrating that such response sets as bias in favor of a particular alternative, tendency to guess, working for speed rather than accuracy, and the like operate in conventional objective tests. Not only are such sets wide-spread, but they reduce the validity of test scores. The response set can be altered readily by alteration of the directions or by coaching. Some studies show that response sets are somewhat correlated from one test to another (but not if the tests differ greatly in content), and that they are correlated with important external variables. While response-set variance may under certain circumstances enhance logical and empirical validity, it appears that its general effect is to reduce the saturation of the test and to limit its possible validity.

The following recommendations for practice, most of which were previously suggested, are reinforced by the present findings:

1. Response sets should be avoided with the occasional exception of some tests measuring carefulness or other personality traits which are psychologically similar to response sets.

2. The forced-choice, paired-comparison, or "do-guess" multiple-choice test should be given preference over other forms of test item.

3. When a form of item is used in which response sets are possible,

(a) Directions should be worded so as to reduce ambiguity and to force every student to respond with the same set.
(b) The test should not be given to a group of students for whom it is quite difficult.
(c) A response-set score should be obtained and used to identify subjects whose scores are probably invalid.

4. Where response sets are present, attempts should be made to correct for or to capitalize on the response set by an appropriate empirical procedure.

In view of the overwhelming evidence that many common item forms invite response sets, and in view of the probability that these sets interfere with accurate measurement, it will rarely be wise to build new tests around item forms such as A-U-D, Yes-No-?, and "check all correct answers." It is to be hoped that the tests forthcoming in the future will be designed to increase their saturation with the factors the test is seeking to measure.

VIII

INTERPRETING TEST SCORES

The inclusion of a chapter on interpreting test scores is, to some extent misleading. In trying to give meaning to a particular test score, the interpreter must draw upon his knowledge of the background of the examinee(s), validity, and reliability as they relate to both the particular test with which he is concerned and to testing in general. He must keep in mind the purposes for which the test is being used, such as the decisions which are to be made. He should consider the various factors which influence test scores. Even without delving into the kinds of information and approaches which would be supplied by various researchers and theorists, it can obviously be seen that a list of vital data necessary for a specific test interpretation would be lengthy.

Nevertheless, the interpretation of test scores deserves separate, deliberate consideration, as evidenced, for example, by the widespread reception of Dr. Howard Lyman's (1963) text, *Test Scores and What They Mean*. Certain cautions and certain techniques in the interpretive chain demand emphasis; indeed, are prerequisites for the practice of test interpretation. Often tests are blamed when the user is the unsophisticated link.

Let us hint briefly at the necessity of and types of information for interpretation. An illustration outside the field of testing will be used. Suppose you ask a man from Outer Myskania, "How long did you attend college?" and he replies, "Seventeen ercs." You probably have added little to your knowledge. Some kind of a base is needed for interpreting this statement; as examples, the number of ercs which equal a year, the amount of time in college typical for the residents of the country, and the average amount of time spent in college historically.

In the first article in this chapter Dr. Eric Gardner underlines the lack of interpretability which results when only a test score is given. He specifies some types of information which should be available and types of interpretations which are hazardous.

Additional hazardous types of interpretations are indicated by Dr. Junius Davis. He addresses specifically the problem of using *Scholastic Aptitude Test* norms for college decisions, although the generalizations to other situations are easily recognized. The probability of making some of the unjustified types of statements which the author notes could be decreased with the help of expectancy tables. This topic will be discussed in the third article of the chapter.

Often we wish to estimate how an individual might perform in the future. Probably the most comprehensible procedure for relating predictor and criterion is the construction of expectancy tables. Dr. William Schrader presents examples of such tables along with a set of characteristics that differentiate among various types that have been developed.

The frequent misinterpretations of the *Kuder Preference Record—Form C* alone would more than justify the article by Professor Robert Bauernfeind. He carefully describes the forced-choice item type and ipsative scoring. After reading this paper, a test user should have a better idea of the kind of statements which are legitimate for expressing the meaning of scores from such tests, although admittedly the illegitimate statements are easier to make.

After digesting the techniques and cautions expressed in the above-mentioned articles contained in this chapter, the reader may wish to consider the communication of test information to others. Certainly it can be argued that the testee and others concerned with his welfare often deserve to know, and can make use of, the information for further decision-making. Dr. James Ricks presents relevant guidelines and specific suggestions for transmitting test results to pupils and parents.

In the final article of the chapter, a paper by Dr. Frank Womer, the importance of establishing goals for testing programs and the proper use of test results are stressed, and the two topics are meaningfully integrated. He considers ten common misconceptions and misuses of test results.

29   *Some Significant Factors in Test Interpretation*

ERIC F. GARDNER

Intelligent test interpretation is a complex and demanding task. Many important factors need to be considered if test scores are to be made meaningful. The significant factors mentioned below by Dr. Gardner represent only a few of many possible sources of error or misunderstanding. What are some of the test interpretation factors which might be unique to the application of an intelligence test, personality or interest inventory, or a classroom achievement test?

It is commonly accepted that a single isolated test score is of little or no value. For a score to have meaning and be of social or scientific utility, some frame of reference is needed. A number of different frames of reference have been proposed and found to have value. Some are based upon a consideration of the specific content sampled by the test, and others, on the performance of a particular group of subjects.

Suppose Johnny, who is in your school, tells you that he obtained a score of 40 on an arithmetic test (let's say a standardized test). What does this score mean to you? Just what information does it convey? The score might be a percentage, but unless you knew how difficult the test was, the material sampled, and how other people with certain amounts of training had done on it, even a percentage would be relatively meaningless. It might be a raw score, in which case it would convey even less meaning. You would not know whether this represented 40 items right out of 80 or 40 out of 40. Neither would you know whether or not these were very difficult items or very easy items, nor would you know the content sampled. In order to interpret this test score some frame of reference is necessary.

The authors of most tests provide tables for interpreting a raw score in relation to normal or typical performance. These conversion tables are based on computations from scores on a normative or standardization group. Basically, a raw score can be given meaning only by referring it to some group or groups of subjects. A score is not high or low, good or bad; it is higher or lower, better or worse.

The importance of the particular reference population which is used to determine any such scales cannot be overemphasized. A person scoring at the eighty-fourth percentile or obtaining a T score of 60 in an arithmetic test where the score is calculated for a typical seventh grade is obviously not performing equally

Reprinted and abridged with permission of author and publisher from Arthur E. Traxler, (editor), *Improving the Effectiveness and Quality of Learning.* Report of the 26th Educational Conference, sponsored by the Educational Records Bureau and the American Council on Education, Washington D. C.: American Council on Education, 1961, pp. 95–98.

to one whose standing at the eighty-fourth percentile on the same test is calculated for a below-average seventh grade. Likewise a pupil with a vocabulary grade score of 5.2 obtained from a representative sample of fifth graders in Mississippi for example, is certainly not comparable to a pupil making a score of 5.2 based on a national representative sample.

As we know, there are a number of patterns for interpreting the score of an individual. All of these have value, depending upon the situation.

Test scores are used by administrators, teachers, and research workers to make comparisons in terms of rank, level of development, growth, and trait differences among both individuals and groups. Hence, many types of scales have been developed, depending upon the intended use. Each is consistent within itself, but the properties of the scales are not completely consistent from one type of scale to another. For example, a grade scale is not appropriate for measuring growth in a function unless one is willing to accept the assumption that growth is linearly related to grade.

Although we continually strive for a single scale with the maximum of desirable properties, it would seem inadvisable to abandon useful scales designed for a specific purpose merely because they are not adequate for additional purposes for which they were not designed. It should be emphasized that the adoption by a test user of any one of the scales available does not exclude the use of any of the others.

A point which has been stressed many times in the past is the fact that any test score is a fallible measure and contains an error of measurement. Any difference measure between two obtained scores involves two errors of measurement, one contributed by each obtained score. Since the information needed to make recommendations and decisions is that given by true scores, it is extremely important to take the error of measurement into account.

One of the greatest abuses occurs when teachers, counselors, or school psychologists use profiles. There is a much too common tendency to use only inspection to determine whether Johnny is better in reading than he is in spelling or arithmetic. Two points that appear to be well separated are assumed to represent actual differential ability in the functions portrayed. Such is not the case. Any difference, large or small, can be made to appear large simply by the artifice of increasing the scale the way a photographer would make an enlargement of a print. A minute difference can in this way be made to appear gigantic. Only by considering the magnitude of the error of measurement associated with the points of a profile can you comment with any degree of certainty on the meaning of an observed difference. If Johnny had a T score of 60 in reading on a test with a standard error of measurement of 7 and a T score of 55 in arithmetic on a test with a standard error of measurement of 5, you would be making a very hazardous statement indeed if you asserted he was better in reading than arithmetic. The errors of measurement here are sufficiently large that on a subsequent retesting the scores could easily be reversed.

A second abuse is one committed sometimes by a test publisher or author. It is essentially an attempt to convince the test user he is getting something for nothing (a most attractive kind of salesmanship). As an illustration let us consider an achievement test battery of the usual length, but promising many diagnostic features obtained by grouping the items into a large number of categories each containing a handful of items. Unless these so-called diagnostic measures have substantial reliability and scores obtained on them, small errors of measurement, they have about the same value for individual diagnosis as one would get by tossing a coin. Unfortunately, in the past the test user has often been not sufficiently sophisticated to ask this vital question about reliability, and the publisher has ignored it.

The term "diagnostic" as applied to tests is one fraught with danger and ambiguity. Some professional educators will consider a certain test as being diagnostic, while others will claim with equal vehemence that it has no diagnostic characteristics. A diagnostic test undertakes to provide a picture of strengths and weaknesses. Hence, any test that yields more than a single over-all score is, in a sense, diagnostic. Even if there are only two part scores, for example, one for arithmetic computation and one for arithmetic reasoning, the test makes it possible to say that Johnny performed better on computation than in reasoning answers to problems. This information provides one diagnostic cue. Diagnosis is essentially a matter of degree. We may examine and analyze with varying degrees of thoroughness and detail.

As illustrative of the use of tests in diagnosis let us consider the case of Jane, a seventh grader, who late in the spring reported at home that she hated school and especially arithmetic. This announcement came as a surprise to her parents, since she was bright, mentally alert, and had always been a good student, with arithmetic as one of her favorite subjects. An examination of her scores on the *Stanford Achievement Test*, which she had just taken, showed that she was well above the norm in reading, vocabulary, and, in fact, all subjects except arithmetic. In arithmetic reasoning she was slightly above the norm and in arithmetic computation, slightly below. The previous year she had been two grades above the norm on both arithmetic tests. The information supplied by the achievement test battery can be considered diagnostic at a very general level. There is evidence that her arithmetic performance, although above average, had dropped relative to her previous year's performance and relative to her work in other subjects.

A more refined diagnostic arithmetic test containing many items on different computational procedures was then administered to her. On this test she did reasonably well but showed a rather inconsistent pattern on items involving fractions and decimals. As a still more refined attempt at diagnosis, the teacher asked her to "think out loud" while doing some additional problems on fractions and decimals. The kinds of errors and the thought processes used were recorded systematically. The teacher discovered that Jane apparently did not understand the role of the denominator in working with fractions. She also showed little basic understanding of the processes involving the use and manipulation of the decimal point. Remedial work, including reteaching of certain processes in fractions and decimals, was undertaken. The success experiences Jane gained in arithmetic after overcoming her deficiencies were reflected in her general attitude toward school.

The preceding account is an illustration of successful diagnosis achieved rather readily. *Frequently satisfactory results are not so readily attained.* In general, results from diagnostic testing must be interpreted with caution. This is especially true when detailed diagnostic properties are claimed for an achievement test battery. Even the best specifically designed diagnostic tests have very modest reliabilities. Hence, the tests provide some rough and tentative suggestions concerning the individual's strengths and weaknesses. They must be clearly recognized as tentative hypotheses and nothing more. If the remedial activities are successful, well and good. If not, the teacher must stand ready to review what he has done and explore other leads. It is most helpful to think of diagnostic test results as suggestions, not commands.

There are a few standardized diagnostic tests in reading and arithmetic. In fact, there are very few published diagnostic tests outside these fields. Even here relatively little information about these tests is provided by the authors. Much diagnosis must be done by teachers using tests developed by themselves. In general, diagnosis should be made with particular care and much tentativeness. General achievement test batteries are useful in the over-all problem of diagnosis but at only the first stage of the process.

30   Non-Apparent Limitations of Normative Data

JUNIUS A. DAVIS

How often we fail to realize the limitations of a set of data. We may make certain inferences without noting that the information is somewhat irrelevant. The misuse of normative data is one example, and Dr. Davis in the following article notes certain limitations of such data and some potential sources of illegitimate interpretation. These limitations are generally relevant to the use of test-norms information as used in the college selection process. The problems to which the author addresses himself will be of special concern to guidance personnel, but others involved with higher education, including students, should also gain informative insights.

Reprinted and abridged from an article appearing in *Personnel and Guidance Journal*, 1959, Vol. 37, pp. 656–659, with permission of the author and publisher.

Is it safe to judge the quality of an institution by the quality of its freshmen? Why might norms for an institution become outdated in a short time? How does the desire and the capability of the interpreter affect the type of information which he presents?

Recent emphasis on testing at state, regional, and national levels, and hope nourished by leaders in the professional organizations and state and federal agencies seem to guarantee not only an increase in testing activity, but also a wealth of research data which may make test scores more useful in counseling. It may be expected that normative data on more geographic areas and more institutions will be available than ever before. As colleges become generally more selective, there will be less fear about releasing normative data; as more college officials find good normative data to be of real value in dealing with admissions and guidance problems, an increased number of institutions will make these data available to off-campus colleagues.

With regard to pre-college counseling, this seems to promise that long-sought goals are in sight. We have suffered through advising college-oriented youth with the knowledge that colleges do differ tremendously in competitiveness; yet we have had to guess the climate of intellectual ability from rumor and the degree of severity of admission policy statements in the catalog.

In the University System of Georgia, after a year of sifting data on the 16 tax-supported colleges, it has been found that College Board test scores are related to grades. A variety of comparable data for each of the colleges has been assembled, and every counselor in the high schools of Georgia may now be provided with norms for entering freshmen in these institutions. With institutional averages on the College Board SAT ranging from 250 to 550, there has been great temptation to do so, for it would seem that such would be in the best interests of all.

However, the range of experience which the 16 colleges have provided also demonstrates that accurate normative descriptions in themselves may be quite misleading, even dangerously so.

A FIRST FALLACY

An error which the most sophisticated and well-meaning counselor may make is that of too ready generalization from test scores to assumptions about the merits of the college. Non-guidance personnel in colleges have feared that the naive, upon seeing a panorama of test data on a range of colleges, may jump to the conclusion that intellectual quality of entering freshmen is somehow synonymous with the quality of the institution. Some counselors may scan the data and write off the lower-level colleges as too mediocre for consideration by anyone in a serious frame of mind. The fallacy here is that the quality of a college can be determined only in terms of *growth* of students along societal value lines, not by what students were upon entrance. It is reasonable to assume that some colleges with brilliant freshmen release four years later brilliant seniors who have grown little in the interim beyond what normal maturation elsewhere would have afforded. Thus, to avoid this error the counselor must not only continuously examine the variety of institutions against variety of college aspirants, but he must also retain his searching curiosity into the significant but sometimes subjective elements which signal a strong learning environment, regardless of position of college on the intellectual totem pole.

TEST SCORES AND GRADES

A second limiting characteristic of conventional normative data is not as apparent but is far more likely to mislead counselors or their counselees. Let us say that we have found from normative tables that a given counselee ranks at the 97th percentile on a given intelligence test at College A, at the 70th percentile at College B, and the 45th percentile at College C. On the basis of this information most counselors would seek some effective way of letting the counselee feel he would be in the most advantageous competitive position at College A, where he stands in the top 3 percent of his class. Yet, if there is no relationship between the test score and grades at College A, standing in the top 3 percent is of no advantage.

ATTRITION PHILOSOPHY

A third limitation of conventional normative data may become readily apparent from comparisons of several colleges. Let us take three actual liberal arts colleges in Georgia which are such that a high school senior reasonably might be attracted to all three. Let us say our subject has a College Board SAT-V score of 400, which at College A is at the 80th percentile of entering freshmen, at College B the 70th percentile, and at College C the 74th percentile. At each college the relationship between SAT-V scores and grades is about the same (in the high .40's). On the basis of this information, most counselors would seek good ways of leading the counselee to believe that his chances for success are about equal, or are slightly better at College A than at Colleges B and C. *Yet, an analysis of grades of fall-quarter students at these three colleges shows this is not true.* At these three colleges 54 percent of freshmen with the given SAT-V score of 400 made satisfactory grades their first quarter at College B, 73 percent of the same group achieved the same level or better at College C, *while only 42 percent of freshmen with SAT-V scores of 400 made satisfactory grades at College A.* Thus, in actuality the odds against satisfactory work would be highest at the college at which our counselee looked best among entering freshmen.

The reason for this has to do with differential attrition rates. Of all entering freshmen, College A gave satisfactory first-quarter grades to only 32 percent of the class, while Colleges B and C gave 41 and 63 percent of entering freshmen satisfactory fall-quarter averages. The level of entering freshmen on tests of intelligence or achievement gives no indication, in itself, of the philosophy of the college in regard to what its faculty regards as reasonable proportions of academic failures. Some colleges with low institutional averages on intelligence tests for entering freshmen may deal sternly with all students and permit only a small proportion of beginners to graduate. There need to be orderly ways of dealing with this problem, or great misinformation of potential harm to the college and the applicant can accrue. The answer may lie in the preparation of probability tables showing survival expectancies for persons with different test scores, rather than the percentile rank of various scores as in our conventional norms.

A DOUBLE VARIABLE

The fourth limitation is as dangerous as the others and may be just as difficult to detect from conventional normative descriptions. Let us consider the actual facts concerning one well-known Georgia institution of national standing, and those concerning a small state junior college offering solace in the form of efforts toward effective remedial teaching for applicants fearful of starting college in the big league. At both institutions the high school average had been found to be a good predictor of grades. At both institutions the average entering freshman averaged about B in high school. At both institutions about 50 percent of the entering freshmen had unsatisfactory fall-quarter averages, and at each, 50 percent of students with B high school averages did unsatisfactory academic work. The counselor avoiding some of the limitations of norm tables by using such probability data might "validly" infer that the little junior college would provide just as difficult and competitive an environment as the big league institution for a counselee with a B high school average.

For the colleges in the example (these institutions do exist), our counselor is falling into an easy error which the normative tables or probability data do not expose. All counselees with B averages do *not* have equal chances of survival at either college. In terms of high school record one might stand average at either institution; yet the big institution attracts students not only with good high school records but also with high test scores, while the little college has always attracted students with good records but low test scores. Thus, students with B high school averages at one college had College Board SAT scores averaging about 525, while similar students at the little school had SAT averages of about 380. In technical terms we make the assumption when using norm tables that our counselee may legitimately be considered to be a member of the same population as that reflected by the norms sample, and this does not always hold. Advising the counselee on the basis of one datum alone, such as a single-test score, may ignore other factors related to the spectrum of traits which are important in academic performance. Normative or probability tables on one class of variable alone can divert attention from other important characteristics of students in a given college group.

THE UNEXPECTED VARIABLE

A fifth limitation may become increasingly important in the next few years of tightening college admissions practices. Let us consider a table of norms for College X, based on last year's freshman class, readied quickly for use in the current year. A College Board SAT score of 525 places an applicant in the top fifth of the normative distribution. We send seven seniors at or above this level to College X with our blessings, only to learn that all find the going is too rough for easy survival. College X turns out to be an institution in which the admissions office has sustained in a single year a 40 percent increase in applications and the loss of a dormitory by fire. Thus, the SAT was grasped as a tool for exclusion of applicants, and although a score of 525 was equivalent to the 80th percentile in 1957, it is below the 50th percentile for the class entering in 1958. The faculty at College X suspected a better class in 1958 but could not break away from rules of thumb like "the bottom 10 percent on the final exam in Biology 101 shall fail." The limitations from temporal variation, like limburger cheese, grow stronger with age. Even good local norms can become outdated rather quickly.

DIFFERENT COLLEGE CULTURES

A sixth limitation may grow out of the convincing discoveries made about the usefulness of complete and versatile statistical data. We find our delighted and persevering counselor now a knight in statistical armor, replete with probability tables, multiple regression equations, and armed to the teeth with errors of estimate and the multiple discriminant function. His counselee can get the best varied facts on his probability for survival at a number of colleges.

The counselee may take the statistically safest course of action only to find himself at a school unknown to him three months before, which offers no curricula of interest, and with social and extracurricular patterns the antithesis of what he had hoped to find. The counselee had excellent facts dispensed to him, but the counselor's enthusiasm for the impressive welter of statistical data made these seem to be the only facts worth considering.

USING TECHNICAL DATA

Some counselors feel that the information-imparting aspect of counseling is relatively unimportant and, in fact, incompatible with the crucial clarification of feeling function. In this therapeutic frame of reference test data of any kind are generally held to be relatively unimportant. Other workers of more statistical bent will continue to seek varied but generally highly technical ways of presenting test data in such form as to make their limitations apparent; yet, too often these researchers speak a strange tongue unintelligible to all but their own sect.

Counselors must certainly be able to go beyond the ability to define "percentile" in writing or to know that intelligence tests generally are good predictors of grades. Enough has been learned about validity studies to permit, in the academic situation at least, a potential wealth of tremendously useful data. Counselors must be capable of recognizing the finer technical aspects of the data with which they work to capitalize on these findings, and they must then be versatile and communicative enough to translate the concepts for the counselee, who seldom will have had courses in the statistics of inference.

31   *A Taxonomy of Expectancy Tables*

WILLIAM B. SCHRADER

The results of test validation studies are usually reported as correlation coefficients. These coefficients, although meaningful, are for some test users too abstract. One method devised to facilitate the interpretation of test validity is the application of expectancy tables (Bittner & Wilder, 1946). Although at times technical, the following discussion should provide an informative overview of how expectancy tables are developed and applied. A less technical discussion of the topic may be found in an article by Wesman (1949). The author considers both "theoretical" vs. "concrete" approaches to table development and describes four bases which may be used to classify expectancy tables. How might the use of expectancy tables prove valuable for (a) a classroom teacher, (b) a college admissions officer and (c) a clinical or counseling psychologist?

Before attempting to classify expectancy tables, it might be well to formulate a working definition and to look at some examples. I would like to propose the following definition. "An expectancy table expresses the relation between two (or more) variables by stating the probability that individuals who belong to each of a set of subgroups defined on the basis of one (or more) variables will belong to each of a set of subgroups defined on the basis of another variable." Usually, one of the variables will be the predictor and the other the criterion. It will be noted, however, that the proposed definition is not restricted to this case.

Reprinted and abridged with permission of author and publisher from the *Journal of Educational Measurement*, 1965, Vol. 2, pp. 29–35.

Figure 8 illustrates an *abac* designed to aid in the prediction of law school

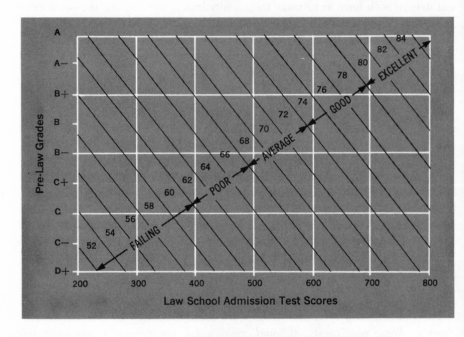

Figure 8. Sample Abac for Predicting First-Year Grades in Law School
from Law School Admission Test Scores and Pre-Law Grades

grades at a particular law school. To determine a student's predicted grade it is
necessary to locate his Law School Admission Test score along the horizontal
axis and to locate his undergraduate average grade along the vertical axis. The
point determined by the intersection of the vertical line through his LSAT score
and the horizontal line through his pre-law average grade will be located in one
of the diagonal bands running from upper left to lower right. The band in which
the point falls corresponds to the student's predicted grade. For example, a student with an LSAT score of 500 and a pre-law average grade of B— would have
a predicted grade of 68, which is described as "average." Since the prediction
chart is based directly on the multiple regression equation, we may assert that the
probability is .5 that he will equal or excel his predicted grade. Table 1 makes it
possible to estimate the probability that a particular student will equal or excel
a number of different grades. Thus, his chances of earning honors or failing
grades may be estimated, once his predicted grade is known. A prediction chart
and table of this kind would enable a guidance counselor or admissions officer to
translate test scores and pre-law grades into the more familiar units of the law
school's grading system. At the same time it would remind him of the limitations
of the available predictions.

TABLE 1. *Chances in 100 That Students with Various Predicted Grades (Based on Figure 1) Will Equal or Excel Various First-Year Average Grades in Law School*

Predicted Grade	Chances in 100 That a Student Will Earn an Average of at Least:														
	54	56	58	60	62	64	66	68	70	72	74	76	78	80	82
84										99	97	94	87	78	65
82									99	97	94	87	78	65	50
80								99	97	94	87	78	65	50	35
78							99	97	94	87	78	65	50	35	22
76						99	97	94	87	78	65	50	35	22	13
74					99	97	94	87	78	65	50	35	22	13	6
72				99	97	94	87	78	65	50	35	22	13	6	3
70			99	97	94	87	78	65	50	35	22	13	6	3	1
68		99	97	94	87	78	65	50	35	22	13	6	3	1	
66	99	97	94	87	78	65	50	35	22	13	6	3	1		
64	97	94	87	78	65	50	35	22	13	6	3	1			
62	94	87	78	65	50	35	22	13	6	3	1				
60	87	78	65	50	35	22	13	6	3	1					
58	78	65	50	35	22	13	6	3	1						
56	65	50	35	22	13	6	3	1							
54	50	35	22	13	6	3	1								
52	35	22	13	6	3	1									

In constructing Table 1, the difference between each average grade and the predicted grade was calculated. This difference was divided by the standard error of estimate, and the resulting normal deviate was looked up in a table of the normal curve. In Table 1 the probabilities have been allowed to range from 1 to 99, as determined by the calculations. There might be some advantage in cutting them off at, say, 5 and 95 to avoid a suggestion that the table is more precise than the data warrant.

Quite a different approach to expectancy is shown in Table 2. Here we have for correlation coefficients ranging from .10 to .90 probabilities that students scoring at different levels on a predictor would have various standings on the criterion. In each instance the rows add to 100. Thus, if the correlation coefficient were .60, a student who ranked in the top fifth on the predictor would have 50 chances in 100 of ranking in the top fifth on the criterion and only 2 chances in 100 of ranking in the bottom fifth. Table 2 helps to make it clear why an improvement in validity from .40 to .70 is well worth-while. With a correlation coefficient of .40, 7 students in 100 who rank in the top fifth on the predictor rank in the bottom fifth on the criterion. When the correlation is .70, errors of this type occur only once in 100 times.

Part of Table 2 was originally developed using the computing charts for tetrachoric correlation coefficients prepared by Chesire, Saffir, and Thurstone (1933). Subsequently, it was recomputed and extended using the extensive tables of the

TABLE 2. *Relation Between Standing on Predictor and Standing on Criterion for Various Values of the Correlation Coefficient*

Representative Correlation Coefficients	Standing on Predictor	Percent of Students Standing in Each Criterion Group		
		Bottom Fifth	Middle Three-Fifths	Top Fifth
.10	Top Fifth	16	60	24
	Middle Three-Fifths	20	60	20
	Bottom Fifth	24	60	16
.30	Top Fifth	10	57	33
	Middle Three-Fifths	19	62	19
	Bottom Fifth	33	57	10
.40	Top Fifth	7	55	38
	Middle Three-Fifths	18	64	18
	Bottom Fifth	38	55	7
.60	Top Fifth	2	48	50
	Middle Three-Fifths	16	68	16
	Bottom Fifth	50	48	2
.70	Top Fifth	1	43	56
	Middle Three-Fifths	14	72	14
	Bottom Fifth	56	43	1
.90	Top Fifth	(0.002)	25.2	74.8
	Middle Three-Fifths	8.4	83.2	8.4
	Bottom Fifth	74.8	25.2	(0.002)

bivariate normal distribution prepared by the National Bureau of Standards (1959).

Among the various bases on which expectancy tables might be classified, four seem to be particularly relevant. Stated in the form of questions, the criteria are:

(1) Has the table been derived from correlation or regression results or obtained directly from the scatter diagram?

(2) Is the predictor variable expressed in terms of points, of three or more mutually exclusive and exhaustive class intervals, or of one or more dichotomies?

(3) Is the criterion variable expressed in terms of points, of three or more mutually exclusive and exhaustive class intervals, or of one or more dichotomies?

(4) Is each variable expressed in the original measurement units or in terms of relative standing in a defined group?

Of the four bases for classification, the most vexatious issues arise in the first. Is it preferable to derive the tables on a *theoretical* basis using correlation and regression theory or to take a concrete approach sticking closely to the original scatter diagram? If the figures for the table are derived from the correlation or regression results, the obtained figures will display a regular progression, free of the detailed idiosyncracies of the data in hand. Thus the dangers of capitalizing on chance by identifying peculiar features of the data are minimized. Moreover, scatter diagrams are difficult to evaluate without the help of the correlation coefficient. Finally, the availability of tables of the normal distribution, of tetrachoric correlation coefficients, and of the normal bivariate distribution permits great flexibility in the design of a table. If regression is used, the derived results may be extrapolated into regions where data are very scanty. Correlation coefficients corrected for restriction of range and multiple correlations may be used directly in computing an expectancy table.

On the other hand, the preparation of expectancy tables directly from the scatter diagram has two very substantial advantages: first, the resulting tables are more readily understood by the non-statistician; and, second, the necessity of making various (possibly unrealistic) assumptions of normality, linearity of regression, or both is avoided. Certainly there is much to be said for computing the probability figures directly from the scatter diagram if a large number of cases is available and if the analysis is kept simple.

The choice between the theoretical and concrete approaches will necessarily depend on the specific purpose for which the table is prepared, the willingness of the audience to accept results involving a relatively complex and perhaps unfamiliar chain of reasoning, and the nature of the available data. Ideally, tests of linearity and homogeneity of the variance of residuals or at least a careful scrutiny of the scatter diagram might precede the use of the theoretical approach. By the same token, users of the concrete approach with relatively small samples should warn readers of the dangers of capitalizing on chance.

The second basis for classification depends on whether the predictor is to be expressed in terms of points, intervals, or a dichotomy. The use of a series of points seems logical when the regression equation is the basis for the table and when the primary purpose of the table is to aid in the interpretation of individual performance. On the other hand, if the scatter diagram is used to make the table, the predictor would be expressed as a series of points only if the predictor itself were measured in this way. Admittedly, the distinction between points and intervals is made somewhat ambiguous by the customary practice of letting the midpoint of an interval represent the entire interval. However, a clear difference between points and intervals emerges when only a few intervals are used for the predictor. Use of a small number of intervals is highly desirable when the goal is to give a clear indication of the effectiveness of prediction. Table 2 shows how this may be done with the theoretical approach. With the concrete approach we have found it useful to divide the group into equal thirds (interpolating if necessary) on one or more predictors to permit an evaluation of predictive effectiveness. Use of a small number of intervals is especially advantageous in this approach when the number of cases is 100 or less.

The dichotomous form of the predictor is most useful when cutting scores are being considered. Essentially, this kind of table answers the question: What would happen if we selected the group more and more stringently on the basis of the predictor? It will be recalled that the familiar Taylor-Russell tables (Taylor & Russell, 1939) treat the predictor in terms of selection ratios and thus reflect the fact that selection is inherently dichotomous. For general institutional planning, this method is probably the most realistic, since it takes the characteristics of the applicant group directly into account. However, in view of the well-known disadvantages of using a rigid cutting score in selection, tables prepared in this form should be used mainly for exploratory work.

The third basis for classification is also concerned with whether the variable is expressed in terms of points, intervals, or dichotomously. For the criterion, the dichotomous form seems preferable for many purposes. For example, percent passing, percent failing, and percent equaling or excelling the average criterion score are frequently used. Even more interesting is the possibility of treating the criterion as a whole series of dichotomies, as in Table 1. Indeed, the dichotomous form is probably the most widely used basis for expressing the criterion. The use of a small number of class intervals (for example, "honors," "acceptable," "failing") is effective, but the use of a large number of class intervals for the criterion is likely to be confusing.

To express the criterion in terms of points, the points corresponding to selected probabilities are calculated. Thus, in one recent study we showed for selected predictor scores the range of scores on the criterion test which would be expected to include 68 percent of the cases. McCabe (1956) published a useful table showing for selected percentiles and selected correlation coefficients the range of percentiles on the criterion corresponding to plus or minus one standard error of estimate from the prediction based on the regression equation. When the scatter diagram approach is used, selected percentiles on the criterion are computed for each subgroup defined by predictor scores. This kind of table also shows the general trend of relation of criterion to predictor scores.

Finally, expectancy tables may be classified according to whether the variables are expressed in their original units or in terms of relative standings within a defined group. Thus, Figure 1 and Table 1 express both predictor and criterion variables in the original units, while Table 2 expresses both variables as percentages of the total group. The use of the original units is most advantageous when results of a single study in a single school or college are to be presented. Here the table gains in meaningfulness from the fact that the units are already familiar to the persons using the table. On the other hand, when comparisons are to be made for different predictors or for the same predictors in different colleges, the use of percentage groupings is virtually essential. This is evident from a consideration of tetrachoric correlation tables. Suppose that one predictor is used to divide the group into the top 15 percent, the middle 70 percent, and the bottom 15 percent while another is used to divide the same group into thirds. Comparison of the tables for these two predictors would certainly be misleading. Only if the percentage splits both on predictors and criteria are the same may expectancy tables be used with confidence in comparing predictive effectiveness. The percentage approach is also advantageous for variables which are not familiar to the audience for whom the tables are intended.

One conclusion which might be drawn from this discussion is that the making of expectancy tables is an art. Hopefully, the conclusion may also be drawn that it is an art based on statistical principles.

32   *The Matter of Ipsative Scores*

ROBERT H. BAUERNFEIND

Whether selecting a test or interpreting its results, the user must investigate the type of items and the type of scoring which are used. Interest and personality instruments are likely to require the selection of one activity, for example, from each of successive groups of two or three activities. Such a "forced-choice" arrangement leads to "ipsative" scoring. Dr. Bauernfeind compares ipsative, normative, and absolute scoring procedures, and compares forced-choice with free-response items. How are these bases for scoring and types of items defined and illustrated? What are the author's recommendations? Which type of information would be most helpful in decision-making? How do response sets affect the two procedures? How might the two types of items be combined in one instrument?

Many high school and college counselors have elected to measure interests or personality inclinations with forced-choice techniques. Such techniques require a counselee to respond to each item by choosing a statement or activity that is most consistent with his view of himself. Each choice is made at the expense of other statements or activities. Forced-choice instruments in popular usage today include the *Kuder Preference Records,* the *Lee-Thorpe Occupational Interest Inventory,* the *Edwards Personal Preference Schedule,* the *Allport-Vernon Study of Values,* and others—all of which present items forcing choices from among two or more statements or activities.

The concept of "ipsative"[1] scores is inherent in each such instrument. In this article the ipsative matter will be defined and discussed as it relates to student scores on the *Kuder Preference Record,* but the problems raised apply with equal force to all other instruments using a forced-choice format.

Reprinted and abridged with permission of author and publisher from the *Personnel and Guidance Journal,* 1962, Vol. 40, pp. 210–217.

[1] The term "ipsative" was coined by Raymond Cattell in 1944. Cattell provides a detailed development of this concept in his 1957 book, *Personality and Motivation Structure and Measurement.*

ABSOLUTE, NORMATIVE, AND IPSATIVE SCORES

In some types of measurement three different types of score interpretation are possible. These three interpretations are the "absolute," "normative," and "ipsative," often with a systematic progression from one to another.

In a season of baseball, for example, we can obtain absolute measures of performance in three areas: singles per 100 times at bat, extra-base hits per 100 times at bat, and error-free fieldings per 100 chances. Suppose, for baseball-player Jones, that his scores on these three measures are as follows:

	Absolute Score
Singles per 100 times at bat	17
Extra-base hits per 100 times at bat	4
Error-free fieldings per 100 chances	92

These absolute measures tell a great deal about Jones' performance: His sureness of fielding is greatly superior to his sureness of hitting, and he is more likely generally to hit a single than to obtain an extra-base hit. Each measure has a true zero point that allows for absolute comparisons of the three scores.

A normative interpretation adds further information about Jones' performance. In this type of analysis these same three measures are applied to a representative sample of players in the same league, and percentile norms are obtained. It may be found that the average player obtains 22 singles per 100 times at bat, 5 extra-base hits per 100 times at bat, and 97 error-free fieldings per 100 chances. Jones' percentile-rank scores are as follows:

	Absolute Score	Percentile Rank
Singles per 100 times at bat	17	28
Extra-base hits per 100 times at bat	4	40
Error-free fieldings per 100 chances	92	1

These normative measures indicate that Jones' low absolute score in extra-base hits actually represents his best performance on the norm (within the baseball culture, so to speak), and that his high absolute performance in fielding is very low on the baseball norm.

The ipsative interpretation inquires into the individual's baseball skills that are normatively higher or lower than his personal normative average of baseball skills. Using just these three measures, it is noted that Jones' median percentile rank is in singles per 100 times at bat. We interpret his three scores on an ipsative basis as follows:

	Ipsative Interpretation
Singles per 100 times at bat	Average
Extra-base hits per 100 times at bat	High
Error-free fieldings per 100 chances	Low

These ipsative scores tell us nothing about Jones' absolute performances, and they tell us nothing about how good or poor a player Jones may be within the baseball norms group. Another player whose respective percentile rank scores are 98, 99, and 97 would obtain exactly the same ipsative interpretations as Jones, and a third player whose respective percentile rank scores are 2, 3, and 1 would also obtain exactly the same ipsative interpretations.

Given only the ipsative interpretations cited above, our comments on Jones' performance would have to run something like this: "Your performance in extra-base hits is higher—we don't know how much higher—than your own average performance—whatever that is—relative to the performance of other players in this league."

SCORES OF FORCED-CHOICE INSTRUMENTS

Forced-choice instruments provide ipsative scores only. Each of these instruments partials out energy and enthusiasm (in the same way as the above report for player Jones partialled out the actual quality of his performance), leaving an "interest profile" that centers on a 50th percentile point with scores ranging upward and downward from the student's personal average score in a series of normative measurements.

The point can be illustrated quickly by considering the item format of the *Kuder Preference Record* (1947):

Mark M for the activity you like Most.
Mark L for the activity you like Least.

Eat strawberry ice cream .... M   L
Eat chocolate ice cream .... M   L
Eat vanilla ice cream .... M   L

In forced-choice testing, each choice is made at the expense of other statements or activities, and all students obtain the same (or nearly the same) average score for the instrument as a whole. Scoring two points for an M response, one point for a blank response, and zero points for an L response, what is your average score for the three preferences cited above? What will be the average score of a man who eats one quart of ice cream daily? What will be the average score of a man who never eats ice cream?

The essential characteristics of ipsative scores is the equation of means from one student to another. It does not matter whether this equation of means is accomplished statistically, proceeding from normative scores (as in the baseball example), or whether it is accomplished directly through choice of item format. Interest inventories automatically produce ipsative scores if they involve systematic pairings of choices, systematic variation of triads from which choices are made, rank-ordering of all items, or control of distributions of responses to items for each student.

Since forced-choice instruments produce ipsative scores only, it may be well to review the important properties of such scores: Intercorrelations are low and tend to be slightly negative; every tested student will have the same mean interest score computed across all categories, so that he will necessarily be below average in some areas and above average in others (or at average in all areas); differences in scores from one area to another within a student reflect only relative strengths of interests for that student; and differences in scores from one student to another for a particular interest category cannot be interpreted normatively, since each score may be related to a different mean.

STUDIES OF FORCED-CHOICE VS. FREE-RESPONSE MEASURES

The *Brainard Occupational Preference Inventory* (Brainard & Brainard, 1945) provides interest items in a free-response format, as follows:

Mark SD if you Strongly Dislike the activity.
Mark D if you Dislike the activity.
Mark N if you are Neutral about the activity.
Mark L if you Like the activity.
Mark SL if you Strongly Like the activity.

Eat strawberry ice cream .... SD	D	N	L	SL
Eat chocolate ice cream .... SD	D	N	L	SL
Eat vanilla ice cream .... SD	D	N	L	SL

A comparison of the Brainard type of item with the previous Kuder type of item illustrates the difference between normative interest scores and ipsative interest scores. With the Brainard instrument it is possible for a student to obtain all high scores or all low scores.

How do similarly named scores of these two instruments correspond? The Brainard manual reports two studies of eleventh-grade groups that help to answer this question (Brainard & Brainard, 1956).

	BOYS	*GIRLS*
Brainard "Commercial" vs. Kuder "Clerical"	0.12	0.32
Brainard "Mechanical" vs. Kuder "Mechanical" ...	0.58	0.51
Brainard "Professional" vs. Kuder "Soc. Service" ..	0.39	0.51
Brainard "Esthetic" vs. Kuder "Artistic"	0.19	0.31
Brainard "Scientific" vs. Kuder "Scientific"	0.53	0.58
Brainard "Agricultural" vs. Kuder "Outdoor"	0.53	....

Since the Brainard items are different from those in the Kuder, some of this independence between similarly named scores may be a function of the test questions rather than the response format. However, a study by Way (1953) demonstrates that the matter of response format *does* constitute an important issue. Way first reported complete forced-choice intercorrelation data for groups of college men and college women tested with the Kuder-Vocational-Form B. This analysis yielded rather typical ipsative intercorrelation data, with a median of −0.06 for the men and −0.11 for the women.

Way then administered the same Form B items to the same groups using a free-response format. This testing yielded high positive correlations among the nine scores for both groups. For the men, the intercorrelations ranged from 0.92 (Persuasive-Clerical) to 0.37 (Computational-Musical), with a median of 0.72. For the women, the intercorrelations ranged from 0.91 (Persuasive-Clerical) to 0.40 (Computational-Musical), with a median of 0.73.

All correlations between the same scales obtained by the two techniques were positive but only moderately high, ranging from 0.57 (Musical scores for men) to 0.09 (Clerical scores for women). Using the same Kuder items assigned to the same Kuder categories, the median correlation between forced-choice and free-response Kuder testings for the men was 0.26; the median for the women was 0.33. In view of these data, a counselor may reasonably ask which testing best measured the students' interests.

ARGUMENTS FAVORING FORCED-CHOICE AND FREE-RESPONSE MEASUREMENTS

Arguments favoring the use of "forced-choice" instruments usually run as follows:

1. The forced-choice technique operates to keep intercorrelations among interest categories at a low level, thus providing the instrument a greater potential for validity.

2. The forced-choice technique parallels more closely actual life situations where one cannot do all things he would like to do, but rather where he regularly elects one course of action in preference to alternatives—even fairly attractive alternatives. In this sense forced-choice testing functions as a realistic microcosm of everyday behavior.

3. The forced-choice technique tends to control "response set"—differences in response enthusiasm between individuals and also from occasion to occasion within one individual. Additionally, the forced-choice technique is likely to be more resistant to faking than is the free-response technique.

4. The forced-choice technique usually provides higher reliabilities than the free-response technique. Kuder (1939) has shown that the forced-choice format evokes a high level of behavioral reliability in responding to the items, and the consistent evidence of high reliability for various forced-choice instruments is quite convincing.

5. The research literature indicates clearly that such instruments as the Kuder-Vocational yield useful validities in terms of discriminating among various vocational groups.

Arguments favoring the use of "free-response" instruments usually run as follows:

1. The forced-choice technique is frustrating to students in that it does not permit expressions of high enthusiasm for interest items that are especially appealing to them.

2. Because energy and enthusiasm undoubtedly represent basic components of human behavior, denial of energy and enthusiasm in forced-choice instruments creates artificial test scores. Granted that forced-choice scores show near-zero intercorrelations and high reliabilities, it is argued that the scores are spurious, contrived—that they fail to represent real-life behaviors. If free-response intercorrelations run moderately high, it is because human enthusiasms in real life probably show moderately high intercorrelations. Just as we expect (and find) positive correlations among achievement scores, aptitude scores, and school grades, we should expect to find positive correlations among areas of interest.

3. Free-response instruments not only have a potential for validity in terms of discriminating among various occupational groups, but they also have a further potential for discriminating enthusiasms *within* occupational groups.

A BROADER ISSUE

While these arguments bring certain issues into focus, there appears to be a still broader issue: Before taking a position for or against forced-choice testing, we need to identify carefully the criterion behaviors we are trying to predict. Only then can we seek to identify the testing technique that holds the most promise for approximating the criterion behaviors. We can divide our analysis into three parts:

1. *Criterion behaviors that are themselves forced-choice in nature.* In these cases forced-choice testing instruments should evoke more behaviors common to the subsequent criterion behaviors. Job entry is a case in point: Job entry represents a force-choice situation (one cannot enter all jobs that interest him), and we may therefore expect that forced-choice measures will provide useful predictions of these behaviors. In the case of the Kuder this contention is at least partially borne out by various studies. Selection of school electives is another case in point: In high school or college one cannot elect to take all of the courses he would like to; he is confronted with forced-choice situations, and we therefore expect that forced-choice instruments should provide useful predictions of these behaviors. This contention also is borne out by research. Illustrative of this general point, Frandsen (1947) reported a correlation of 0.54 between the Kuder-Vocational Scientific score and percent of natural science courses taken in high school, and a correlation of 0.32 between the Kuder Social Service score and percent of social studies courses taken in high school.

2. *Criterion behaviors that are themselves free-response in nature.* In these cases free-response testing instruments should evoke more behaviors common to subsequent criterion behaviors. Because there are so few free-response instruments available,[2] it is not possible to document this contention at the present time.

---

[2] The *Strong Vocational Interest Blank* presents a combination of forced-choice and free-response items. Since the purpose of this discussion is to compare the merits of the two-item types, it seems preferable to exclude the Strong from this discussion.

This contention is consistent with correlation theory, and it is supported indirectly by evidence that forced-choice instruments at best yield only anemic predictions of subsequent free-response behaviors. Illustrative of this general point, Kuder (1947) compared the Kuder-Vocational scores of "satisfied workers" and "dissatisfied workers" in five occupational fields: For laborers, no significant differences were obtained; for engineers, no significant differences were obtained; for laboratory workers, no significant differences were obtained; for managers, the "dissatisfied" group showed a significantly higher mean score on the Persuasive scale than did the "satisfied" group; for salesmen, the "satisfied" group showed a significantly higher score on the Persuasive scale than did the "dissatisfied" group. In these last two studies none of the other forced-choice scores showed significant differences between the "satisfied" and "dissatisfied" groups.

3. *Criterion behaviors that represent power of performance.* In these cases—where the criteria are school grades, foremen's ratings, sales records, etc.—it is expected that neither type of interest measurement would yield especially strong predictions of the criteria. A ceiling validity of about 0.30 has been observed in such studies of the forced-choice Kuder-Vocational scores. Illustrative of this general point, Maier (1957) correlated each of the Kuder-Vocational scores with subject-matter grades in 19 areas of the college undergraduate program. The *highest* correlation obtained in this study was 0.26, between the Kuder Mechanical scores and grades in engineering. In the case of mathematics grades, none of the Kuder scores yielded validities exceeding 0.08. Using total grade-point averages as a criterion, the highest prediction (r = 0.15) was obtained from the Kuder Literary scores.

Since Kuder scores are ipsative and school grades are not ipsative, it is clearly dead-end research—even for masters' theses—to correlate Kuder scores with a variety of school grades and expect to come up with findings of psychological significance. While free-response measures occasionally yield somewhat higher validities against power-of-performance criterion behaviors (e.g., Frederiksen and Melville, 1954), it is doubtful that counselors should rely heavily on any interest scores for these types of predictions.

DEVELOPING A POINT OF VIEW

While all counselors need to know something about students' interests, the foregoing analysis shows that the purposes must be more specific. If the counselor intends to predict future forced-choice behaviors, a forced-choice interest instrument may be helpful. If he intends to predict free-response behaviors, a free-response interest instrument may be helpful. If he intends to predict future power-of-performance behaviors, it is doubtful that any type of interest instrument will be especially helpful.

What about the case of ninth-grade testings for the purpose of helping the counselor to understand the student better—to "come to know" the student more quickly? In these cases we would recommend use of a free-response instrument such as the Brainard. The reasons for this recommendation are as follows:

1. Personal enthusiasm, which is denied by the forced-choice instruments, is vital to the counselor's work of "getting acquainted with" each student. Most counselors want to be alerted to the fact that one student enjoys a great many activities in life while another enjoys few; that one student has a fire of conviction for his beliefs and preferences while another does not. To present the counselor with a long series of interest profiles, each showing interests neatly balanced around some 50th percentile point, is to deny the strong possibility that certain of the students are more active, more alert, more interested than others.

2. The forced-choice technique is frustrating to many high school and college students. With respect to work with the Kuder-Vocational, Johnson (1952) comments:

> During my tenure of punch counting I observed that some marks were decisive and vigorous; others were hesitant and barely penetrated the paper. Some were bull's-eyes and others appeared on the periphery. Why a configuration of faint punches near the circle's edge should count as much as those accurately made and with sufficient force to mar the table and blunt the pin is indeed hard for me to understand. It seems rather apparent that a count of perforations is a pretty crude measure of interest.

3. One can reject categorically the contention that forced-choice testing functions as a realistic microcosm of everyday behavior. Many interested students, faced with forced-choice situations in signing up for high school or college electives, choose to attend summer school in order to pursue their other interests. Many workers, faced with forced-choice situations in deciding on a career, develop outside jobs, hobbies, and community activities in support of their other interests. Some students join as many as eight or ten school and community clubs; others join none. Some students arrange to attend two or three educational/social functions in a single evening; others attend only one, and still others do not leave home at all. If these types of behaviors are worth predicting, free-response instruments at least hold promise of predicting them; forced-choice instruments cannot predict them.

4. To the extent that free-response intercorrelations depart from zero, they represent realities of human behavior. Enthusiasm and energy are common denominators of human behavior, and the denial of energy and enthusiasm in forced-choice instruments creates artificial test scores. Such scores are more things than approximations of behavior; and their failure to provide substantial predictions of performance behaviors is undoubtedly in large part a function of their breed.

5. Finally, and perhaps most important, forced-choice scores utterly defy straightforward interpretations to students. With a free-response instrument one is able to say, "You indicated interest in Mechanical activities exceeding that of 75 percent of other boys in the national norms group." But referring to the

Kuder-Vocational profile, what are we to say? "Your interests in Artistic activities are higher than your interests in Mechanical activities." No, these are not absolute scores. "Your interests in Artistic activities exceed those of 90 percent of other boys in the national norms group." No, these are not normative scores; the Kuder national percentiles simply provide a means for identifying "high" and "low" ipsative scores. "Your interests in Artistic activities are higher—we don't know how much higher—than your own average of interests—wherever that is—relative to the interests of other boys in the national norms group." This type of statement comes close. It represents a conscientious effort to interpret the Kuder profile honestly; and it also represents a classic case of communication invalidity.

IMPLICATIONS OF THIS ANALYSIS

In view of the limitations of forced-choice interest scores for prediction and for "get acquainted" counseling, it is surprising to find that there is at present only one inventory yielding a profile of general interest scores that are normative rather than ipsative. This one instrument is the *Brainard Occupation Interest Inventory.* While the present writer makes no brief for the Brainard as such, he would recommend its use to counselors who want general measures of interests for use in the high school program.

If a counselor should decide that he is partial to ipsative scores—perhaps for predictions of future forced-choice behaviors—he can always develop ipsative conversions from normative scores, as was shown in the case of baseball-player Jones. To illustrate, suppose that a student obtains the following normative scores on the Brainard instrument:

	Percentile
Commercial	88th
Mechanical	92nd
Professional	70th
Esthetic	52nd
Scientific	78th
Agricultural	48th

These normative scores can be readily converted to Kuder-type ipsative scores, as follows:

Commercial	High
Mechanical	High
Professional	Average
Esthetic	Low
Scientific	Average
Agricultural	Low

The normative scores show a profile of interests, and also show a relatively high level of enthusiasm on the part of this one student. The ipsative transformations bring the student's scores to a personal average within the culture—with half of his scores "below average" and half of his scores "above average."

Ipsative scores can thus be obtained from normative scores, but normative scores cannot be inferred from ipsative scores. As with the question of buying whole eggs or scrambled eggs, only in the former instance does one have flexibility in deciding on their use.

While we readily acknowledge the probable value of forced-choice scores for predicting future forced-choice behaviors, we may also ask whether this is the best line of development for other test authors to follow. As alternatives, might we not redouble our efforts to develop absolute measures of interests—measures of interests irrespective of cultural norms? Or failing this, should we not plan to construct more instruments along the line of the Brainard—to see what can be done with different item types to provide better predictions of job tenure, job satisfaction, and power-of-performance behaviors?

In summary: Free-response interest scores can be interpreted in a straightforward way, whereas ipsative scores cannot. Free-response scores have more potential for predicting free-response and power-of-performance behaviors than do ipsative scores. And, free-response scores can be readily converted to ipsative scores if one wants to. Alerted to the issues presented in this article, however, we wonder how many counselors will want to.

33 *On Telling Parents About Test Results*

JAMES H. RICKS, JR.

With increasing frequency parents are requesting that the results of school testing programs be communicated to them. Indeed in some areas courts have ruled that a child's school records, which typically contain test scores, must be open to his parents.

School personnel are often hard pressed to find the most efficient and understandable techniques by which this request might be met. The following article presents some non-technical and common-sense suggestions that might be used in interpreting test scores to parents.

Like any other organization dealing with people, a school has many confidences to keep. School administrators, teachers, and especially guidance workers inev-

Reprinted with permission of the publisher from *Test Service Bulletin No. 54*, published by the Psychological Corporations, 1959 (December), pp. 1–4.

itably come to know items of private information. A gossip who carelessly passes such information around abuses his position and his relationship with his students. It is both right and important that some kinds of information be kept in confidence.

What about test results? Do they belong in the category of secrets, to be seen only by professional eyes and mentioned only in whispers? Or is their proper function best served when they become common knowledge in the school and its community? (In some towns, names and scores have been listed in the local newspaper, much like the results of an athletic contest.)

We think neither extreme is a good rule. Sometimes there is reason to make group data—figures such as the average and the range from high to low—generally public. Seldom should individual results be published except for the happy announcement of a prize won, a scholarship awarded, and the like. But short of general publication, school guidance workers face a particularly important question: Should parents be told their children's test results?

Hard questions often are hard because they deal with genuinely complicated problems. Simple "solutions" to such questions are likely to be a trap rather than an aid if their effect is to divert our attention from the difficulties we truly face. Simple rules or principles, on the other hand, can be of real help as one tackles complex problems and situations. This article will present some rules that we have found useful in facing questions such as—"What should I say when a mother wants to know her son's IQ?" "Should we send aptitude test profiles home with the children?" "We feel that parents in our school ought to know the results of the achievement tests we give, but then it's hard to explain the discrepancies between these and the teachers' grades."

No single procedure, obviously, can be appropriate for every kind of test. Nor for every kind of parent. To Mr. Jones, a well-adjusted and well-educated father, a report of his daughter's test scores may enhance his understanding of her capacities and of what the school has been giving her. To Mr. Green, a somewhat insecure and less knowledgeable man, the identical information may spark an explosion damaging to both child and school. And the counselor or teacher often has no sure way of knowing which kind of parent he will be reporting to.

Two principles and one verbal technique seem to us to provide a sound basis for communicating the information obtained from testing. The two "commandments" are absolutely interdependent—without the second the first is empty, and without the first the second is pointless.

The first: PARENTS HAVE THE RIGHT TO KNOW WHATEVER THE SCHOOL KNOWS ABOUT THE ABILITIES, THE PERFORMANCE, AND THE PROBLEMS OF THEIR CHILDREN.

The second: THE SCHOOL HAS THE OBLIGATION TO SEE THAT IT COMMUNICATES UNDERSTANDABLE AND USABLE KNOWLEDGE. Whether by written report or by individual conference, the school must make sure it is giving real information—not just the illusion of information that bare numbers or canned interpretations often afford. And the information must be in terms that parents can absorb and use.

Few educators will dispute the first principle. It is in parents that the final responsibility for the upbringing and education of the children must lie. This responsibility requires access to all available information bearing on educational and vocational decisions to be made for and by the child. The school is the agent to which parents have delegated part of the educational process—but the responsibility has been delegated, not abdicated. Thoughtful parents do not take these responsibilities and rights lightly.

The parents' right to know, then, we regard as indisputable. But, to know what?

Suppose that as a result of judicious testings the school knows that Sally has mastered social studies and general science better than many in her ninth grade class, but that few do as poorly as she in math. In English usage she stands about in the middle, but her reading level is barely up to the lower border of the students who successfully complete college preparatory work in her high school. The best prediction that can be made of her probable scores on the College Boards three years hence is that they will fall in the range which makes her eligible for the two-year community college, but not for the university. She grasps mechanical concepts better than most boys, far better than most girls. Looking over the test results and her records, her experienced teacher recognizes that good habits and neatness of work have earned Sally grades somewhat better than would be expected from her test scores.

All of these are things Sally's parents should know. Will they know them if they are given the numbers—Sally's IQ score, percentiles for two reading scores, percentiles on another set of norms for several aptitude tests, and grade-placement figures on an achievement battery?

Telling someone something he does not understand does not increase his knowledge (at least not his correct and usable knowledge—we are reminded of the guide's observation about the tenderfoot, "It ain't so much what he don't know, it's what he knows that ain't so that gits him in trouble."). Transmitting genuine knowledge requires attention to content, language, and audience. We have already referred to some of the characteristics of parents as an audience. Let's look at the other two elements.

Content means that to begin with we must ourselves know what we are trying to get across.

We need to know just what evidence there is to show that these test results deserve any consideration at all. We need equally to know the margins and probabilities of error in predictions based on tests. If we don't know both what the scores mean and how much confidence may properly be placed in them, we are in trouble at the start—neither our own use of the information nor our transmission of it to others will be very good.

Content—what we are going to say—and language—how we are going to put it—are inseparable when we undertake to tell somebody something. In giving information about test results, we need to think about the general content and language we shall use and also about the specific terms we shall use.

To illustrate the general content-and-language planning, a guidance director may decide that he wants first to get across a sense of both the values and the weaknesses of test scores. One excellent device for his purpose would be an expectancy table or chart. Such a chart can make it clear to persons without training in statistics that test results are useful predictors and that the predictions will not always be precise. Local studies in one's school or community are of greatest interest. But the guidance director who lacks local data may still find illustrative tables from other places helpful in preparing parents and students to use test results in a sensible way.

Specific terms used in expressing test results vary considerably in the problems they pose. Consider, for example, the different kinds of numbers in which test results may be reported.

IQ's are regarded as numbers that should rarely if ever be reported as such to students or to their parents. The reason is that an IQ is likely to be seen as a fixed characteristic of the person tested, as somehow something more than the test score it really represents. The effect, too often, is that of a final conclusion about the individual rather than that of a piece of information useful in further thinking and planning. Few things interfere more effectively with real understanding than indiscriminate reporting of IQ scores to parents.

Grade-placement scores or standard scores of various kinds are less likely to cause trouble than IQ scores are. Still, they may substitute an illusion of communication for real communication. Standard scores have no more meaning to most parents than raw scores unless there is opportunity for extensive explanations. Grade placements seem so simple and straightforward that serious misunderstandings may result from their use. As noted in a very helpful pamphlet (Katz, 1958), a sixth-grade pupil with grade-placement scores of 10.0 for reading and 8.5 for arithmetic does not necessarily rank higher in reading than he does in arithmetic when compared to the other sixth-graders. (Both scores may be at the 95th percentile for his class—arithmetic progress much more than reading progress tends to be dependent on what has been taught, and thus to spread over a narrower range at any one grade.)

Percentiles probably are the safest and most informative numbers to use provided their two essential characteristics are made clear: (1) that they refer not to percent of questions answered correctly but to percent of people whose performance the student has equaled or surpassed, and (2) who specifically are the people with whom the student is being compared. The second point—a definite description of the comparison or "norm" group— is especially important in making the meaning of test results clear.

Much more can be said about the kinds of numbers used to convey test score information. But a more fundamental question remains—are any numbers necessary?

We intend nothing so foolish as suggesting a ban on the use of numbers in reporting test results. But we have been struck repeatedly by the fact that some of the very best counselors and many of the best-written reports present numerical data only incidentally or not at all.

Along with the two "commandments" at the beginning of this article, we mentioned a verbal technique. Generally we dislike formulas for writing or speaking. This one, however, seems to have advantages that outweigh the risks attending its suggestion. It's just a few words: "YOU SCORE LIKE PEOPLE WHO . . ." Or, to a parent, "Your son (or daughter) scores like students who . . ."

The sentence, of course, requires completion. The completion depends on the test or other instrument, the reason for testing, and the person to whom the report is being given. Some sample completions:

YOU SCORE LIKE

". . . people who don't find selling insurance a very satisfactory choice. Three out of four who score as you do and become insurance salesmen leave the job for something else in less than a year."

". . . people who are pretty good at office work, fast and accurate enough to hold a job and do it well."

". . . students who find getting into liberal arts college and getting a B.A. degree something they can attain only with extra hard work. On the other hand, they find a year or two of technical school interesting and they probably do well in the jobs to which that leads."

". . . students who are disappointed later if they don't begin a language in the ninth grade and plan to take some more math and science. It's easier to head toward business later if you still want to than to go from the commercial course into a good college."

". . . students who don't often—only about one out of four—manage to earn a C average their freshman year at State."

". . . students who have more than average difficulty passing in arithmetic —you (or, to a parent, he) may need some extra help on this in the next few years."

Many more samples will come readily to mind. The most important thing to note is that a satisfactory report combines two kinds of information:

1) the test results of the individual person, and
2) something known about the test or battery and its relationship to the subsequent performance of others who have taken it.

Also, a satisfactory completion puts the school or the counselor out on a limb, at least a little. Some variant of "That's not so!" or, more politely, "How do you know?" will be the reaction in some cases, probably less frequently voiced than it is felt.

Well, let's face it. The decision to use a test at all is a step out on a limb. Some limbs are broad and solid and the climber need feel little or no anxiety. Some are so frail that they offer only hazard, with the bait of an improbable reward. We climb out on some limbs of medium safety because there is evidence of a real chance that they will help us, and those whom we test, toward a worthwhile goal. The words of the formula need not actually be used in each case. Sometimes percentiles, grade placement scores, or a profile may be what the parents should receive. But it is well to try first mentally stating the meaning of the results in the language suggested above. If this proves difficult or discomforting, a warning signal is on—reporting the numbers is likely not to be constructive in the case at hand!

The audience of parents to which our test-based information is to be transmitted includes an enormous range and variety of minds and emotions. Some are ready and able to absorb what we have to say. Reaching others may be as hopeless as reaching TV watchers with an AM radio broadcast. Still others may hear what we say, but clothe the message with their own special needs, ideas, and predilections.

The habit of using the formula and of thinking a bit about what answer to give if the response is a challenging or doubting one puts the interpreter of test scores in the strongest position he can occupy. In the case of achievement tests it requires him to understand why and how the particular test or battery was chosen as appropriate for his school and his purpose. In the case of aptitude (including scholastic aptitude or intelligence) tests it requires him to examine the evidence offered in the test manual and research studies to back up the test's claim to usefulness. And it reminds him always that it is in the end his thinking, his weighing of the evidence, his soundness and helpfulness as an educator or counselor that is exposed for judgment—not the sometimes wistful ideas of the test author or publisher.

The school—or the counselor—is exposed for judgment when telling parents about the abilities and performances of their children. The parents have the right to know. And knowledge in terms they can understand and absorb is what the school must give.

34   *Tests: Misconception, Misuse, and Overuse*

FRANK B. WOMER

Placing a reliable and valid test in the hands of an untrained and ignorant test interpreter can have serious and unfortunate consequences. If sound procedures for developing and evaluating a testing program are not followed, some of the misuses of tests and test data discussed by Womer in the following article may

Reprinted with permission of author from the *Michigan Journal of Secondary Education*, 1961, Vol. 2, pp. 153–161.

result. Several recommendations are implicit in the article. Development of an effective testing program requires highly trained, intelligent, and motivated personnel. It is very often the case that an in-service training program in test administration and interpretation should be undertaken concurrently with the establishment of the testing program. Students as well as faculty need to be informed as to the purposes of the program by specifying the ways in which the results will be used.

We are in a boom period of standardized testing in elementary and secondary schools. Millions of tests are administered each year to pupils at all grade levels —achievement tests, mental ability tests, aptitude tests, and interest inventories, as well as several other types of tests and inventories. Some of these tests are given for college scholarship purposes and some for college admissions purposes. Title V of the National Defense Education Act has stimulated, and in some instances required additions to testing programs at the secondary level. In general, however, these external influences account for a relatively small percentage of the total standardized testing undertaken by a school system.

There are at least two factors which have had a greater impact upon the amount of testing done in the schools than NDEA or college requirements. First, there has been and continues to be a natural growth of standardized testing at all grade levels. Second, the rapid growth of the guidance movement has meant a corresponding rapid growth in testing. This latter influence may well be the most influential one operating, for in many schools the testing program is developed by and operated by guidance personnel.

Inauguration or expansion of a testing program is relatively easy. Decisions made one day can be implemented within a week or two. The only time lag is that of the United States mail in delivering orders for tests and getting test materials from the publisher to the school. Machine methods for test scoring have reduced and, in many cases, eliminated objections that a testing program is a burden upon individual teachers. The school budget and allocation of time for testing are the only real problems to face if an administrator or faculty decides to enlarge the testing program. Thus it is relatively easy to test.

The values of standardized testing, however, cannot be dismissed so quickly. Such values are dependent upon two processes: (1) establishment of proper goals of testing and the development of a testing program to meet those goals, and (2) proper use of test results. Both of these processes are essential to the operation of a successful testing program. Most educators feel, and rightfully so, that the major weakness of testing today is in the area of test use.

Many writers have made this point, and most school administrators are acutely aware of the fact that the ultimate criterion for judging the effectiveness of their testing programs is the correct use of test results. Accumulating test scores in cumulative files is not evidence of test use. Correct use depends upon getting test results into the hands of counselors, teachers, administrators, pupils, and parents and of being sure that each consumer of these results is made knowledgeable enough to interpret them. In this latter statement—"made knowledgeable enough to interpret them"—lies the key to proper test use.

There are a number of ways that test scores are misused or overused and there are a number of misconceptions about tests and test scores that are common enough to warrant special attention. While one could think of innumerable examples of specific errors in test interpretation, the purpose of this article is to point up some of the more common mistakes in order to help increase the knowledgeable use of test results. Ten points have been selected for discussion; others could have been added.

CATEGORIZING A PUPIL AT A SPECIFIC LEVEL OF ACHIEVEMENT OR ABILITY

One of the most common mistakes made by persons unskilled in interpreting test results is the assumption of perfect reliability of a test score. Too often it is assumed that an IQ of 105 represents performance definitely superior to that represented by an IQ of 104 and definitely inferior to that represented by 106. Too often we fail to realize that a test score is best interpreted as a good estimate of the general level of performance, and that it will vary from test to test and from time to time. Test users must accept the concept of variability of test scores over time and over tests. The assessment of human traits and abilities is not at the same level of accuracy as that found in a physics laboratory. It probably is closer to the level of accuracy found in the predictions of weather, in which temperature predictions are generally within a few degrees of actual temperatures, but in which differences of ten or more degrees are common enough to be remembered vividly by critics.

Another aspect of this assumption of greater accuracy than actually prevails is the use of a single estimate (test score) to predict human performance. It is generally wise to insist on having two or three reading scores, or two or three aptitude scores, before putting much confidence in them. This is a direct result of the unreliability present in all test scores. If a pupil receives percentiles of 35 and of 40 on arithmetic tests given in two different years, one can have greater confidence that his level of achievement in arithmetic is in the average range than if only one of these scores is available.

CONFUSION OF NORMS AND STANDARDS

Norms are test scores which tell us the level of performance attained by an average or typical group of pupils. Standards represent human judgments of the level of performance that "should be" attained by a group of pupils. A test user should not assume that "typical" pupil performance is automatically the "proper" level of performance for pupils in a particular school system. It is reasonable, of course, to assume that pupils in many school systems will tend to perform at a level close to the level of test norms. In others, however, it is reasonable to assume that pupils will perform at a higher level or at a lower level.

One occasionally finds a test user who completely fails to grasp the conception of what a test norm is. Since a test norm represents "typical" performance, then of necessity half of the pupils in a typical or average group will have scores at or below the average score. If a teacher of a typical group of pupils finds that 40 percent of his pupils are below grade level in reading, he is to be congratulated. In the norm group for whatever test is being used, 50 percent of all the pupils were at or below grade level. The assumption that all pupils in a class should be at grade level is patently impossible, unless one knows that the poorest achieving pupil in one's class is in the top 50 percent of all pupils his own age or grade.

ASSUMPTION THAT TEST SCORES PREDICT SUCCESS OR FAILURE FOR INDIVIDUAL PUPILS

One way that test results often are overused is based on the assumption that a particular score or series of scores does in fact predict success or failure with unfailing accuracy. It is well established that students who succeed in colleges of engineering generally make high scores on numerical ability tests. Yet it is not correct to conclude from such data that Johnny, with a 50th percentile rank on a test of numerical ability, will not succeed in an engineering course. It is correct to conclude that of every one hundred students with numerical ability scores the same as Johnny's only a small percentage will succeed in an engineering curriculum. The test score does provide information of a probability type; it enables a student or parent or counselor to know the odds for success or failure. It is a well-known fact that long shots occasionally win the Kentucky Derby, but year in, year out the favorites generally win.

It is not unusual for two counselors to look at the same test scores for an individual pupil and to come to somewhat different conclusions. For this reason it is well to face the fact that while test scores do provide information that can be helpful in decision making, the decisions for courses of action are made by human beings, not by the scores.

Added to this overuse of test scores is the failure of some people to utilize all pertinent data available about a student when test scores are known. To allow test scores to outweigh all other judgmental data is a misuse of these scores; to ignore test scores in favor of other judgmental data also is a misuse of these scores.

DETERMINATION OF VOCATIONAL GOALS

"Mary's scores from a clerical speed and accuracy test and from a spelling test are only average. Therefore, Mary should not consider secretarial work as a career possibility." Or, "Since Jim's interest profile shows high scores in 'Scientific' and 'Social Service' he should elect a pre-med course in college." How often can vocational counseling be summed up in just such simple statements? It is so easy to make the jump from test score to occupation, and it seems so logical that this type of interpretation should be accurate. Unfortunately, the predictive validity of test scores in high school for success in specific occupations is not good enough to permit such interpretations. Most evidence of the predictive efficiency of test scores relates those scores to academic curricula. We can say with a fair degree of accuracy that certain patterns of test scores predict fairly well in different curricula. That is the type of validity data that is generally available.

The use of test scores in vocational counseling should tend to open doors of possible occupations rather than close them. Again, presenting the relationship between test scores and occupational areas on a probability basis can be helpful, and is certainly more accurate than making the assumption that certain test scores assure success in one field and failure in another.

ASSUMPTION THAT INTELLIGENCE AND ACHIEVEMENT ARE SEPARATE AND DISTINCT

Here are two sample questions from standardized tests:

1. Extraneous
   a. extra   b. foreign   c. transparent   d. noisy

2. Make *indelible* means
   a. indistinct   b. permanent   c. purple   d. identical

Both are vocabulary items. One of them is taken from a widely used intelligence test (*California Test of Mental Maturity*) and the other from a widely used achievement battery (*Iowa Tests of Educational Development*). Vocabulary items measure the learned meanings of words; vocabulary items are our best single measure of general intelligence or scholastic aptitude. Arithmetic items and general information items are also found in both achievement tests and intelligence tests. It is true, of course, that some items suitable for an intelligence test (number series, verbal analogies) are not good measures of achievement. It also is true that many direct measures of achievement (capitalization, punctuation, spelling) are not good measures of intellectual potential.

There is considerable overlap between standardized tests of achievement and standardized intelligence tests. One of the important differences between the two is the way the results are used. When analyzing achievement test scores one is generally considering past performance, what has been accomplished. When analyzing intelligence test scores one is generally looking forward to the future, predicting performance.

It is well to keep in mind the fact that intelligence is inferred from achievement. We have no direct measures of intelligence completely divorced from achievement.

ASSUMPTION THAT INTERESTS AND APTITUDES ARE SYNONYMOUS

Probably few users of standardized tests would acknowledge a belief in clearly different domains. Yet how many users of standardized interest inventories can truthfully say that they have never made the jump from a high percentile score in "Persuasive" to the suggestion that Bill probably could succeed in sales activities? To say that Bill seems to be interested in many of the same things that are of interest to people who work in occupations that require influencing other people may be accurate. But to say that Bill will likely succeed in one of these occupations is to make the unwarranted jump from interest to aptitude.

There is evidence that interests and aptitudes are correlated, but not at a level that allows us to predict one from the other with a high degree of accuracy. This is not to say that interest inventories are useless, but their use might well center on their motivational attributes, on their power to stimulate pupil concern over long-range planning.

MISCONCEPTION OF THE MEANINGS OF CERTAIN TYPES OF DERIVED SCORES

Students of education have been and are continuing to be taught that an intelligence quotient is obtained by dividing mental age by chronological age, and that mental age is determined by the test performance of students at different age levels. Yet, as a matter of fact, very few of the IQ's to be found in the cumulative folders of elementary and secondary schools today are quotient scores at all. IQ's are standard scores, just as are z scores, T scores, stanines, College Board scores, and others for almost every widely used intelligence test.

It is true that IQ's originally were quotient scores. But, primarily for statistical reasons, the deviation IQ was developed some years ago and has since met with almost universal adoption. Even the Stanford-Binet test switched to a deviation IQ in 1959. The change from a quotient score to a standard score has not necessitated any drastic change in interpretation. Yet it seems to the writer that test users would be well advised to stop paying lip service to a type of score that no longer exists, and to become familiar with standard scores, the type of scores actually being used with our intelligence tests.

The grade-placement or grade-equivalent score is another type of derived score that is frequently misinterpreted or overused. All too often it is assumed that a grade-placement score is an indication of the grade to which a pupil should be assigned. It does not provide that type of information; it simply tells a user whether a pupil is doing high, average, or low quality work. A percentile rank also provides the same assessment of level of work, yet avoids the danger of overinterpretation. If one wishes to compare a pupil's achievement on two different tests in an achievement battery (e.g., reading level versus arithmetic level), a grade-equivalent score may lead one to an important misinterpretation. Because of the variability (standard deviation) of grade-placement scores from test to test it is possible for a sixth-grade pupil to be at the 90th percentile in both reading and arithmetic, yet receive grade-placement scores of 8.8 in reading and 8.0 in arithmetic.[1] If a teacher sees only the grade placement scores of 8.8 and 8.0 he may assume superiority in reading, whereas the two scores represent equivalent performance. For test-by-test comparisons in elementary-level achievement batteries, percentile scores should be used.

GRADING OR PROMOTING PUPILS

Standardized achievement tests are designed with certain purposes in mind. In general, test authors attempt to identify those skills and understandings that are common to most educational programs. They look for the common denominators; they make no attempt to cover those unique aspects of content that a particular school system may incorporate in its curricula offering. They cannot attempt to reflect a particular teacher's goals for his own pupils. Thus, while achievement test results represent very useful assessment of certain skills and understandings that are common to many classrooms, they should not be used to replace a teacher's own assessment devices.

In many schools standardized achievement tests are given toward the beginning of the school year. They are used to look ahead rather than to look back, to diagnose rather than to evaluate or grade. In those schools that use standardized achievement tests at the end of the year, it may be interesting for a teacher to compare the results with his own judgments. It is not wise for the test results to be used to replace his judgments, in either grading or promotion.

JUDGING EFFECTIVENESS OF INSTRUCTION

Just as standardized tests are not designed to be used for grading pupils, they are not designed to be used for grading teachers. Many of the outcomes of classroom instruction cannot be programmed in standardized tests. Those that can be programmed in tests may not be meaningful because of different emphases, different content, and different grade placement in a particular school.

Of special concern is the attitude engendered in teachers in a school attempting to assess instruction through achievement tests. When test results are used to judge teachers, teachers soon learn to teach for the tests.

It is interesting to note that in some instances teachers even feel compelled to "teach for" ability tests. They somehow feel that it isn't respectable to turn in a set of IQ scores for filing in a cumulative record unless all or almost all of them are at least 100. Such a feeling, of course, is based on a misconception of the meaning of intelligence. A teacher may be cutting his own throat with such high scores, for if his pupils all are above average in ability, they may be expected to show equally high achievement levels.

---

[1] *Iowa Tests of Basic Skills*, end-of-year percentile norms for sixth-grade pupils.

COMPARING RESULTS FROM DIFFERENT TESTS

There is a very natural tendency for test users to assume that a language usage score from one test is directly comparable to a language usage score from another test, that an IQ from one test means the same thing as an IQ from another. When making such assumptions one tends to forget two very important characteristics of standardized tests:

1. Test authors do not build their tests on the same specifications, following the same blueprints. Each one develops his own specifications for test construction. There usually is considerable overlap between the plans for a language usage test developed by one author, and the plans developed by another. However, there is never a complete overlap. Scores from two tests measuring the same attribute vary to a certain extent because the test designs vary.

2. The norms for different tests are based upon different groups of pupils. Each test author aims at securing a truly random population of pupils for use in standardizing his test. Each author falls somewhat short of his goal. While it is correct to assume that test norms for two different arithmetic tests are based on groups with considerable overlap in achievement, it is not correct to assume 100 percent overlap.

Thus, two IQ's derived from two different intelligence tests are not exactly equivalent. It has been demonstrated that IQ's can vary as much as 5 or 10 points between different tests for no other reason than that they are different tests.

Sometimes one hears this objection: "But how can IQ's be different from different tests? I thought that all good intelligence tests correlated well with each other." It is true that the correlation between different intelligence tests are generally sizable, and many times are almost as high as the reliability of the separate tests. Such correlations do not guarantee comparability of norms. Such correlations simply say that pupils taking the different tests will tend to get scores putting them in the same relative rank order but not with the same scores. For example, suppose one were to take a set of IQ's (or any other test score) and add 50 points to each score. The correlation between the original IQ's and the new scores would be perfect, yet the two sets of scores would be 50 points apart.

As was mentioned earlier, we are in the middle of a boom period of testing. If the users of tests do a good job of interpreting the results for the improvement of our understanding of boys and girls and for the improvement of instruction, the boom will level off on a satisfactory plateau of test use. If the users of test results fall into the various misuses, overuses, and misconceptions that are possible, the boom will most certainly be followed by a "bust."

It is the thesis of this article that the consumers of test scores must be thoroughly conversant with proper methods of test use and must studiously avoid misuses, overuses, and misconceptions.

"A little knowledge is a dangerous thing."

IX

APPLICATION OF TESTS
IN PREDICTION AND
DECISION MAKING

So much that we do, both in our professional and our everyday lives, involves prediction and decision making. Even though much of the time we act without the benefit of quality information which is statistically treated, we still must act. For example, one must decide whether to purchase a particular automobile. Included in his decision making would be predictions concerning cost, comfort, and so on. Even though these predictions are based on rather casual information and procedures, the decision still must be made. The articles which follow may better enable the reader to handle such informal situations in addition to those instances when the information and procedures are of a more formal nature.

If decisions need making, should information be combined statistically, i.e. by a precise set of rules, or should one subjectively combine test data and additional information according to his "clinical" judgment? Often the stand is taken that the merits of the statistical approach are only practical, i.e., while there is a saving of time and money the results are inferior. The studies that have been done (see, for example, the summary of research by Meehl, 1954) indicate the "statistical" approach to be at least as good as the "clinical" approach.

The articles included in this chapter were selected to illustrate the problems encountered in prediction and decision making. The first paper, an article by Dr. Sarbin, illustrates, for example, studies in which the statistical and clinical approaches are compared. Not only does his paper typify the comparative results obtained, but it illustrates the methodology of prediction. Dr. Sarbin also refutes a frequent criticism of statistical prediction, i.e., that it is an economical but second-best approach.

The next two articles demonstrate prediction using independent (predictor) variables to predict a single dependent (criterion) variable. Jacobs used intellective predictors while Payne, et al. added non-intellective predictors. These studies, in addition to those summarized by Fishman and Pasanella (1960), indicate the kinds of expectations one may have for intellective predictors, and the hopes that one may have for non-intellective predictors.

In the article by Dr. Paul Horst, the fourth in the chapter, several predictors are simultaneously used to predict several criteria. This additional level of complexity depends and builds upon the single-predictor, single-criterion approach utilized in the previous two articles.

A caution regarding either of the foregoing approaches is introduced in the next paper by Dr. Kazmier. A relationship or a procedure established on one sample may greatly reflect idiosyncracies of that sample. To check on this possibility an independent sample may be drawn from the same population, and the proposed predictor or procedure developed on one sample may be tested on the second. Such cross-validation is desirable before a particular predictor or procedure is recommended for use in making "real-life" decisions.

Often we are interested in *making decisions* rather than merely predicting. Tests provide information from which we may make predictions, but the predictions are frequently made to emphasize the alternatives and probabilities that enter into the making of particular decisions. The article included by Dr. Wickert introduces the reader to decision theory and its application to measurement problems. To reassure the reader, it should be noted that definitions and discussions of the concepts rather than the mathematical procedures are presented.

In the final article of this chapter, a paper by Professor Farr, a prediction problem is treated using decision theory as a basis. One should be stimulated by a knowledge of decision theory to take account of the types of the "losses" that may occur under various possible strategies. Farr's concern for one of the errors often disregarded when selection occurs may stimulate others to estimate these same losses for situations in which they have a direct interest.

In summarizing, the author of the first article presents a justification for and an illustration of prediction using statistical procedures. Then two examples of "simple" prediction are followed by a more complex procedure. After a caution concerning cross-validation is noted, attention is turned to decision theory. A general discussion is followed by an application of the concepts.

35 A Contribution to the Study of Actuarial and Individual Methods of Prediction

THEODORE R. SARBIN

It has long been felt by many case workers, clinicians, and counselors that predictions based on a subjective integration and evaluation of test and non-test data, carefully weighed, will prove more valid than predictions based on the statistical treatment of test data alone. To the chagrin of many, the evidence does not seem to support this view (Meehl, 1954). The following definitive research reported by Dr. Sarbin identifies and analyzes the contribution of a number of significant factors in the prediction of academic achievement. Which technique— the clinical (individual) or the actuarial (statistical)—is more valid, reliable, and efficient? Why do counselors tend to overestimate expected performance? Do the results of the study suggest that the counselor or clinician should not be concerned with prediction? Why?

The object of this paper is to illuminate some of the dark corners of the concept of prediction in the social sciences. In recent years a number of writers have expressed themselves to the effect that the clinical or individual method of predicting behavior is superior to the actuarial or statistical method. In order to determine the soundness of this assertion, one would have to test a hypothesis which might be formulated somewhat as follows: A complete case study will increase the accuracy of prediction of behavior over that obtained from the use of statistical tables based on experience with relatively few variables.

That this hypothesis is too general to submit to experimental analysis becomes immediately evident. First, the term "behavior" here means too much. Second, no standards exist to tell us when a case study is complete. Third, statistical indices and regression equations are not available for the prediction of many forms of behavior. In order to make the hypothesis testable, we must narrow it down to coincide with these requirements: (a) the criterion to be predicted must be subject to definition and measurement; (b) experience tables or regression equations must be available beforehand in order to make statistical predictions; (c) the individuals whose behavior is to be predicted must have had at least one clinical interview; and (d) in addition to the statistically determined variables, other data which are presumably associated with the criterion must be made available to the clinician.

Reprinted and abridged with permission of author and publisher (the University of Chicago Press) from the *American Journal of Sociology*, 1942, Vol. 48, pp. 593–602.

In performing their daily activities clinical counselors[1] make predictions of academic achievement. They provide a situation whereby the general hypothesis may be tested and where the four requirements just mentioned are satisfied. The criterion of success is honor-point ratio, admittedly not a highly reliable measurement, but nonetheless one that is in use in most institutions of higher learning. It is defined as the ratio of credits to grades which have been converted into honor points. Previously derived regression equations were available in which academic achievement is predicted by a combination of two variables: rank in high school graduating class and college aptitude test. All subjects had one interview with the clinician prior to exposure to college classes. Data available to the predictors in addition to the measurement variables were in the form of additional tests of aptitude, achievement, vocational interest, and personality; an eight-page individual record form; a preliminary interviewer's form and impressions; and finally, the counselor's own observations. Now the hypothesis may be stated more specifically: *By virtue of the case-study method employed, clinical counselors' predictions of academic success will be more accurate than those determined from regression equations.* In short, the testing of the hypothesis involves comparing the predictions made from regression equations on two variables to the predictions made by clinicians from an innumerable assortment of variables.

DATA AND RESULTS

Predictions of academic achievement were made for 162 Freshmen—73 men and 89 women—who matriculated in the fall of 1939 in the arts college of the University of Minnesota. These predictions were made by five clinical counselors on the basis of tests, information obtained from the individual record forms, preliminary interviewer's reports, and whatever data might be gathered and summarized in the interview. These were made on an eight-point scale and were correlated with the actual honor-point ratios at the end of the quarter. Statistical predictions were made by the simple process of substituting the values of the two variables—high-school rank and college aptitude test— in the previously derived regression equation and then solving for the most probable honor-point ratio. These predictions were likewise correlated with honor-point ratios. Table 1 gives the results.

TABLE 1. *Coefficients of Correlation Between Actual Honor-Point Ratios and Clinical and Statistical Predictions*

Type of Prediction	Men	Women
Clinical	.35	.69
Statistical	.45	.70

[1] Clinical counselors are clinical psychologists with experience and training in working with college students. Four of the five clinicians in this study possessed the Ph.D. degree or its equivalent. All five had had considerable experience in clinical counseling work with university students.

By comparing the correlations obtained by the clinical method with those obtained from the actuarial method, we see that the correlations are not significantly different. The apparent differences which seem to favor the statistical mode of prediction are shown to be not significant,[2] by the application of Fisher's z test. If the trend were to remain the same with larger numbers of cases, we could safely conclude that statistical predictions are more accurate. At any rate, we can draw the conclusion that the clinical counselors in this study did not predict college achievement more accurately than did the statistical method.

The plausibility of the hypothesis that case-study predictions are superior is not without foundation. Starting from a position which is logically acceptable—namely, that items in the history of an individual are associated with subsequent behavior—clinicians seek to discover and weight items in the client's previous and current history. Information gathered from a survey of an individual's past, then, should have value for predicting events in the future. That two items in the regression equation—high-school rank and college aptitude test—could summarize all the pertinent and significant data that can be used does not seem plausible. So many other variables seem to be untouched. What of strivings, habits of work and play, special aptitudes, emotional patterns, systematic distractions, and the hundreds of other conditions which seem to be related to this complex form of social psychological behavior known as academic achievement? Have these forms of behavior no influence on the criterion other than that accounted for by the two variables? The answer is usually given in the affirmative —that these traits are associated with the criterion of academic achievement and, further, that these subtle factors can be identified and weighted by skillful interviewers.

Some of these so-called "non-intellective" factors were systematically observed in each of the cases in this study by means of the *Strong Vocational Interest Blank* and the *Darley Personal Inventory*. Four measures derived from the Strong blank were correlated with (a) actual achievement and (b) clinical predictions. None of the correlations obtained was significantly different from zero.

That these variables are not associated with college achievement is no new finding. Harris (1940) has reviewed several hundred studies in which tests and estimates of traits other than those determined by aptitude tests were correlated with achievement. His report shows essentially negative results. Whatever the value of these data for predicting other forms of behavior, they seem to be valueless for predicting achievement in college.

The data just mentioned were, of course, only a few of the many kinds that are available to the clinician. The question still remains: Of the wealth of data available to the interviewer, how much is used systematically in making predictions of academic success? The knowledge that all this case-study information

---

[2] The usual significance levels are used in this study. If a difference is significant at the 1 percent point, we consider it a real difference. A difference that is significant to the 5 percent point is suggestive and calls for further experimentation.

is at hand in contrast to the usual few variables in regression equations has led many interviewers to work from a hypothesis such as the following: Approximately correct average weights are applied to test and other data by clinicians—even to the measurements for which regression weights have been determined. If this hypothesis is true, then the multiple correlation coefficients between the criterion and the measures in the regression equation will not differ significantly from the multiple correlation coefficients of the clinical predictions with the same measures.

One method of testing this hypothesis is described below. The two measures in the regression equation can be correlated with actual grade averages and also with clinical predictions. By using R^2, the coefficient of multiple determination, we can make rough comparisons to see the proportion of the variance accounted for by the two measures. First we examine Table 2 to see if the multiple R values appear different.

TABLE 2. *Multiple Correlation Coefficients of Clinical Predictions and of Honor-Point Ratios with High-School Rank and College Aptitude Test*

	Men	Women
Honor-point ratios with high-school rank and aptitude test	.56	.68
Clinical predictions with high-school rank and aptitude test	.70	.81

The coefficients of correlation (R) are easily converted into coefficients of multiple determination by squaring. For men the R^2 values are .31 and .49, respectively. Interpreting, we would say that the high-school rank and college aptitude test account for 31 percent of the variance in honor-point ratio and for 49 percent in the clinical predictions. For women the figures are 40 and 66 percent, respectively. It would appear, then, that at least 18 or 20 percent of the variance in the clinical predictions was due to "other factors" if the two variables had been given efficient weights by the clinicians. However, the previously submitted evidence on the non-intellective factors systematically studied shows that those "other factors" at least have no consistent relationship with the criterion. At this point we may safely say that the clinicians overestimate the contribution of the two measurable variables.

The data, to this point, demonstrate that because they are no more accurate, clinical predictions cannot replace statistical predictions. This leads to the question: If the clinician cannot replace the statistical prediction, can he serve as a complement to it? This question can be answered quite easily by pooling the clinical predictions with the high-school rank and the college aptitude test. By comparing the multiple correlation coefficients with and without the clinical predictions, we can answer the question (see Table 3).

Neither of the differences shown in Table 3 is statistically significant. These results are to be expected in view of the high intercorrelations between clinical

TABLE 3. *Multiple Correlation Coefficients of Honor-Point Ratios with High-School Rank and Aptitude Test and with High-School Rank, Aptitude Test, and Predictions*

	Men	Women
Honor-point ratios with high-school rank and aptitude test	.56	.68
Honor-point ratios with high-school rank, aptitude test, and clinical predictions	.57	.73

predictions and high-school rank and college aptitude test. As reported before, the predictions of the counselors are based for the most part on the same data as go into the regression equation. We can draw the conclusion, then, that clinical predictions do not add to the validity of statistical predictions of academic achievement.

The clinical predictions were made on an eight-step scale. Some clinical workers maintain that predicting involves too much guesswork when dealing with so fine a scale. After all, they say, in practice we make predictions in terms of success or failure, not usually in terms of degree of success or failure. We can do better, they continue, if we can make predictions on a two-point scale where success is considered to be "C" average or better and failure less than "C" average. Success would then be defined as 1.01 honor-point ratio or higher; failure, as any value below.

The predictions of the counselors and those of the regression equation were assembled in fourfold tables, as shown in Table 4. The chi-square method was

TABLE 4. *Analysis of Clinical Predictions and Actuarial Predictions in Terms of Success and Failure*

Prediction	Honor-Point Ratio			
	Men		Women	
	Success	Failure	Success	Failure
Clinical Predictions:				
Success	25	15	49	20
Failure	11	21	2	18
Statistical Predictions:				
Success	27	12	48	14
Failure	10	24	3	24

used to test the hypothesis. The actuarial predictions are taken for the hypothetical or standard distribution; the clinical predictions, as the experimental distribution.

This analysis reveals that for men the clinical predictions are not significantly different from the statistical predictions. For women the chi-square value shows a doubtful difference—favoring the actuarial predictions in regard to accuracy. (When the predictions for the men and the women are combined, the chi-square value is below the 2 percent point of significance, again favoring the actuarial method.) The obvious conclusion is that the interviewers in this experiment could predict academic achievement no better than a simple regression equation, whether the criterion was scaled in eight steps or in two.

Up to now we have considered the validity of clinical predictions as compared with actuarial predictions. Nothing has been said with regard to the reliability or consistency of the two modes of prediction. In the plan of this experiment it was possible to determine the consistency of the predictions by two methods: (a) a case-reader read each case and made predictions independently of the counselors and (b) six months later the same case-reader reread all but his own cases and again made predictions. In this way we had determinations of reliability analogous to the "alternate form" and "test-retest" methods used in computing test reliability.

We must not confuse the reliability of statistical predictions as represented by such a statistic as the standard error of estimate with the consistency of establishing a prediction from a regression equation. Given the equation and the values of the predictor variables, the consistency of such predictions would be represented by a coefficient of unity. That is to say, the regression equation will always yield the same result for a given set of scores. This is not so in the case of clinical predictions where the correlations between counselors' predictions with case-readers' predictions ranged from .64 to .88, and the correlation of one case-reader with himself is only .78, and of counselors with case-readers, .68.

From the point of view of efficiency in the practical situation where predictions serve as the basis for employment or college admissions, the regression equation is to be preferred. The margin of error is known for the regression equation (S.E.$_{est.}$) ; for clinical predictions the margin of error varies from one interviewer to another, and this error is added to that which is inherent in the data used. In terms of consistency of prediction, then, the actuarial is to be preferred to the clinical method.

None of the previous evidence provides detailed information with regard to the nature of errors committed by the clinicians in making predictions. To determine in detail the causes for clinical predictions being less accurate is beyond the scope of the present paper. The experimental design does allow, however, for comparisons to be made of two important statistics, namely, the mean and the variance. In order to point the way to better predictions, we should know, for example, whether interviewers overestimate or underestimate in their predictions, and whether their predictions follow the same dispersion as the criterion.

The questions to be answered are two: "Are the means of the clinical predictions underestimations or overestimations of the actual honor-point ratios?" and "Are the means of the actuarial predictions underestimations or overestimations?"

It was found that the interviewers significantly overestimated the college achievement of the group studied. The means of the statistical predictions, however, were not significantly different from the criterion. We may conclude, then, that on the average clinical interviewers overestimate the grades their clients will receive.

One more question: "Are the dispersions of the clinical predictions and of the statistical predictions less than the dispersions of the honor-point ratios?" This question is stimulated by the claim of some advocates of the case-study method of prediction that the regression equation demonstrates the well-known phenomenon of statistical regression—predictions are therefore bunched too close to the mean. The case-study method can allow for this and make predictions which follow the distribution curve of the criterion. If we can show that the variance of the clinical predictions is close to the variance of the criterion, then the case-study method has a remarkably unique property. We know beforehand that the distribution of predictions from the regression equation will not be the same as the distribution of the criterion, although its form will be similar.

The distributions of both the statistical and the clinical predictions were found to be significantly different from the distribution of the honor-point ratios.

The reasons for the decreased variance in the clinical predictions are difficult to establish. One suggestion is that the interviewers wanted to "play safe." The closer to the mean, the safer the prediction. As a matter of fact, the interviewers used the uppermost two intervals only a few times; the lowest two, hardly at all.

SUMMARY OF RESULTS

1. Many well-known social scientists maintain, expressly or by implication, that the case-study method of prediction is superior to the actuarial method. Evidence is submitted in this study which shows that clinical predictions of academic achievement, made on an eight-step scale, are not more accurate than statistical predictions.

2. Factors such as interest, inferred level of aspiration, and personality traits as measured in this experiment appear not to be related to achievement in college. Furthermore, clinical interviewers do not use these measures systematically, so that actually they give little or no weight to them in making predictions.

3. In formulating predictions, counselors rely for the most part on rank in high-school graduating class and college aptitude test results—the same variables in the regression equation—although many different kinds of data are available.

4. Case-study predictions—at least on the grounds of efficiency—should not be substituted for actuarial predictions. As a complement to the actuarial predictions, the clinical predictions add nothing.

5. When cast in the form of success-failure instead of the eight-interval scale, clinical predictions are shown to be no more valid than the more easily obtained statistical predictions.

6. The reliability of clinical predictions varies from .64 to .88 (correlation between interviewer and case-reader). Predictions made by the same case-reader from two readings of the same cases correlated to .78.

7. Clinical predictions overestimate the criterion by about a third of a letter-grade; the differences are statistically reliable. Statistical predictions do not overestimate the criterion by any significant amount.

8. As expected, the variance of the predictions made by statistical methods is significantly less than the variance of the criterion (a result of the phenomenon of statistical regression). The variance of the predictions made by the case-study method is likewise significantly less than the variance of the criterion.

Any jury sitting in judgment on the case of the clinical versus the actuarial methods must on the basis of efficiency and economy declare overwhelmingly in favor of the statistical method for predicting academic achievement. Even though the small differences which uniformly favor the actuarial method are not statistically reliable, the factor of time and efficiency will decide in favor of the regression equation with its known margin of error.

DISCUSSION AND IMPLICATIONS

What are the implications of the findings as they relate to the more specific problem of prediction in academic achievement? Since prediction serves as an aid to the control of events, the results of prediction studies can be utilized in the selection and distribution procedures within institutions of higher learning. Admissions officers can decide on the basis of prediction tables derived from regression equations at what level of ability to accept students. Some have argued that the clinical interview must supplement the test procedures so that so-called "intangible" factors which go into achievement may be appropriately weighted. From the evidence of this study this clinical step is unnecessary. Predictions of college grades can be made with as much accuracy by the simple device of placing a straightedge on an alignment chart. In short, a competent statistical clerk can make predictions as well as a highly trained clinical worker.

Can we generalize and say that this set of procedures can be used in industrial selection as well? Not only on the basis of data presented here but also because of the logic of prediction is the answer in the affirmative. Some years ago Viteles (1925) submitted arguments against the actuarial approach, which were logically controverted by Freyd (1925). Notwithstanding, the so-called "clinical" interpretations of objective measurement have continued unchecked. If the trained psychologist, sociologist, vocational counselor, or case-worker can tell any better than a test whether a man is fit for a particular job, he should make explicit the factors upon which he disregards the objective measurements and then submit his predictions to experimental validation. Unless checked by statistical studies, the case-study method in the social sciences will become intellectually bankrupt.

May we go further and declare that statistical procedures shall be substituted for clinical procedures in the diagnosis and treatment of all behavior disorders? If we interpret the statistical method more broadly than the administration of mental tests, then we can again answer in the affirmative. As a matter of fact,

Wittman has presented evidence which fully supports this proposition. She compared the prognoses of patients in a mental hospital made by attending psychiatrists with prognoses made from a well-constructed rating scale. The results showed the statistical predictions to be superior to the "intuitive" judgments of the psychiatrists.

Realistic clinicians and case-workers know that their predictions are made on the basis of an informal statistical method. Those who hold that the case-study method can do more than the statistical method, even in the prediction of human behavior problems, must submit evidence. The *onus probandis* seems to fall upon those who advocate the individual mode of prediction.

A word is in order here relevant to the clinical method as used in this study. Predictions were made on the basis of the tests and other written data together with information gathered in the face-to-face interview. The author would agree with any critic who says that more interviewing would probably produce better predictions. The better predictions, however, would be made on the basis of the frequency interpretation of probability—the same basis upon which the regression equation is built. As the number of clinical periods is increased, the number of observations is likewise increased. Similar observations are ordered to a class, and the interviewer then makes a statistical prediction on the basis of many instances. It is conceivable that the clinician might discover certain traits which are not apparent from one interview. But he can only test the adequacy of his deductions by submitting his generalizations to test—by predicting future behavior and by comparing his predictions with events as they occur.

If advocates of the case study can identify traits, dispositions, attitudes, or motivations, then let these be put in the form of a hypothesis and tested. If predictions from the hypothesis are shown to correspond to events, then the traits identified can be included with other measures in a regression equation. This is considered by the author to be one of the chief functions of the clinician: the formulating of hypotheses to be tested by him or by others in the field or in the laboratory. Another important function is that of serving as an agent of treatment. By the same statistical method we can predict which treatment method is most appropriate for a given symptom complex. Where the treatment involves a second person, such as play therapy, relationship therapy, group therapy, etc., the interviewer has a definite role. In diagnosis, however, his role is a secondary one. Except as he gathers data to include in the formal or informal regression equation, his diagnoses can be made from experience tables. If such an item as "Does your father beat your mother?" were found to have predictive value, then the clinician would serve to ask the question and to record the answer. The weight it would have in the regression equation, however, would be determined by considerations other than what the clinician intuitively thought the weight should be. This conclusion follows from evidence presented elsewhere which demonstrates that a diagnosis without a future referent has no utility so far as treatment or control is concerned. As soon as a diagnosis is made meaningful, it takes the form—implicitly or explicitly—of a prediction. As shown by Reichenbach (1938), predictions are expressed as probability statements. Only after statistical manipulations have taken place, either informally, generalizing from clinical experience, or formally, regression equations, can we derive such a probability statement.

The implications of these paragraphs for psychologists and other social scientists may be summarized:

1. Statistical predictions, being more easily determined and at least as accurate, are to be preferred to predictions made by the clinical method.
2. If clinical predictions can be shown to be more valid, the data which are used by the clinician should be made explicit, so that they may be quantified and included in prediction tables.
3. One of the chief tasks of the clinician is to formulate hypotheses to be tested by experimental methods.
4. Another task is that of serving as an agent of treatment.
5. Diagnosis is a secondary function in that predictive diagnoses are more readily made by the actuarial method; the clinician, however, may collect data called for by his formal or crude equations.

For the training of case-workers and clinicians this study has an important contribution. If the proposition is accepted that the diagnostic function belongs appropriately to the statistician (since meaningful diagnoses are predictions of future behavior), then the clinician-in-training or apprentice case-worker will spend more of his training time in two activities: (a) learning from empirical studies which treatment devices are appropriate to certain symptom complexes and (b) learning how to administer the various types of therapy. In addition, he must learn how as an interviewer he can be a diagnostic tool. But the diagnosis itself should be made from experience tables, regression equations, or similar mathematical aids.

36   *Aptitude and Achievement Measures in Predicting High School Academic Success*

JAMES N. JACOBS

Probably the most frequently made application of tests is in the area of achievement prediction. If an educational organization can predict future success with a high degree of consistency, activities such as selection, classification, and evaluation can be carried on with greater efficiency. The following study by Jacobs is

Reprinted and abridged with permission of author and publisher from The *Personnel and Guidance Journal*, 1959, Vol. 37, pp. 334–341.

representative of the kinds of academic forecasting frequently undertaken at the high school and college level. It should be noted that it is a truly predictive study, in that a three-year period elapsed between test administration and gathering of criteria. The effectiveness of several of the tests is, therefore, quite remarkable. Many similar types of studies reported in the literature are actually "status" or "concurrent" validity studies, although the term "predictive" may have been used in the title and liberally throughout the article.

How can you account for the high validity of the Arithmetic Proficiency test in predicting the seemingly unrelated criteria of grades in foreign language and social studies? Are the grade criteria more predictable than the test criteria? How can you account for the marked sex differences in and above the reasons offered by the author? Are the two types of criteria measuring the same thing? In responding to this question, the reader may wish to integrate the material presented in the Brogden and Taylor article of Chapter IV.

This study was inaugurated to evaluate the effectiveness of certain aptitude and achievement tests in predicting academic success in the Cincinnati public high schools, since curricular, administrative, and instructional decisions are often based on information of this kind. The particular problem of this study was to evaluate seven specific measures of aptitude and achievement in predicting general academic success and success in eight high school subject areas: English, social studies, science, mathematics, foreign language, industrial arts, home economics, and business education.

DESCRIPTION OF TESTS AND SAMPLE

During the school year 1952–1953, Grade 8 (the senior class of 1956–1957) was given the *Terman-McNemar Test of Mental Ability*, Form C, and the English Proficiency and Arithmetic Proficiency tests[1] of *Metropolitan Achievement Tests*. These are a regular part of the city-wide testing program conducted by the Division of Appraisal Services of the Department of Instruction. In addition, during the same year this group was given the Verbal Reasoning, Numerical Ability, Mechanical Reasoning, and Language Usage subtests of the *Differential Aptitude Tests*, Form A, to determine experimentally their possible value in the testing program. In May of their junior year these pupils were given the *Essential High School Content Battery*, which was used as an alternate criterion of academic success. All tests except the English and Arithmetic Proficiency tests were administered by trained examiners.

From analyses of co-variance of grade point averages (GPA) and scholastic

---

[1] These are special editions of the *Metropolitan Achievement Tests*, Advanced Battery, Form R, published under special cover for the Cincinnati Public Schools by Harcourt, Brace, & World, Inc.

ability scores (*American Council on Education Psychological Examination*) in each of six comprehensive public high schools in Cincinnati, three schools were selected whose marking practices were sufficiently consistent in relation to ability to justify pooling of the senior pupil populations. These pupils were believed to be representative of the Cincinnati 12th grade population as a whole. From these schools a sample of 595 pupils was taken, consisting of 266 boys and 329 girls. The correlation data presented in this study were derived from this sample, treating boys and girls separately.

THE CRITERIA

For purposes of this study, high school academic success was "measured" in two ways: by the use of grade point averages, and by the *Essential High School Content Battery* (EHSCB). The former is the usual subjective teacher rating of pupil performance as represented by marks; the latter, a standardized achievement test, represents an objective estimate of student achievement.

General academic success was measured by averaging the year-end marks made by each pupil in all the subjects taken in high school (except subjects giving only one-half credit, such as health and physical education). The grades given in subjects taken during the senior year were estimated from the first two marking period reports. In general, the total grade point average (TGPA) consisted of the average of from 15 to 18 marks in various subjects taken during high school, here defined as grades 9 through 12.

Academic success in subject areas was measured by averaging marks in three or more courses taken within a subject area. In other words, a pupil must have majored in a subject area before he could have a GPA in that area. A major may consist of any combination of three or more courses taken in a subject area. For example, a science major may consist of a combination of biology, physics, and chemistry, or general science, physiology, and botany, etc.

All marks were obtained from the school files of each of the six high schools. Since all predictor tests were administered before the pupils entered the 9th grade, a true prediction situation existed over at least a three-year period of time.

PREDICTION OF GENERAL ACADEMIC SUCCESS

PREDICTION OF TOTAL GRADE POINT AVERAGE ■ The degree of relationship between each aptitude and achievement test predictor used and TGPA is seen in Table 1.

Considering the complexity of the criterion, the relationships shown in Table 1 are high, particularly between the Arithmetic Proficiency, Numerical Ability, and Terman-McNemar predictors with the criterion. For both boys and girls these three tests correlated highest with the total grade point average criterion. For boys the correlations ranged from .310 to .657, while for girls the range was

TABLE 1. *Correlations Between the Predictor Variables and Total Grade Point Average for 12th Grade Boys and Girls, Cincinnati Public Schools, 1956–1957*

Predictor Variable		Boys N=266	Girls N=329
Verbal Reasoning		.510	.596
Numerical Ability		.613	.636
Mechanical Reasoning	DAT	.310	.437
Spelling ⎫ Language		.438	.582
Sentences ⎭ Usage		.544	.588
Terman-McNemar IQ		.582	.611
English Proficiency ⎫	MAT	.539	.638
Arithmetic Proficiency ⎭		.657	.716

between .437 and .716. There were no significant differences between the correlations of boys and girls shown in Table 1 except for the Spelling Test.

An important aspect of Table 1 is the general consistency of higher relationships existing between the predictor test variables and criterion variable for girls more than for boys. In no case are the correlations higher for boys. In addition, it will be noticed that a ranking of the "validity" coefficients for girls and boys results in a very similar ordering. Since these data were obtained independently, the latter fact leads to an acceptance of the statistics as reliable measures of the relationships.

Regarding the higher relationships among girls, a probable explanation lies in the fact that the boys represent a more homogeneous group than do the girls. Since correlation is a function of group variability, the correlations would be expected to be somewhat higher among girls than among boys. A possible explanation of this is the larger number of drop-outs among boys than among girls. Since these drop-outs largely are among the boys of lower academic caliber, the remaining group is not only relatively homogeneous but also represents the academically better pupils on the whole.

PREDICTION OF THE COMPOSITE SCORE OF EHSCB ■ The composite score of EHSCB represents the median among performance scores on the four subtests: mathematics, science, social studies, and English. By comparison, the total grade point average is a more complex and inclusive composite of performance than the EHSCB criterion. The latter is more a composite of the "fundamental" or "tool" academic subjects.

Again, it was found without exception that the correlations are higher among girls than among boys. In only two instances, however, were the differences significant, namely, for the Spelling and the Terman-McNemar predictors. The best three predictors are the Terman-McNemar, English Proficiency, and Arithmetic Proficiency tests for both boys and girls. It is interesting to note the fact that the best two predictors of total grade point average, the Terman-McNemar and the Arithmetic Proficiency tests, are also two of the best three predictors of the EHSCB criterion. The data suggest that this criterion is generally consistent with the total grade point average criterion. This idea was partially confirmed by correlating these two criteria: for boys $r = .744$, and for girls $r = .765$. Considering the differences in these two criteria, their relationship is fairly high.

For boys the correlations ranged from .455 to .803, while for girls the correlations ranged from .557 to .858. On the whole it was found that the *Differential Aptitude Test* predictors were relatively better predictors of the EHSCB criterion than they were of the TGPA criterion.

The relationships between the test predictors and the EHSCB criterion are higher than those of TGPA. This probably is due to the greater objectivity and reliability of a test score over a grade point average. It is also to be expected that a test is more likely to correlate highly with another test than it is with teachers' ratings as reflected in school marks because of their common limitations of sampling performance.

It was found that the Terman-McNemar and the Arithmetic Proficiency tests produced a multiple correlation of .703 and .742 for boys and girls, respectively, in the prediction of total grade point averages. In predicting the composite score of EHSCB, these same two tests produced multiple correlations of .858 and .875 for boys and girls, respectively. This degree of relationship is unusually high, even though it is based on the correlation between test scores. The multiple correlations derived from using all eight predictor tests were not found to be significantly higher than the two test predictor combinations above.

PREDICTION OF ACADEMIC SUCCESS IN SUBJECT AREAS

PREDICTION OF GRADE POINT AVERAGES ▪ Direct correlations of each test predictor variable with each high school subject area within which pupils have selected majors are seen in Table 2.

The most striking aspect of Table 2 is the generally higher relationships between the test predictors and GPA's among girls than among boys. This phenomenon was noted also in the prediction of TGPA's.

In determining the significance of difference of correlations between the sexes, the greatest differences in prediction were found in the subject areas of English and foreign language: In the case of English, only two of the eight test predictors (Verbal Reasoning and Spelling) failed to show a significant difference between the sexes.

In the area of foreign language, the Spelling, Sentences, Terman-McNemar, and English Proficiency tests showed a significant differential prediction. It is interesting to note that these predictors are all measures of verbal facilities. These same tests failed to prove significantly different from zero correlation with foreign language achievement of boys. In general, the predictor tests showed substantial correlations with foreign language achievement of girls.

TABLE 2. *Correlations Between the Predictor Variables and Grade Point Averages in Each of the Subject Areas for 12th Grade Boys and Girls, Cincinnati Public Schools, 1956–1957*

Subject Area	Sex	N	*Verb Reas.*	*Num. Abil.*	*Mech. Reas.*	*Spelling*	*Sent.*	*Terman IQ*	*Eng. Prof.*	*Arith. Prof.*
English	Boys	266	.496	.499	.125	.448	.455	.520	.514	.520
	Girls	329	.568	.661	.411	.570	.584	.687	.647	.690
Social Studies	Boys	171	.485	.495	.199	.361	.481	.553	.528	.538
	Girls	209	.554	.554	.389	.504	.551	.623	.595	.633
Science	Boys	173	.493	.527	.438	.308	.501	.541	.509	.627
	Girls	137	.570	.582	.422	.526	.524	.651	.590	.663
Mathematics	Boys	107	.379	.495	.271	.401	.428	.433	.408	.610
	Girls	71	.566	.654	.506	.624	.566	.622	.617	.671
Foreign Language	Boys	33	.051*	.485	.219*	.032*	.019*	.023*	.046*	.411
	Girls	62	.421	.633	.219	.637	.498	.529	.517	.628
Industrial Arts	Boys	74	.268	.222*	.194*	.322	.307	.307	.290	.364
Home Economics	Girls	49	.359	.486	.167*	.215*	.415	.511	.589	.409
Business Education	Girls	187	.390	.525	.330	.403	.371	.466	.456	.571

* These correlations are *not* significantly different from zero at the five percent level of significance.

In only two other instances, namely, the Mechanical Reasoning Test in predicting social studies grades and the Spelling Test in predicting science grades, did the differences in the correlations between boys and girls prove to be statistically significant. Although only 12 out of 40 differences were statistically significant, the cumulative probabilities would reflect a tendency for girls to be a more predictable group than boys with the type of tests and criteria used in this study.

An examination of Table 2 will reveal that in 9 out of 13 cases the Arithmetic Proficiency Test is the best single predictor of GPA's. This instrument is one of the best three predictors in every instance except in the case of predicting home economics GPA's. The Terman-McNemar, Numerical Ability, Spelling, and English Proficiency tests proved to be the best single predictors in the subject areas of social studies (girls), foreign language (boys and girls), and home economics (girls), respectively.

It may seem surprising that an arithmetic achievement test is among the best predictors in areas such as English, social studies, and foreign language, since in terms of course content at least this relationship is not apparent.

The subject areas where the highest correlations were found are English, social studies, science, and mathematics, or what are commonly called the tool subjects. Every correlation presented in these subject areas is statistically significant.

PREDICTION OF EHSCB CRITERIA ■ As was the case in the prediction of general academic success, scores on the *Essential High School Content Battery* also were considered as alternate criteria of success. Because this test measures achievement in only four subject areas (English, mathematics, social studies, and science), it could be used for comparative purposes and as an alternate criterion in these four areas only.

In general the relationships are high, especially when compared to the results of similarly reported investigations. As was the case in the prediction of grade point averages, the prediction of girls' achievement is consistently higher than that for boys. Another notable aspect was the consistently higher prediction of achievement using the EHSCB criteria than was found when grade point averages were used as the criteria of academic success.

Although the correlations with the EHSCB criteria were higher, it is interesting to note that a ranking of the subject areas in order of their predictability is similar with both criteria. Thus, English is in general the area of highest prediction, followed by science, mathematics, and social studies. *Terman-McNemar Intelligence Test* is one of the best predictors in each of the subject areas for both boys and girls. The English Proficiency Test seems to be the second best all-around predictor, followed by the Verbal Reasoning Test, the Arithmetic Proficiency Test, and the Numerical Ability Test.

In comparing the predictability of the two types of criteria, one finds a general difference in the type of predictors which are most effective. For example, in comparing these four subject areas only, if the predictors were dichotomized into a "number" or quantitative group and another group measuring "verbal" abilities, it would be found that for the prediction of grade point averages the "number" tests, i.e., the Arithmetic Proficiency Test and the Numerical Ability Test, are generally the better predictors. Conversely, the remaining "verbal" type tests, particularly the Verbal Reasoning and the English Proficiency tests, are generally better predictors of the EHSCB criteria. If one assumes that verbal (primarily reading) skills are to a large extent the factors being measured by the typical paper-and-pencil achievement test, then a logical basis for the higher relationships between the verbal tests and EHSCB criteria is formed. The EHSCB criterion, measuring verbal skills and abilities to a large extent, finds as its best predictors those instruments measuring these very abilities. On the other hand, grade point averages, apparently based to a larger extent upon quantitative abilities, find as their best predictors those tests measuring number abilities. The Terman-McNemar Test is one of the best predictors for both of the criteria. Since verbal abilities are inherent in both criteria, and since Terman-McNemar is a verbal intelligence test, it probably reflects a general intelligence factor permeating all achievement. The correlations between both criteria are shown in Table 3.

The coefficients shown in Table 3 express moderately high relationships between the EHSCB criteria and the GPA criteria. It is seen that the highest relationship between the two criteria is in mathematics. A possible explanation is that this area is more factorially pure than the other subject areas.

The lowest relationship between the criteria is in social studies. Considering the difference between the two criteria, however, all the relationships shown in Table 3 are high, ranging from .589 to .749. By comparing the multiple R's

TABLE 3. *Correlations Between EHSCB Criteria and Grade Point Averages in Corresponding Subject Areas for 12th Grade Boys and Girls, Cincinnati Public Schools, 1956–1957*

| | Boys | | Girls | |
Variables	N	r	N	r
EHSCB English Test vs. English Grade Point Averages	266	.613	329	.734
EHSCB Social Studies Test vs. Social Studies Grade Point Averages	171	.677	209	.722
EHSCB Science Test vs. Science Grade Point Averages	173	.589	137	.678
EHSCB Mathematics Test vs. Mathematics Grade Point Averages	107	.736	51	.749

derived from the best two predictor test combinations, usually found to be the Terman-McNemar and Arithmetic Proficiency tests and the combination of all eight predictor tests, it was found that the former predictive combinations were not significantly lower than the latter.

CONCLUSIONS

In view of the findings of this study, the following conclusions seem warranted:

1. In predicting general academic success, the Arithmetic Proficiency Test proved to be the best predictor of total grade point average, while the Terman-McNemar Test was the best single predictor of the composite score of EHSCB.

2. The subject areas in which the highest prediction occurred were English, mathematics, science, and social studies, or what are commonly known as "tool" studies. Vocational subject areas were predicted less well.

3. In general, quantitative measures seemed to be better predictors of grade point averages in subject areas, while verbal tests were better predictors of the EHSCB criteria. The Terman-McNemar Test proved to be a good predictor of success for both types of criteria.

4. One the whole, girls represent a more predictable group than do boys.

5. *Terman-McNemar Test of Mental Ability* (a verbal general intelligence test) and the Arithmetic Proficiency Test (a "quantitative" measure of mathematics achievement in *Metropolitan Achievement Tests*) make an effective pair of predictors of high school achievement.

37   Academic Achievement Motivation: Development of Objective Measures and Their Application to High School and College Samples

DAVID A. PAYNE, WILLIAM W. FARQUHAR, AND ROBERT F. JASTRAB

Over the years there have been innumerable achievement prediction studies, and the results have often been inconsistent and even contradictory. All manner and form of independent variables have been used singly and in combination. A cursory review of the literature indicates the wide variety of measurement approaches have been used, e.g., aptitude and past achievement, parental attitudes, study habits, level of aspiration, biographical data, interests, socioeconomic status, and personality factors. A recent book by Lavin (1965) presents a cogent review of the theoretical and practical problems involved in prediction studies.

In the following paper, prepared specifically for this book, an attempt is made to bring both theory and modern measurement techniques to bear in the development of an instrument which will have greater relevance to academic criteria than devices previously available.[1]

In what ways have content, criterion-related and construct validity been investigated in this research? Why was cross-validation important in this study? What kinds of future validity and reliability studies are suggested by the data?

It is only within the last decade and a half that any concerted effort has been put forth in investigating the predictive efficiency of various motivational measures relative to academic criteria. The paucity of definitive motivational studies can probably be attributed to the failure of psychometric technology to keep pace with theoretical developments. McClelland, et al. (1953), have presented both theoretical and psychometric material related to the measurement of achievement motivation. The appearance of these materials has stimulated predictive studies related to academic achievement criteria, but these studies have generally yielded erratic results. Investigators have reported both strong positive relationships between McClelland's instrument and grade point averages (Morgan, 1952; Weiss, Wertheimer, & Groesbeck, 1960), and non-significant relationships (Lowell, 1952; Shaw, 1961). The inconclusive results might be explained in the light of data reported by Krumboltz and Farquhar (1957) which cast doubt on both the reliability and validity of McClelland's modified *Thematic Apperception Test (TAT)* instrument. It is reasonable to assume that the erratic results using the *TAT* instrument can be traced to the measurement problems inherent in pro-

---

[1] For a more detailed report of the theory, and data related to the high school sample of the present study, see Farquhar, 1963, and Farquhar & Payne, 1963.

jective devices, i.e., lack of stability, consistency, and objectivity in scoring, which are due for the most part to the small number of items in the devices. These problems are further compounded by the fact that the McClelland group conceived of achievement motivation as a broad construct. The prediction of academic achievement, which is a narrowly defined criterion, would presumably suffer as a consequence of this broadness of definition. An attempt was made to take account of the above problems in the present investigation.

The purpose of this paper is to present data concerning the internal consistency and the construct and criterion-related validity (using high school and college samples) of a recently developed theory-based battery of subtests (the M-Scales) purporting to measure academic achievement motivation.

THEORY

Recent analyses by Michael, Jones, and Trembly (1959) and Mitchell (1961) have indicated the highly complex nature of the achievement motivation construct. No single factor could be identified in these studies which would adequately describe the motivational phenomena. It seemed logical then to develop a battery of instruments, each of which could make a unique contribution to the measurement of motivation (Farquhar, 1963).

For purposes of this research, academic motivation was defined as *a combination of forces which initiate, direct, and sustain behavior toward a scholarly goal.*

For conceptual reasons theory was assumed to be tripartite, with focusing, predictive, and integrative levels. The present study was concerned with the first two levels. At Level One (focusing), past studies were examined to pinpoint sufficiently refined concepts for testing null hypotheses. Level One Theory was used particularly in attempting to relate personality structure and self-concept to academic motivation. Theory was conceived at this level as functioning to spotlight the variables which might have a high likelihood of relating to the criterion.

Theory employed at Level Two (predictive) requires sufficient clarification to specify directional alternate hypotheses—one-tailed tests. Three factors were abstracted from the writings of McClelland, et al. (1953), and were extended and polarized to predict extremes in academic motivation; i.e., need for (a) long-term *vs.* short-term involvement; (b) unique *vs.* common accomplishment; and (c) competing with a maximal *vs.* minimal standard of excellence. Level Two Theory was used to relate occupational aspiration and elements of the motivational situation to the academic achievement criterion.

METHODOLOGY

INSTRUMENTATION ▪ The original project began with six experimental instruments, only four of which were found to be functional. Two inventories, one dealing with perceived parental attitudes and child-rearing practices, and one with preferred teacher characteristics, were eliminated because of inadequate reliability.

The items of each subtest were validated and cross-validated by chi-square analyses of the responses of statistically defined criterion groups of *eleventh* grade under- and over-achieving students (Farquhar & Payne, 1964). Because a significant number of items were found to discriminate between such criterion groups, it was felt that construct validity of the battery had been demonstrated to some extent for the high school level.

Following is a brief description of the four functional instruments which constituted the motivational battery (the *M*-Scales). Sample items are presented in Table 1. The first two test scales were intended to represent Level Two Theory, and the second two scales to represent Level One.

TABLE 1. *Sample Items from Four Functional Subtests of the* M-Scale

Generalized Situational Choice Inventory (GSCI)	Preferred Job Characteristics Scale (PJCS)
I would prefer to:	I prefer:
1. A) receive a grade on the basis of how well I did on the teacher's test, or B) get a grade on the basis of how hard I tried.	3. A) a job which does not require a college education, or B) a job where I solve problems no one else can.
2. A) learn by losing to an expert, or B) learn by defeating an experienced player.	4. A) a job where my opinion is valued, or B) a job where I could not be fired.
Word-Rating List (WRL) Teachers feel that I am: 5. Competitive. 6. Competent.	*Human Trait Inventory (HTI)* 7. I worry about my grades. 8. It is difficult for me to keep interested in most of my school studies.

Key for High Motivation Responses: 1 (A), 2 (B), 3 (B), 4 (A), 5, 6 & 7 (rating of usually or always), 8 (ratings of never or sometimes).

Generalized Situational Choice Inventory (GSCI): A measure of motivational factors operative in the academic situation. Originally a 200-item, two-alternative, forced-choice instrument developed from the extended McClelland theory. Item content was related to the motivational situation, particularly in an academic context. Forty-five items for males and 30 items for females remained after cross-validation, with 13 in common. (Thorpe, 1961)

Preferred Job Characteristics Scale (PJCS): A measure of academic-occupational aspiration. Again, based on the extended McClelland theory, eight items characterizing high, and eight characterizing low achievement motivation were developed. Every high motivation alternative was then paired with every low motivation alternative. These item-pairs, each with an occupational referent, were randomly ordered into a 64-item, two-alternative forced-choice instrument. Twenty and 33 items were found to be significant discriminators for males and females, respectively, with 10 in common. (Farquhar & Payne, 1964).

Word Rating List (WRL): A measure of academic self-concept. Following from the assumption that self-concept is an intervening variable, operational between motivation and achievement, a 119-item word rating list was developed. One-, two-, or three-word concepts or phrases were rated on a four-point scale by the student as he thought his teachers would rate them in describing him as a student. Forty-eight items remained after cross-validation for males and females, with 30 in common. (Payne, 1962; Payne & Farquhar, 1962).

Human Trait Inventory (HTI): A generalized measure of the academic personality. Personality test items from both standardized and non-standardized tests, which had previously been shown to be associated with academic achievement, were assembled into a 125-item single statement inventory. The student was required to assign a rating from 1 to 4 indicating the degree to which he perceived each of the statements as being true of him. Twenty-six and 25 items were significant discriminators for males and females, respectively, with 12 in common. (Taylor, 1962).

Two different aptitude measures were used in the present study. For the high school samples, scores on the *Verbal Reasoning* subtest of the *Differential Aptitude Tests (DAT-VR)* were gathered. Total scores on the *College Qualification Test (CQT)* were available for the college samples.

SAMPLES ▪ In view of the fact that McClelland, et al. (1953), and Verhoff, Wilcox, and Atkinson (1953) have noted sex differences in achievement motivation, and that Seashore (1962) has noted higher achievement predictability for females than for males, all analyses of the present study were conducted separately for males and females. Kazmier (1961) (Appearing in the present volume as article #39) emphasized the importance of using cross-validation groups in predictive validity studies. This caution was heeded in the present investigation.

High School Samples: Approximately 4200 eleventh-grade students constituted the population of the high school group. These students, who were from nine high schools located in eight Michigan cities, were selected to represent the full range of socio-economic environments. From this population, validation groups of 254 males and 261 females were randomly selected. Random samples of 118 males and 117 females were obtained for cross-validation purposes.

College Samples: The college samples were selected from two sections of introductory educational psychology students at Michigan State University. These students were primarily sophomores, but representatives of other academic levels were also present. Because of the limited number of subjects available, it was necessary to combine sections. No significant differences on predictor or criterion measures were noted between sections. The randomly determined validation samples contained 41 males and 75 females. Cross-validation samples contained 42 males and 74 females.

ANALYSIS PROCEDURES ■ Internal consistency was estimated by the analysis of variance technique detailed by Hoyt (1941).

Initially the means of the M-Scale total scores and individual subtest scores were contrasted by t-tests, within each sex group across the two academic levels, to determine motivational differences. Direct sex comparisons could not be made in view of the fact that different items were found on the male and female forms of the M-Scales.

Zero-order correlations of the M-Scale individual subtest scores with cumulative GPA were considered evidence of criterion-related validity. Further, if a significant increase of the multiple correlations over zero-order aptitude-GPA correlations was noted, additional evidence concerning criterion-related validity was considered to have been provided.

To determine whether a reliable (stable) and valid set of score weights had been evolved, the regression weights from the validation samples were used to predict the achievement of the cross-validation samples.

A significance level of .05 was selected for all statistical analyses of the study.

RESULTS

RELIABILITY ANALYSES ■ Data on the internal consistency of the individual subtest and total M-Scale scores for the high school and college samples are presented in Table 2. For the high school samples, the internal consistency estimates are

TABLE 2. *Summary of Hoyt's Analyses-of-Variance Reliability Estimates for Individual Subtests and Total M-Scale Scores for High School and College Samples*

	Subtest								Total M-Scale	
	GSCI		PJCS		WRL		HTI			
Sample	N	r_{tt}	N	r_{tt}	N	r_{tt}	N	r_{tt}	N	r_{tt}
Males										
High School	62	.82	66	.76	66	.92	66	.80	240	.94
College	50	.67	50	.62	50	.87	50	.45	50	.77
Females										
High School	66	.85	66	.60	66	.90	66	.76	240	.93
College	50	.52	50	.58	50	.87	50	.81	50	.79

generally within an acceptable range. The number of items in the $PJCS$, however, needs to be increased for both males and females. The HTI also needs some increase in length, particularly for the females. In contrast, only moderately satisfactory reliability estimates were obtained for the college samples. Satisfactory reliability was attained for the WRL for both males and females (this subtest yielding consistently better results for both high school and college samples). The results of the reliability analyses indicate that revision is necessary if the *M*-Scale is to be used as a measure of academic motivation at the college level.

CONSTRUCT VALIDITY ■ In analyzing the descriptive data of the present study, it was hypothesized that the college samples, in view of the effect of selectivity, would score significantly higher on the total and subtests of the motivational battery than would the high school samples. It was argued that one of the primary reasons for an individual's presence at an institution of higher learning was motivational in nature. If the construct of academic achievement motivation is operational in the *M*-Scale, significant differences should be found between high school and college groups. Data pertaining to this hypothesis are summarized in Table 3.

TABLE 3. *Means and Standard Deviations of Data Used in Study for High School and College Samples*

				Sample				
		Males				Females		
	High School (N=254)		College (N=41)		High School (N=261)		College (N=75)	
Variable	$\overline{X}$	S. D.	$\overline{X}$	S. D.	$\overline{X}$	S. D.	$\overline{X}$	S. D.
GPA	2.94	.72	3.41*	.41	3.27†	.66	3.52*	.47
Aptitude‡	19.91	8.59	127.77	24.62	20.00	7.76	123.09	25.95
GSCI	30.76	6.89	35.17*	4.80	20.45	5.11	23.55*	3.36
PJCS	16.20	4.32	18.90*	1.43	27.44	5.78	31.26*	2.57
WRL	30.41	9.69	38.37*	6.21	28.99	8.29	37.31*	6.50
HTI	18.97	4.41	20.80*	2.73	17.51	3.60	20.49*	3.58
Total M-Scale	96.39	20.01	113.24*	11.29	94.93	18.69	112.85*	11.26

‡ Aptitude measure for high school samples was the Verbal Reasoning subtest of *DAT*; for the college sample it was total score from *CQT*.

* Higher mean of this academic level, within sex (p < .05)

† Higher mean for this sex, within academic level (p < .05)

As anticipated, the means for all motivational variables for both college males and females are significantly higher than for their high school counterparts. Aptitude comparisons could not be made because of the lack of comparability of the measures. It should also be noted that the high school GPA's for females were significantly higher than for males. Such contrasts are not strictly legitimate, because of the lack of comparability of achievement data. They were completed, however, to provide a crude indication of relative levels of performance. The *M*-Scale measures have a relatively normal distribution for the high school samples, with the exception of the *PJCS*, which is negatively skewed. All *M*-Scale distributions for the college samples evidence negative skewness, which is again most pronounced in the *PJCS*. The *WRL* consistently shows the greatest mean discrepancy between academic levels. This is interpreted as underscoring the importance of academic self-concept in influencing scholastic performance. It might also support the assumption that self-concept is functioning as an intervening variable operant between motivation and achievement. The data of Table 3, in conjunction with the fact that a significant number of items held up upon item cross-validation in the original study, support the construct validity of the M-Scale and its subtests.

CRITERION-RELATED VALIDITY ■ Intercorrelational data for M-Scale subtests, achievement, and aptitude tests are summarized in Table 4. Two general trends

TABLE 4. *Intercorrelations Among* M-*Scale Subtests,* GPA, *and Aptitude Measures* (APT) *for High School* (HS) *and College* (C) *Validation Samples*

		GPA	APT‡	GSCI	PJCS	WRL	HTI
				FEMALES			
				(High School $N=261$)		(College $N=75$)	
GPA							
HS		—	.60*	.32*	.27*	.42*	.36*
C		—	.62*	.42*	.24*	.10	.10
APT‡							
HS		.62*	—	.21*	.18*	.34*	.29*
C		.22	—	.27*	.23*	.00	.00
GSCI							
HS		.50*	.39*	—	.53*	.43*	.53*
C		.41*	.46*	—	.48*	.15	.27*
PJCS							
HS		.32*	.30*	.51*	—	.32*	.43*
C		.54*	.25	.40	—	.07	.12
WRL							
HS		.51*	.42*	.51*	.32*	—	.50*
C		.01	.25	.32*	.32*	—	.54*
HTI							
HS		.42*	.25*	.47*	.39*	.47*	—
C		.24	.19	.34*	.55*	.29*	—

(Left margin labels, rotated: (College $N=41$) · MALES (High School $N=254$) · (High School))

* Correlations significantly different from zero at .05 level for one-tailed test.

‡ Aptitude measure for high school samples was the *Verbal Reasoning* subtest of *DAT*; for college samples, total score from *CQT*.

Note: Dotted lines separate subtest intercorrelations.

among the M-Scale subtest and achievement criterion (GPA) correlations are evident. Correlations with GPA are generally higher for the high school ($\bar{x}_r = .40$)[1] than the college samples ($\bar{x}_r = .25$), and for high school males ($\bar{x}_r = .44$) than for any of the other three samples ($\bar{x}_r = .32$). The *GSCI* and *PJCS*, both of which are Level Two (predictive) theory instruments, yield consistently higher rela-

---

[1] Mean correlations ($\bar{x}_r$) were computed through use of an appropriate z transformation.

tionships. Support for the use of theory in instrument construction seems evident. Subtest intercorrelations indicate no noticeable trends, with the possible exception of the somewhat erratic relationships seen among the college female sample $(.07 \leqq r \leqq .49)$. All subtests show moderate relationship with each other $(.07 \leqq r \leqq .55, \bar{x}_r = .43)$. It is also seen that the motivational subtests are reasonably independent of aptitude $(\bar{x}_r = .28)$, particularly for college males $(\bar{x}_r = .29)$ and females $(\bar{x}_r = .13)$.

In summarizing the results reported in Table 4, one may see that the degree of criterion-related validity of the M-Scale and its subtests is generally in an acceptable range, particularly for the high school samples. Such a conclusion seems reasonable despite the general lack of sensitivity of significance tests for correlations. Of the 16 possible subtest-criterion correlations, 12 are significantly different from zero.

Further evidence of criterion-related validity was derived from multiple-regression analyses. When the M-Scale subtests are treated individually in the regression equation, multiple correlations with GPA of .74 (High School) and .63 (college) were found for males. When the regression weights derived from the validation sample were used to predict GPA's for the cross-validation sample, correlations of .70 (High School) and .49 (college) between actual and predicted criterion scores were found.

Similar patterns were observed for the female samples. The initial multiple correlations of .63 (High School) and .68 (college) decreased to .62 and .50 upon cross-validation.

All multiple correlations were significantly different from the zero-order aptitude-GPA correlations. When aptitude measures are disregarded, the weightings of WRL and $GSCI$ are generally the largest, a fact which suggests the high relative importance of academic self-concept and of motivational situation factors in the determination of the level of scholastic success. The degree of consistency of weightings, which was found to be greater within the female samples than within the male samples, was also noted to be higher within academic groups.

DISCUSSION AND CONCLUSIONS

Several factors may have significantly influenced the results of the present study. The small number of subjects in the college samples, particularly in the instance of males, may have adversely affected internal consistency of subtests as well as the stability of score weights. The influences of social desirability, response set, and test sophistication have not been controlled in the M-Scale. These factors may have been more operative in the college samples and they may have been masked and interpreted as higher motivation. The skewed distributions of the $PJCS$ might be explained as an artifact of the items developed. It may be that in item writing, social desirability or conformity was equated with high motivation. And finally, the interaction of reliability, of both the independent and the dependent measures, and validity must not be overlooked. It may be that the upper limits of validity have been reached in relation to the moderate reliability.

Despite these imperfections, the basic measurement approach used here to assess academic motivation seems to be functional. It appears that selected generalized situational factors in the academic setting (GSCI) and the way in which an individual student views his ability (WRL) play a significant role in school performance. These factors seem especially important at the secondary level. Controlled investigations of the interaction of these and other variables might yield even more conclusive evidence of their academic importance. Although the validity coefficients of the individual M-Scale subtests are not so large as those of such predictors as aptitude or past achievement, they are significantly higher than those usually encountered with non-cognitive measures. Although the ability to predict achievement with objective motivational measures has limited application, their use in other ways is easily conceived.

Contemporary practice in education includes grouping or tracking on the basis of ability or achievement. The research using these approaches has been inconclusive. Perhaps grouping on the basis of motivation might yield more fruitful results. Additionally, the application of diagnostic motivational measures by the school counselor should prove useful. The results of this study seem to indicate that through the use of theory and elementary construct validation procedures a beginning has been made in isolating unique, stable, and psychologically interpretable contributors to the prediction of scholastic success.

38 Differential Prediction in College Admissions

PAUL HORST

Academic criteria frequently suffer from many shortcomings. As several writers (e.g., Bloom and Peters, 1961) have pointed out, one approach to the criterion problem is to use many different measures of related criteria instead of a single criterion. In the two preceding papers in this chapter, one criterion at a time was predicted. In the following article the prediction of multiple-criteria is considered. Dr. Horst differentiates between multiple absolute prediction, where concern is with estimating performance with respect to each of several criteria, and multiple differential prediction, where differences in success among various criteria are estimated. To consider the application made by Dr. Horst, one might

Reprinted and abridged with permission of author and publisher from the *College Board Review*, Fall, 1957, Vol. 33, pp. 19–23. (Published by the College Entrance Examination Board, New York.)

ask why the prediction of an over-all grade-point average might not be as helpful as predicting averages for several fields or the differences among those averages. While we realize that positive traits tend to be positively related, these relationships are imperfect. We would, therefore, expect various patterns of abilities to be present in a group of individuals; e.g., some individuals would be better in English than in science, while others would be better in science than in English. How then would a predicted over-all grade-point average be inadequate from the standpoint of the student, the university, and society as a whole? Can the procedures described serve the needs of the student as well as those of the university and of society?

A contemporary problem of higher education is to determine who should go to college. The admissions policies of certain private colleges tend to admit only students who are brilliant in everything. Until recently many of our state-supported institutions have implied by their admissions requirements that only those students who are stupid in everything should be rejected. Both of these policies ignore the phenomenon of intra-individual differences as distinguished from inter-individual differences. It is well known that a person may show great differences in the extent to which he possesses various abilities and competencies. It seems to me admissions policies should reflect this phenomenon.

We know that society needs a lot of different kinds of people. No one person needs to excel in a lot of different kinds of things. But very superior people tend to be superior in almost everything, and very inferior people tend to be inferior in almost everything. Actually these are mere tautologies, because it is the fact that a person is superior in everything that makes him seem very superior, and the fact that a person is inferior in everything that makes him seem inferior. It is in the large middle group between the very superior and the very inferior where there is room for a person to excel in one thing and not in another or to show great variation in his abilities. Therefore, the average person may be superior in some things and relatively inferior in others.

We cannot observe the frantic recruiting competition of large industrial organizations on our college campuses without being convinced of the varied and voluminous demands which society is placing upon the crops of graduates from our higher educational institutions. We cannot afford to be profligate with our student resources on the one hand so that we throw away all but those who excel in everything. Neither can we afford to be profligate with our educational resources so that we squander them on individuals who have little aptitude or promise for any particular thing.

However, if we consider that there are many demands for many different kinds of abilities, then the problem of differential guidance in college becomes extremely important, and it is only on the basis of differential prediction of success that differential guidance can be offered. Differential guidance and differential prediction of success should be the keystone of admissions policies. The question is not whether a person will be able to succeed in almost any subject he might attempt in college; neither is it whether he will be only slightly better than poor in everything. The real question is whether there are certain areas in which he might succeed in college and presumably make an important contribution to society.

DIFFERENTIAL METHOD EXPLAINED

I do not believe, therefore, that we can have intelligent and rational admissions policies, nor sound guidance, nor effective utilization of our manpower resources without an effective program of differential prediction of success in college. And what do we mean by the differential prediction of success? Rather obviously we do not mean simply predicting over-all success in college irrespective of what a person happens to major in, but rather we mean predicting success specifically with reference to each of a number of different areas of study.

When we talk about predicting success we imply that we have a set of predictor variables from which to predict. In the limiting case we may have only one predictor variable. If we have only one predictor variable then it is possible to determine empirically how well we can predict success in each of a number of criterion activities. We may have a single test score by means of which we attempt to make multiple predictions. Certainly, however, such a test cannot predict success differentially among these criteria because the correlations among the different predictions must by necessity be perfect, since they are all linear functions of the test score.

We must, therefore, consider the more typical case of a battery of predictor variables which may consist of a number of different kinds of tests. By means of multiple regression techniques we can find how well this battery of tests will predict success in each of a number of different criteria such as different areas of study in college. Techniques readily available to us will also determine the best set of regression weights for predicting success in each criterion area from the single set of predictor variables.

Instead of trying to get the best absolute prediction of success from a battery of tests for each of a number of different criteria, we may rather wish to get a set of predictions which will estimate the *differences* between all possible pairs of criterion variables as accurately as possible. The first case we have called the problem of multiple absolute prediction (Horst, 1955). The second case we have called the problem of multiple differential prediction (Horst, 1954).

It can be shown that for a given battery of tests or predictors the weights used for best multiple absolute prediction are precisely those used for multiple differential prediction. The conventional least-square multiple regression techniques apply to the case of multiple absolute prediction as well as to that of multiple differential prediction for the same set of predictor and criterion variables. However, if our problem is not to get the best possible prediction of success for each of a number of different criterion activities but rather to predict differences in the criterion activities, then we can prove that a different set of tests will serve the latter purposes better than the former.

Essentially, for the problem of multiple absolute prediction we may well have one or more general factors involved in the criterion variables which make for high intercorrelations among them. In differential prediction we are not concerned with these general factors, but only with the specific and group factors which differentiate the criterion abilities from one another. It is for this reason that techniques for constructing predictor batteries for multiple absolute prediction and multiple differential prediction tend to yield different sets of measures. In the case of a society which purports to utilize optimally all of its human resources the technique of multiple differential prediction would seem more appropriate than that of multiple absolute prediction.

There are other kinds of prediction with which we may be concerned in using a multiple set of predictors and a multiple set of criterion variables. One of these types of multiple prediction is involved in the problem of optimal classification. This is sometimes called differential classification as distinguished from differential prediction. In the problem of optimal classification we are concerned with allocating individuals to a number of different activities so that the over-all success of the group will be a maximum. The problems in defining over-all maximum success are not simple and in themselves involve some rather technical considerations. However, the problem of optimal classification is basic to the problem of maximizing the effective use of human resources.

The essential difference between the optimal classification problem and the differential prediction problems may be indicated briefly. In the differential prediction problem we are concerned primarily with predicting a person's relative success in each of a number of different criterion activities. But the differential classification problem involves further restrictions. We cannot assume that each person should engage in the activity in which he has the most ability, aptitude, and other personal qualities relevant to success in that activity. If persons were assigned on this basis, there would in general be a wide disparity between the number of people assigned to the various activities and the number of persons required by society to perform those activities.

The optimal classification problem, therefore, requires us to place a restriction on the number of persons assigned to a particular activity. The problem, then, is how can people be assigned to the various activities so that the quotas or requirements are met and yet so that the over-all expected proficiency or effectiveness of the total group will be a maximum?

As yet there is no entirely satisfactory solution to the optimal classification problem. However, a great deal of work has been done on it and the next few years may yield some practical solutions. These should prove extremely useful in guidance work at colleges and universities. If it is possible to obtain reasonably satisfactory estimates of the approximate number of persons who should be trained in each of a number of different areas, and if reasonable predictions of their success in these areas could be made before admission to college, then each person's prediction of success could be adjusted or modified according to the demand for persons in that category. Then, if persons tended to follow the indications of their adjusted predictions, we could expect that approximately the correct number of persons would select each line of training and the over-all chances of their success could be increased.

The question has been asked me frequently, "Do you really think that it is possible practically to get differential prediction of success in college?" This question always comes to me as something of a shock because it asks essentially, "Do I really think that there are some people who can do some things better than they can do other things?"

Well, of course I think so, and so do most people. You don't need a college education to know this, even though people with college educations sometimes ask the question. One of the things on which the theory and practice of factor analysis is based is the fact that some people can do some things better than they can do other things. The experimental studies in factor analysis are replete with the evidence that the number of statistically independent and socially significant things which some people can do better than they can do other things may be as high as 30 or 40.

Or we can go directly to criterion variables themselves, such as academic activities. Even a common-sense type of analysis would lead us to believe that more than just verbal and mathematical ability are involved in scholastic aptitudes. Certainly we know that some people can use words effectively on a public platform or in social intercourse but cannot write well; other people can write well but cannot speak well. We also know that some people can use words effectively in narration but are poor in the presentation of abstract ideas. People who are good with figures may be poor in algebra, people who are good in algebra may loathe geometry, or be entirely inept with spatial relations or with factors involving mechanical comprehension.

In the field of career activities it is obvious that some people can do some jobs better than they can do other jobs even in the same economic or social status levels. Few would seriously argue that these differences are based solely on training and experience.

So far the evidence for differential ability which we have considered has been of an *a priori* nature. We may consider briefly some experimental evidence from the University of Washington Differential Grade Prediction Program. In this program, college course grades in each of 33 different college course areas are estimated from 15 different predictor variables. The answer to the question of how effective these predictions are from the differential point of view must be based on two considerations. First, how well do the predictions agree with actual success? But, as we pointed out earlier, the intercorrelations of these predictions will be unity if based on a single test or a single set of weights. Second, it is therefore important to know also the intercorrelations of these predicted course grades.

To state briefly the results, average validity for the 33 predicted criteria on the experimental group was .58, with a range from .33 to .89. As was to be expected on subsequent cross-validation, these validities dropped considerably. The average validity for the cross-validation group was .45, with a range from .13 to .71. Although cross-validation studies are frequently not reported, it is believed that in most of those quoted, cross-validities of .45 are reasonably high for this type of criterion. The average intercorrelation of the 33 different predicted criteria was .67. Admittedly, .67 is not a low average intercorrelation but on the other hand it is far from unity. When we consider that the cross-validation of .45 is probably a lower limit to what we may expect in future research and the intercorrelation of .67 an upper limit of what we may expect for the intercorrelations of the predicted criteria, the prospect for useful differential prediction based on current experimental results appears encouraging.

The question of how we may evaluate college success is a perennial one. Without apology, we recommend that actual course grades provide the best available criterion of success in college. It would only be threshing over old straw to point out the well-known limitations of college grades. However, the problems of these limitations is not to be solved by looking for other criteria such as personality improvement, qualities of leadership, and other vague and high-flown phrases, however useful they may be in securing research grants or increasing college endowments. We have consistently taken the position that when better criteria of college success are available, they will consist of better grading methods.

FORECASTS OF COURSE AND AREA GRADES

What, then, specifically are those grades which we might wish to predict? Certainly a most interesting and useful grade is over-all college grade-point average. This, however, gives us no indication of differential success. It would be of limited use only for admissions purposes and of no use whatever for guidance purposes. It would indicate only how successful the person might be expected to be in college provided he had no specific guidance, and it would not help to indicate what particular courses of study he should choose.

Another type of grade-point average which may be considered is the over-all university average for subgroups according to majors. This, I think, is an unsatisfactory criterion for any attempt at differential prediction. Each major requires courses in many different subject areas. Such a criterion may not be much better than over-all university grade-point average and would result in highly correlated predicted grade-point averages. Furthermore, the number of cases on which the weighting formulas can be based is limited to the numbers of persons in each major.

The only feasible method on the basis of which to develop a differential grade prediction program is, in my opinion, to establish criteria by course areas. The grade-point average in each course should constitute the fundamental criterion variable. I realize that this presents problems in deciding just what to call a course area. Special problems arise in the case of particular schools or colleges such as engineering and business administration. Should we, for example, break down engineering into different kinds of engineering, such as chemical, mechanical, aeronautical, ceramic, and metallurgical? Should we break down business administration into personnel, accounting, finance, transportation, and so on? The answer to this question must be based primarily upon the number of cases available on which to establish the prediction formulas. If the course areas are broken down too finely, there may not be enough cases in some of them on which to establish reliable regression weights.

To reduce the number of criterion variables it may be desirable to define groups of course areas in which there is some reason to believe that the courses are fairly homogeneous. For example, one might group the social sciences, the biological sciences, the physical sciences, foreign languages, and so forth. Admittedly, there are problems in effecting these groupings, but I do not believe they are insurmountable. One of the chief objections from the student's point of view to forming groups of course areas is the problem of deciding which particular course in the group should constitute the major. For example, if the group in question is the social sciences, the student may well want to know whether his prediction in psychology is better than in sociology or anthropology.

BASES FOR PREDICTION

The kinds of predictor variables which may be considered in a differential grade prediction program are as broad as the availability of measures. The essential requirement of a good differential predictor is that it shall predict well for one or for a few criteria and poorly for others. If it predicts well for all criteria, it is in effect predicting the part common or general to most of the criteria, and so will not be useful for differential prediction.

In the past, high school grade-point average has been used for predicting college success. It is true that this has been found to correlate well with over-all college grade-point average, but here again it is not useful for differential prediction. In the University of Washington program, we have therefore broken down high school grade-point average into six different course areas: English, mathematics, social science, natural science, foreign languages, and electives. It is only when the grades are broken down in this way that they can serve any useful purpose for differential prediction.

In addition to high school grades, personal data can also be used. So far we have used only the factors of age and sex, but I suspect that other biographical data variables may also be useful for differential prediction.

In the way of actual tests, we have relied so far on conventional aptitude and achievement tests published by commercial and educational institutions. We do not attempt to distinguish sharply between aptitude and achievement tests, for we believe essentially that achievement tests measure what students learn in school and aptitude tests measure what students learn out of school. It is still a hope, although founded on some research, that personality measures will contribute to the differential prediction of success in college. We have concluded a study involving 700 students in 20 different course areas in which the Strong, the Kuder, and the Michigan Vocabulary Test were included along with the American Council on Education test and eight of the Educational Testing Service's Cooperative tests. (The Michigan Vocabulary Test is sometimes regarded as primarily a test of interest.)

It is interesting to note that in this study involving 30 different variables all five parts of the Michigan Vocabulary Profile and four of the 14 Strong scales were selected while three of the eight Cooperative tests failed to be selected using the predictor selection technique which we have developed.

To sketch briefly the research on which our present differential grade prediction program is based, we started by developing a technique for the selection of a battery of tests which would yield maximum differential prediction efficiency for any subset of predictors of specified size. On a group of 2,000 freshmen entering in 1948, 27 predictor variables were available. These included seven tests from the Guilford-Zimmerman Aptitude Survey, the two parts of the ACE test, three parts of the Cooperative English Test Form OM, and six of the Cooperative General Achievement Tests. In addition the variables of age and sex were also included, as were high school grade-point averages in English, mathematics, foreign language, social studies, natural science, and electives.

At the end of four years the university grade-point average of each student who took courses in one or more of 33 different university subject areas was calculated. These subject areas ranged from anthropology through zoology. The subject areas were those in which at least 50 persons had taken course work during their four years of college. On the basis of these 33 different criterion variables and the 27 predictor variables, the predictor selection technique was used to select the 16 best predictors from the point of view of differential prediction efficiency.

The tests which were selected by the technique were verbal comprehension, numerical operations, mechanical knowledge, English usage, spelling, ACE quantitative, Co-op social studies part 2, and Co-op mathematics part 1. In addition to these, age, sex, and most of the high school grade-point variables were also selected.

The prediction formulas based on this group and the selected predictors were used to provide differential grade predictors for the entering class of 1953. At the end of three years a cross-validation was carried out on the grade prediction and the actual achieved grades in the various course areas. As indicated earlier, an average cross-validity of .45 was obtained. The intercorrelation of the predicted grade-point averages was calculated for only the first group and this, as I have indicated, was .67.

We are constantly confronted with requests from other institutions and individuals asking how they might take advantage of our results or engage in a similar program. One of the main considerations is to make sure that the institution is large enough so that enough cases will be available to give stable results for most of the important subject areas. Otherwise, it will not be possible to establish and validate a dependable differential prediction program.

The question of how long after the tests are administered they should be validated cannot be answered simply. Many of the validation studies on prediction of college success are based on freshman grade-point averages, sometimes at the end of the first semester or first quarter. I do not think this is a long enough time on which to base a differential grade prediction program. Perhaps at the end of two years enough course grades in enough different course areas would be available to provide reasonably sound criterion measures for differential prediction purposes. I think, however, that it is better to wait until the end of the third year to attempt to get validity data. The results from the third and fourth year will usually be so similar that it would not be worthwhile waiting until the end of the fourth year to complete the necessary research.

In any case, a big problem from the point of view of clerical labor is that of collecting and processing the criterion data. The sheer job of segregating grades by course areas and calculating the averages for each individual student involves a great deal of time and expense, and no study should be undertaken unless the availability of such data can be guaranteed. One of the biggest handicaps to the development of differential prediction studies is the lack of availability of these criterion data and the complicated problems involved in processing them. Obviously, therefore, the development of an effective differential grade prediction program requires very close cooperation and assistance on the part of the registrar's office.

Before closing, I would like to contrast the differential prediction approach with a current and highly publicized approach. This approach is concerned with and identified by such phrases as "National Merit," "Talent Search," "The Gifted Student," and so on. My own feeling is that if we are concerned primarily with having our institutions of higher learning make their maximum contributions to the best utilization of our human resources, then these programs are missing the mark.

Is a talent search really necessary? Do we need to go to great lengths to identify the gifted or exceptional student? I think not. I think these students who excel in everything, far from having to be searched for, cannot possibly be hidden. They stand out in their high schools and in their communities so that anyone could name them. Suppose, however, that they don't have to be searched for, that they were discovered away back in grammar school, should we not go to great lengths to make it possible for them to go to college? I suspect that even here we are on the wrong track. I would guess that 95 percent of the students identified and subsidized by the formal programs now operating would go to college without these programs' aid.

39   The Importance of Cross-Validation in Achievement Prediction

LEONARD J. KAZMIER

In an earlier article in this volume Cattell discussed the importance of generalizability as a test parameter. The following research bears directly on this discussion. As will be seen, the need to cross-validate total or composite scores is crucial if we are to have any confidence in the weightings we attach to each predictor. Cross-validation is also crucial in the early stages of test development when we are concerned with initially selecting test items. Following such procedures allows for greater confidence in the final product.

By cross-validation we mean the experimental tryout of a procedure on a second sample drawn independently from the same population as was the sample used initially to validate the test. Why is it important that the second or cross-validation group be independent of the original group? In addition to independence, what other factors will dictate our selection of the second sample? What are the implications of not cross-validating? What frequently happens to many of our statistics when we do cross-validate? (The reader may wish to refer to articles by Langmuir (1954) and Mosier (1951) for further clarification of the topic.)

There has come to be considerable concern about the widespread use of extreme groups in hypothesis testing. As McNemar has indicated (1960), such tests of significance are misleading and may represent only a small degree of relationship between the two variables. The primary purpose of the present study was to investigate the relationship between the *Edwards Personal Preference Schedule* (Edwards, 1957) scales and a criterion of academic achievement when scores of all subjects are utilized, not just those of selected extreme groups. The correlation technique was used throughout because it provides a measure of the degree of relationship as well as its signfcance. To ascertain that the measured relationships of the several scales with the criterion are not due to chance factors, a cross-validation group was included in the study.

PROCEDURE

The sample consisted of 140 students enrolled in two sections of introductory psychology at Ohio State University during the spring quarter of 1960. Both

Reprinted and abridged from, Leonard J. Kazmier "Cross-Validation Groups, Extreme Groups, and the Prediction of Academic Achievement", *Journal of Educational Psychology*, 1961, Vol. 52, pp. 195–198. Copyright 1961, by the American Psychological Association and reproduced by permission of author and publisher.

sections were taught by the author of the present report. For use as a predictor, six paragraphs of material, including a total of 36 questions on the contents thereof, were chosen from old forms of the *Ohio State Psychological Examination* (OSPE). The criterion for success in the psychology course was the total number of points accumulated at the end of the quarter from three departmental examinations and four class quizzes.

In order to achieve comparability of the experimental and cross-validation groups, all class cards for the subjects were segregated by sex, and then categorized according to college year. Within the college year the cards were arranged in order of percentile scores on the OSPE. Seven students for whom these scores were not available were arbitrarily placed at the end of their respective college-year groups, after the highest percentile scores. Then the over-all sample was subdivided into two groups of 70 subjects each by alternatively putting one card in the experimental group and the following card in the cross-validation group. Comparability of the two groups in terms of their standing on the reading comprehension test, the criterion, and the 15 EPPS scales was ascertained.[1]

The correlation of each of the 15 scales with the criterion of success was determined for each of the groups and for the entire sample, and the Wherry-Doolittle test selection technique (Garrett, 1958, pp. 426–440) was then applied to the experimental group of subjects in order to determine the best selection and weighting of EPPS scales for maximum predictiveness. The applicability of this result to the cross-validation group was investigated by computing a composite correlation for that group by using the scales and weights derived from the experimental group.

RESULTS

The split-half reliability coefficient (odd vs. even) for the reading comprehension test is .813, while the coefficient of correlation between this predictor and the criterion of total points in the psychology course is .593, which is significant at the .001 level for the 140 subjects involved in this study.

The correlation coefficients between the criterion of success in the psychology course and each of the 15 scales of the EPPS are indicated in Table 1 for the experimental and cross-validation groups as well as for the total sample. For the experimental group, the correlation coefficients for Succorance and Dominance were significant at the .10 level, while that for Change was significant at the .05 level. The cross-validation group yielded a somewhat different pattern of correlations, resulting in significance at the .10 level for the Order and Dominance scales. For the total sample of subjects, the correlation coefficients for Achievement, Affiliation, and Nurturance were significant at the .10 level, while that for Dominance was significant at the .05 level.

---

[1] No significant differences were noted between the experimental and cross-validation groups with respect to the means and standard deviation of the predictor, criterion, or 15 EPPS scores.

TABLE 1. *Correlation of the EPPS Scales with the Criterion of Success in Psychology*

Scale	Experimental Group (N=70)	Cross-Validation Group (N=70)	Total Sample (N=140)
Achievement	.113	.191	.153*
Deference	.013	−.109	−.043
Order	.029	−.214*	−.080
Exhibition	.027	.157	.092
Autonomy	.073	−.040	.013
Affiliation	−.139	−.161	−.149*
Intraception	.022	.099	.059
Succorance	−.205*	.078	−.087
Dominance	.209*	.226*	.213†
Abasement	−.054	−.068	−.060
Nurturance	−.167	−.163	−.164*
Change	−.244†	.035	−.114
Endurance	.088	−.061	.018
Heterosexuality	.192	.037	.114
Aggressiveness	.115	−.034	.043

* $p < .10$.
† $p < .05$.

It would appear that the desired stability of relationship of the EPPS scales with the criterion is lacking in this study. For example, of the three scales whose relationship with the criterion was significant at the .10 level or better in the experimental group, only one scale "held up" for the cross-validation group, while the algebraic signs of the correlation coefficients for the other two groups actually were reversed. In order to verify this conclusion statistically, the Wherry-Doolittle technique was utilized to ascertain the best selection of scales for the experimental group and the appropriate beta weights to be used in conjunction with each scale. Stability of the scales is then indicated by the extent to which these beta weights apply for use with the cross-validation group. As indicated by Table 2, for the experimental group it was found that the use of the Change,

TABLE 2. *Best Selection of EPPS Scales for the Experimental Group by the Wherry-Doolittle Method*

Scales	$_s\bar{R}$
Change	.244
Change + Succorance	.313
Change + Succorance + Heterosexuality	.345

Succorance, and Heterosexuality scales results in the maximal coefficient of multiple correlation corrected for shrinkage.

The beta weights obtained by the Wherry-Doolittle test selection method are

—.252 for Change, —.233 for Succorance, and .181 for Heterosexuality. Utilizing these weights derived for the experimental group and the correlation coefficients of the chosen scales with the criterion in the cross-validation group results in a composite coefficient of correlation for the cross-validation group of —.058. Thus, the validity evidenced for the EPPS scales in the experimental group did not at all hold up in the cross-validation group, in that the scales and weights that resulted in a multiple R of .345 for the experimental group yielded a slightly negative composite coefficient of —.058 for the second group.

The results of the study do not necessarily indicate a lack of usefulness for the EPPS, but they do highlight the shortcomings of many of the research studies which have reported success in prediction with the EPPS scales.

40   Some Implications of Decision Theory for Occupational Selection

FREDERIC R. WICKERT

A relatively new way of viewing testing is in terms of the potential contributions of test results to the making of specific decisions. The following brief introduction to decision theory should assist the reader in considering concepts such as validity and reliability within a decision-making context. Viewing conventional testing concepts in this context provides new insights; often traditional approaches in testing are challenged by decision theory. For example, are there instances where accuracy in testing should be sacrificed? Might it be more efficient to use a sequence of tests rather than one long test? What new criteria are required when evaluating tests within a decision theory framework?

Until recently little thought was generally given by test users to the question of how tests could best serve in making decisions. Instead, tests were thought of primarily as measuring instruments. Test theory concerned itself with the accuracy with which tests measured. It was found, for example, that a well-made test of achievement in mathematics or an intelligence test would usually measure rather accurately. However, personality tests, especially when they were tried out for the first time after just having been constructed (even when the best-known principles of test construction were utilized), sometimes gave surprisingly

Reprinted and abridged with permission of author and publisher from an article entitled, "Some Implications of Decision Theory for Occupational Selection in West Africa," which appeared in A. Taylor, ed., *Educational and Occupational Selection in West Africa*, London: Oxford University Press, 1962, pp. 127–138.

inaccurate, inconsistent measurements. After numbers of experiences of this kind, it is little wonder that psychologists became preoccupied with accuracy of measurement.

According to decision theory, the purpose of tests is to help administrators and teachers make decisions about people rather than give the test psychologist the satisfaction of having made the most accurate possible measurement. The usefulness of accurate measurement is recognized under decision theory, but at the same time the value of a test is seen to depend on many qualities in addition to its accuracy. These other qualities include the relevance of the measurement to the particular decision being made and the loss resulting from an erroneous decision. Even more important may be the fact that the decision maker is both reminded of the possible courses of action available to him and helped in choosing from among them. With respect to the making of personnel selection decisions, for example, the decision maker can see the relative value of such alternative courses of action as getting a little but highly accurate test information, or getting more but less accurate test information.

SOME DEFINITIONS AND TERMS FROM DECISION THEORY

Certain familiar words take on new meanings in decision theory. A definition of such words will serve as a good introduction to decision theory as applied to occupational selection.

Let us begin with the word *treatment.* A decision in personnel work concerns what is to be done, that is, what treatment to give one or more persons. Should an individual be hired or rejected, for what job should he be trained, to what counselling or therapy or educational course should he be assigned? The word treatment takes on a broad meaning. "Every personnel decision involves assigning each individual to an appropriate treatment." The number of individuals and the number of treatments available in any one decision problem may be large or small.

Next, three terms often encountered in personnel work—*selection, classification,* and *placement*—can be more sharply defined in the light of decision theory, and especially in the light of the concept of treatment as just defined.

In a *selection decision* an institution decides to accept some persons (give them the acceptance treatment) and to reject others (give them the rejection treatment). Hiring or not hiring candidates for employment, or admitting or turning away persons who have applied for admittance to a school would be examples of selection.

In *classification,* the decision is made regarding which one of many possible, dissimilar assignments (or treatments) an individual is given. An applicant at a store may be assigned to a clerical job, or to selling in the store, or to receiving incoming goods, or to guarding the store after hours, etc.

When persons are assigned to different levels of treatment rather than to quite different types of treatment, a *placement* decision is said to have been made. An example of placement would be the sectioning of students into several classes according to their ability to learn as determined by a general intelligence test.

One should differentiate between the two-category placement treatment: for example, sectioning students into two classes according to their ability to learn as determined by a general intelligence test; and the selection-rejection treatment, for example, admitting some candidates into a school and rejecting the others on the basis of scores on a test, possibly again a general intelligence test. In placement, the persons remain within the institution; in selection, one group enters or remains in the institution while the other group has no further association with the institution. It will be seen from time to time farther on in this paper that the decision theory implications differ appreciably for the non-selection as compared with the selection problem.

Personnel decisions matters, whether they are concerned with selection or classification or placement, may be characterized on still another basis, namely, the presence of certain common constraints on the kind of decision that can be made. Two broad types of constraints on personnel decisions are encountered: (1) the number of treatments per man, and (2) the number of men per treatment. Mostly each man is assigned to a single treatment: one job, one training program, or one diagnosis. When a man is assigned to more than one treatment, these treatments are usually interrelated. For example, a university student may be enrolled in three related subjects in any one trimester. In this case the personnel decision problem becomes one of finding for the individual the best pattern of treatments among those available.

On the other hand, the number of men per treatment may be constrained by a quota. The quota may be absolute or relative. An absolute quota is set when a definite number of vacancies has been established. For example, the establishment may provide for three clerks. A relative quota is set when a certain proportion of the group being considered is assigned to a treatment. Examples would be hiring a set of percentage of applicants, or releasing a set percentage of soldiers from further military service, or promoting a set percentage of civil servants in a given year.

Strategy is another term frequently encountered in discussions of decision theory. A strategy is defined as a rule for arriving at a decision. One possible classification of strategies is into sequential as compared with non-sequential strategies. A sequential strategy involves not making an irrevocable assignment of an individual to a treatment. Instead, information is gathered during each stage of an individual's treatment and this information in turn is used to help form a decision about what his next treatment will be. For instance, an employee may be assigned to a job, that is, a terminal treatment, after just one test has been given to him; or he may be given additional tests, that is, assigned to additional treatments to get more information about him. These "tests" may include not only the usual psychological tests but such treatments as job tryouts, or psychotherapy, or counselling, or training, or even sending him at the institution's expense to get more education. We shall see later that sequential strategies are often better from a decision-making point of view than non-sequential ones.

It is obvious that we are continually making decisions as we go about our day-to-day work of occupational and educational selection and administration, but seldom do we go to the trouble of stating our strategy. Cronbach and Gleser (1965) point out that strategies can be made explicit—often laid out in tabular form. When this is done, the decision maker has revealed possibilities of which he may have been previously unaware.

Two related terms, the last ones to which we are formally introduced in this discussion of decision theory, are *outcome* and *payoff*. The outcome of a strategy consists of the consequences of a decision to assign a person to a given treatment. Further, any specific outcome is expressed in terms of some criterion (or set of criteria). In a textile mill, for example, the outcome of hiring an individual could be measured in terms of such criteria as his hourly production, how much trouble he was to supervise, how much material he wasted, the amount of time the machines he was assigned to tend were idle, the amount of training time to achieve some expected standard of production, etc.

There are some difficulties with decision theory at this point. Almost never is the decision maker able to anticipate the outcome for each person under each possible treatment. At best, he can only predict the probability distribution of the outcomes. Empirical results from previous cases are needed to determine how the information about a person is related to the criterion.

But outcomes alone are not enough. We need to go beyond outcome to payoff. An evaluated outcome is called a payoff. For example, it is clear that in the case of a factory operative the higher the proportion of perfect objects he produces, the more valuable he is. Cronbach and Gleser cite a hypothetical case in which a 2 percent rise in quality from 94 percent to 96 percent might be of great value because this rise might be just enough to permit the factory management to eliminate routine inspection altogether, but a gain of 2 percent from 74 percent to 76 percent might mean relatively little because complete inspection of the whole output would still be required. In other words, gain on the criterion measure may not be a linear function.

A strategy may be evaluated by considering its payoff, and two or more strategies can be evaluated by comparing their respective payoffs. It is important that the cost of a test or other information-producing procedure be expressed in monetary or utility units and deducted from the expected payoff in each instance.

INSIGHTS INTO OCCUPATIONAL SELECTION PROVIDED BY DECISION THEORY

Now that we have some notion of what decision theory is and we understand some of its main concepts and terms, we shall turn to a few of the insights from decision theory regarding occupational selection. To a certain extent these are quite technical, but every attempt will be made to present these implications in as non-technical a manner as possible. Here, as previously, much of what is said is a paraphrase of the Cronbach-Gleser argument.

The first of the insights from decision theory to consider concerns comparing a "fixed" with an "adaptive" treatment following a given selection procedure. In fixed-treatment selection individuals are chosen for one specified treatment which cannot be modified. In adaptive-treatment selection, the treatment is modified depending on the improved quality of the people selected. A good selection procedure becomes much more valuable when it is followed by a treatment which takes advantage of the improved quality of the persons selected. All too often following the installation of more effective educational selection procedures in a school system, the level of instruction remains the same. Decision theory indicates that improved educational selection will give greatest benefit when the methods of instruction are adjusted by introducing whatever pace and procedures are most appropriate for students of the quality selected. Most test theory to date has limited itself to fixed treatments and may have underrated the contribution better personnel procedures could make. The utility from selected persons is always greater with adaptive treatment than with fixed treatment as long as the selection method has some validity and the adaptations are appropriate.

The optimal strategy in any personnel situation would be a complex mixture of adaptation and selection. Decision theory asks in each instance in which selection and adaptation are manipulated that the payoff functions for the several possible arrangements be determined empirically. Only then can one make appropriate decisions.

Before dismissing all this as impractical, we should consider some of the truly important implications of the above reasoning for the making of personnel decisions in industry and government. The traditional sequence in personnel research that has been designed to bring about a better quality of personnel decisions has been first to establish a job and an associated training procedure, and then to look for tests or other selection procedures which would weed out applicants likely to perform poorly. Under decision theory there would be no reason to regard the job organization or the training procedure as being independent of the selection procedure. All three are regarded as variables on the same level. Personnel research should seek to identify the best combination of tests, training method, and job organization, as well as such other possible significant factors as the incentive plan and other motivational factors. The initial recruitment methods and sources might also be useful to include as variables.

A closer look at the relation between two of these personnel variables, job organization and selection, will serve to exemplify the power of the decision theory approach. In recent years in highly industrialized countries two new professions, job simplification expert and human engineer, have come into existence. Frequently these experts seek to organize the job so that any unselected man can do the work. The greater their success, the less the value of occupational selection. The tester is competing with the treatment simplifier, whose methods may be the more economical because his changes may be relatively permanent, while the tester must evaluate new employees forever. However, if the tester and the job simplifier were to cooperate and use decision theory, they should be able to arrive at a better combination of treatments.

All too often managers of institutions throughout the world stress occupational selection as a method for solving their personnel problems. They assume that their problems of managing people will be minimal if they can somehow limit the people in their organizations to those who are already able, intelligent, well trained, and easily satisfied. Unfortunately not enough such people exist. Managers must take into their organizations mostly imperfect people like the majority of us. The processes of training people, carefully organizing their jobs, and skill-fully motivating imperfect people may be more difficult, expensive, and time-consuming for managers, but it is frequently more realistic to stress these processes rather than selection. Such stress may well yield a greater payoff. Some experts on developing areas of the world like West Africa, where adequate numbers of experienced, well-trained people are rarely available, recommend that more effort and money be put into training and motivating people and less into selection. According to decision theory, however, all these personnel activities are profitable. It is the best combination that has to be worked out in each case.

A second set of insights of decision theory are those associated with sequential testing. Efficiency of testing is often improved by a sequential scheme which allows the decision maker to continue testing whenever he is in doubt about accepting or rejecting an individual. The mathematical statistics of sequential testing was first worked out in the field of industrial inspection in manufacturing. The striking similarity, from a statistical point of view, between industrial inspection and personnel selection was discovered later. Sequential testing is useful because it costs something to gather information. Obviously it would always be better to administer the full series of tests to every person if observations cost nothing. But testing does cost. Theoretical considerations suggest that sequential procedures can provide a given level of accuracy of decisions with about half the amount of testing required by non-sequential procedures.

It will be realized that sequential procedures can be applied within a test as well as within a group of tests. Instead of having all persons taking a test take all the items in a standardized way as in the past, each person answers questions only until the required decision can be made about him.

Another set of insights of decision theory relates to further improving the efficiency of testing. The personnel director who is concerned with selecting men for different assignments must decide under what conditions tests can make the greatest contribution. In the past he might have selected those tests with the highest validity, that is, those tests with the greatest measured accuracy in predicting success on the criterion. In the light of decision theory, however, he now knows that the importance of an assignment can justify using a test of low validity. "Tests for important decisions which fall far short of the ideal predictor may be much more worth using (and improving) than tests which give excellent guidance in making minor decisions."

Another variable to work with in improving testing efficiency is the length of the test. In traditional test theory it was long ago determined that the longer a test (within very broad limits), provided it had some validity to start with, the greater the validity of the test. But decision theory has begun to suggest ways to determine the optimal length of a test, that is, that point beyond which "increases in cost outweigh benefits from greater validity."

The benefits of greater validity might also be sacrificed for a greater variety of test information. Variety of information is especially likely to be of value when, for example, test scores are to be used to select for many different jobs from among the same pool of applicants—in other words, situations in which multiple decisions have to be made. To get a greater variety of information in a given, usually limited amount of testing time, personnel men in the United States are increasingly turning to batteries made up of several relatively short tests not closely related to each other in what they test. One of these test batteries has been developed by the American government and is enjoying wide usage. It is called the General Aptitude Test Battery.

One last type of insight of decision theory we consider here has to do with the implications of decision theory for several types of tests. The first of these types of tests we might consider are the general ability tests, that is, those measures of academic and intellectual ability widely used to predict performance in schools and on the job. Decision theory shows such tests to have certain hitherto not clearly formulated advantages and disadvantages. On the advantage side of the ledger the criteria or outcomes which the general ability test predicts are usually of the highest importance, and we have seen earlier that the importance of a decision frequently constitutes adequate grounds to accept a test of lower validity. Also, decision theory indicates that a test which contributes to many decisions may be more valuable than a test which contributes to few or but one decision. The general ability test does contribute to many decisions. The intelligence test score of a secondary school student may tell teachers of several subjects whether or not the student is under-achieving, what range of occupations the student might appropriately consider, whether or not to think of going on to the university, etc.

The disadvantages of general ability tests, as revealed by decision theory, turn out to be quite damaging, despite their advantages. If valid decisions can be made using information at hand or cheaply available, any test should be judged by the increase in validity it offers. But because the general ability test deals with qualities required in a wide range of performances, information on those qualities can be obtained from past performances. In England, for example, Professor Vernon has reported that success in grammar school has been very closely predicted from primary school ratings, and that the best general ability tests added almost nothing, even though the measured validity of the general ability tests was high. What may well be more useful might be tests which have lower validity but which might contribute to decision where substitute information is not so readily available, e.g., tests on motivational patterns, emotional functioning, interests, and the like. Consider briefly the use of general ability tests in doing occupational counselling with university students in the United States. The common problem in this situation is the choice of a curriculum. Since general ability tests predict success in about all curricula to about the same degree, they provide no useful information toward the decision regarding which curriculum to follow. What is needed are differential predictors. The same weakness of general ability tests applies to the classification of military personnel.

Another weakness of general ability tests becomes apparent from a point made earlier in this paper. In the world of work, job simplification experts may so simplify work that men, unselected with respect to general ability, could do the work readily. Under such circumstances selection by general ability test would add little. Even at university level the elimination through careful planning of intellectual hurdles, which are irrelevant to a person's later performance, could reduce the importance of selection on general intellectual characteristics. It can be concluded that general ability tests have their strengths and weaknesses, and that their use in the future could better be associated with the kind of decisions to which they were expected to contribute.

The second and last type of test for which we are to consider the implications of decision theory are called *wide-band* procedures, a term from the information theory recently developed for the study of electronic communication systems. Band-width, or greater coverage, is obtained only at the cost of lowered fidelity or dependability. For any decision problem there is optimum band-width, although in conventional selection theory it has been assumed that it is always desirable to maximize dependability. Important wide-band procedures include (1) the interview, as used in guidance, counselling, and therapy, and in both educational and occupational selection, and (2) the projective techniques. These tend to be unsatisfactory when judged by conventional standards of predictive efficiency and dependability. Nevertheless, they continue to be widely used. One may infer from decision theory that their value lies in arriving at reversible, or investigatory, rather than terminal decisions. They are especially useful in situations where sequential procedures can be used. "A sequential process makes ideal use of fallible data, trusting them only to the extent that they deserve." The wide-band procedures are especially useful for directing the decision-maker's subsequent observations so that he finds what is pertinent. Consequently these wide-band procedures have the value of the wide-ranging, initial survey. Following the survey, the decision-maker can turn to the more dependable, narrow-band test procedures. He will have learned which narrow-band procedures to use in order to arrive at a reasonably dependable terminal decision.

41   *Selection and a Better Use for Tests*

S. DAVID FARR

In the following article Professor Farr considers the use of tests in selection for teacher education programs, comments upon the loss of potentially successful candidates when selection occurs, and argues that frequently the wrong questions have been considered important. He suggests that we ask which instructional technique is best for the individual student, and that this question be raised with respect to fairly limited units of instruction. Does this appear to be more psychologically and philosophically defensible than using tests and grades as incentives to motivate learning? To what extent does the effectiveness of this approach depend upon the criteria employed? How much of a loss is it to have a teacher using an approach which is inefficient for a number of his students, i.e., how much cost is the improvement of instruction worth? The reader should note in this paper the practical application of the decision theory concepts presented in the previous article by Wickert, and elements of the prediction problem discussed earlier by Horst.

I would like to begin by considering the usefulness of selection and evaluation in teacher education programs. Turning first to selection, I would propose that in a shortage field like science education we should not practice selection unless it is forced on us by limited accommodations for students, and in that case we should select according to the well-known predictors of academic success.

This last point depends on our lack of a good criterion measure of effective teaching. Even though Medley and Mitzel, Flanders, and others have made some progress in providing ways of describing teaching, teacher educators are properly skeptical of their ability to specify what teaching behaviors are preferred. On the other hand, when we take the obvious criterion of student achievement, we have had little success in finding useful relationships between that criterion and characteristics of the teachers which might be observed at the time they are selected for pre-service programs. Similarly we have been essentially unsuccessful in finding predictors of the tendency to remain in teaching. As a result we tend to fall back on a criterion which is defined by graduation from our institution, certification by appropriate agencies, and placement in a beginning teaching job. Since the latter two of these are conditional and heavily dependent on the first, we can make use of our knowledge of various measures of ability in predicting academic success.

Reprinted and abridged with permission of the author from a speech entitled "Selection and Evaluation in Teacher Education Programs," presented in October 1965 to a meeting in New York City, of the Eastern Regional Division of the Association for the Education of Teachers in Science.

Moving to the independent question of whether selection should be practiced in a field like science education regardless of the definition of the criterion, I must point out that my thoughts on the wisdom of selection go back to a classic 1939 paper by Taylor and Russell as interpreted by Rabinowitz and Mitzel (1961). The background of these two papers is decision theory, although its application here would have to be described as most elementary. The basic point which will be illustrated, however, is that unless there is a perfect relationship between the selection information and the criterion measures, selection aimed at improving the proportion of candidates who are successful will necessarily result in some loss of potentially successful candidates who did not meet the selection criterion. Some illustrations adopted from the Rabinowitz-Mitzel paper may serve to illustrate this point for situations realistic to the selection of students for teacher preparation.

In order to save words later, let me define the *success ratio* as the proportion of those students who choose to prepare for teaching and are acceptable to the university on general admission standards, who complete the program, graduate, are certified, and are placed in beginning teaching jobs. In other words, this success ratio essentially defines the ability of the standard selection program of the institution to select successful students for our program. Let me also define the *selection ratio* as the proportion of those students choosing to prepare for teaching and are acceptable to the university who will be selected on the basis of some further selection procedure. In other words a selection ratio of 50 percent means, then, that we select on the basis of extra information only half of those students interested in education who would have been admitted by the university. Let us further assume that if this extra selection information and the criterion data could each be expressed as continuous variables, their joint distribution is the bivariate normal distribution characterized by a correlation coefficient of .40, probably a reasonable figure in terms of our past success at predicting academic performance. I am assuming too that the proportion of students defined as "successful" is a dichotomization of the continuous criterion distribution, as the selection process is of the selection information distribution.

I would like now to consider the consequences of selection ratios of 90 percent, 50 percent and 10 percent in situations where the success ratio without added selection is 90 percent and 50 percent. I will phrase some of these results in terms of a hypothetical one thousand students admitted by the university, and therefore any number of students I report relate directly to that total. Let us look first at the situation where 90 percent of those students selected by the institution would succeed in our program, and we decide that in addition to this we will select 90 percent of those admitted by the university. Under the 90 percent success ratio 90 percent selection ratio plan, 93 percent of the selected students will be successful, a slight increase from the 90 percent expected in the unselected group. However, the productivity of our program in terms of successful candidates has dropped from 900 to 827, since we removed 73 potentially successful students from our program by means of our selection process and in fact removed only 27 unsuccessful students. Hence, we are making a slight improvement in the percent of students who are successful at the loss of a considerable absolute number of such students.

Suppose that the same university, that is, the one with a 90 percent success ratio for "unselected" students, decides that in their education program they will become more highly selected and choose only 50 percent of those students who meet the general university requirements. Under this plan the proportion of students in the program who are successful goes up to 96 percent, that is, 478 of the 500 students selected. On the other hand the loss of potentially successful education students jumps dramatically to 422. In other words, 422 of the 900 potentially successful students have been removed by our selection system. If the same university decides to run a "small high quality program based on extremely strict selection," let us say selecting only the top 10 percent of those admitted by the university, the percent of success within the program goes to 98 percent, but 802 of the 900 potentially successful candidates are eliminated.

Let us look at the same question at another hypothetical institution where the general admissions procedures are less effective and only 50 percent of those admitted succeed in the education program; in other words, let us describe an institution with a success ratio of 50 percent. If we use a 90 percent selection ratio, our batting average increases from 50 percent to 53 percent with the loss of 23 of the 500 potentially successful candidates and the screening out of 77 potentially unsuccessful students, a somewhat more pleasing picture than we found in the other university. Similarly if we apply a 50 percent selection ratio, we find that 317 or 63 percent of those selected are successful as opposed to the 50 percent expected in the unselected group. On the other hand, we have eliminated 183 of the potentially successful candidates from our program. Assuming that we choose or are forced to use the stringent policy of selecting only 10 percent of the pool of students, we find that the percent successful jumps to 77 percent, but at the tremendous cost of eliminating 423 of the 500 potentially successful students.

In summary I would observe that smaller quality programs based on strict selection among the applicants will not answer the problems of education, as they will produce only a slightly greater percentage of success among those admitted to the programs at a tremendous cost in absolute numbers of teachers provided. I must agree with Rabinowitz and Mitzel that we must look to other approaches for improving the quality of people who are entering the teaching profession. I might add as a footnote that the citerion problem is irrelevant to this argument. If we were able to develop a good criterion of success in teaching, exactly the same arguments could be applied using that rather than the academic success criterion.

Before trying to provide a more attractive answer to our problems, let me turn to the question of evaluating programs in teacher education and attempt to define in that context a plan which might essentially solve both problems at once.

EVALUATION OF INSTRUCTIONAL PROGRAMS

I would like to begin this discussion by proposing that the traditional approaches to evaluation are generally unsatisfactory and in fact might well be considered unscientific.

Let us consider the questions asked in evaluation. These can generally be summarized under the general phrasing "Is our program good?" or "Is our program satisfactory?" There appear to be two difficulties with these questions. First of all, the questions seem to be based on the assumption that all students are treated alike or at least are treated according to a specific formula, that is, we are evaluating "the program." Second, the definition of good or satisfactory has always been a problem to those evaluators who prefer the more scientific approach of defining these terms before looking at the data. Usually there is no alternative to arbitrary (or perhaps it is more polite to say logical) definition of the performances to be judged good or satisfactory.

A second approach to evaluation is the comparison of the average performance of similar students under different programs of instruction. This approach partially solves the problem by revising the concepts of "good" or "satisfactory" to the more manageable concept of "better than." However, it still tends to result in gross conclusions for gross units of instruction, for example "the program" as it applies to gross groups of students, for example all students in the institution.

Let me make a couple of assumptions which should not be too hard to accept. First of all, let us assume that we must work within known techniques of instruction, that is, we do not expect our approach to magically produce new instructional methods. Second, let us assume that we are willing to offer variations in instruction when there is empirical evidence to support its utility. Under this assumption we are faced with either a choice among methods for each student or perhaps a choice among students of those who will respond best to our method. As to the reality of this assumption, I think that it is certainly possible to offer variation at some level. For example, at the very least, different institutions can offer different instruction, and it is very likely possible to vary instruction within an institution at least to the extent of different sets of courses. It is even possible, I have heard, to vary instruction within a single classroom, and it seems to me that the most ordinary elementary school teacher could surely teach all of us something on that point.

Let us make one further assumption for this discussion, that is, that we have a single, continuously measured criterion variable and a set of continuous predictor variables through which we characterize the students. This restriction however is merely a convenience so that we may talk in terms of familiar models, and can be relaxed considerably without causing serious problems.

Under these circumstances we can re-state the evaluation question in the following form. We now ask "Which instructional techniques result in the highest criterion performance for which students?," and we hope that this question will lead us to the planning of research which will have direct application in developing a highly effective "teaching strategy."

Let us look first at the basic information which can be generated as we use teaching or instructional techniques for particular units of subject matter. With the question defined in this way it becomes quite clear that a reasonable approach is to study the regression of the criterion on a set of predictors which we accept as a psychometric description of the student. This enables us to compute the expected criterion performance of a given student in a given subject-matter unit for each of the instructional techniques under study. We may then apply these expectancies in what might be called a "maximum expected performance" strategy, selecting for the student that instructional method for which his expected performance is highest on this particular unit of subject matter. Cronbach and Gleser (1965) would describe this as the making of "classification decisions."

Let us take a look at a simple example of this principle, drawn from a study of instruction in secondary school English. It is oversimplified in that it uses a

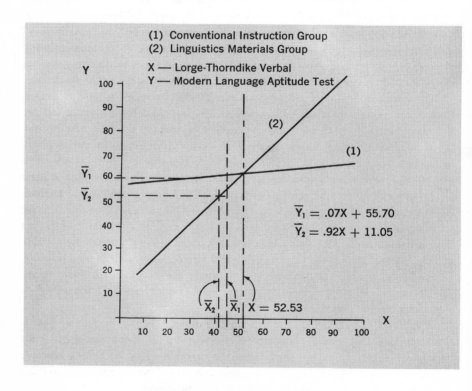

$$X = 52.53$$

$\bar{X}_1 = 46.22$		$\bar{X}_2 = 52.36$
$\bar{Y}_1 = 58.95$		$\bar{Y}_2 = 50.85$
$N_1 = 290$		$N_2 = 248$

Figure 9. Regression of Y on X for Two Groups

single predictor variable and that it deals with performance at the end of a program of instruction several months long, while I would generally prefer much shorter units of instruction. Regardless, it provides a sharp example of the possibilities.

The criterion test is the *Modern Language Aptitude Test* and the predictor the Verbal Battery score of the *Lorge-Thorndike Intelligence Test*. The first treatment is conventional instruction and the second involves the use of linguistics-based teaching materials. Assuming that linear regression lines are reasonable representation of the data (see Figure 9), it seems obvious that students with Lorge-Thorndike (raw) scores less than or equal to 52 would be expected to perform better under the standard method, while those with scores greater than 52 will on the average do better under the linguistics-based program. The obvious thing to do, then, is to pretest students on the Lorge-Thorndike and offer them differential treatment according to their score. This might be done by assignment to different sections of the course or by differentiation of treatment in each classroom.

Another advantage of this approach is that it does not lead to unnecessary differentiation of instruction. When the regression lines are parallel or when one line is consistently higher over the useful range of the predictor, the maximum expected performance strategy would call for use of one instructional technique with all students. Under this plan, however, the decision to treat students alike is rationally arrived at, not just a matter of expediency.

A variety of extensions of this model is apparent. A natural concern is for the use of several predictor scores or non-linear regression models. While these make the problem more complex, they certainly do not put it out of reach.

The inevitable existence of multiple criteria in educational endeavors is a slightly more complex problem, but again decision theory has an answer. We must specify weights so that the weighted sum constitutes a single continuum ordering the various sets of outcomes according to their over-all value. This determination of values is a difficult rational task, with some empirical support to be gained from the psychological scaling techniques.

In summary, let me review a few points. First, I believe that looking to testing for answers to problems of teacher education is essentially a fruitless approach, doomed to failure because it does not direct itself toward the proper questions. Second, in any shortage field, selection, especially the creation of "small quality programs," can not be justified because of the large losses of potentially successful students. Finally, in my opinion the best approach to producing a quality product from our teacher education programs is to study the question of "which instructional technique is best for which students in which subject matter units" and to apply our knowledge according to the "maximum expected performance" strategy. Only through this scientific improvement of program do we have the possibility of feeling confident that we are producing the best possible product under conditions which will allow us to provide an adequate supply of new teachers.

X

SPECIAL PROBLEMS
IN TEST USAGE

While the previous chapter was devoted specifically to the use of tests for prediction and decision-making, the present chapter contains a sampling of articles concerned with a variety of applications of measurement data. The problems with which these authors deal often have had a long history but nevertheless are problems of contemporary importance and interest. These problems range from estimating gains to the mundane matter of assigning grades, to measuring two extreme groups (the culturally deprived on one hand, college students on the other), and to answering important educational questions with modern computers.

These are all crucial topics in today's world. To illustrate, although measuring achievement status is of importance, educational objectives are frequently phrased in terms of growth; basic decisions of extreme importance are often based on faulty grades; the effective use of education as an agency for social and individual advance is needed at all levels of ability; computers permit assessments and operations not previously feasible, but pose significant threats as well. It is with problems such as these that the papers assembled in this chapter are concerned.

An example of an enduring topic is treated in the first paper. Both educators and psychologists consider changes in behavior as indicative of learning, and therefore must concern themselves with the measurement of gains. Dr. Paul Diederich notes three reasons why the assessment of gains, which might appear so simple, is so difficult to accomplish well.

The assignment of grades is another perennial problem for the classroom teacher, and like the assessment of gains, involves procedures which may appear to the uninitiated to be simple and exact. The second paper in this chapter examines in a unique way the matter of grading. The reader should enjoy as well as profit from Dr. Orville Palmer's delightful instructions on how *not* to accomplish the task.

A further topic of importance in the schools is the testing of minority group children. The current concern with the education of minority groups leads thoughtful people to be apprehensive lest decisions made regarding the schooling of the groups are politically or emotionally rather than professionally based. A working group, with Dr. Joshua Fishman as chairman, has provided professional advice for testing this special class of students. Their guidelines should prove helpful not only in the construction and selection of instruments for special groups of children but in the interpretation of scores which the instruments yield.

Society's equal concern with the more advantaged student is reflected in much research dealing with undergraduate education. Representative of this research is the third paper in this chapter, an article dealing with college environments. Drs. Pace and Stern have described differences in college environments and hypothesized the importance of these differences among campuses: e.g., some are characterized as "party schools," some as being strongly social conscious, and some as having a businesslike, no-nonsense air. The degree of success and satisfaction experienced by individual students may be expected to be related to their "fit" in their particular college environments.

The final paper in the chapter illustrates the potential value of technological advance in the testing field, in this instance, the use of computers. Indeed, many of the tasks identified in other papers in this book can only be accomplished efficiently by modern data processing procedures. Certainly it is well recognized that much of the routine work can thus be delegated. But Dr. William Cooley, the author of the paper included here, maintains that better solutions to many educational and psychological problems are now attainable by more unique employment of computers. Some of his illustrations should further stimulate consideration of some of the broad issues which concern us all, particularly those associated with test interpretation and the classification of individuals.

42   Pitfalls in the Measurement of Achievement Gains

PAUL B. DIEDERICH

A technique frequently used to secure data for purposes of evaluating teaching effectiveness and learning involves the testing of pupils before and after an educational experience. Intuitively it would seem that a measure of growth, thus

Reprinted and abridged with permission of author and publisher (The University of Chicago Press) from the *School Review*, 1956, Vol. 64, pp. 59–63.

made possible, should provide a more equitable base for judging performance than final class standing. Consideration of three major difficulties encountered in using growth scores, pointed out in the following nontechnical discussion, should lead the reader to a clearer perspective of a very complex topic. (For a more comprehensive and technical treatment of the topic, the reader is referred to a recent volume edited by Harris, 1963.) How can the major difficulties met in using change scores be overcome? Would the effort be justified? In addition to their application to learning situations, where else in the behavioral sciences might the study of change or growth scores prove valuable?

When a teacher gives a published test of almost any skill that develops more or less continuously, such as reading, writing, or arithmetic, at the beginning of the school year and a parallel form of the same test at the end, the average score is practically certain to rise. In addition to the fact that teachers are better at their jobs than most people realize, all the forces of growth are on their side, just as all the recuperative powers of the body are on the side of the physician. If we ever need evidence to confound our critics, we can find it in the difference between initial and final averages on standardized tests.

If it should occur to the critic, however, or even to a friendly inquirer to find out how much the lowest fifth on the initial test had gained, then the middle fifth, and then the highest fifth, he could upset our apple cart. In most cases it would turn out that the students who made the lowest initial scores had gained by far the most, those in the middle had gained less, and those at the top had gained little or nothing. Some of the latter would even appear to have lost ground. The obvious conclusion would be that instruction had been pitched at the level of the least able, the brighter students had not been stimulated and had loafed on the job, and almost all of the average gain to which we pointed with such pride could be attributed to the fact that the bottom of the distribution had been hauled up to about the level of the initial average.

COOPERATIVE STUDY DATA

That this is not a fanciful or unusual situation is shown by the 1954 Final Report of the Cooperative Study of Evaluation in General Education (Dressel & Mayhew, 1954). The data presented in Table 1 reflects average gains from the beginning to the end of the freshman year for an average of 1,400 students in nine colleges, from the lowest fifth on the pretest up to the highest fifth, on all instruments developed during the Cooperative Study.

Whatever tests or inventories were used, and wherever they were used, students with the lowest initial scores appeared to gain the most; students with the highest initial scores appeared either to have gained least or to have lost ground. This was true not only of cognitive tests but of instruments attempting to measure appreciations, attitudes, and insight into human relations.

TABLE 1. *Average Gains of Students on Post-Tests, Classified According to Pretest Standing*[1]

Test	Low Group	Low Middle Group	Middle Group	High Middle Group	High Group
Critical Thinking in Social Science	6.89	5.48	3.68	4.20	2.26
Science Reasoning and Understanding	6.26	5.16	2.93	2.04	0.31
Humanities Participation Inventory	18.00	5.05	4.94	1.39	−2.07
Analysis of Reading and Writing	5.33	2.89	1.81	1.22	0.25
Critical Thinking	6.68	4.65	3.47	2.60	1.59
Inventory of Beliefs	9.09	5.31	4.65	3.32	1.01
Problems in Human Relations	3.19	1.67	1.31	1.51	−0.36

[1] Adapted from Paul L. Dressel and Lewis B. Mayhew, 1954.

So many students in so many different colleges were tested that the consistent downward trend in the data on gains, from initially lowest to initially highest, cannot be attributed to the population tested. The fact that the same trend is shown by all instruments developed in the study suggests that it cannot be attributed to poor test construction. The colleges participating in the study were selected for the excellence of their general education programs; they could not all have done a poor job of teaching. It is contrary to all teaching experience to suppose that the initially weak students were, in every case, more highly motivated than the initially strong. The data seem unassailable; yet we cannot accept the conclusion that "poor" students regularly learn more than "good" students. Something in the nature of present test construction or of the test-retest situation gives initial low scorers an advantage. What is it?

PROPHECIES DISCREDITED

Unless we can find answers to this question and do something about them, two of our most hopeful prophecies connected with testing are likely to be discredited. The first may be stated in the form of an incomplete sentence: "When testing turns from the measurement of status to the measurement of growth . . ." What will happen is not very clear, but we assume that it is bound to be good. The data just cited suggest that is bound to be bad. By some quirk in the test-retest situation, poor students will uniformly appear to have grown more than have the good students no matter who teaches them or what is tested.

The second prophecy is that when marks are based on growth rather than on final status, the inequities of the present marking system will disappear. So they will, it seems, but only to be replaced by a great inequity: the guaranteed superiority of the least able. The only way in which good students will be able to get good marks will be to select the most obviously absurd answers to all the items on their pretests.

These prospects, we trust, will not come to pass; the good sense of the profession will reject such outrageous conclusions. But at the same time teachers and administrators are likely to reject testing. They cannot put their faith in instruments that lead to absurd conclusions.

The true conclusion emerging from these considerations, I suggest, is that we do not know very much about the measurement of growth. Testing and retesting will have to be put on some different basis before we can find out and truly evaluate how much students have learned. I do not know how this will be done, but I can review three of the most obvious difficulties that will have to be surmounted.

CEILING EFFECT

The first difficulty is that the pretests may have been too easy for the high-scoring students, and their initial scores were so near the maximum possible scores as to leave little room for improvement. We usually discard this hypothesis far too hastily when we find that the highest final score was 90 percent correct and the average went up only from 50 to 60 percent correct. What we overlook is that the maximum attainable score may be a good deal lower than 100 percent correct.

Good tests of such complex skills as reading and writing go beyond matters on which everyone can agree into questions calling for insight, judgment, and taste—the very qualities in which we hope our best students will show their greatest improvement. On such questions, however, it is impossible to secure 100 percent agreement among qualified critics of the test. On the test of Critical Analysis of Reading and Writing used in the Cooperative Study, for example, no item was admitted to the final form of the test on which fewer than eleven out of the thirteen critics agreed. Restricting the test to items on which everyone agreed would have resulted in a very dull test, unlikely to challenge the brighter students. While the standard of agreement seemed strict enough, there were a good many items that only 84 percent of competent English teachers answered correctly. In such a case we should regard 84 percent correct as the maximum attainable score. Many of the students in the highest fifth came perilously close to this figure in the pretest.

Even so, the highest fifth should have been able to show more than the average gain of a quarter of a point that was reported in the study, for the lowest members of this group got only half the items right on the pretest. Some other explanation is needed.

REGRESSION

The most likely explanation of the apparently unfavorable difference in gains is the phenomenon known as "regression." Scores on all objective tests are determined partly by ability and partly by luck. The items presented to the students are only a sample drawn from an almost infinite number of similar questions that might have been asked. The particular sample that happens to be chosen is bound to favor some students more than others. They have had more experience with these kinds of questions or have given more thought to them. But when a different sample is drawn, luck is not likely to favor the same students to the same degree.

Moreover, students are rarely certain in their choice of answers. On a five-choice item they may eliminate one as absurd and two others as common errors of which they have learned to beware. The remaining two appear equally plausible, and they decide by a mental "flip of a coin." The initial high scorers were lucky in their guesses; the initial low scorers were not. On a second test the proportion of chance success may be reversed.

The phenomenon of regression has been studied by the statisticians, and they have provided an easy-to-use formula to predict what final score is to be expected on the basis of any given initial score—to the extent that chance is involved in both. I can explain how the principle works with a minimum of numbers if we imagine the following situation.

A class has been given a test of reading and writing on their first day in school and a parallel form of the same test on the second day. It is parallel in all respects: covers the same type of content with the same types of items, and the mean, standard deviation, and reliability of the second test are all equal to those of the first. The students have had sufficient practice in taking machine-scored objective tests so that marking the answer spaces is not a problem in either test. They are not told their scores on the first test, nor which answers are correct. They learn nothing about reading and writing in the interim. Let us imagine that the average score on the first test is 16; the average of the lowest fifth is 8; of the highest fifth, 24; and the reliability of the tests, as indicated by the correlation between them, is .70. What average scores of the lowest and the highest fifths may be expected on the second test when chance alone is involved?

In such a situation final scores may be predicted by multplying initial differences from the average by the reliability of the tests.[2] Take the difference of the lowest fifth from the average of the total group: it is —8. Multiply this by the reliability (.70), and you get —5.6. Take 5.6 from the initial average (16), and the predicted score of the lowest fifth on the second test will be 10.4. Since their initial average was 8, they will appear to have gained 2.4 points.

Similarly, take the difference of the highest fifth from the initial average (+8), multiply by the reliability (.70), and you get 5.6. Add this to the initial average (16), and the predicted score of the highest fifth on the second test will be 21.6. Since their initial average was 24, they will appear to have lost 2.4 points.

While the situation we have imagined is artificial, the same chance factors will operate to the same extent when the tests are given at the beginning and end of

---

[2] The actual prediction formula is a bit more complicated, but this simplification is valid for the situation described and illustrates the basic principle that is involved.

the school year—provided that the two tests are strictly parallel. In the ordinary course of events, of course, they are not strictly parallel, and then chance differences will be even greater. We usually do not realize the magnitude of the differences in test-retest scores that may be attributed to chance alone. The figures I have cited were very close to the actual figures for the test of Critical Analysis of Reading and Writing used in the Cooperative Study, rounded for the sake of simplicity. We regarded with some horror the finding that the lowest fifth gained 5.33 points while the highest fifth gained only 0.25 points. But when we consider what might be expected to happen on the basis of chance alone, the lowest group should have gained 2.4 points; it actually gained 5.33; therefore it exceeded a chance gain by 2.93 points. The highest group would be expected to lose 2.4 points; it actually gained 0.25 points; therefore the best approximation of the actual gain is 2.65 points.

We can now view the gains of both groups in better perspective. When set against what would have happened by chance, if no learning whatever had taken place, the lowest fifth gained 2.93 points; the highest fifth gained 2.65 points. Such a finding comes closer, although not close enough, to our intuitive judgment of what these two groups probably learned.

Teachers regard such manipulations uneasily. The raw scores seem to be real; the converted scores, hypothetical. But there is nothing fanciful about the phenomenon of regression. It was originally deduced from observations that children of extremely tall parents tend to be shorter and children of extremely short parents tend to be taller than their parents. The formula expressing this principle can be proved as rigorously as any proposition in geometry, and study after study has shown that this principle must be taken into account if the results are to seem reasonable.

Teachers may wonder why fortune uniformly smiles upon the weakest students and frowns upon the strongest in the test-retest situation. It does nothing of the sort. Both groups will "regress" toward the average to precisely the same extent: their distance from the average multiplied by the reliability of the test. The direction of this regression quite naturally has to be upward for low-scoring students and downward for high-scoring students.

My only quarrel with the use of the regression formula is that, if we stop there, we have not gone far enough. We have wiped out the spurious gains and losses that may be attributed to chance, but the usual result is that the weakest and the strongest groups appear to have gained about the same amount. We have good reason to believe that this is not true. What else keeps the initially high students from showing how much more they have learned than the initially low?

UNEQUAL UNITS OF MEASUREMENT

A further explanation of the discrepancy in gains may lie in the way in which objective tests are constructed. In a four-choice test we tend to put in one best answer, one that is likely to deceive all but the elect, one common error that students make, and one absurd answer that I shall refer to as a "booby trap." These four types of answers may not appear in every item, but let us suppose that there are equal numbers of each in the total test. Consider the case of the boy who in the beginning can rule out only half the booby traps and has to choose among the remaining answers by chance. The part of his score that may be attributed to knowledge or skill is one-eighth. But merely by staying awake in class he may learn to rule out all the booby traps and to avoid the most common types of errors that students make, for these will be emphasized most heavily in class. Hence in the final test he will be able to rule out two out of every four responses on the average and will have to choose, by chance, only between the right and the nearly right. The part of his score that may be attributed to knowledge is now 50 percent. He has gone from one-eighth correct to one-half correct —a gain of 38 percentage points—on the basis of minimum ability and minimum effort.

Now consider the student who can do this well in the beginning. He can already rule out booby traps and common errors; the only way he can improve his score is by learning to distinguish best answers from those that are equally plausible and almost as good. These are hard choices. While the poor student can gain 38 points in a test of 100 items by learning to make easy choices, the good student may have a harder time gaining 10 points, for he has much harder problems to cope with.

Unfortunately there is not yet any precise way to translate responses to test items into equal units of growth. Standard scores based on the normal curve are an improvement on percentiles in estimating growth, but they do not solve the problem, because they rest on the assumption that equal gains of raw-score points represent equal increments in ability, and the whole purpose of this section has been to demonstrate that this is not the case. It is harder to get from the mean up to plus one standard deviation than it is to get from minus one standard deviation up to the mean. All the data presented from the Cooperative Study attest that this is not a fanciful or theoretical argument but a fact, for many students were able to do the latter but relatively few were able to do the former.

The only ultimate answer to this question that I can now foresee is to get norms for gains as well as for status, starting from any given initial score. Until such norms are provided, the best we can do as teachers is to become as familiar with records on our tests as our students are with records in sports. It may be that a gain from 30 to 60 percent correct, while creditable, is nothing to get excited about, for almost everyone who starts at 30 percent correct can make it. But a gain from 80 to 85 percent correct on a difficult test may be breathtaking, for no one has ever made it before.

This plan will not settle the metaphysical argument as to whether a gain from stupidity to mediocrity is better than a gain from competence to brilliance, but at least it will not automatically stack the cards in favor of the former.

43   Seven Classic Ways of Grading Dishonestly

ORVILLE PALMER

The applications of measurement data in the process of evaluation or decision-making are many and varied. In the following article important uses and misuses of test data in the assignment of grades are discussed. Sources of data used in the marking process should, of course, not be limited to tests or examinations. Any evidence related to a course, as long as it was gathered to determine if certain instructional objectives had been attained, should be considered legitimate data. Such a suggestion, however, can lead to a troublesome problem. On the one hand, a teacher desires a common basis for the evaluation of his pupils. Such efforts as outside readings or independent research projects might not be considered, as they may have a different meaning for different students. It is also true that the failure to reward "extra effort" is contrary to the known positive relationships between reinforcement, motivation, and learning. Dr. Palmer's discussion underscores a widely known fact but one which is not generally part of a teacher's conscious awareness, namely, that the assignment of grades involves philosophical decisions. Each teacher must determine what data are germane, what proportion of the class will receive A's, B's, etc. The shortcomings of many marking practices highlighted in the following article are well worth considering. In addition, the reader may wish to consider the following questions: (1) What principles should guide the teacher in marking? (2) How can grading practices be improved? (3) How does the assignment of marks relate to the over-all instructional process?

No two marking systems of teachers are quite alike, even as no two teachers are identical. Nevertheless, the major kinds of bad evaluation systems, or quasi-systems, may be identified.

A first, and wholly indefensible way of grading dishonestly is by abdication. Because of inexperience, inadequate training, or overwork, the teacher in effect abdicates his responsibility for grading fairly and creatively. Such a teacher may claim that an adequate testing program would take more time than he can spare, or that test-making is an art for which he has no talent. At the last moment such a teacher will put together a crude, inadequate test, or use anything he can lay his hands on: a workbook unit test, a dog-eared commercial test; or he may assign an essay topic thought up on the spur of the moment. Rather than tailor his tests to his course, he may tailor his course to any available set of tests. But

Reprinted and abridged from *The English Journal*, October, 1962, pp. 464–467, with permission of the National Council of Teachers of English and Orville Palmer.

such a teacher clearly knows very little about student evaluation. He shirks real responsibility in the matter, and unfortunately all too often he does nothing to improve his competence.

The second method of grading dishonestly is by means of what can be called "the carrots and clubs" system. In this system, grades may be raised by performing designated added tasks, or lowered by failure to avoid certain prejudices of the teacher. Here we find the teacher who fails every theme that contains a run-on sentence or, say two spelling errors. And here we meet up with bonuses for good behavior and added effort.

In grade school, I suppose, a teacher may properly grade, in part at least, on "attitude and effort." But in high school and college surely the academic grade should be based on academic performance and little else. It is a mistaken and dangerous kindness—or mode of discipline—to do otherwise. I dare say I shall affront more teachers on this point than any other. I can only urge that the line between rewarded good attitude and effort and favoritism is a treacherous one. I can only say that the more blatantly a teacher "buys" good behavior or extra effort, the greater the damage to class morale, to student ethics, and to academic standards. Beyond any question, the more extraneous factors that enter into the marking system, the less meaning an academic grade possesses. Any grade becomes debased coinage to the same degree that it represents nonacademic effort and attainment. By extraneous factors I mean such things as classroom deportment, neatness of penmanship, imaginative covers for reports and similar artwork, extra credit for reading, and the like. Not that any one of these things is bad or even suspect in itself. My point is simply this: everything of an academic nature that the teacher grades—quizzes, themes, oral and written reports, required or volunteer work—should be graded on its merits and nothing else.

There does not exist a teacher who has wholly freed himself of "halo effect," of all those tangibles and intangibles of personal approval or disapproval of students' attitudes and conduct. Teaching is not, and should not be an impersonal, cold-blooded enterprise. To the extent that it is not, however, it becomes increasingly difficult to make evaluation wholly impersonal. Yet I have observed that one excellent measure of a teacher's honesty and rectitude is the respect that students give to grades bestowed by the teacher known for his fairness and scrupulousness in marking.

A third way to grade dishonestly is by default. This teacher gives as little time to tests as possible. In graduate school we find the professor who reluctantly gives a single term-end test. In secondary schools the teacher who hates tests and claims they are meaningless or farcical or an infernal nuisance will give as few of them as possible. Sometimes his students are in a state of near-panic because the base for grades is so narrow a single misstep could spell disaster. Curiously enough, the teacher who hates tests very often also hates reading student themes, and his students consequently write few themes or none. (Such an arrangement is probably the best single guarantee that students will not learn how to write competently.)

The dishonesty lies precisely in the unfair base. Any test, of whatever nature, is but a limited and inadequate sampling of the student's knowledge and achievement. Every test will have its defects of validity and reliability.

A student instinctively knows that the odds for a valid evaluation improve when he takes four tests rather than a single test. He knows that the chances are better that he will be able to demonstrate his skills and understanding—because the base is broader.

The testing zealots furnish a fourth system of grading unwisely. The zealot sets his students to racing with a vengeance—daily quizzes, almost daily written assignments, weekly tests, quarter-term, mid-term, final examinations, reports of all sorts. He grades everything short of classroom posture. At its extreme, in such systems everything becomes an ordeal, the course an endurance contest or a problem in survival.

The zealot's quizzes check whether the students have read their assigned pages of text, whether assigned short stories or novels were read carefully. They are, in short, a policing device. Even notebooks may be called in and graded.

A certain amount of such police work may be necessary, of course. It should, however, stop well short of constant surveillance and the spirit of the police officer administering a lie detector test.

Until the sheer weight of oversize classes or the scythe of Father Time cuts down these teachers, they average up their dozens of minor and major grades, using elaborate formulas of computation and weighting, secure in the belief they have evolved a scientific, fair system of evaluation. Possibly they have, but I would suggest they have paid too high a price for it. The good will, the student rapport, the main purposes of instruction have been lost somewhere in the process.

Changing the rules in mid-game is a fifth way to grade dishonestly. It is always a temptation to a harried or uncertain teacher. It amounts to shifting the grading standards, either up or down, for workbook tests, themes, examinations, and so on. The teacher may start off the course by distributing quantities of low or failing grades to frighten the students into greater effort, then ease his standards later. He may tighten his grading at mid-term to put spurs into the lazy and laggard, to discipline an unruly class, to merely rectify a grading curve that threatens to be top-heavy with A's and B's and unballasted with failures.

Here, too, we discover the irate teacher who decides to "get tough" about bad spelling or bad grammar. Henceforward it will be an automatic F for every theme with two or more misspelled words, an F for any essay examination with a run-on sentence, and so on.

Strewing with booby traps the field across which the student must march, making a hazard-cluttered obstacle course of every theme—this may or may not eliminate misspelled words and rambling sentences. It can usually be counted on to put frost on the fragile flower of student creativity and enthusiasm, to put greater tension between teacher and student, even to make learning an ordeal.

A sixth kind of dishonesty is displayed by the psychic grader. His is an ingenuous method—it can scarcely be called a system since it is neither structured nor organic. Undoubtedly it is an ultimate variety or extension of halo effect grading. (Halo effect probably constitutes the chief weakness of teacher-made tests and evaluation.)

The psychic teacher may inform you that he, for one, has no need for anything so coarse-meshed as a test to catch his fish in. You are given to understand that he can tell almost immediately in his bones or by means inscrutable to ordinary man who the A students will be, who the B. And he will swear by the distinction between the two. To this teacher tests are superfluous or at best mere window dressing.

A final classic method of grading dishonestly is anchored in a system of impossible perfection. Teachers adhering to this system inform their students, in effect, that an A is out of the question, and that only the most brilliant and industrious can hope for the accolade of a B. Often this teacher can be counted on to fail twice as many students as anyone else in his department. He prides himself on his high standards. And he grumbles at his soft-hearted colleagues' habit of debasing departmental standards by the indiscriminate bestowal of high grades and by a rabbit-hearted reluctance to fail the dullards.

When you challenge their use of one or more of the above systems or ways of grading, some teachers stubbornly and even angrily reply that it is perfectly fair to use any set of rules you like, so long as you have all your students running the same race and abiding by the same set of rules. This of course has a sporting air to it and seems to doff its cap to egalitarian democracy and our American way of life.

The fact remains that such a reply is specious. The students in any high school class are not running one race but several. They are also racing all the other academic classes in their school, and (if college-bound) they are racing all the other students in all the other high schools in the land.

If every teacher makes his own set of rules and answers to no one's conscience but his own, there can only be anarchy in these races. This, in a very real sense, is the state of affairs today.

Of course nothing can be more corrosive of values and goals than the concept of academic courses as "races" in which the winners snatch the A's, the runners-up win the B's, and the also-rans receive only C's and worse. When the grade becomes more important than the learning itself, education itself is subverted.

44   *Guidelines for Testing Minority Group Children*

MARTIN DEUTSCH, JOSHUA A. FISHMAN, LEONARD S. KOGAN,
ROBERT D. NORTH, AND MARTIN WHITMAN

The usefulness of a test depends in part on appropriate and intelligent admin-istration and interpretation. But perhaps even more important is the compati-bility of the group or individual to be examined relative to the test content and its standardization population. With the increased public, private, and governmental concern surrounding the social and educational problems of minority groups, the need to reappraise our testing practices becomes mandatory. The following paper, prepared by a work group of the Society for the Psychological Study of Social Issues under the chairmanship of Dr. Joshua Fishman, makes a very important contribution to the reappraisal process. This report highlights some very signifi-cant sources of error originating from implicit and explicit cultural bias that must be taken into account in test development and interpretation.

What are some of the sources of error that may influence test reliability that are somewhat unique to minority groups? How might these influences be controlled? Are interest and personality tests more or less susceptible to bias than achieve-ment and aptitude measures? Why? What are the three kinds of factors the authors indicate may influence predictive validity? What are the major sources of error in test interpretation? In general, what are the major implications of this article for test selection?

Responsible educational authorities recognize that it is as unwise to put educa-tional and psychological tests in the hands of untrained and unskilled personnel as it is to permit the automobile or any highly technical and powerful tool to be handled by individuals who are untrained in its use and unaware of the damage that it can cause if improperly used.

The necessity for caution is doubly merited when tests are administered to members of minority groups. Unfortunately, there is no single and readily avail-able reference source to which test users can turn in order to become more fully acquainted with the requirements and cautions to be observed in such cases. The purpose of this committee's effort is to provide an introduction to the many con-siderations germane to selection, use, and interpretation of educational and psy-chological tests with minority group children, as well as to refer educators and their associates to other more technical discussions of various aspects of the same topic.

The term "minority group" as we are using it here is not primarily a quantita-

Reprinted and abridged with permission of first named author and the publisher (the Society for Psychological Study of Social Issues) from *The Journal of Social Issues*, 1964, Vol. 20, pp. 129–145.

tive designation. Rather it is a status designation referring to cultural or social disadvantage. Since many Negro, Indian, lower-class white, and immigrant children have not had most of the usual middle-class opportunities to grow up in home, neighborhood, and school environments that might enable them to utilize their ability and personality potentials fully, they are at a disadvantage in school, and in after-school and out-of-school situations as well. It is because of these disadvantages, reflecting environmental deprivations and experiential atypicalities, that certain children may be referred to as minority group children.

CRITICAL ISSUES IN TESTING MINORITY GROUPS

Standardized tests currently in use present three principal difficulties when they are used with disadvantaged minority groups: (1) they may not provide reliable differentiation in the range of the minority group's scores, (2) their predictive validity for minority groups may be quite different from that for the standardization and validation groups, and (3) the validity of their interpretation is strongly dependent upon an adequate understanding of the social and cultural background of the group in question.

I. RELIABILITY OF DIFFERENTIATION ■ In the literature of educational and psychological testing, relatively little attention has been given to the possible dependence of test reliability upon subcultural differences. It is considered essential for a test publisher to describe the reliability sample (the reference group upon which reliability statements are based) in terms of factors such as age, sex, and grade level composition, and there is a growing tendency on the part of test publishers to report subgroup reliabilities. But to the best of our knowledge, none of the test manuals for the widely used tests give separate reliability data for specific minority groups. Institutions that use tests regularly and routinely for particular minority groups would do well to make their own reliability studies in order to determine whether the tests are reliable enough when used with these groups.

RELIABILITY AFFECTED BY SPREAD OF SCORES ■ In addition to being dependent on test length and the specific procedure used for estimating reliability (e.g., split-half or retest), the reliability coefficient for a particular test is strongly affected by the spread of test scores in the group for which the reliability is established. In general, the greater the spread of scores in the reliability sample, the higher the reliability coefficient. Consequently, if the tester attempts to make differentiations within a group which is more homogeneous than the reference or norm group for which reliability is reported, the actual effectiveness of the test will be found to be lower than the reported reliability coefficient appears to promise. For many tests there is abundant evidence that children from the lower socio-economic levels commonly associated with minority group status tend to have a smaller spread of scores than do children from middle-income families, and such restriction in the distribution of scores tends to lower reliability so far as differentiation of measurement with such groups is concerned.

CHARACTERISTICS OF MINORITY GROUP CHILDREN THAT AFFECT TEST PERFORM-ANCE ∎ Most of the evidence relating to the contention that the majority of educational and psychological tests tend to be more unreliable, i.e., more characterized by what is technically called "error variance," for minority group children, is indirect, being based on studies of social class and socio-economic differences rather than on minority group performance per se. Nevertheless, the particular kinds of minority groups that we have in mind are closely associated with the lower levels of socio-economic status.

For children who come from lower socio-economic levels, what characteristics may be expected to affect test performance in general, and the accuracy or precision of test results in particular? The list of reported characteristics is long, and it is not always consistent from one investigation to another. But at least it may be hypothesized that in contrast to the middle-class child the lower-class child will tend to be less verbal, more fearful of strangers, less self-confident, less motivated toward scholastic and academic achievement, less competitive in the intellectual realm, more "irritable," less conforming to middle-class norms of behavior and conduct, more apt to be bilingual, less exposed to intellectually stimulating materials in the home, less varied in recreational outlets, less knowledgeable about the world outside his immediate neighborhood, and more likely to attend inferior schools.

Some Examples. Can it be doubted that such characteristics—even if only some of them apply to each "deprived" minority group—will indeed be reflected in test taking and test performance? Obviously, the primary effect will be shown in terms of test validity for such children. In many cases, however, the lowering of test validity may be indirectly a result of lowered test reliability. This would be particularly true if such characteristics interfere with the consistency of performance from test to retest for a single examiner or for different examiners. Consider the following examples and probable results:

Example: A Negro child has had little contact with white adults other than as distant and punitive authority figures. *Probable Result:* Such a child might have difficulty in gaining rapport with a white examiner or reacting without emotional upset to his close presence. Even in an individual testing situation he might not respond other than with monosyllables, failing to give adequate answers even when he knows them. The examiner, reacting in terms of his own stereotypes, might also lower the reliability and validity of the test results by assuming that the child's performance will naturally be inferior, and by revealing this attitude to the child.

Example: Children from a particular minority group are given little reason to believe that doing well in the school situation will affect their chance for attaining better jobs and higher income later in life. *Probable Result:* Such children will see little purpose in schooling, dislike school, and will reject anything associated with school. In taking tests their primary objective is to get through as rapidly as possible and escape from what for them might be an uncomfortable situation. Their test performance might, therefore, be characterized by a much greater amount of guessing, skipping, and random responses than is shown by the middle-class child who never doubts the importance of the test, wants to please his teacher and parents, and tries his best.

SPECIAL NORMS OFTEN NEEDED

When the national norms do not provide adequate differentiation at the lower end of the aptitude or ability scale, special norms established locally are often useful. For instance, if a substantial number of underprivileged or foreign-background pupils in a school or school district rank in the lowest 5 percent on the national norms, local norms might serve to provide a special scale within this range. If the score distribution with the first few percentiles of the national norms is mainly a function of chance factors, however, a lower level of the test or an easier type of test is needed for accurate measurement of the low-scoring children.

RESPONSIBILITIES OF TEST USERS ▪ The sensitive test user should be alert to reliability considerations in regard to the particular group involved and the intended use of the tests. In assessing reports on test reliability provided by test manuals and other sources, he will not be satisfied with high reliability coefficients alone. He will consider not only the size of the reliability samples, but also the nature and composition of the samples and the procedures used to estimate reliability. He will try to determine whether the standard error of measurement varies with score levels, and whether his testing conditions are similar to those of the reliability samples. He will ask whether the evidence on reliability is relevant to the persons and purposes with which he is concerned. He will know that high reliability does not guarantee validity of the measures for the purpose in hand, but he will realize that low reliability may destroy validity.

The examiner should be well aware that test results are characteristically influenced by cultural and subcultural differentials and that the performance of underprivileged minority group children is often handicapped by what should be test-extraneous preconditions and response patterns. He should not necessarily assume that the child from a minority group family will be as test-sophisticated and motivated to do his best as are the majority of environment-rich, middle-class children.

If the examiner finds—and this will be typical—that the reliability sample does not provide him with information about the reliability of the test for the kind of children he is testing, he should urge that the test results not be taken at face value in connection with critical decisions concerning the children. Very often careful examination of responses to individual test items will indicate to him that the apparent performance of the child is not adequately reflecting the child's actual competence or personality because of certain subcultural group factors.

II. Validity ▪ Of course if an individual's test scores were to be used only to describe his relative standing with respect to a specified norm group, the fact that the individual had a minority group background would not be important. It is when an explanation of his standing is attempted, or when long-range predictions enter the picture (as they usually do) that background factors become important.

For example, no inequity is necessarily involved if a culturally disadvantaged child is simply reported to have an IQ of 84 and a percentile rank of 16 on the national norms for a certain intelligence test. However, if this is interpreted as meaning that the child ranks or will rank no higher in learning ability than does a middle-class, native-born American child of the same IQ, the interpretation might well be erroneous.

Factors Impairing Test Validity ▪ Three kinds of factors may impair a test's predictive validity. First, there are test-related factors—factors or conditions that affect the test scores but which may have relatively little relation to the criterion. Such factors may include test-taking skills, anxiety, motivation, speed, understanding of test instructions, degree of item or format novelty, examiner-examinee rapport, and other general or specific abilities that underlie test performance but which are irrelevant to the criterion. Examples of the operation of such factors are found in the literature describing the problems of white examiners testing Negro children (Dreger and Miller, 1960), of American Indian children taking unfamiliar, timed tests (Klineberg, 1935), and of children of certain disadvantaged groups being exposed for the first time to test-taking procedures (Haggard, 1954).

It should be noted that some test-related factors may not be prejudicial to disadvantaged groups. For example, test-taking anxiety of a disruptive nature (Sarason et al., 1960) may be more prevalent in some middle-class groups than in lower-class groups. In general, however, the bias attributable to test-related factors accrues to the detriment of the culturally disadvantaged groups.

Interest and Personality Inventory Scores ▪ When standardized interest inventories are used, special caution should be observed in making normative interpretations of the scores of culturally disadvantaged individuals. When a child has not had opportunities to gain satisfaction or rewards from certain pursuits, he is not likely to show interest in these areas. For example, adolescent children in a particular slum neighborhood might rank consistently low in scientific, literary, musical, and artistic interests on the Kuder Preference Record if their home and school environments fail to stimulate them in these areas. With improved cultural opportunities, these children might rapidly develop interests in vocations or avocations related to these areas.

Scores on personality inventories may also have very different significance for minority group members than for the population in general (Auld, 1952). Whenever the inventory items tap areas such as home or social adjustment, motivation, religious beliefs, or social customs, the appropriateness of the national norms for minority groups should be questioned. Local norms for the various minority groups involved might again be very much in order here.

PREDICTING COMPLEX CRITERIA ▪ A second class of factors contributing to low predictive validity is associated with the complexity of criteria. Criteria generally represent "real life" indices of adjustment or achievement and therefore they commonly sample more complex and more variegated behaviors than do the tests. An obvious example is the criterion of school grades. Grades are likely to reflect motivation, classroom behavior, personal appearance, and study habits, as well as intelligence and achievement. Even if a test measured scholastic aptitude sensitively and accurately, its validity for predicting school marks would be attenuated because of the contribution of many other factors to the criterion. It is important, therefore, to recognize the influence of other factors, not measured by the tests, which may contribute to criterion success. Since disadvantaged groups tend to fare poorly on ability and achievement tests, there is particular merit in exploring the background, personality, and motivation of members of such groups for compensatory factors, untapped by the tests, which may be related to criterion performance.

In some instances, such as in making scholarship awards on a statewide or national basis, test scores are used rigidly for screening or cut-off purposes to satisfy demands for objectivity and "impartiality." The culturally disadvantaged child (quite possibly a "diamond-in-the-rough") is often the victim of this automatic and autocratic system. Recourse lies in providing opportunities where the hurdles are less standardized and where a more individualized evaluation of his qualifications for meeting the criterion may prove to be fairer for him.

EFFECTS OF INTERVENING EVENTS ON PREDICTIONS ▪ A third set of contributors to low criterion validity is related to the nature of intervening events and contingencies. This class of conditions is particularly important when the criterion measure is obtained considerably later than the testing—when predictive rather than concurrent validity is at stake. If the time interval between the test administration and the criterial assessment is lengthy, a host of situational, motivational, and maturational changes may occur in the interim. An illness, an inspiring teacher, a shift in aspiration level or in direction of interest, remedial training, an economic misfortune, an emotional crisis, a growth spurt or retrogression in the abilities sampled by the test—any of these changes intervening between the testing and the point or points of criterion assessment may decrease the predictive power of the test.

One of the more consistent findings in research with disadvantaged children is the decline in academic aptitude and achievement test scores of such children with time (Masland, Sarason, and Gladwin, 1958). The decline is, of course, in relation to the performance of advantaged groups or of the general population. It is plausible to assume that this decline represents the cumulative effects of diminished opportunities and decreasing motivation for acquiring academic knowledge and skills. When such cumulative effects are not taken into consideration, the predictive power of academic aptitude and achievement tests is impaired. If it were known in advance that certain individuals or groups would be exposed to deleterious environmental conditions, and if allowances could be made for such contingencies in connection with predictions, the test's criterion validity could be improved.

Looking in another direction, the normative interpretation of the test results cannot reveal how much the status of underprivileged individuals might be changed if their environmental opportunities and incentives for learning and acquiring skills were to be improved significantly.

In situations where minority group members are likely to have to continue competing with others under much the same cultural handicaps that they have faced in the past, normative interpretation of their aptitude and achievement test scores will probably yield a fairly dependable basis for short-term predictive purposes. When special guidance or training is offered to help such individuals overcome their handicaps, however, achievement beyond the normative expectancies may well be obtained, and predictions should be based on expectancies derived specifically from the local situation. In this connection it should be recognized that attempts to appraise human "potential" without defining the milieu in which it will be given an opportunity to materialize are as futile as attempts to specify the horsepower of an engine without knowing how it will be energized.

"CULTURE FAIR" AND "UNFAIR" IN THE TEST AND IN SOCIETY ■ The fact that a test differentiates between culturally disadvantaged and advantaged groups does not necessarily mean that the test is invalid. "Culturally unfair" tests may be valid predictors of culturally unfair but nevertheless highly important criteria. Educational attainment, to the degree that it reflects social inequities rather than intrinsic merit, might be considered culturally unfair. However, a test must share this bias to qualify as a valid predictor. Making a test culture-fair may decrease its bias, but may also eliminate its criterion validity. The remedy may lie in the elimination of unequal learning opportunities, which may remove the bias in the criterion as well as in the test. This becomes more a matter of social policy and amelioration rather than a psychometric problem, however.

The situation is quite different for a test that differentiates between disadvantaged and advantaged groups even more sharply than does the criterion. The extreme case would be a test that discriminated between disadvantaged and advantaged groups but did not have any validity for the desired criterion. An example of this would be an academic aptitude test that called for the identification of objects, where this task would be particularly difficult for disadvantaged children but would not be a valid predictor of academic achievement. Here, one could justifiably speak of a true "test bias." The test would be spuriously responsive to factors associated with cultural disadvantage but unrelated to the criterion. Such a test would not only be useless for predicting academic achievement but would be stigmatizing as well.

While certain aptitude and ability tests may have excellent criterion validity for some purposes, even the best of them are unlikely to reflect the true *capacity for development* of underprivileged children. For, to the extent that these tests measure factors that are related to academic success, they must tap abilities that have been molded by the cultural setting. Furthermore, the test content, the mode of communication involved in responding to test items, and the motivation needed for making the responses are intrinsically dependent upon the cultural content.

ELIXIR OF "CULTURE-FAIR" TESTS ■ The elixir of the "culture-fair" or "culture-free" test has been pursued through attempts to minimize the educational loading of test content and to reduce the premium on speed of response. However, these efforts have usually resulted in tests that have low validities for academic prediction purposes and little power to uncover hidden potentialities of children who do poorly on the common run of academic aptitude and achievement tests.

In spite of their typical cultural bias, standardized tests should not be sold short as a means for making objective assessments of the traits of minority-group children (italics ours, eds.). Many bright, non-conforming pupils, with backgrounds different from those of their teachers, make favorable showings on achievement tests in contrast to their low classroom marks. These are very often children whose cultural handicaps are most evident in their overt social and interpersonal behavior. Without the intervention of standardized tests, many such children would be stigmatized by the adverse subjective ratings of teachers who tend to reward conformist behavior of middle-class character.

III. TEST INTERPRETATION ■ *The most important consideration of all is one that applies to the use of tests in general—namely, that test results should be interpreted by competently trained and knowledgeable persons wherever important issues or decisions are at stake* (italic ours, eds.). Here, an analogy may be drawn from medical case history information that is entered on a child's record. Certain features of this record, such as the contagious disease history, constitute factual data that are easily understood by school staff members who have not had medical training. But other aspects of the medical records, as well as the constellation of factors that contribute to the child's general state of health, are not readily interpretable by persons outside the medical profession. Consequently, the judgment of a doctor is customarily sought when an over-all evaluation of the child's physical condition is needed for important diagnostic or predictive purposes. So, too, the psychological and educational test records of children should be interpreted by competently trained professional personnel when the test results are to be used as a basis for decisions that are likely to have a major influence on the child's future.

There are several sources of error in test interpretation stemming from a lack of recognition of the special features of culturally disadvantaged groups. One of these may be called the "deviation error." By this is meant the tendency to infer maladjustment or personality difficulty from responses which are deviant from the viewpoint of a majority culture, but which may be typical of a minority group. The results of a test might accurately reflect a child's performance or quality of ideation, but still the results should be interpreted in the light of the child's particular circumstance in life and the range of his experiences. For example, a minister's son whose test responses indicate that he sees all women as prostitutes, and a prostitute's son whose test responses give the same indication may both be accurately characterized in one sense by the test. The two boys may or may not be equally disturbed, however. Clinically, a safer inference might be that the minister's son is the one who is more likely to be seriously disturbed by fantasies involving sex and women.

There is evidence to indicate that members of a tribe that has experienced periodic famine would be likely to give an inordinate number of food responses on the Rorschach. So too might dieting Palm Beach matrons, but their underlying anxiety patterns would be quite different than those of the tribesmen. Or to take still another example, the verbalized self-concept of the son of an unemployed immigrant might have to be interpreted very differently from that of a similar verbalization of a boy from a comfortable, middle-class, native-American home.

A performance IQ that is high in relation to the individual's verbal IQ on the Wechsler scales *may* signify psychopathic tendencies but it also may signify a poverty of educational experience. Perceiving drunken males beating up women on the Thematic Apperception Test may imply a projection of idiosyncratic fantasy or wish, but it may also imply a background of rather realistic observation and experience common to some minority group children.

For children in certain situations, test responses indicating a low degree of motivation or an over-submissive self-image are realistic reflections of their life conditions. If these children were to give responses more typical of the general population, they might well be regarded as subgroup deviants. In short, whether test responses reflect secondary defenses against anxiety or are the direct result of a socialization process has profound diagnostic import, so that knowledge of the social and cultural background of the individual becomes quite significant.

WHAT DOES THE TEST REALLY MEASURE ▪ A second type of error, from the viewpoint of construct and content validity, might be called the "simple determinant error." The error consists in thinking of the test content as reflecting some absolute or pure trait, process, factor, or construct, irrespective of the conditions of measurement or of the population being studied. Thus, a fifth-grade achievement test may measure arithmetical knowledge in a middle-class neighborhood where most children are reading up to grade level, but the same test with the same content may be strongly affected by a reading comprehension factor in a lower-class school and therefore may be measuring something quite different than what appears to be indicated by the test scores.

Generally, the test-taking motivation present in a middle-class group allows the responses to test content to reflect the differences in intelligence, achievement, or whatever the test is designed to measure. On the other hand, in a population where test success has much less reward-value and where degree of test-taking effort is much more variable from individual to individual, the test content may tap motivation as well as the trait purportedly being measured.

Caution and knowledge are necessary for understanding and taking into account testing conditions and test-taking behavior when test results are being interpreted for children from varying backgrounds. A child coming from a particular cultural subgroup might have very little motivation to do well in most test situations, but under certain conditions or with special kinds of materials he might have a relatively high level of motivation. As a result, considerable variability might be evident in his test scores from one situation to another, and his scores might be difficult to reconcile and interpret.

How a question is asked is undoubtedly another important factor to consider in interpreting test results. A child might be able to recognize an object, but not be able to name it. Or he might be able to identify a geometric figure, but not be able to reproduce it. Thus, different results might be obtained in a test depending upon whether the child is asked to point to the triangle in a set of geometric figures or whether he is required to draw a triangle.

RESPONSE SETS MAY AFFECT TEST RESULTS ▪ In attitude or personality questionnaires, response sets such as the tendency to agree indiscriminately with items or to give socially desirable responses may contribute error variance from the viewpoint of the content of behavior it is desired to sample. To the extent that such sets discriminate between socially advantaged and disadvantaged groups, the target content area may be confounded by specific test format. Thus, a scale of authoritarianism may be found to differentiate among social classes, but if the scale is so keyed that a high score on authoritarianism is obtained from agreement with items, the social class differences may be more reflective of an agreement set rather than an authoritarian tendency. If authoritarian content is logically distinct from agreement content, these two sources of test variance should be kept distinct either through statistical control, by a change in the item format, or by having more than one approach to measurement of the trait in question.

From the standpoint of content validity, there is a third type of error. This may be termed the "incompleteness of content coverage" error. This refers to a circumscribed sampling of the content areas in a particular domain. In the area of intelligence, for instance, Guilford (1966) has identified many factors besides the "primary mental abilities" of Thurstone and certainly more than is implied in the unitary concept of intelligence reflected by a single IQ score. As Dreger and Miller (1960) point out, differences in intellectual functioning among various groups cannot be clearly defined or understood until all components of a particular content area have been systematically measured.

Familiarity with the cultural and social background of minority-group children not only helps to avoid under-evaluating the test performance of some children, but also helps to prevent over-evaluating the performance of others. For example, children who have been trained in certain religious observances involving particular vocabularies and objects, or those who have been encouraged to develop particular skills because of their cultural orientations, might conceivably score "spuriously" high on some tests or on particular items. In other words, any special overlap between the subgroup value-system of the child and the performances tapped by the test is likely to be an important determinant of the outcome of the test.

FAILURE BARRIERS MAY BE ENCOUNTERED ■ Failure-inducing barriers are often set up for the minority-group child in a testing situation by requiring him to solve problems with unfamiliar tools, or by asking him to use tools in a manner that is too advanced for him. To draw an analogy, if a medical student were handed a scalpel to lance a wound, and if the student were to do the lancing properly but were to fail to sterilize the instrument first, how should he be scored for his accomplishment? If he had never heard of sterilization, should his skillful performance with the instrument nevertheless be given a "zero" score? Similarly, if a child from a disadvantaged social group shows a considerable degree of verbal facility in oral communication with his peers but does very poorly on tests that stress academic vocabulary, can he justifiably be ranked low in verbal aptitude?

In a broad sense, most intelligence test items tap abilities involving language and symbol systems, although opportunities for developing these abilities vary considerably from one social group to another. One might reasonably expect that a child living in a community that minimizes language skills—or, as depicted by Bernstein (1960), a community that uses a language form that is highly concrete —will earn a score that has a meaning very different from that of the score of a child in a community where language skills are highly developed and replete with abstract symbolism. It is important, therefore, to interpret test results in relation to the range of situations and behaviors found in the environments of specific minority groups.

SOME SUGGESTED REMEDIES ■ While this analysis of the problems involved in the use and interpretation of tests for minority group children may lead to considerable uneasiness and skepticism about the value of the results for such children, it also points up potential ways of improving the situation. For example, one of these ways might consist of measuring separate skills first, gradually building up to more and more complex items and tests which require the exercise of more than one basic skill at a time. With enough effort and ingenuity, a sizable universe of items might be developed by this procedure. Special attention should also be given to the selection or development of items and tests that maximize criterial differentiations and minimize irrelevant discriminations. If a test is likely to be biased against certain types of minority groups, or if its validity for minority groups has not been ascertained, a distinct caveat to that effect should appear in the manual for the test.

Furthermore, we should depart from too narrow a conception of the purpose and function of testing. We should re-emphasize the concept of the test as an integral component of teaching and training whereby a floor of communication and understanding is established and learning capabilities are measured in repeated and cyclical fashion.

Finally, we should think in terms of making more use of everyday behavior as evidence of the coping abilities and competence of children who do not come from the cultural mainstream. Conventional tests may be fair predictors of academic success in a narrow sense, but when children are being selected for special aid programs or when academic prediction is not the primary concern, other kinds of behavioral evidence are commonly needed to modulate the results and implications of standardized tests.

CONCLUSION ■ Tests are among the most important evaluative and prognostic tools that educators have at their disposal. How unfortunate, then, that these tools are often used so routinely and mechanically that some educators have stopped thinking about their limitations and their benefits. Since the minority group child is so often handicapped in many ways, his test scores may have meanings different from those of non-minority children, even when they are numerically the same. The task of the conscientious educator is to ponder what lies behind the test scores. Rather than accepting test scores as indicating fixed levels of either performance or potential, educators should plan remedial activities which will free the child from as many of his handicaps as possible. Good schools will employ well-qualified persons to use good tests as one means of accomplishing this task.

In testing the minority group child it is sometimes appropriate to compare his performance with that of advantaged children to determine the magnitude of the deprivation to be overcome. At other times it is appropriate to compare his test performance with that of other disadvantaged children—to determine his relative deprivation in comparison with others who have also been denied good homes, good neighborhoods, good diets, good schools, and good teachers. In most instances it is especially appropriate to compare the child's test performance with his previous test performance. Utilizing the individual child as his own control and using the test norms principally as "bench marks," we are best able to gauge the success of our efforts to move the minority group child forward on the long, hard road of overcoming the deficiencies which have been forced upon him. Many comparisons depend upon tests, but they also depend upon our intelligence, our good will, and our sense of responsibility to make the proper comparison at the proper time and to undertake proper remedial and compensatory action as a result. The misuse of tests with minority group children, or in any situation, is a serious breach of professional ethics. Their proper use is a sign of professional and personal maturity.

45   *An Approach to the Measurement of Psychological Characteristics of College Environments*

C. ROBERT PACE AND GEORGE G. STERN

Traditional social psychology has always been concerned with the interaction of individuals and institutions. At least intuitively one would agree that the methodological problems involved in assessment in this area are formidable. Only recently have concerted attempts been made to systematically measure institutional environments. These attempts have generally been concerned with college environments (Astin & Holland, 1961; Nunnally, Thistlethwaite & Wolfe, 1963). The following paper by Professors Pace and Stern describes one of the earlier and more interesting procedures. As the authors note, the application possibilities of the technique are virtually limitless and exciting, as we are now becoming able to begin drawing fascinating and useful pictures of colleges and universities just as we have done with individual students. Are the authors justified in using the idea of "construct validity" in connection with their scale? Why or why not? How would you test the validity and reliability of the CCI? How could you apply the technique in selection or classification of college students?

The present article considers the idea that college cultures may be seen as a complex of environmental press which, in turn, may be related to a corresponding complex of personal needs. In the psychological literature one is indebted to Henry Murray (1938) for the dual concept of personal needs and environmental press. In the broadest sense the term "need" refers to denotable characteristics of individuals, including drives, motives, goals, etc. The term "press" can similarly be regarded as a general label for stimulus, treatment, or process variables.

DEVELOPMENT OF THE COLLEGE CHARACTERISTICS INDEX

Using Murray's classification of needs as a model, Stern has constructed several experimental editions of a needs inventory, called the Activities Index. In its current form the Activities Index consists of 300 statements of commonplace,

Reprinted and abridged from, C. Robert Pace and George G. Stern "An Approach to the Measurement of Psychological Characteristics of College Environments," *Journal of Educational Psychology*, 1958, Vol. 49, pp. 269–277. Copyright 1958 by the American Psychological Association and reproduced by permission of publisher and first-named author.

socially acceptable activities to which responses of "like-dislike" are given. There are 30 scales of 10 items each, corresponding to 30 needs in Murray's taxonomy. Some scales can be scored positively or negatively, as for example conjunctivity-disjunctivity, succorance-autonomy, impulsion-deliberation, etc., so that the total number of needs to which scores can be attached is 42 rather than 30.

A corresponding test for describing college environments, called the College Characteristics Index, was subsequently constructed. It consists of 300 statements about college environments to which responses of "True-False" are given. The statements are organized into 30 ten-item scales, with a press scale for each need scale that was included in the Activities Index. The following kind of question guided the writing of items: What might be characteristic of an environment which exerted a press toward order, or toward autonomy, or toward nurturance, or understanding, or play, etc.? Stated in another way, what might there be in a college environment which would be satisfying to or tend to reinforce or reward an individual who had a high need for order, or autonomy, or nurturance, or understanding, or play, etc.? The items themselves are statements about college life. They refer to the curriculum, to college teaching and classroom activities, to rules and regulations and policies, to student organizations and activities and interests, to features of the campus, etc.

Sample items from corresponding Need and Press scales will illustrate the parallelism.

A need for Order would be inferred from liking such activities as: "Arranging my clothes neatly before going to bed. Having a special place for everything and seeing that each thing is in its place. Keeping a calendar or notebook of the things I have done or plan to do." What might such a person like to find in a college environment or what features of a college environment might be rewarding or frustrating to such a need? The following items from the press scale for Order might be relevant: "Faculty members and administration have definite and clearly posted office hours. In many classes students have an assigned seat. Professors usually take attendance in class."

A high need for Energy is inferred from liking such activities as: "Taking up a very active sport. Having something to do every minute of the day. Giving all of my energy to whatever I happen to be doing." The needs of such a person might be expected to find fulfillment and satisfaction in a college environment where: "There is an extensive program of intramural sports and informal athletic activities. Student gathering places are typically active and noisy. Class discussions are typically vigorous and intense."

Just as needs are inferred from the characteristic modes of response of an individual, so press are reflected in the characteristic pressures, stresses, rewards, conformity-demanding influences of the college culture. Operationally, press are the characteristic demands or features as perceived by those who live in the particular environment. To each statement in the College Characteristics Index a person marks the test answers true if he believes it is generally characteristic of the college, is something which occurs or might occur, is the way people tend to feel or act; and he answers false if he believes it is not characteristic of the college, is something which is not likely to occur, is not the way people typically feel or act.

A STUDY OF FIVE INSTITUTIONS

A first draft of the College Characteristics Index was administered in May, 1957, to groups of students at five institutions and to smaller groups of faculty members at four of the five institutions. In all, 423 students and 71 faculty members responded to the instrument. Neither student nor faculty groups were representative samples. Most of the students were upperclassmen and most of the faculty members were in the upper academic ranks. It was argued that if a dominant press really exists in a particular environment, almost any group of people living in the environment would probably identify it. The testing program was, in any case, intended only as a preliminary tryout of the model from which some information would be gained about the types of items, the possible reliability and validity of the scales, and the potential utility of this approach to measuring college characteristics.

The five institutions, although not identified here, were selected because observers would probably agree that they are rather different from one another, with the selection of colleges thus providing some evidence about the construct validity of the test. One was a large Midwestern state university. The second was a large Midwestern private university. The third institution was a large Eastern private university. The fourth was a moderate-sized Eastern private college for men. The fifth institution was a publicly supported college in the metropolitan New York area.

TEST RESULTS ■ Saying that a particular press is or is not characteristic of an institution is an arbitrary matter. There exist no conventions or experience to guide the decision. The basis for the tentative decisions that were made, together with other statistical information about the scales and the items are given in the following paragraphs.

In examining means, or a profile on which mean scores are plotted, one naturally looks for what appear to be high and low points. And in examining variances of distributions in the context of press identification, one naturally looks for some concentration of scores or a low variance, suggesting a consistency of impression rather than a wide dispersal of scores, suggesting divergent impressions about the press.

The means and standard deviations on each of the press scales, computed from the students' responses at the five institutions studied are presented in Table 1. Each of these 30 scales has a maximum possible range of 0 to 10. The median of these means scores is approximately 5.5. The median of the standard deviations

TABLE 1. *Means and Standard Deviations on the Various Press Scales from Students' Responses at Five Institutions*

Press Scales	College A (N=100) M	SD	College B (N=44) M	SD	College C (N=100) M	SD	College D (N=68) M	SD	College E (N=111) M	SD
Abasement	4.0	2.2	3.6	1.7	3.3	1.9	3.4	1.7	4.3	2.1
Achievement	4.9	1.9	5.3	1.4	4.4	1.9	5.4	1.9	5.5	1.8
Adaptiveness	6.3	1.8	7.9	1.4	6.9	1.5	6.3	1.5	5.3	1.6
Affiliation	5.4	2.0	5.6	2.2	5.8	1.7	4.2	2.1	3.8	2.0
Aggression-Blameavoidance	4.4	1.9	5.8	1.4	5.6	1.6	4.7	1.6	3.5	2.0
Change-Sameness	5.6	1.3	7.1	1.4	5.1	1.7	5.1	1.4	4.8	1.4
Conjunctivity-Disjunctivity	6.7	2.0	5.8	2.3	7.4	1.7	5.8	2.1	6.9	1.9
Counteraction	6.1	1.4	6.5	1.4	5.0	1.5	5.4	1.6	5.9	1.4
Deference	5.6	1.7	5.1	1.4	5.6	1.7	5.4	1.4	5.5	1.5
Dominance	5.5	1.5	3.5	1.5	4.9	1.7	5.7	1.6	4.3	1.8
Ego-Achievement[a]	6.9	2.0	5.2	1.5	5.6	1.7	6.9	1.8	4.9	2.2
Emotionality-Placidity	6.3	1.5	5.8	1.6	6.3	1.5	5.9	1.9	5.3	1.8
Energy-Passivity	5.1	1.9	6.0	1.7	4.4	1.8	5.0	1.6	4.8	1.7
Exhibitionism	6.7	1.7	5.8	1.6	6.2	1.4	6.3	1.5	5.6	1.8
Fantasied Achievement[b]	6.0	1.8	6.5	1.6	5.7	1.6	4.6	1.7	5.7	1.6
Harmavoidance	4.7	1.5	4.8	.9	3.4	1.3	3.9	1.3	5.5	1.5
Humanism[c]	5.7	1.9	8.5	1.3	6.0	1.8	6.8	1.8	6.6	2.0
Impulsion-Deliberation	3.5	1.5	4.3	1.5	4.1	1.5	4.2	1.3	3.3	1.4
Narcissism	5.8	1.5	3.2	1.3	3.8	1.6	5.3	1.7	5.5	1.7
Nurturance	7.4	1.6	5.8	1.8	6.7	1.7	6.9	1.7	6.5	1.7
Objectivity-Projectivity	6.6	1.9	8.1	1.4	7.4	1.9	6.7	1.9	6.4	2.1
Order	7.3	1.5	3.3	1.5	5.8	1.4	6.2	1.4	7.1	1.3
Play	7.4	1.5	3.8	1.6	6.1	1.4	7.8	1.6	5.9	1.9
Pragmatism[d]	4.6	1.6	1.7	1.1	4.9	1.6	4.7	1.5	3.8	1.6
Reflectiveness[e]	5.5	1.9	8.0	1.4	4.9	1.9	5.5	1.9	5.6	1.9
Scientism[f]	6.3	1.9	8.4	1.5	5.1	2.0	6.5	2.0	6.5	1.7
Sentience	5.3	1.8	6.5	1.5	3.5	1.6	5.2	2.0	5.0	1.8
Sex	6.2	1.4	4.9	1.5	5.7	1.3	7.0	1.3	4.7	1.3
Succorance-Autonomy	5.8	1.3	4.6	1.6	5.2	1.4	5.1	1.9	5.1	1.6
Understanding	4.8	1.8	8.6	1.2	5.1	1.7	4.7	1.6	5.8	1.8

a Derived from Exocathection-Intraception.
b Derived from Ego Ideal.
c Derived from Endocathection-Extraception: Social Sciences and Humanities.
d Derived from Exocathection-Extraception.
e Derived from Endocathection-Intraception.
f Derived from Endocathection-Extraception: Natural Sciences.

is approximately 1.7. Putting this information together, one might suggest that for the five institutions represented, a fairly reasonable definition of a noticeable press (or its absence) would be one which required a mean score falling in the upper or lower one-fourth of the total distribution. Mean scores of 6.6 or higher and mean scores of 4.4 or lower would thus be suggestive of a press. In Table 1, means which meet this criterion are in bold-face type.

A corresponding table showing faculty means and sigmas is not presented, mainly because the number of cases is quite small. Also, from an educational view it may be argued that the effective press of an environment is what the students say it is, not what the faculty say, or what the catalogue says, etc. Nevertheless, in the four colleges where both student and faculty responses to the CCI were obtained, marked similarity was noted.

RELIABILITY ■ Conventional estimates of reliability from a single administration may not be appropriate for an instrument on which one hopes to find skewed distributions and minimal dispersion of scores. Faculty-student agreement within the same institution is of some relevance, but one might argue that the perceptions of these two groups could differ on individual items or scales, yet each could be reliable within itself.

Item analysis data are more directly relevant to the reliability of scales. An item analysis was made of each scale, separately for each of the five institutions, using the students' responses. Each of the 30 scales was subjected to item analysis in five different samples, and since there are 10 items in each scale, the total number of item discrimination indexes obtained was 1500. Of these 1500 discrimination indexes, 1 percent were negative, 18 percent fell between .0 and .19, 30 percent fell between .20 and .39, and 51 percent were .40 or higher. In other words, 81 percent of the items had, on the average, moderate to high discrimination in their respective scales.

Perhaps the most important approach is one which treats reliability and validity as inseparable and deals with the instrument as a whole. For example, do different people characterize the institution in the same way? This involves the reliability of profiles, with all their interrelationships. As a first approximation of this, the rank order of mean scores from the students' responses can be compared with the rank order of mean scores from faculty responses within the same institution. Thus, do these groups see the institution in relatively the same pattern? For the two colleges (Colleges B and C) which had the largest number of faculty respondents, these rank order correlations were .96 and .88.

VALIDITY ■ To illustrate the sort of interpretation and description of a college environment which can be derived from the CCI, the press of two colleges are presented. The comments are based entirely on the arbitrary definitions of what levels of scores constitute a press (which was explained earlier); and the nature of these press is further illustrated by citing some of the specific items which most clearly define them. No estimate is presently available of the validity of these descriptions against a systematic outside criterion. But the descriptions show quite clearly that these are very different environments, and that the test is therefore capable of revealing some sharp distinctions between colleges which qualified observers would expect to be different. The evidence is therefore relevant to the property of validity.

COLLEGE A ▪ The major press in College A are toward orderliness and friendly helpfulness, with overtones of spirited social activity. This is suggested by high scores in the scales for Order, Objectivity, Conjunctivity, Nurturance, Play, Ego Achievement, Exhibitionism, and by low scores on the scales for Abasement, Impulsion, and Aggression.

The stress on Order, Deliberation (opposite of impulsion), and Conjunctivity is indicated by such highly shared observations as the following: students have assigned seats in some classes, professors often take attendance, papers and reports must be neat, buildings are clearly marked, students plan their programs with an adviser and select their courses before registration, courses proceed systematically, it is easy to take clear notes, student activities are organized and planned ahead.

Within this orderliness, student life is spirited and a center of interest. For example, big college events draw lots of enthusiasm, parties are colorful and lively, there is lots to do besides going to classes and studying, students spend a lot of time in snack bars and in one another's rooms, and when students run a project everyone knows about it.

At the same time, amid this student-centered culture there is a stress on idealism and service. Students are expected to develop an awareness of their role in social and political life, be effective citizens, understand the problems of less privileged people, be interested in charities, etc.

The total picture of the environment, then, is one of high social activity, esprit de corps, and enthusiasm combined with an emphasis on helping others and idealistic social action and all within a fairly well understood set of rules and expectations which are deliberative and orderly. One would expect some of the explicit objectives of such an institution to stress personal and social development, idealism and social action, and civic responsibility.

COLLEGE B ▪ Here the dominant press of the environment fall in the theoretical-intellectual category—Reflectiveness, Humanism, Scientism, Understanding, and Objectivity. This dominant press occurs in an environment also characterized by Change, non-defensive acceptance of criticism (Adaptiveness), and by resistance to any abject acceptance of criticism or presumed low status (Abasement). Moreover, on two of the scales which defined a high press at College A (Play and Order), the press at B is exactly opposite. There is further a minimum of importance to social status or manipulation for tangible ends (Pragmatism), preoccupation with self and personal appearance (Narcissism), and bossing or directing others (Dominance). There is, however, a generally consistent and high press toward Deliberation or planning and thinking ahead.

It is clear that the most pervasive press is directed toward the pursuit of understanding for its own sake, abstract and unencumbered by requirements for practical utility or social action.

The theoretical-intellectual press of the environment at College B is more specifically suggested by the following observations with which, generally, more than nine-tenths of both faculty and students agree: there are excellent library resources in natural science and social science, a lecture by an outstanding philosopher or scientist would draw a capacity audience, many students are planning graduate work or careers in science or social science, there are many opportunities for students to see and hear and criticize modern art and music, reasoning and logic are valued highly in student reports and discussions, students who spend a lot of time in a science laboratory or in trying to analyze or classify art or music or in seeking to develop a personal system of values are not regarded as odd, scholarship and intellectual skills are regarded as more important than social poice and adjustment, there is time for private thought and reflection, one need not be afraid of expressing extreme views, the faculty and administration are tolerant and understanding in interpreting regulations.

In contrast with College A students at B do not have an assigned seat in class, professors do not take attendance, students are likely to study over the weekend, big college events draw no great enthusiasm, and the place is not described as one where "everyone has a lot of fun."

Moreover, student leaders have no special privileges, family status is not important, students are not much concerned about personal appearance and grooming, and an intellectual is not an "egghead."

And finally, exams are not based on factual material from a textbook, classes are not characterized by recitation and drills, grade lists are not publicly posted, students are not publicly reprimanded for mistakes, student organizations are not closely supervised, students tend to stay up late at night, work all the harder if they have received a low grade, and if confronted with a regulation they do not like they will try to get it changed.

One would expect the explicit objectives of such an institution to stress the acquisition of knowledge and theory, critical judgment and independence, and a sense of the significance of intellectual life.

CONCLUSIONS AND IMPLICATIONS

After completing the preliminary studies reported thus far, a revised form of the College Characteristics Index was produced in which 58 percent of the original items were retained, 13 percent were slightly modified, and 29 percent of the items were new. The revised form, at the time of writing this article, has been administered to approximately 1200 students distributed among more than 30 institutions. Further research and more intensive analysis have been planned. Before commenting on specific plans, however, certain broad values and implications in this psychological approach to the measurement of college environments are suggested.

One potential value, for example, is in institutional self-analysis. Administrators and faculty members should be able to learn something useful about the dynamics of the college environment from studying students' responses to the College Characteristics Index. Institutional press should have some clear relationship to institutional purpose. The objectives of a college are formal or explicit statements of intent: they indicate the directions in which a college means to influence the behavior of students. They find expression in curricula, practices, services, policies, and other aspects of the college environment. The press, as measured by the method described, constitute what Stern, Stein and Bloom (1956) have referred to as an operational definition of objectives, or the implicit influence of the environment upon the students. Implicit press and explicit objectives should reinforce one another, for an institution should operate in reality the way it means to operate in theory. Consequently, a serious lack of congruence between implicit press and explicit objectives would suggest to faculty members and administrators that certain aspects of the environment ought to be changed in order to make the total impact of the institution more consistent or more effective. Pace has commented elsewhere on the disintegrative effect of discrepancy between stated objectives and actual practices.

Some aspects of an environment can be changed more readily than others. The College Characteristics Index provides some direct indications of the psychological implications of various policies and practices. Roughly, one-fourth to one-third of the items in the Index state specific practices which an administration or faculty could more or less easily change if they did not like the implications. For example, being able to drop a course in which one is having difficulty, or to substitute another course for one which has been failed, is associated with Counteraction; insisting that students' reports or papers be neat, or giving students an assigned seat in class, or taking attendance regularly is associated with Order. As the relationships among press variables and between these variables and institutional objectives as well as personal needs are established, the significance of such specific practices will become clarified. Other items in the Index are more indirect in their implications about the effect of various policies or practices. But the clues can be investigated and can thus be the starting point for serious discussions about the impact of the environment on the student and the relation of this impact to the intended objectives.

Another set of implications from this approach to describing college environments relates to the problem of assessment and prediction. Assessment studies have often failed because the situations of environments in which assessed modes of behavior were supposed to occur have been inadequately described or differentiated. The interaction between person and environment was not successfully predicted because the environment was not measured as analytically and systematically as the person. The whole field of college prediction studies provides a good example. The criterion is typically a grade-point average. No fundamental improvement in predicting against this criterion has been made in the last 25 years. Prediction studies should be concerned with performance in the environment as a whole. The complexity of relationship between person and environment is inevitably obscured by the simplified and often inappropriate symbolism of correlation between scholastic aptitude test and grade-point average. The press of a college environment represents what must be faced and dealt with by the student. It is possible that the total pattern of congruence between personal needs and environmental press will be more predictive of achievement, growth, and change than any single aspect of either the person or the environment.

It will be a long time before admissions officers or guidance counselors can benefit from the results of these more complex analyses. This requires the establishment of known relationships between kinds of persons and kinds of environments. But conceivably advisers within an institution may be better able to help students find an effective and rewarding role within the operative environment of the college, or to see more clearly the ways in which environments need to be modified if different kinds of students are to grow within them most effectively.

46   *A Computer-Measurement System for Guidance*

WILLIAM W. COOLEY

Dr. Cooley extends a challenge to the education profession to use the computer for other than routine tasks such as completing report cards and scheduling students. He suggests that with a computer we can assist the individual student by estimating the extent of his resemblance to a particular group, by warning of inconsistencies between expectations and performances of the student, by recommending appropriate learning experiences, by assisting in his placement, and by identifying skills or concepts needing remediation or relearning. Further, considering groups of students, we can examine student growth and its relationship to instruction, and formulate dynamic, longitudinal norms. Beginnings have fortunately been made in some of these areas, involving multivariate analyses such as discriminant analysis. This emphasis upon resemblance of an individual to a group, shown when a discriminant analysis is performed, may be contrasted with concern for the likelihood of success for an individual in the group, indicated by regression analysis, as illustrated by Horst's earlier article in Chapter IX.

Which types of information specified by Cooley would be most crucial in guiding the individual student? How might a guidance counselor, for example, be able to do a better job with some of the information specified than without it? How does information concerning human behavior (in general) contribute toward the guidance of the individual? How can psychologists and other researchers contribute to the generation of such knowledge?

Reprinted and abridged with permission of author and publisher from the *Harvard Educational Review*, 1964, Vol. 34, pp. 559–572.

The special guidance issue of the *Harvard Educational Review* (Fall, 1962) leaves the reader with the impression that the individual counseling of students is the only legitimate activity of today's guidance programs. Testing and the interpretation of test scores were not considered in any of the articles, and one could also be left with the idea that testing is no longer an aspect of guidance. The opposite is found when schools are visited. There, the testing program is the dominating and expanding aspect of guidance. The apparent trend has been documented by recent *Project Talent* data (Flanagan, et al., 1962) which show the increasing use of tests in most high schools, the trend being much more pronounced than that for the addition of counselors, for example.

Although it is expected that counseling will continue to be an important and integral aspect of guidance, many of the time-consuming details can now be automated, freeing time for busy people to do a good job of counseling in those cases where it is most necessary. As they become more aware of these changes, school systems are turning more and more to testing programs as a means of assisting counselors.

Recently many books and articles have appeared which seem to be a reaction against too much testing, and undoubtedly there has been much wasted and misguided effort in school testing. I should like to consider here some of the ways by which we might improve our ability to deal with test scores and thus reconsider the school testing program. The computer, methods of examining many test scores simultaneously (multivariate analysis), and results of longitudinal studies make it possible to take a new look at potential improvements.

Perhaps it would be useful to consider briefly the current situation regarding measurement in guidance and the use of computers in the schools. School testing programs today are primarily concerned with achievement testing. Generally, a battery of four or five tests is used to sample a student's knowledge in the major curriculum areas. Also, a general test of scholastic aptitude is administered about every other year. As a result the student is assigned some sort of number or set of numbers, generally a percentile, a score which tells the percentage of students who received lower scores than he did. Often neither the students nor the parents are told anything regarding the outcome of the tests. A major reason for the testing program seems to be of sectioning students on the basis of previous achievement as measured by these tests. One thing we can be fairly sure of is that a student's test scores are recorded in indelible ink in his cumulative record so that in case some teacher or counselor wants to know how this student "is doing," the record is pulled and the scores are there.

The computer is now being used in many school systems, and more are joining this bandwagon every day. In every installation I know about, the computer applications have been almost exclusively a simple automation of clerical tasks previously done by hand, such as report cards, school attendance, scheduling, test scoring, etc. Those schools which have transferred the student cumulative record to the computer have done so in a very routine fashion. In fact, in many cases one wonders why the computer is involved at all. Information is read into the computer, the computer then prepares a gummed label containing the student's grades or test scores, and this is placed onto the student's record card. However, if there is no attempt to ask questions which would assist in interpreting the data, the need for the computer is dubious. School testing programs need to shift from a system of recording sets of numbers on student cumulative records to a procedure of "flashing red lights" which indicates when certain students seem to be in particular types of danger.

CAREER GUIDANCE

For some time psychologists have been convincing guidance workers that one test score alone is not sufficient evidence to conclude much of anything about a student. Their recommendation was to consider several test scores as a profile of the student. This resulted in the familiar "parallel stalks" model, each stalk standing for a test, with a line passing from stalk to stalk representing a particular student's score combination. Although this gives the impression that all the test score information available on a student is being considered simultaneously, anyone who has worked with this approach knows that it is only a slight graphical improvement over this same set of scores recorded in a cumulative record. What has been needed is a summary of this test score evidence with respect to particular questions, questions with educational and career relevance for each student.

I certainly do not visualize a system where the student's test scores are the input and prescribed curriculum and career are the output. Rather, the input consists of test scores, grades, biographical (including family) information, and the student's school and career plans. Output from the system would include, for example, certain information regarding students who appear to have high-risk plans. The actual form of this computer output could include explanatory paragraphs, if that seemed desirable. The task of the guidance program then, given this information, would be to plan experiences for such students which would give them more information about their plans, and about themselves in relation to those plans.

One key component of the output would be the probable success and satisfaction associated with a particular student plan. Most students seem quite willing and able to make plans and to discuss their plans in terms of probabilities. Interviews with the 700 boys of the *Scientific Careers Study,* a five-year study of career development, consistently found them talking in terms of their chances of doing this or that (Cooley, 1963). "Although I would rather be a doctor, I think I have a better chance of getting into a dental school." "With my grades, what are my chances of making it as a physicist?" "Do boys like me tend to go into law?" The students seemed to be continually searching for the type of data which a computer-measurement system could provide them.

Perhaps a specific example would help to clarify the points being made here. A case was drawn from the *Scientific Careers Study*, and it illustrates a frequent guidance problem. Selection of the case was quite simple. A brief inspection of computer output quickly identified several students with the characteristics needed. The files of that five-year study contained folders on each of 700 boys, and each folder contained about 100 scale scores, 4 questionnaires and 2 interviews. Only with the aid of the computer can students with particular combinations of characteristics be identified quickly and easily from a file of data this extensive.

THE CASE OF ROBERT S. ▪ Bob S. was first contacted in the 8th grade. Our file contains his achievement data prior to 8th grade, as well as the data which were collected from grades 8 to 12 as part of the study.

Bob lives with his natural mother and step-father. He has two younger brothers and no sisters. His father is a typewriter repairman and his mother does not work.

Ability and achievement information available on Bob when he was in 8th grade gave every indication that he had the potential for further schooling beyond 12th grade. A multivariate statistical summary of his ability and achievement profile indicated that about 83 percent of the boys with his particular combination of scores do enter some type of college.

Interest and temperament data available indicate that Bob "looks" very much like other boys who have entered careers in some field of science and technology. Of the boys with his pattern of interests, 73 percent enter some science-technical field. About one-half of the boys who responded to the Temperament Survey as he did were pursuing careers in science-technology.

A summary of socio-economic data showed that 87 percent of the boys with Bob's family background do *not* go to college. These data include such variables as parents' education, father's occupational level, and the parents' expectations with respect to further schooling for the boy.

Notice that the numbers reported above tell something about Bob with respect to such questions as whether he is likely to go to college and/or become an engineer. Those percentages can be thought of as the probabilities associated with a particular type of prediction based upon a certain set of data. The data upon which these predictions are based were available when Bob was in eighth grade. Previously used techniques tend to report test results in terms like, "Bob did better on the mathematics test than did 50 percent of his classmates," or perhaps simply, "Bob received a score of 500 on the SCRAP mathematics test." It is difficult to decide what to think about such test scores. They are static. No implications are discernible.

Bob's career plans when first contacted in eighth grade were to enter the Coast Guard. He had an uncle and a cousin in the Coast Guard and felt "they had a good life." Otherwise, he might become an airline pilot. At grade 9, he was still talking about the Coast Guard but was also considering becoming a mechanic or engineer. He thought it might be a good idea to be a mechanic in the service because it is "more organized and less chance of business collapsing." In 10th grade he talked about "becoming a mechanical engineer because he liked to work on cars." This goal continued through 11th grade, but when he was last contacted in grade 12, he was planning to enter the service after high school graduation and become an airplane mechanic.

The point of this particular case is to illustrate a high-risk in the sense that if Bob developed realistic college goals later during high school (as he did during grades 10 and 11), he would discover that his 8th and 9th grade behavior (e.g., course selection) was not consistent with those goals.

PROGRAMMED EXPERIENCES ▪ By a systematic examination of several different types of data, a variety of potential problem cases can easily be uncovered today among a very large group of students. A computer-measurement system could allow the early identification of potential problems soon enough to do something about them. The problem then is what to do once a trouble spot has been observed. The recommendation here is to develop a system of programmed experiences.

In Bob's case, for example, general mechanical-technical orientation was quite clear. What was not clear was the level at which he might operate. A sequence of experiences could be designed to show the broad range of jobs open to boys like Bob, including the training required. For common problems, such as this one, films could be an excellent method. Included in these experiences would be some indication of the types of financial aid available to the boys like Bob, so that college is not unrealistically discounted too early for financial reasons.

Included in this program of experiences would be a talk with a counselor. In fact, this might be the first experience in the sequence, to make sure that the established measurement-computer system did not miss something important, and to examine the prescribed sequence to see if it made sense. It is beyond the scope of this paper to consider other facets of the counseling interview. The plea here is that we do not rely too exclusively on such talks for either diagnosis or "treatment."

ADDITIONAL APPLICATIONS ▪ The college placement function is a big consumer of counselor time. College finding services, for example, have demonstrated that much of this problem can be automated. Also, the computer-measurement system could identify trouble spots which, if acted upon immediately, the counselor could easily help remedy. If not identified early, the problem could grow until the student's situation required extensive remedial action.

One case occasionally observed is the student who is planning to apply to only two colleges and the chances of his being accepted at either one is something like one chance in one thousand. It would not be difficult to develop experiences which could point out to the student the desirability of also applying to a college for which he has a much higher probability of being admitted. Counselors are already using a type of intuitive estimate of such probabilities, so they should welcome assistance in this area.

The case just mentioned illustrates the problem of "over-aspiring," whereas Bob's problem, cited earlier, was a type of "under-aspiring." Both are frequent problems in educational and vocational planning, and if identified early, they might be remedied with suitable student experiences. The student may decide not to change his plans, but at least he will know he is pursuing a high-risk path. He may even decide to do something about some of the predictors (e.g., grades), thus changing his probability in that way. The main thing is that he have a rational basis for whatever plan he develops. As Kogan and Wallach (1964) have recently shown, the amount of risk a person is willing to take is a function of his personality, and this aspect could also be built into the computer-measurement system.

Another area in which an active computer-measurement system could accomplish much is in the analysis of student achievement. It is now possible for schools to develop a type of dynamic norm, which would make it possible to detect, for example, a student whose achievement-growth curve has suddenly slacked off. If this is done on a continuous basis, problems can be anticipated before they become serious, such as leading to another drop-out. The need for dynamic norms is considered in the next section.

A computer-measurement system could perform other very important diagnostic functions. Testing programs of the past have tended to assess "how much" the student knows instead of asking what missing skills or concepts are interfering with his school progress. Perhaps a few weeks' review of fractions would help fill a gap which is currently giving some students trouble in shop work, for example.

THE NEED FOR DYNAMIC NORMS

Although there have been several factors which have limited the effective use of measurement in guidance, the problem of obtaining sufficient normative data has been one of the more serious problems. For one thing, norms have been allowed to get out of date. Funds are only now becoming available in the amounts needed to provide their continued updating, Another problem is that norms have been insufficiently developed, limiting the questions which can be asked. Norms are needed which are based upon multiple observations of the same students over time, and these need to be developed on a continuous basis. Also, counselors have not had the information needed for understanding the validity of test scores or the predictive implications of particular test score combinations.

Project TALENT (Flanagan, et al., 1962) has shown that it is now possible to develop truly representative norms. These norms are also dynamic in the sense that they are based upon follow-up data which make it possible to ask questions about the subsequent educational or vocational implications of current behavioral and environmental observations, including the current plans of the student.

At regular intervals (say every three years) a five percent sample of schools could be selected for participation in a national "norming" study. The students would take a battery of tests which broadly sampled student behavior and determined their plans.

Periodic follow-up studies could then determine the pattern of events which followed the testing. The first follow-up might be conducted five years later, when most of the original group will have graduated from high school. This is more or less the current plan of *Project TALENT*, and so the feasibility of such an operation is now being demonstrated.

The computer-measurement system being proposed here is completely dependent upon obtaining such adequate normative data. The *Scientific Careers Study* (Cooley, 1963) has shown the potential utility and validity of the probability predictions for individual students based upon multivariate information, but only the *techniques* used there have generalizability. The actual prediction equations from that study are appropriate for a very restricted population (boys of above-average ability in eastern Massachusetts). Undertakings such as *Project TALENT* can now provide the type of normative data which has been lacking.

Not all applications of a computer-measurement system require national norms. In fact, "norming" can and should be frequently done on a regional basis. However, follow-up data must be made an aspect of this norming procedure if we expect to be able to utilize the test results in the manner described here.

This proposed periodic, mass testing program may sound expensive. It certainly is when viewed in terms of the amount of money which has previously been spent on establishing norms and other validating information for tests. Yet it would cost only about $500,000 annually, which is about what it would cost to add only 50 more counselors to the entire United States, a number which would not even make a dent in the current student-counselor ratio. If we really want to learn more about students from the millions of dollars annually spent on school testing programs, if we want to provide the type of information which students seem to want and need, then such undertakings seem necessary and feasible.

The skeptic may also claim that although computers and multivariate methods are available today, they are out of the financial reach of most school systems. There are ways to solve this financial problem, however. Through establishment of regional data processing centers such as the New England Education Data Systems (NEEDS) project, a central computer facility is able to service many school systems, including the analysis of test scores for guidance purposes. In a few years each school could be directly connected to a central computer by a remote typewriter-type terminal which would enable school personnel to ask questions of their school data stored at the central computer center.

THEORETICAL BASIS

The discussion thus far has been more or less exclusively about rather vague operations. By now the reader is probably concerned about the theoretical basis for this type of wild talk. Actually there are several bases, depending upon the area of application for the computer-measurement system. Perhaps it would be useful to examine the view of man which is behind the recommendations for applications in the area of student educational and vocational planning.

The basic proposition is that different plans are appropriate for different people. This proposition requires a taxonomy for plans and people, and a method for dealing with relationships between types of plans and kinds of people.

Factor theory provides a more operational basis for talking about people differences and their relationship to plans. In the factorial conceptualization of human behavior, personality has its locus in an m-dimensional space. An individual's personality is his unique location in this space, the location determined by the total pattern of the m behavioral measures which are available for that individual. In this context, personality encompasses all behavior, including intellectual functioning. People who have similar patterns of scores will occupy similar regions of this m-dimensional space. That is, people who behave similarly have similar personalities. Career planning and decision making is one aspect of behavior. People with similar personalities tend to make similar types of career decisions. Once the regions of the personality space occupied by people who have made particular types of career decisions are defined, the probability that another person will make a certain decision can be estimated.

Before this theoretical position can be further developed, it is necessary to explain the test space concept, and the probability classification procedures which are the analytical techniques employed in the factor approach advocated here.

Say, for example, the task is to distinguish future scientists from non-scientists; Figure 10 represents a one-dimensional test space. An individual's location along axis X depends upon his score on test X. The height of the curve for the scientist

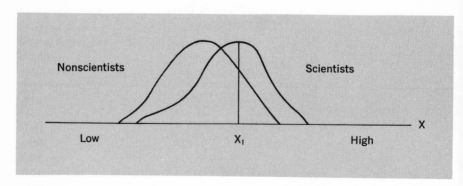

Figure 10. A One-Dimensional Test Space

group at some point, for example at x_j, is the frequency with which scientists receive that particular score on X. Knowing only the test score, you would predict that the person was a non-scientist if the score was low, and a scientist if the score was high. Knowing the heights of the two curves at score x_j, it is possible to compute the proportion of people receiving that score who are scientists, and the proportion who are non-scientists. With new test scores from a person for whom the scientist-non-scientist designation is unknown, the proportions become probabilities of group membership for that person.

For example, if one-third of the people having a score of x_i are non-scientists, and two-thirds are scientists, then the probability that a person with score x_i is a scientist is .67, and .33 is the probability of non-scientist. This assumes that the two categories exhaust the possibilities for the population under consideration. If the areas under the two curves are equal, this also assumes that the two groups exist in equal numbers within that population. These two conditions (that there are only two categories of people in the mixed population and that they are of equal frequency) are peculiar to this example and are not limitations of the technique.

Of course, a single test score yields inadequate information, so a method is needed for handling more than one test score. Consider the next most simple case, that of two tests. This results in a two-dimensional space similar to

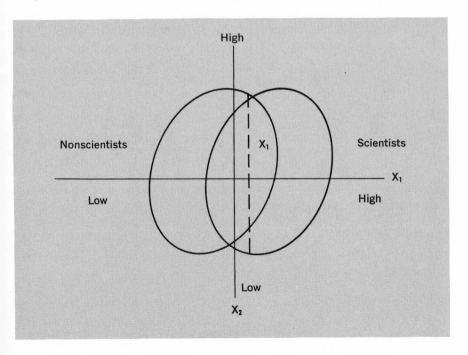

Figure 11. A Two-Dimensional Test Space

Figure 11. In this space, each individual can be represented as a point with a unique location depending upon his combination of scores on X_1 and X_2. This time questions can be asked about people receiving a particular combination of test scores: what proportion are scientists, and what proportion are non-scientists? These proportions are computed from the relative densities of "scientist points" and "non-scientist points" for a given score combination.

The importance of score combinations can be seen in this example. A score of x_i on test X_1 could have different implications depending upon the score X_2. High scores on X_2 with x_i on X_1 indicate the student is more like a non-scientist. Low scores on X_2 with a score of x_i on X_1 indicates greater similarity to the scientist group. If a score on X_2 is viewed alone, nothing can be concluded about the student's resemblance to these two groups. Multivariate procedures make use of this combinational aspect of scores.

Consider another example. If a decision between two alternatives has been made by individuals located in the behavioral space, such as A) college preparatory curriculum in high school and B) non-college preparatory, the behavioral space will contain regions in which many individuals chose A over B, other regions in which choice B was preferred to A. There may be at least some A choosers in all regions of the personality space, but the A density varies from region to region. Comparison of the density of A choosers to B choosers at a

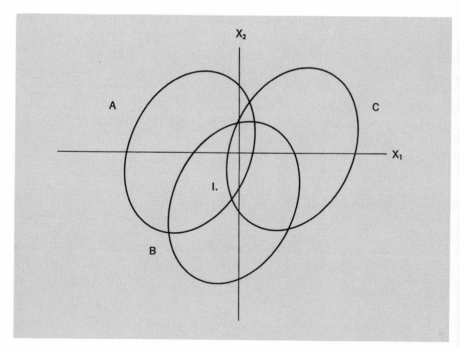

Figure 12. Three Group Dispersions in a Two-Dimensional Space

particular point in the space determines the probability that choice A will be made by persons at or near that point. This scheme of analysis is generalizable to decision-making situations involving more than two alternatives and/or two variables. Each new variable adds a new axis to the system. The bivariate normal distributions for three groups on tests X_1 and X_2 are outlined in Figure 12. Once the means and dispersions of these three groups have been estimated, the probability that individual i is a member of group A, B, or C can also be estimated. The computations become rather extensive as the number of variables increases, but this is where the computer comes in. It is certainly not necessary for counselors to become familiar with the details of this type of multivariate analysis. The nature of these techniques were hinted at here for purposes of illustrating the type of thinking and analysis behind the computer output that would monitor student plans.

IMPLICATIONS

As recently as 1960 participants at a conference on measurement and research (Traxler, ed., 1961) have pleaded that counselors and teachers be taught how to interpret test scores in relation to all other data available on the same student. Although this is a noble goal, it is unrealistic. Even if they had the follow-up data which would make predictive interpretations possible, people are just not able to process that much information reliably.

It is possible to achieve this goal of sounder interpretation by use of the computer, methods of multivariate analysis, and results of continuous, normative, longitudinal studies. I do not mean to imply that such a system is ready to be installed tomorrow in any school that wants a computer-measurement system. The point is that for the first time the parts are all clearly discernible and feasible.

This paper and these arguments seem necessary because of the emphasis today on the counseling process. There seem to be too few people in guidance today who are concerned with the role of measurement in guidance and the ways in which new techniques might assist counselors in the task of helping our millions of students through school and into careers. The hope is that this type of article might stimulate renewed action along these lines.

XI

INITIATING AND CONDUCTING A TESTING PROGRAM

Almost everyone is aware of the increasing blocks of time that are being given over to formal and informal testing in our schools and colleges. In addition, external testing programs (e.g., scholarship and admissions testing) appear to be taking on increased importance. One wonders whether the public, or a great proportion of school personnel for that matter, are really aware of the economic, social and psychological implications of increased test "use." The word "use" is purposefully enclosed in quotation marks as it may take on many definitions in a testing context. All too often tests are administered, scored, and then filed away, never to be seen by teacher, counselor, or student. Unfortunately, many individuals involved in establishing and administering the testing programs, be it for the purpose of curriculum evaluation or counseling, are not trained in measurement. Many of the problems in test "use" can, therefore, be traced to ill-conceived, poorly administered, and inefficient testing programs.

The papers in this chapter are concerned with general and specific considerations in designing and implementing a school-wide testing program. The chapter has been placed toward the end of the book as it is expected to serve as a kind of synthesis for all of the articles that have gone before. We have described how to construct and analyze a test. We have illustrated how test scores can be interpreted and used in prediction and decision making. We have noted the factors which can significantly influence test performance. All of the principles involved in these chapters must be considered in initiating and conducting a testing program.

Four major purposes for testing are outlined in the first paper, which was authored by the Guidance and Counseling Staff of the College of Education at Michigan State University. After the general steps for the establishment of a testing program are discussed, the procedures for selecting the specific tests are enumerated. The article closes with a comment on the on-going nature of the testing program.

As the program undergoes periodic reappraisal, the criteria supplied by Dr. Arthur Traxler in the second article in this chapter might be applied. The criterion questions raised by Traxler are for the most part of a common-sense variety. But often because questions are viewed as common sense, their importance is overlooked. The author does a commendable job in emphasizing their importance. The necessity of involving the total faculty in conducting the testing program is a particular point worth underscoring.

The first two papers in this chapter deal with broad general perspectives on testing programs. The final two papers, however, deal with more narrowly defined topics of contemporary concern. In the third paper of the chapter, Dr. Frank B. Womer considers the advantages and disadvantages of external testing programs. It is only within the last several decades that the impact of these programs has been felt. There are obvious administrative, economic, and philosophical problems associated with these kinds of programs. After careful study of Dr. Womer's paper, the reader may agree that the advantages usually outweigh the several disadvantages of such programs.

There is no simple answer to the problems surrounding the use of external tests. Some concerned individuals have proposed the elimination of these programs. One possible result of such a decision would be the proliferation of admissions and scholarship testing programs by individual colleges and universities. From the student's standpoint, this result could only be described as anarchy. Even today the scores on different external tests cannot be considered comparable. One solution that has been offered for the excessive and burdensome testing is the computation of equivalency tables which would allow the conversion of scores obtained on the test of one publisher to the score scale of another publisher. While such a procedure has important advantages, it also poses certain problems. In the final paper in this chapter Dr. William Angoff discusses many technical and some philosophical problems in the development of equivalency tables.

47   *Designing and Implementing a Testing Program*

MICHIGAN STATE UNIVERSITY GUIDANCE DEPARTMENT

Since the intelligent application of tests provides pertinent data useful to student, school, and community, careful attention must be given by school officials to the problem of specific tests to be used, the times at which they should be administered, and how the results are to be collated for school use. The following article presents a general overview of the purposes and procedures for establishing a testing program. It provides a set of sound guidelines based on expert recommendations and common sense and considers questions such as the following: What are the general purposes of a testing program? What criteria should be applied in selecting tests? What kinds of administrative errors in handling the mechanical details of a testing program could lead to meaningless test results?

The reader is referred to a book by Bauernfeind (1963) and one edited by Findley (1963) for more extensive treatments of the topic of testing programs.

What is a good testing program? This question implies that an absolute standard exists by which all testing programs may be measured. Such a quest for certainty is characteristic of many human endeavors and often leads to fallacious and superficial answers. Essentially a basic testing program provides the information which the faculty is prepared to use and is capable of using to improve the total educational program. It follows from this definition that a testing program may be good for school X and poor for school Y.

WHY HAVE A TESTING PROGRAM?

For development of a good testing program the proper purposes of testing must be considered. Four major purposes have been identified as basic.

1. Tests may be given to improve the instructional program. The school's prime reason for gathering information about students is to aid the teacher in planning the work of the class and in evaluating teaching. This purpose will be fulfilled only if the teacher believes in differentiating instruction. If he believes that he will need to vary his materials, techniques, and goals in keeping with the nature of the child, then a testing program can be most helpful. If, however, his belief is that he should teach the same things in the same way with the same materials regardless of the ability and achievement of the children, then nothing is achieved by providing him with information about children.

Reprinted and abridged with permission from the pamphlet, "Let's Look at Our Testing Program," published by the Bureau of Educational Research, Michigan State University, 1959. The pamphlet was authored by the staff of the Michigan State University Guidance Department.

2. Tests may be given to facilitate curriculum revision. By learning the ability and achievement levels of the students, curriculum planners may make wiser judgments regarding the scope and the sequence of learning experiences which are to be offered to various groups of children. Results of a testing program alone are not sufficient basis for curriculum revision. No test expert will be sufficiently acquainted with the local situation to build a test which will properly measure all the objectives of the school system.

3. Tests provide information for educational and vocational counseling. This purpose needs little stressing, since too often the testing program has been totally associated with counseling at the expense of instruction and administration. This purpose is legitimate and important, but is by no means the only reason for giving tests.

4. Tests may be given to help the administrative staff appraise the educational program. Testing is not by itself an evaluation. Tests may supply some information which, when added to other information, may permit a realistic judgment of the extent to which the total school is fulfilling its educational purposes. Tests should never be used, however, to evaluate teaching effectiveness of staff.

These four purposes must be clarified before a testing program can be properly developed. Many testing programs have been unsuccessful because the purposes were not made clear.

HOW IS A TESTING PROGRAM DEVELOPED?

A three-step process of development is likely to be most workable. What information is needed? Who will use the information? How will it be used?

1. The first step is to formulate clearly what information is needed and desired. This step is probably best taken by a staff committee representing instruction, personnel, curriculum, and administration. A group such as this may decide that the teacher at the fifth-grade level should know the spelling achievement of the class; that the counselor at the twelfth-grade level should know the students' vocational interests, etc. When they have described in detail the information they need at the various grade levels, the first step is completed.

2. The second step is to specify who will use the information. It is possible that an intelligence test may provide the administrator with an over-all judgment about the nature of the school population. At the same time, the intelligence tests may provide the curriculum specialist with hints as to the kind of program which would be more appropriate. The counselor may use the same test, which, when interpreted to the child and his parent, will be useful in making a vocational decision. Finally, the test data will be useful to the teacher in selecting materials and methods appropriate to the individual child.

3. The third step is to designate specifically how the information will be used. Will other texts be used with the children who deviate from the class average in reading ability? Will the counselor provide scholarship information to students

of high ability? It is unwise to proceed with a testing program in the vague hope that somehow the obtained information will be used to the advantage of the child.

HOW ARE TESTS SELECTED?

When the three questions of what, who, and how have been answered, the simpler but more technical phase of development follows.

Decisions will need to be made regarding which test, if any, will offer information the staff is prepared to use.

Those who are developing the testing program may consult personnel from county offices, departments of public instruction, colleges and universities, or representatives of major test publishing agencies. Further objective help can be obtained from reference books (e.g. Buros, 1959).

In conjunction with consultants the staff will consider whether various tests meet proper standards of usability, reliability, and validity. Such questions will be asked as "How well does the test measure what we want it to measure?," "How consistent are these results?," and "How practical is it to use this test?" An expert in testing may be most valuable at this stage by interpreting reliability and validity data in meaningful terms. It is extremely important that the consultant not move prematurely and set up a testing program apart from the philosophy of the school and the sophistication of the staff.

In considering the usability of a test, attention will be given to such factors as how much does it cost and how long does it take to administer and score. Even though a more reliable result is generally achieved with long tests, there are practical limits in each school situation, and some reliability may need to be sacrificed because adequate time is not available.

Reliability must be weighed carefully, particularly when test results are used as a basis for making decisions about individuals. Test scores low in reliability may fluctuate radically; the consequence of this use will be grossly inadequate judgments. Conversely, it is just as important that reliability not be overemphasized to the exclusion of validity considerations.

In considering the matter of validity the test administrator will need to be most aware of how he is going to use test results. Tests are not thought of as being "valid" or "non-valid" but as valid for certain purposes and not valid for others. For example, in using scholastic ability tests, the validity which is desired is that which allows prediction of the degree of student academic success. On the other hand, a valid achievement test is one which measures the student's acquisition of the kind of information the school is trying to impart.

Some of the important factors to consider in developing a specific testing program are outlined in the following section: Seven Guidelines for Selecting Tests. The guidelines represent only a few of the major test principles and should be used as a rough assessment of the over-all testing process.

SEVEN GUIDELINES FOR SELECTING TESTS

1. The practice of measuring achievement in arithmetic and language in the primary grades is a questionable one, because (a) scores are heavily dependent on reading ability, (b) rote memory tends to play an unduly important role in the scores and, (c) too much pressure may be placed on the child at an age when his attitude toward school is of great importance in determining his success during the next several years.

2. The older the child the closer the agreement between his current measured intelligence and his adult intelligence; the results of intelligence tests in the early grades should be interpreted in the light of their relative unreliability.

3. Interests are usually not stable until middle or late adolescence, so interest inventories are of questionable value before then.

4. Regular intelligence and achievement tests often provide information which can be used to predict the probable degrees of academic success. A so-called "prognosis" test may only duplicate such information.

5. Some achievement tests measure isolated aspects of formal education, and some emphasize the use of information in critical thinking and problem-solving. The appropriate test will reflect the philosophy of education of the school using it.

6. Since the reliability of a test is related to its length, a shortened version of a test gives convenience at the expense of consistency. A school must balance these two factors in deciding between a longer and a shorter test form.

7. Before making routine use of "personality" or "adjustment" tests, a school should (a) carefully examine the evidence of validity for the test to be used, (b) make certain that the community understands the purpose and function of such tests, and (c) be prepared to follow up identification with treatment or referral to available psychological or psychiatric resources.

PRACTICAL PROBLEMS OF ADMINISTERING THE TESTING PROGRAM

After the total testing program has been developed, the practical problems of administering the program follow. It will be necessary to determine who will record the test results and who will be primarily responsible for interpreting the scores. The answers to these questions need to be sought at the local level, because the best answers are those which take into account the skill of the school personnel and the nature of the local organization. It is most important that the administrator have a mature understanding of the advantages and limitations of test information. Clear thinking and wise decision-making on his part can greatly enhance the development of the program. Generally the administrator's responsibilities in relation to the testing program center on:

1. Clarifying the school's philosophy and purpose in evaluation.
2. Involving staff in the development of the program.

3. Communicating to all faculty the nature, extent, and purpose of the testing program.
4. Defining responsibilities for the execution of the program.
5. Securing financial and moral support for the program.
6. Providing the administrative machinery for re-evaluation of the program.
7. Interpreting the program to the community.

USING THE TESTS

An important phase of the development of a good testing program consists of increasing understanding of the proper use of tests. The administrator who fails to develop a testing program because his staff is not prepared to use the results has not assumed his full administrative responsibilities. He has recognized the practicalities of the situation, but has not extended his responsibility to in-service education and professional upgrading of his staff.

ACCESSIBILITY OF TEST DATA

The success of a testing program is directly related to the availability of the test results. Ideally, all teachers should have a file folder for each student containing summary information from the cumulative record which includes test scores. (When key information is added to the cumulative record, a carbon copy is placed in the teacher's personal file.) Individual considerations will have to be taken into account when determining the location of the central file. In general, when deciding on the location of records, the people who use them most should be considered first.

Just as important as accessibility is the confidentialness of test information. It is easy for the test administrator to become so concerned about having the school staff use the test results that he fails to take the necessary precautions insuring that contact with the records is made only by people who have legitimate professional interest in the students. The most frequent offenses against confidentialness occur when high school students are used for supplementary clerical help.

THE ON-GOING PROGRAM

The testing program must be constantly strengthened and reappraised. New and better tests must be reviewed as they are developed. The tests in use must be evaluated, and frequently local norms should be built for achievement and aptitude measures. The construction of local norms is of particular value in making comparisons within the school or community.

48   Fifteen Criteria of a Testing Program

....

ARTHUR E. TRAXLER

In the previous article the purposes of and procedures for implementing a testing program were detailed. The evaluation of the effectiveness of the program is, of course, an on-going process. It will not only improve periodic subjective appraisals, but will hopefully stimulate frequent empirical investigations into program utility as well. The fifteen significant questions posed by Dr. Traxler in the following article are ones which every school administrator, teacher, and guidance staff member should ask about his own testing program.

The criteria of a testing program are dependent, in part, upon the nature of the school and the grade level of the pupils involved. Certain general criteria, however, are applicable to nearly all kinds of schools and practically all grade levels. These criteria may be phrased in the form of questions.

Is the testing program comprehensive? Does it include different kinds of tests? It is difficult to interpret a test score in one area, for example, reading comprehension, unless it can be compared with scores in other areas. The level of a pupil's score in a given subject is not as important as the pattern or profile of his scores indicating his strengths and weaknesses.

Does the testing program include all pupils in the school? If the tests are placed on a voluntary basis, or if they are given only to the pupils who are having difficulty, or if they are administered only to selected groups, or if a large number of pupils are designated as special pupils and are excluded from the class distributions, erroneous conclusions may be drawn concerning the ability and achievement in the school as a whole. What is more important, if some pupils are excluded from the testing, their educational guidance may be impaired by the fact that their records are incomplete. Following each testing program there is a need for a careful check-up and testing of absentees, even though this procedure will inevitably involve a large amount of extra work for the person in charge of the testing program.

Are the tests given at regular intervals? Are there regular fall and spring testing programs in the school, or are the tests given in a haphazard manner whenever it suits the convenience of the staff member in charge of testing? If the tests are administered at regular intervals, it is possible to study the growth of the pupils from year to year or from the beginning of the school term to the end. But if they are given irregularly, growth studies are likely to be difficult to make and of little value.

Reprinted and abridged with permission of author and publisher from *The Clearing House.* 1950, Vol. 25, pp. 3–7.

Are the tests well timed? Is the time of administering the different types of tests carefully planned so that the results will be of maximum usefulness? For instance, are tests of reading ability and arithmetic skills given fairly early in the fall so that there will be time to plan and carry out corrective work for pupils found to be retarded in certain skills? Are tests in one-year subjects, such as plane geometry and biology, given toward the end of the year so that the results can readily be reported to the teachers who have the pupils in class, and yet far enough from the end of the term to enable the teachers to make practical use of the results?

Are the tests in the school's testing program comparable? Are the various tests in a particular fall or spring testing program constructed along similar lines and standardized on similar populations so that it is possible to make comparisons among the results on the different tests? Is an attempt made to keep the tests from year to year comparable through the use of different forms of the same battery?

It has been observed that occasionally a school will deliberately vary its testing program from one year to the next in an effort to get as many different kinds of measures on its pupils as possible. While a certain amount of experimentation, particularly with new and promising tests, is necessary, frequent changes in the tests used are ordinarily undesirable. Such frequent changes are likely to give the test results for the school as a whole a confused picture which even test specialists find difficult to interpret.

Do the tests used agree with the objectives and the curriculum of the school? In planning a testing program, it is advisable for a school, first of all, to state its objectives, not merely in general terms but specifically and in detail, and then to try to choose tests that are in line with the objectives and the course of study that has been formulated to carry out these objectives. For instance, if a school has an integrated program in the social studies, it will likely find that a general achievement test in social studies is better suited to its program and needs than separate tests in American history, world history, and other specific subjects. No set of standardized tests will fit the objectives and program of an individual school exactly, but there should be a reasonable amount of agreement if the results are to be meaningful.

Are the specific tests carefully chosen? Does a competent group of persons go over the tests themselves with care and study the available statistical data concerning them? Many different tests are available for various fields, and there is often a great deal of difference in the value of these tests. The work of studying and choosing among specific tests is so time-consuming and has so many technical ramifications that oftentimes it is preferable to have this work done by a committee appointed to represent a group of schools with similar objectives and programs.

Are the tests carefully administered to each group? No matter how reliable and valid the tests are, the results may be rendered almost worthless by indifferent and careless administration. The question of whether the tests should be administered in large, specially scheduled groups or in the regular classes is one that can be decided only on the basis of local conditions. If the physical equipment of the school is suitable, probably more nearly standard conditions can be achieved through the use of a small number of large groups. But a more natural and less tense atmosphere may attend the administration of the tests in the regular classes.

If the tests are given in the regular classes with all or nearly all the teachers participating, it is important to precede the testing program with a special period of instruction and training of the teachers in test administration. It is highly desirable to make sure that the teachers understand the purpose and value of the tests and that their attitude toward the testing situation is favorable, for an indifferent attitude on the part of a teacher may be reflected in indifference in his pupils. Even with these precautions, it may be necessary to leave some teachers out of the test-giving process, for some excellent teachers seem constitutionally unable to administer tests according to a definite and rigid time schedule.

Are the tests scored accurately? Test scoring is a difficult and wearisome clerical task. It calls for careful attention to detail, not only in the original scoring but also in the rescoring and checking, and it requires vigilant supervision if large errors in the scores of individual pupils are to be avoided. As a rule, a clerical staff, specially chosen and trained for this task, can score objective tests more rapidly and accurately than the most intelligent group of teachers a school can assemble. It is doubtful whether a school can ever feel confident of the accuracy of the test scores on its records unless it either specially plans and carries through a thoroughly supervised local scoring program or makes use of the services of an outside scoring agency.

Are the test results interpreted in terms of appropriate norms? National norms based on a meticulous statistical sampling of public schools throughout the country are likely to be very useful for an average public school, but these norms may be almost useless for a public school in a remote rural area of the South or Mid-west, a school in an underprivileged area of a large city, or a college-preparatory group in a suburban public school, or an independent school. The test scores of an individual pupil or a class group should be compared with norms appropriate to the background, training, and educational and vocational goals of that individual or group.

Are the test results quickly reported to teachers and counselors in understandable terms? If the test results are to be of maximum value to the school, they must be placed in the hands of the person in a position to use them while the interest in the tests is still strong and while there is still time in the school year to act upon the needs indicated by the results. The scores should reach the teachers and counselors in not more than a few weeks at the most. The test data should be organized in the form of class distributions and alphabetical lists so that the results for both groups and individuals can be quickly and easily apprehended.

The results should be expressed in terms that the individuals who are to use them can understand. For most classroom teachers and many counselors, percentile ranks are the best medium of expression of the results. Where there is a high degree of sophistication concerning tests, the results may be expressed in units whose statistical properties are superior to percentiles, such as standard scores or scaled scores.

Are the test results recorded on individual cumulative record forms? The results of each testing program have an immediate usefulness, but they also have a long-term value, and this value is enhanced as data are accumulated from year to year. The point cannot be over-emphasized that while it is important to know the level of ability and achievement of a pupil at a given time, it is much more important to know how he is growing in the different areas measured by the tests. Growth can be noted and appraised only when the test results are systematically recorded on individual forms. A school may either prepare its own cumulative record form or use forms generally available through such organizations as the Educational Records Bureau or the American Council on Education. The cumulative record should include not only test data but also many other kinds of information about the individual.

Is a definite attempt made to relate the test scores to other kinds of information? Even the most enthusiastic proponent of testing must concede that test results cannot stand alone. They can never give a complete picture of a pupil. There are areas such as effectiveness of oral expression, ability to bring ideas together and synthesize thinking in written expression, various personal factors, and other qualities that are not covered by existing tests. Moreover, even in the skills and understandings that can be measured well by the better objective tests, it is often true that test results can be adequately interpreted only if there is information on some of the less tangible areas which the tests do not cover. For instance, the development of a situation leading to the personal and social maladjustment of an individual may explain what would otherwise be a puzzling and alarming decline in achievement test scores. Up-to-date cumulative records are invaluable in the study of these interrelationships, although even the best cumulative record must oftentimes be supplemented by the collection of current information and case-study procedures for specific individuals.

In addition to the regular testing program, is there provision for special testing as needed? The all-school testing program should be supplemented by a variety of tests to meet special needs. Several specific needs may be cited by way of illustration. Usually the testing of intelligence or scholastic aptitude in the regular all-school testing program is based on group tests of mental ability, most of which depend rather heavily upon ability to read. Where a reading handicap is suspected, it may be necessary to give a pupil an individual Stanford-Binet Scale to obtain an accurate measure of his intellectual capacity. A pupil who is having difficulty with the usual academic subjects may be given tests of mechanical and clerical aptitude in order to identify aptitudes that have positive significance for educational and vocational guidance.

Guidance of both an educational and a vocational nature may be enhanced by measures of interests, such as the *Kuder Preference Record* or the *Strong Vocational Interest Blank*. In the adjustment counseling of a pupil with whom good rapport has been established, occasional use of inventories of personal qualities, such as the *Bell Adjustment Inventory* or the *California Test of Personality*, may be helpful, provided the counselor has sufficient training and experience to interpret and use the results.

Does the school have an in-service program for educating teachers in the use of test results? This is without a doubt the most important criterion of all. Even a somewhat inadequate testing program from the standpoint of number and kind of tests used may be very helpful to a school if the teachers are prepared to make full use of the test results. But the most thorough and elaborate testing program ever devised will fall flat and be largely a waste of time if the results are placed in the hands of persons untrained in and indifferent to their use. Very few teachers can ever expect to be experts in testing, but every school should have on its staff one person who makes it his special job to thoroughly understand the testing field, and this person should assume responsibility for training the rest of the faculty. All teachers, even those least mathematically inclined, can learn enough about test scores, class medians, and percentile ranks to interpret and use intelligently the results of the tests in their own subject fields. Understanding of test results can be increased through group discussions, lectures based on lantern slides, non-technical staff clinics, and case studies.

The use of test results is an all-faculty function. When it is accepted as such, pupils and teachers alike can benefit greatly from a comprehensive, regular, systematic testing program.

49   *Pros and Cons of External Testing Programs*

FRANK B. WOMER

Within the past two decades the number of "external" tests being administered to high school students has spiraled dramatically. The reasons offered for the existence of such programs are varied, but are primarily concerned with college admissions and the granting of scholarships. Objections to external tests are voiced by many local school administrators, for it is frequently upon their shoulders, as far as the public is concerned, that the burden of proof falls regarding the legitimacy and validity of such programs. What are the major problems

Reprinted and abridged with permission of author and publisher from the *North Central Association Quarterly*, 1961, Vol. 36, pp. 201–210.

in using external testing programs? Are the objections "real" or "imagined"? What can be said in support of the programs? How can a school principal answer the critics? A careful reading of the following objective analysis of the situation by a test consultant should provide answers or at least clues to possible solutions to the foregoing questions and problems.

THE EXTERNAL TESTING PROGRAMS

External testing programs cannot be identified by the types of tests that are used. Any school may purchase for its own internal testing program tests that are similar to the ones used in external testing programs.

There is one organizational aspect of two of the external testing programs that sets them apart from internal programs. The College Board tests and the American College Testing Program are given under "secure" conditions. That is, there are a limited number of testing centers in a state, the test administrator is someone trained to administer standardized tests, the administrator and proctors are reimbursed for their efforts, and strenuous attempts are made to see that the test items used in these tests do not become available to anyone outside the sponsoring agencies.

The tests designed primarily for scholarship purposes, however, are not given in testing centers, but in each participating school. They are administered and proctored by local school personnel. Of course, efforts are made to maintain the security of test items. But that job is difficult because of the thousands of separate testing units involved.

If external tests cannot be identified by the type of test being used, and only in part by the organization of the programs, how can they be identified? It seems to me that there are at least two distinctive features of the external testing programs: 1) The results of external tests are used primarily by some institution or organization other than the high school, and 2) the local school has or feels no real choice as to whether their students take these tests.

The question of lack of free choice of taking these tests might be argued by some. Technically, no one is physically forcing students to take one test or another. Yet any bright, college-bound student who needs financial assistance would be foolish not to take the National Merit test, and any student aspiring to entry into an institution requiring College Board Tests is hardly in a position to bargain.

By using the definition just outlined at least four tests used in Michigan would qualify as external tests—the College Entrance Examination Board tests (CEEB), tests of the American College Testing Program (ACT), the National Merit Scholarship Qualifying Test (NMSQT), and the Preliminary Scholastic Aptitude Test (PSAT). The first two of these are college entrance examinations, the latter two are primarily college scholarship tests. If one were to use some broader definition, other programs could be classified as being external.

Let us now look briefly at the types of tests that are included in the four instruments we have classified as external tests. Two of these tests are designed to measure scholastic aptitude—the SAT (Scholastic Aptitude Test) portion of the College Boards and the PSAT. In fact the PSAT is a short form of the SAT, using items from the same files. Both tests yield two scores—a linguistic-type ability score, and a numerical-type ability score. Both could be classified as intelligence tests.

One of the four test instruments measures achievement, if one defines achievement as the product of instruction in a specific class. The Achievement Tests of the College Boards include such tests as English Composition, Advanced Mathematics, Chemistry, French, and others.

Two of the four external testing programs measure educational development. The ACT and the NMSQT are both children of the well-known Iowa Tests of Educational Development, at least in philosophy if not in specific items. An educational development test falls someplace between intelligence tests and achievement tests. Items are written that will reflect a pupil's proficiency on his entire educational history (both in school and out of school). Such tests do reflect instruction, but they also reflect general ability.

USES OF EXTERNAL TESTING PROGRAMS

All four of these testing programs may be used to a greater or lesser degree for a variety of purposes. They can be used by high schools for counseling with college-bound students, for the results from any good standardized ability or achievement test taken by a high school student can be helpful in the guidance process.

All four of these tests can and are being used for selection purposes, for which they have at least one characteristic that sets them apart from similar high school level tests. The typical high school test is designed to help make judgments at all ability and achievement levels from very low to very high. Although a group intelligence test may yield IQ's from 50 to 150, half of all the actual IQ's achieved will fall between 90 and 110. An intelligence test author develops a few very easy test items to discriminate between students with IQ's of 60 and 70 and a few difficult items to discriminate between IQ's of 140 and 150.

The most efficient tests designed specifically for college-bound students are those concentrating on the top half of the general population. Some studies have indicated that an average College Board score of 500 is approximately equivalent to a general IQ of about 120. This is the way it should be if the College Boards are to do the best possible job of helping to shed light on college potential. Similarly it doesn't matter whether the NMSQT differentiates accurately between percentiles of 45 and 50 as long as it differentiates between percentiles of 97 and 98.

At least one of the four external tests can be used for placement and/or acceleration purposes at the college level. The achievement portion of the College Boards is probably most amenable to such uses, as they are most like end-of-course examinations. The SAT, NMSQT, and ACT do not yield information of much help in placement in specific courses, although they could be helpful for selection for an honors program when an important basis for judgment is the students' scholastic ability to succeed in such a program.

PROBLEMS

Let us look at some problems that have been associated with external testing.

One of the complaints about external testing is that the pressures to participate are too great to be resisted and that these pressures have a detrimental effect. Publicity about the closing college door has tended to make some parents and pupils feel that participation in admissions and scholarship testing programs is inevitable and that a pupil's whole future rests on the resulting test scores. To say that such fears are entirely groundless is a refusal to face facts. To agree that they are entirely realistic fears is equally rash. Securing a $1,000 a year scholarship may cause Johnny to decide to go to MIT rather than some college nearby. This may well make a difference in Johnny's life. But who can say whether such differences are good or bad? A refusal of admission to one college may result in the choice of another college. Who can say whether the education secured in the second-choice college is poorer than that in the first-choice college? In some instances the second-choice college may actually be a much better selection.

When the pressures on pupils and parents to attain high scores on external tests becomes extreme, perhaps the whole relationship between a school and its constituents needs to be re-examined carefully; perhaps a school's entire guidance and public relations programs need to be scrutinized. There are certainly pressures on schools from other external programs. Yet, most schools seem to be able to handle such pressures satisfactorily.

Another objection that some people raise to external testing programs is that too many pupils are taking the tests. Since only the top 2 percent nationally will get past the first scholarship screening test (NMSQT), perhaps it would be wise to keep the number of students taking the test to a minimum. But some schools prefer to have all of their college-bound students take the tests, and others administer it to all of their juniors. When such conditions prevail, the external test ceases to be external, and as an internal test should no longer be subject to the criticisms leveled at external tests.

A third objection that has been raised is that too much student time is spent taking external tests. The NMSQT, the PSAT, and the ACT each take about a half day, and the complete College Boards take two half-days. Thus, the maximum time spent on these four tests would be the equivalent of two and one-half school days.

Most people probably would agree that students should not be expected to use up two days in testing unless some benefits will result. Considering that important decisions about college scholarships and college admissions are going to be influenced by these two days, it may be a small investment of time for the good that can result. It would be interesting to speculate as to how many days are spent by a typical college-bound student visiting various college campuses—in many instances it would be more than two days.

It is very possible, of course, that many school systems are doing more testing than is warranted. One would need to analyze internal as well as external testing to make a satisfactory judgment.

Some school administrators feel that they are required to spend too much of their time or that their counselors must spend too much time in signing up students for the various external tests, and in actually administering the scholarship tests. There can be no question that it does take administrative and/or counselor time to handle the external testing programs. It is also true that it takes some time to handle the administrative details of all student activities. Whether the administrative time spent on external testing is "too much" must be answered individually by each administrator; it must be answered both in relation to the outcomes of external testing and in relation to his other administrative duties.

Another practical objection that is sometimes raised to external testing is that it costs too much money. NMSQT costs $1.00; PSAT costs $1.00; CEEB costs $5.00 for SAT and $8.00 for the achievement tests; and ACT costs $3.00. This is a total of $18.00 if all four tests are taken. This is a fair amount of money. But consider for a moment how many school pictures, name cards, and graduation announcements one can buy for $18.00. Or consider what portion of the cost of a class ring could be covered for that amount of money. How much money is "too much" is a relative decision.

Another charge that has been made against external testing is that it has grown big because of a fight between two test publishers. It has been inferred that the publishers are more concerned with profits than with educational progress. It would be foolish to say that competition between test publishers does not exist—it does exist and many decisions relative to the marketing of tests are based upon such competition. To infer that such competition necessarily results in poor tests is not warranted; to infer that it sometimes results in duplication of testing is, in my opinion, true.

Both of the publishers involved in this discussion have promoted their scholarship tests as general guidance tools, valuable for all college-bound students at the very least. Yet, both tests were supposedly designed to help do the job of screening scholarship candidates. Proponents of wide use of the scholarship tests claim that it is entirely feasible for one test to be a good guidance tool at several ability levels, yet also be entirely adequate for scholarship screening. Others might challenge that point of view.

Lest I appear to be too negative on this point, it is well to keep in mind that the test publishers have not forced a half million students to take the NMSQT—many other people have been encouraging large groups of students to take the test. It also is important to remember that competition appears in other areas—school textbooks are not produced by entirely disinterested authors or publishers. A good case might be made for defending competition on the basis of improved quality of product.

A major charge that is made against external testing is that it results in standardization of the school program, that it stifles experimentation, that it dictates teaching practices. There are at least three different ways to react to this point: 1) it happens and it is bad; 2) it happens and it is good; 3) it doesn't necessarily happen. Notice that the words "doesn't necessarily" are stressed. Persons taking this position would not say it can't happen, but simply that it doesn't have to happen. They would feel that here, at least, is one aspect of the impact of external testing that is in part at the mercy of the local administrator. They would claim that through working with faculty, with parents, with counselors, and with students, it is possible to eliminate or minimize the effects of testing on the curriculum.

We really don't know how much effect, if any, external testing is having on high school education today. Some say that we already have the effect; others say we don't have it yet but it's coming; still others claim that it will never materialize.

Rather closely allied with the last point is the question of "coaching" for the external tests. The effect of coaching on test taking has been debated far and wide. The research evidence clearly indicates that coaching for intelligence tests very quickly reaches a point of diminishing returns. Research has demonstrated that practice on one ability test is as good as practice on two or more tests, and that coaching classes actually produces less gain than a single practice test. On subject matter tests such as French or Biology, it would be odd indeed if coaching had no effect. Such a statement would mean that formal education has no effect on learning. I am sure that proficiency in any subject area is amenable to change via formal education.

Tests of educational development are probably susceptible to coaching, if coaching is done via regular classwork for an extended period of time. A short series of coaching sessions has very little effect. A student who has taken one or more educational development tests before taking the NMSQT probably has had as much coaching as he can profit from.

Today a great many colleges are becoming more selective than they have ever been before. As they become more selective, admissions officers are faced with decisions that require finer and finer discriminations. In order to maximize correct decisions and minimize incorrect ones, many colleges now feel that they cannot afford to ignore the type of information provided by test scores.

To some critics, if a college says that it wants to add test data to admissions files, this is taken to mean that it wants to replace all previously used criteria with a test score. At this point logical reasoning certainly has broken down for such critics. I don't believe that a college admissions officer could ignore high school records and other pertinent data even if he wanted to, and I've never heard one say that he wanted to. I don't believe he could ignore these other criteria because I think he would make too many mistakes to keep his job very long.

Some critics have said yes, we can see that colleges need test scores and that scholarship agencies need test scores, but why can't they use the scores that are already available in our own school files? They argue that external tests merely duplicate scores already available.

This criticism calls for the exploration of several points. Earlier in this paper the different levels of difficulty at which tests may be aimed were mentioned. Tests such as the old ACE, the SCAT, or the new Kuhlmann-Anderson do yield linguistic and quantitative scores just as the SAT and the PSAT. However, high school tests are geared for all IQ levels, not just those in the upper half or upper third.

Achievement tests such as those in the Cooperative Test Series or the Evaluation and Adjustment Series are available for testing Algebra, Physics, World History, and other subject areas, but they are not at the level of difficulty of the achievement tests in the College Boards. They could hardly be used to help place college students in advanced sections.

Another point that needs to be discussed is uniformity of test administration and security precautions that generally are taken. It probably is impossible to design a testing program that cannot be tampered with if someone is determined enough to do it. However, it is probably true that the so-called "secure" testing programs, College Boards and ACT, do produce less variation in testing practices than any other and that the test items are less apt to fall into the hands of unauthorized personnel.

Suppose that the National Merit Scholarship Corporation were to say tomorrow, "Each high school principal should submit to us percentile ranks for his students from a general ability test, and all of these students with percentiles of 98 and 99 will be semi-finalists." Would this be an acceptable procedure to school administrators? Would they really feel it fair to compare their own Otis percentile rank with a Kuhlmann-Finch given in Arkansas or a TEA given in Hawaii? Is it not possible that such a system could lead to temptations that would be too much for some people to resist? The same condition prevails in college admissions—are all internal testing programs really secure enough if a score is to be used as a part of a competitive selective process?

One major recommendation that has been made by some people is the establishment of equivalency tables. By this is meant a series of tables that would equate test scores for the various widely used ability and achievement tests. This is certainly an appealing idea. It is an idea which I have favored for a number of years for general guidance purposes; it is an idea about which I have serious reservations if test results are to be used to any extent for selective or placement purposes.

The reservations are based on several points. First, there are the different difficulty levels of high school tests and tests designed for college-bound students.

Second, there is the lack of uniformity of test administration and security measures in high school testing. Third, there is the technical question of the reduced reliability of predicted test scores. A College Board score predicted from a DAT (Differential Aptitude Test) is not as reliable as an actual Board score. Fourth, and perhaps most important, the temptation to assume that all standardized tests are alike and that a score on one test is comparable to a score on any other similar test would be overwhelming. One difficulty with statistical treatment of test scores is that it is mathematically easy to equate things that logically should not be equated.

Another practical aspect to this question is the number of different tests now being used by schools for college counseling. In a recent study in Michigan, twenty-one different ability tests were reported in use. A rather extensive series of equivalency tables would have to be developed to relate all of these tests to College Boards and to NMSQT.

Still another criticism of external testing has been the comparisons of school systems that have been made. The selection of the so-called twenty best schools on the basis of number of National Merit semi-finalists ignores completely the ability level of the students enrolled in these schools. If one wanted to compare schools with any degree of fairness, it would be necessary to equate them on various factors, such as average IQ or socio-economic level of the community.

To say that such school-by-school comparisons are not reasonable, however, doesn't keep people from making them. Perhaps the only solutions to this criticism are either: 1) to eliminate the National Merit Scholarship program, or 2) to educate the public to a realistic appraisal of it. It's important to note that elimination of the NMSQT would not eliminate comparisons between schools. If scholarship candidates were chosen on any sort of merit basis, some schools would have more than others.

Some people have suggested that too much publicity has been given to the semi-finalists and winners in the National Merit program. Perhaps that is so; yet, students in our schools are honored for success in other aspects of the educational program. Somehow it would seem odd if the only solution to this problem of school-by-school comparison would be to make a secret operation out of the scholarship program.

At least one national authority has suggested that the double testing of National Merit candidates is unnecessary. He feels that the original screening of high school juniors could be done satisfactorily by the local school administrator. This could be done by allowing each principal to select 2 percent of his own juniors, or to allow him to select as many as he felt would qualify in the top 2 percent on a national basis. Either method would have certain shortcomings, but the practical difficulties could probably be handled. There is a real question, however, whether principals would really want the responsibility and burden associated with personally picking the students who would be eligible for national scholarships.

A final problem associated with external testing is one that has not been discussed very often. The problem is that the critics of external testing cannot agree upon what the "real" problems are.

PROPOSED SOLUTIONS

A number of different solutions have been proposed to meet the various criticisms that are aimed at external testing. Most of them seem to fall into one or the other of two rather broad categories.

One category of solutions involving three alternatives would call for a reduction in the number of programs.

1. The most extreme recommendation in the first category would call for the elimination of all external testing programs. If such a step were undertaken, it would certainly result in a series of adjustments in scholarship selection and college admissions. One possible result could be that many, perhaps most colleges would set up their own scholarship and admissions testing programs, and college applicants would be making treks around the state and the country taking tests wherever the colleges and universities of their choices are located.

2. A less extreme recommendation would call for the establishment of a single national testing program. It is difficult to visualize any test publisher's voluntarily withdrawing his own tests from the field. If there were to be a single national testing program, it probably would have to be a new program that would replace all four of the ones discussed here. This would mean that some new agency would have to be established to do the job—either governmental or educational. The details of such an effort would be many, but would not be unsolvable. Those critics who now question the effect of the present external testing programs on curriculum and instruction might want to consider the potential effects of a single national testing program on a local school's curriculum. Others who object to a single national program claim that competition actually produces better tests and testing programs than monopolistic effort would do.

3. A less extreme recommendation than either of the last two would call for a reduction of the number of external testing programs to two, rather than the elimination of all of them or replacement with a single national program. One rationale for this recommendation says that since there are basically two types of programs, let's have only two. The two types to which I am referring are the educational development type (NMSQT and ACT) and the separate intelligence and achievement type (College Boards and PSAT). If there were only NMSQT or ACT and if there were only College Boards or PSAT, the present four programs would be reduced to two. How could this be accomplished? It seems to me that it could be done only through the cooperative action of states or of regions.

A second category consisting of possible solutions does not attempt to alter or eliminate the programs, but rather to alleviate some or all of the problems associated with them.

1. One widely made suggestion calls for the establishment of equivalency tables so that a school could submit to the scholarship agencies or a college admissions officer a percentile rank or IQ from whatever test is being used in that school. This is certainly possible. Some of the objections have already been discussed and will not be repeated here. However, I would like to mention what my reaction as a test consultant will be if this development takes place. If a high school principal is primarily concerned with giving his students the greatest possible test advantage in getting into the college of his choice, I would suggest that he settle on the intelligence test for his own internal testing program that yields the highest scores. If, on the other hand, a principal is primarily concerned with a student's getting into the college where he will be associating with others of like abilities and achievements, I would recommend that his student take whatever testing program is required by that college in addition to submitting all of the pertinent test scores from his own internal testing program.

2. One suggestion aimed at improving communication calls for more work with pupils and parents. In too many instances neither pupil nor parent knows what the various external tests are about or whether Johnny really should take them. Many of the fears built up in their minds could be reduced by proper information. Too often the impression is left that a scholarship or admissions decision depends wholly on the test score achieved on a particular day. It's no wonder that tensions grow when such impressions are allowed to go unchallenged. Test specialists have long advocated wide dissemination of information about tests and test scores. This applied both to internal and to external tests.

3. The suggestion has been made that all schools shift to Saturday administrations of the various external tests. Many schools already do test on Saturdays. For the school administrator who feels that time spent in testing is time lost from education, Saturday testing is a logical choice. For the school that incorporates any external test into its own testing program, a week day may be more appropriate. It is questionable whether complete agreement could be reached that schools should test on any particular day of the week.

4. Still another suggestion calls for reducing the publicity associated with becoming a scholarship semi-finalist or winner. It is claimed that the greater the publicity, the greater the competition and resulting ill effects. It is also claimed that wide publicity leads to unfair comparisons between schools. Here is an area in which school administrators might be able to establish some policies to govern news releases, if agreement can be reached as to the best course of action. Here, certainly, is an area in which a state or regional association could have an impact. Here, too, is an area in which each high school principal must share some of the responsibility for the effects of external testing.

5. One suggestion for alleviation of the effects of external testing is the holding of appropriate conferences. Their purpose would be to share ideas, to clarify points that may be vague, and to discuss whether some cooperative action should be taken by secondary school and college personnel. There is reason to believe

that this approach to the problems presented by external testing and college articulation can be an effective one.

6. One of the aspects of national scholarship testing is the large numbers of students taking the exams (some half million). Yet approximately 1000 national scholarships are actually awarded each year. To screen a half million students to find 1000 is hardly necessary from the selection point of view. One large city in a North Central state allows only the top 10 percent of its students to take the NMSQT. Their research indicated that their own winners never came from below the top 10 percent; so they recently instituted this policy. One way that criticism involving numbers could be met is by discouraging large numbers of students from taking the tests. Again, it's not certain that everyone would agree that such restrictions would be wise. In fact, it's possible that a majority might feel otherwise. Nevertheless, this is a potential solution to one of the criticisms aimed at external testing.

7. Another practical suggestion that has been made is for schools to take a strong stand against "coaching" for the external tests. One of the major criticisms of external testing is that it influences curriculum, and that teachers will teach for the tests. Is it not possible for such practices to be controlled by high school principals? A strong stand by educators against "coaching" for tests in any form, along with the active cooperation of all school administrators could certainly hold coaching to a minimum. It would be foolish to imply that it can be eliminated since coaching books are available at bookstores. But it certainly could be discouraged by an active campaign that includes working with students and parents.

SOME OBSERVATIONS

In closing, I would like to make some personal observations. I have attempted to approach this whole topic of external testing in as objective a manner as possible. I sincerely feel that we now find ourselves in an uncomfortable position in relation to external testing because of conditions that are beyond the specific control of any one person. However, I also believe that our position is somewhat more uncomfortable than it needs to be, and that each of us must share some of the responsibility for this condition and for future developments in this area.

I believe that test specialists have contributed to the lack of understanding in this area because of their failure to sell educational testing to educators and to the public as a vital part of the educative process. They have not convinced all educators that testing makes a unique contribution to the solution of many educational problems.

I believe that college faculties have created some misunderstanding in the use of test scores for admission to college because of their great concern with academic prestige, and their feeling that highly selective admissions policies are the royal road to that goal.

I believe that test publishers have magnified the problem because of their exploitation of the special purpose scholarship and admissions tests, and their promotion of these tests into overly expanded national programs.

I believe that high school administrators have been overly sensitive to centralized control of testing due to their over-zealous guarding of local autonomy, and their feeling that any program imposed from outside is automatically a bad one.

50   Can Useful General-Purpose Equivalency Tables Be Prepared for Different College Admissions Tests?

WILLIAM H. ANGOFF

With increasing frequency colleges and universities are being faced with the expanding problem of evaluating applicants from secondary institutions of varying quality. One method that has been developed to assist with this problem is to require all applicants to take a common "external" examination. It is legitimately assumed that such a procedure would, to some extent, equate the institutions and provide a fair base for evaluating individual students. It should be emphasized that admissions officers use these test scores as only one additional bit of data to make selections. They do give considerable weight to an individual student's academic record and personality and motivation as reflected in recommendations and if possible personal interviews. Because of the competition for the limited number of openings in a particular freshman class, multiple applications are necessary. But since a student may wish to apply to a number of institutions, and all institutions do not require the same examination, he may have to take three or four different "external" exams. This is obviously inefficient, but if "equivalency tables" allowed conversion of scores obtained on one test to the score scale of another, the situation could be considerably eased.

In the following somewhat technical article, Dr. William Angoff presents probably the most comprehensive discussion available to date of the problems involved in constructing equivalency tables for non-parallel tests. What are the four major sources of error involved in attempting to equate scores on different tests purporting to measure the same characteristics? What are the implications for the table developer and potential examinee of the phenomena known as "regression to the mean"? What are the most frequently used equating methods? What are the three types of groups most frequently used to develop conversion tables?

Reprinted and abridged with permission of author and publisher from the *Proceedings of the 1962 Invitational Conference on Testing Problems*, Princeton, N. J.: Educational Testing Service, 1963, pp. 57–73. (By special arrangement with the American Council on Education)

The development of equivalency tables that would relate the tests of all publishers has some obvious attractions. It also has some objectionable features which may be summarized by saying that such tests will not necessarily be parallel forms—that is, they will not necessarily be measuring precisely the same function—and that in such instances it is not possible to provide a unique conversion that will be appropriate for all groups who are likely to take the tests or for all purposes for which the tests are likely to be given. It is of course reasonable to equate the tests of different publishers when these tests are known to be parallel. And quite possibly some *are*. On the other hand, it is more than likely that in the majority of instances they are not, since they were not constructed with that intention in the first place.

Before going on to consider the problems of equating tests of different function, it may be helpful to say what we mean when we talk about the equating of scores on tests of the *same* function. In this case, in the conversion of scores from one form to a parallel form of a test, say from one form of the *American Council on Education Psychological Examination* to another, or from one form of the *College Board Scholastic Aptitude Tests* to another, we have simply the problem of transforming the system of units. We ordinarily consider this problem as one that is directly analogous to the problem of conversion from centimeters to inches, from Centigrade to Fahrenheit, from pounds to grams, and so on. On the other hand, the question of converting scores across tests of *different* function is another matter. Here we are concerned with the problems of conversion from one kind of dimension to something quite different—from the scale of inches to the scale of pounds, for example. This is not necessarily an extreme or unreasonable example. For instance, the correlation between height and weight for adults of the same age is in the region of the low .50's. The correlation between observed scores on two tests of mathematical ability—for example, SAT-Mathematical and ACE-Quantitative—(both of which, it should be pointed out, were designed to be predictive of scholastic success in the quantitative areas) is in the low .60's. The true-score correlation between these tests is not much higher—around .70. On the face of it, it seems unreasonable to ask for a conversion from inches to pounds. Why then is it not similarly unreasonable (or at least *almost* as unreasonable) to ask for a conversion from SAT-M to ACE-Q? Yet requests for this conversion are not at all unusual.

Even in the conversion of scores across tests of the *same* function we can enumerate at least four sources of error.

SOURCES OF ERROR IN CONVERTING SCORES

(1) One source of error lies in the unreliability of the measuring instruments themselves, and affects the stability of statistics obtained in the collection of data.

(2) A second source of error lies in the design of the equating experiment and the method of treating the data: The various methods of equating are not equally reliable.

(3) A third source of error lies in the choice of samples used to establish the conversion line. Different samples will yield lines that differ randomly from one another.

(4) Finally, there is a source of error that is characteristic of any statistical enterprise—the error associated with the size of the study sample. Obviously larger samples will yield more reliable data.

Nevertheless, in spite of all these kinds of error, it is reasonable in the equating of parallel forms of a test to postulate a unique "true" line and to consider that errors resulting from the unreliability of tests, from design and method, and from the sampling of people only cause random departures from this true line. On the other hand, the problem of "comparable" scores, that is, the conversion of scores of *different* function, has additional complexities. Here, as in the physical analogy in which we convert height to weight, the request for equivalent scores rests on an inappropriate premise—that there is *a single* conversion system—a unique system that exists and needs only to be estimated with the use of appropriate data. While it is certainly true that one can estimate or predict by means of a regression equation the most likely weight of an individual of a given height, or predict scores on the SAT from knowledge of scores on the ACE, in neither case can the prediction be considered simply a tranformation of unit systems. Furthermore, just as regression systems will differ, depending on various considerations like the conditions of measurement and the characteristics of the group measured, so will conversion lines which purport to translate scores across tests of different function differ—and they will differ systematically, that is, in a predictable fashion, depending on certain known considerations.

PROBLEMS IN DERIVING COMPARABLE SCORES FROM NON-PARALLEL TESTS

For one thing, different conversion lines will result, depending on the particular definition of comparability employed. For example, one might ask what the most likely score on one test would be, given a particular score on the other. This would be one definition. Or one might equate standard-score deviates on the two tests. Or one might equate equivalent percentiles. These would be other definitions. Or one might, for example, equate scores that yielded equal-predicted scores on one criterion or another. Here the use of different prediction criteria might yield different conversions. There is probably an unlimited number of definitions, each one conceivably yielding a different conversion. In contrast to this multiplicity of conversions for non-parallel tests, all methods or definitions of equivalent scores for *parallel* tests should lead to the same conversion equation—that is, except for random error of the kind described before.

Secondly, different lines will result when different populations are used to form the basis for deriving the tables of comparable scores. For example, there will be one conversion line between Verbal and Mathematical test scores at the college entrance level for boys and quite another for girls. This fact is immediately apparent if one examines the mean scores of boys and girls on the Verbal and Mathematical sections of the SAT. Girls characteristically score slightly higher than boys on Verbal but considerably lower than boys on Mathematical. The conversion line between Verbal and Mathematical scores when derived from the data for boys would be much different from the conversion line derived from the data for girls. Because they reveal group characteristics and are not independent of the groups on which they are based, these kinds of conversions are themselves another way of representing group profiles.

A third reason for the non-uniqueness of comparable scores is the fact that differential selection will have a pronounced and predictable effect on the conversions. Let us suppose, for example, that we collect data on the SAT and the ACE for a group of individuals in order to construct a conversion table from scores on one of these tests to scores on the other, and let us suppose also that these individuals have been explicitly selected on the SAT. The distribution of resulting SAT scores will, of course, be sharply curtailed. The distribution of ACE scores, on the other hand, will be only moderately curtailed. A conversion line derived from these data could be far different from a line derived from a group of unselected students, or from a group of students who were selected on ACE. Even if the students have not been selected on one of the two tests, but on some third variable, say high school grades, their resulting distributions on the two tests and consequently the conversion of scores on the two tests could be considerably altered. This is so because the two score distributions will be unequally curtailed in rough proportion to the correlation of the two tests with the selection variable. The test that correlates more highly with the selection variable is the test on which the distribution of scores will be more drastically affected by the selection. The unequal effect of this selection is what causes the conversion for the selected group to be different from the conversion for the original unselected group. In contrast, scores taken from parallel tests of equal length will be equally affected by selection on a third variable, since they would correlate equally with that variable. The result is that there would be no predictable effect on the conversion equation.

I should emphasize that these problems are inherent in the derivation of a system of comparable scores, that is to say, in the conversion of scores on non-parallel tests, and that they do not replace or preclude the kinds of sources of error that were mentioned before in connection with equivalent scores that are taken from parallel forms. The problems of comparable scores exist *in addition* to the problems of equivalent scores.

AN ILLUSTRATION OF THE CONVERSION PROBLEM

By referring to appropriate data, it can be demonstrated quite readily that conversions for non-parallel tests are not unique but depend in each case on the nature of the group used to establish the conversion. Table 1 shows two sets of conversions between ACE-Quantitative and SAT-Mathematical, one based on

TABLE 1. *Conversions from ACE-Quantitative to SAT-Mathematical*

ACE-Q Scores*	SAT-M Scores		
	Men Liberal Arts	Women Liberal Arts	Difference
6	250	226	24
9	333	299	34
12	416	373	43
15	499	446	53
18	532	519	63
21	665	592	73
24	748	665	83

* Special scale for ACE; Mean = 13, Standard Deviation = 4.

a group of 333 male students, the other based on a group of 582 women, both enrolled in the liberal arts curriculum at a large western state university. Clearly, each of the ACE-Q scores listed in the column at the left yields two converted scores that differ from each other appreciably. If it were necessary to convert these two tests to a single "common currency" to be used for students of both sexes, there would be considerable doubt as to which one of these two conversions would be the proper one to use. In contrast, Table 2 also shows two sets of con-

TABLE 2. *Conversions from ACE-Linguistic to SAT-Verbal*

ACE-L Scores*	SAT-V Scores		
	Men Liberal Arts	Women Liberal Arts	Difference
6	322	316	6
9	393	383	10
12	464	450	14
15	535	518	17
18	605	585	20
21	676	652	24
24	747	719	28

* Special scale for ACE; Mean = 13, Standard Deviation = 4.

versions for the same two groups of students, this time for tests that correlate more highly: ACE-Linguistic and SAT-Verbal. The results in Table 2 are entirely different from those in Table 1. Here, because the tests are more similar in terms of what they measure than are ACE-Quantitative and SAT-Mathematical, the conversions are in much greater agreement.

INTERPRETIVE PROBLEMS

Added to the systematic effects on comparable score conversions that were discussed earlier—namely, the definition of the kind of comparability in question; the choice and size of the group which would be used to establish the conversion;

and finally, the related effects of selection—there are still other problems to face when we consider the equating of non-parallel tests. Particularly important are the problems of interpretation. For example, there is the danger that converted scores will be assumed to possess the reliability and validity of the scale of scores to which they are converted. While it should go without saying that scores on one test, however well they may be converted to another scale, retain all the basic characteristics of the original test, many test users will assume that, once converted, they should behave in all respects like the test whose scale they have adopted. Obviously, this assumption is unjustified. It becomes evident that this is not an insignificant concern when we reflect that this kind of misinterpretation favors the publishers of the poorer, less reliable test. And it is probably safe to say that scores on the less reliable test would more often be converted to the scale of the more reliable test than vice versa.

Related to this is the very real worry that the existence of tables of comparable scores will favor the test that is readily available for purchase and is sanctioned by the publisher for administration under less secure and less carefully controlled conditions. Here too it is likely that this test would be the one that is converted to the scale of the test in which only the highest standards of control are permitted in and out of the testing room than vice versa. Since it is also reasonable to assume that the test that is administered under less stringent conditions is the one that is likely to yield the higher score, it is easy to see that the candidate for college admission who is given the test under these conditions is the one who stands to gain in comparison with a competing candidate who is required to take the more secure test.

Another kind of error occurs in the interpretation of converted scores when regression methods are used for establishing the conversion line between two tests. Predicted scores are regressed, that is, they have a reduced standard deviation; original scores are unregressed. The pooling of these two kinds of data, one taken from actual obtained scores and the other taken from regressed scores, would be improper. Yet it is for the very purpose of pooling such data, or at least considering them in conjunction, that conversion tables are ordinarily called for. Let us say, for example, that we have a conversion of this sort from ACE to SAT. It is interesting to note here that to adopt the winning strategy good students would be well advised to take the test that does not undergo this type of conversion—the SAT, that is—since by doing so they will avoid the unfavorable effects of regression, in which scores at the upper end of the scale are characteristically depressed. *Their* scores would depend only on their own high level of performance. Poor students, on the other hand, would be well advised to take the ACE, because in the conversion to the SAT their scores would naturally be regressed upward toward the mean. Thus, by following this advice and taking advantage of statistical laws, they manage to achieve a higher score than they deserve—that is, a higher score than would be earned by students of the same ability who are not given this advice. It is important also to note that the lower the correlation between these tests the greater the extent of the regression and the greater the effect of the strategy. The other side of this coin is also worth noting: The good student would be ill-advised to take the ACE because his score would also regress in the conversion process, but downward toward the mean.

There are other situations as well where it would be to a student's advantage to take into consideration the effects of regression. Suppose, for example, a table of comparable scores were developed for two tests of dissimilar validity by defining as equivalent those scores that yielded equal predicted scores on some single criterion, say college grades. Since scores on both tests would inevitably regress toward the mean and since the regression would be more pronounced for the less valid test, it is clear that the winning strategy for the poor student would be to take the less valid test, because it is on this test that his scores would undergo the greater upward regression. The opposite strategy would be appropriate for the good student. His scores would necessarily regress downward in the conversion process, but if he were circumspect and took the more valid test, he would insure himself against substantial loss due to the effects of regression.

In spite of all that has been said so far, there are times, nevertheless, when it is reasonable and appropriate to derive tables of comparable scores for tests of different function. The methods of deriving these tables are much like, and in most instances identical to the methods of equating scores on parallel tests. The ideal plan for equating would be one in which we would select a sample of individuals to whom we would administer both Forms *x* and *y* and see to it that practice on the first form administered did not affect performance on the second form. However, since the ways of doing this are not immediately apparent, we find it more convenient to divide the group into random halves and give Form *x* to one-half of the group and Form *y* to the other half of the group. Then, making the assumption that there are no systematic differences between the groups, we equate the means and standard deviations on the two tests to produce a linear equation relating the two sets of scores. This procedure in effect says that we consider equivalent (or, in the present discussion, comparable) those scores that correspond to equal percentiles. Now, if the distributions on Form *x* and on Form *y* have the same shape, then this latter procedure will result in a straight-line conversion quite similar to the one first described, which assumes that differences in shape are of no consequence. On the other hand, if the distributions are different, then this latter conversion will be curvilinear. Still another method is one in which half the group takes Form *x* followed by Form *y*, the other half taking *y* followed by *x*. Here the assumption is made that the effect of practice is constant and unrelated to score level, and also that the effect on Form *y* performance (in terms of standard scores) is the same as the effect on Form *x* performance. Finally, the conversion between *x* and *y* is achieved by averaging the means and variances on Form *x* and also on Form *y* and setting them equal. Incidentally, the problem of practice effect is a troublesome one in the case of parallel tests. It is particularly troublesome in the case of non-parallel tests for the reason that just as it is logically awkward to compare *performance* on tests that are not designed to measure the same thing, similarly it is logically awkward to compare *changes* on tests that are not designed to measure the same thing.

METHODS OF EQUATING

All other methods of equating that are known to be in frequent use involve the use of anchor tests in one way or another and are variations of a basic method developed by Dr. Ledyard Tucker and also by Dr. Frederic Lord—but with different sets of assumptions. In all of these methods the tests x and y are given to different groups; the function of the anchor test, which is given to both groups, is to adjust for any differences that may be observed in them. Most of these methods may also be used for deriving comparable scores between tests of different function. More recently—within the last two or three years—a method has been suggested by Dr. Lord for making use of anchor tests in estimating frequency distributions for groups on tests that were not actually taken by those groups. This method has been adopted for use with the equipercentile method of equating tests, a method which heretofore was possible only in those situations where the tests could be administered to random groups. I should also add that anchor test scores may be used in a method of equipercentile equating that has been suggested by Dr. E. F. Lindquist. In this method, scores on two tests are taken to be equivalent if they are found to be equivalent to the same score on an anchor test.

CRITERIA FOR EQUATING TESTS

If we attempt to adapt these methods of equating to the problem of non-parallel tests and consider the restriction that was discussed before, that such a conversion is applicable only to the specific conditions under which it was derived, we find that the following questions are pertinent: (1) How similar are the tests for which comparable scores are to be developed? (2) How appropriate is the group on whom the table of comparable scores is based when one considers the person or the group for whom the table is to be used? (3) How much error can we safely tolerate in the particular use we have in mind? These questions are intentionally phrased in terms of degree, because this issue, like so many others, depends on considerations of degree. Categorical answers are inappropriate. Thus, in considering the first of these three questions, if the tests are extremely different— if one is a test of quantitative skills and the other is a measure of interest in sports —then clearly it would be absurd to contemplate a conversion that would make any sense at all. On the other hand, if one is a verbal test heavily loaded with items of the definition type, while the other is a test of reading comprehension, then it is reasonable to consider a table of comparable scores for these two tests.

With regard to the second question, if the group on whom the table is based consists of college seniors majoring in literature, and the group for whom we wish to use the conversion consists of high school sophomores enrolled in a manual training course, then obviously the use is inappropriate. On the other hand, if the groups are both freshmen in liberal arts in colleges that are similarly selective, then the use is probably appropriate.

The third question, which calls for a commitment to a maximum tolerable error, is fundamental to the entire issue. Commitments regarding the amount of difference between the tests that may be allowed, and commitments regarding the difference that may be allowed between the groups under consideration depend ultimately on the demands for precision that are implied by the purpose of the conversion table.

Ordinarily we are confronted with the situation where the tests and the use for which a table of comparable scores is required may not be questioned or altered. In such instances we are free to choose the kind of group we wish to use in forming a conversion table, in order to achieve a degree of error that we say we are willing to tolerate. Three such groups are: (1) the national norms group; (2) a set of differentiated norms groups; and (3) the local norms group. A fourth method—of basing a table of comparable scores on a group of people for whom data happen to be convenient and available—is simply to go through the motions of deriving a table of comparable scores without considering its meaning. The usefulness of such a table—if there is any—is extremely restricted.

Of the various kinds of comparable scores, the one based on differentiated norms groups is probably the most defensible. This procedure would yield a number of conversion tables, each based on and appropriate for a different norms group. If the tests are measures of the same psychological function, then the various conversion tables will for all practical purposes be the same. However, if the tests are measuring different functions, then there will be as many conversions as there are distinguishable and different norms groups. Each conversion, like a profile, will be descriptive of the group on which it is based and applicable only to that group. The user will be forced to choose the appropriate table with care, keeping in mind the group for which he intends to use it and the purpose for which it is to be applied.

The local norms approach to comparable scores is similar to the one involving differentiated norms, and is in general as highly recommended for the purpose of comparable scores as are local norms distributions themselves for the purpose of evaluating relative status. Here the cautions that need to be exercised are: (1) that the group has not been directly selected on either of the scores involved in the conversion; (2) that there are sufficient cases to yield reliable conversions; and (3) that they be applied only in the school where they were developed or in schools known to be similar to it.

The national norms approach is probably the least satisfactory of all, for the reason that it is not likely to be highly appropriate except when the tests in question are quite similar in function. Its primary advantage, however, is that it is the most readily applied method of obtaining rough conversion tables, if for no other reason than the fact that national norms for tests are generally readily available. The significant concern here is that none of the students on whom the comparable scores are based took both the tests in question, and that the norms groups for the different tests may not have been selected in the same fashion in order to satisfy even approximately the requirement of randomly equivalent groups that is ordinarily imposed in parallel-forms equating. And even if they were so selected, there is enough unreliability in norms samples to introduce serious errors in the tables of comparable scores. There are situations in which errors of given magnitude are tolerable in norms, but not at all tolerable in tables of comparable scores—again, of course, depending on the intended use of the tables.

I would like also to mention a method that is appropriate for developing comparable scores for situations in which candidates are permitted to take the particular test that is most appropriate to their own curricular background or interests. As applied to the achievement tests in the College Board program, the procedure is to correlate the SAT-Verbal and Mathematical scores with each achievement test, and use them in combination as a composite control or anchor test in estimating the achievement test performance of a group with certain defined characteristics, as measured by the SAT. The purpose of all this statistical work is to relate the scores on the various achievement tests to one another and to the SAT-Verbal and Mathematical scale, and to enable us to say, for example, that a 600 score on the French test is comparable, in the sense defined by the statistical method, to a 600 score on the physics test. Obviously, there are logical difficulties in expressing this comparability, as there would be with most. However, because of the way in which the achievement test scores are used and have to be used by the admissions officers, some kind of comparable scores must be prepared. And of the various kinds that are available, this one which balances out the effects of differential selection for each of the groups that take the various achievement tests has obvious advantages.

Another approach to the question of comparable scores involves the use of the ordinary correlation and prediction model. This method has at times been suggested for use with tests at the same grade level in order to provide interchangeable scores on different tests. However, as described earlier, it is clearly inappropriate here because it fails in its very purpose. One of the scores is actual and the other is regressed; they cannot be interchanged. On the other hand, when the tests are designed for different grade levels, then the method does have merit. For example, an attempt has been made to use the regression model for relating scores on the *School and College Ability Test* taken in the early years of secondary school to scores earned on the SAT in the twelfth grade. Since these results will be used solely as predictions— to enable students to get a preliminary idea of how well they may expect to do on a test used to select college freshmen, and not to merge or compare them with actual scores—the dangers that were described as inherent in regressed scores are not present here. Furthermore, since the presentation lays great stress on the presence of errors of estimate, it is felt that misinterpretations will be kept to a minimum.

In general, the different uses of comparable scores require different levels of precision. Where, for example, the need for comparable scores arises from a desire to use scores on different tests interchangeably for admissions purposes, the highest degree of precision is required for comparability. Otherwise, a college which gives serious consideration to test scores in admissions decisions might find itself admitting too large a proportion of applicants from one group or another because of the use of an inappropriate conversion table. On the other hand, when scores on different tests are used interchangeably for placement purposes, the demand for precision is less serious, since erroneous placements can be corrected early in the course. Also, the use of conversion tables for estimating the comparative abilities of *groups* of individuals is one that does not ordinarily require a high degree of precision. For one thing, in such comparisons the careers of individuals are seldom at stake (as would be true in admissions decisions). For another, it is a characteristic of conversions that there is relatively little error at the mean. In contrast to this, conversions of scores for individuals of high or low ability are much more likely to be in error.

It probably bears repetition that the problem of comparable scores is simply another one of many other problems about which it is impossible to make categorical evaluations that hold fast in all situations. If the decisions that are made on the basis of a table of comparable scores are made in the central region of the distribution, if the tests are relatively similar in function, if they have approximately equal reliabilities and validities, and finally, if generalizations are restricted to the kind of group that formed the basis of the conversion in the first place, these are the conditions that allow the free use of comparable scores. To demand that all these conditions hold is undoubtedly unrealistic and unnecessarily restrictive as well. At the same time, if in any instance too few of these conditions are operative, then testing organizations would probably do well to heed the advice that they like to give their test users, and proceed with caution.

XII

EDUCATIONAL AND
PSYCHOLOGICAL TESTING
IN SOCIAL PERSPECTIVE

Each year seems to bring a considerable volume of intense critical comment concerning educational and psychological testing. We, of course, have reference to the flood of recent popular magazine and newspaper coverage of testing problems, as well as such books as *The Brain Watchers* (Gross, 1962), *The Tyranny of Testing* (Hoffmann, 1962), and *They Shall Not Pass* (Black, 1963). These publications reflect some real public antipathy, uneasiness, distrust, and ignorance about tests and testing. They are written by the professional and by the layman alike, with occasional words added by hack-journalists. Many of the criticisms are justified, most are not. As in the case with many expositions on somewhat technical or social phenomena intended for public consumption, particularly those related to education, the views expressed are often narrowly defined and biased. It is, therefore, hoped that the papers selected for inclusion in this final chapter of the book will provide the reader with a balanced social-psychological view of the present state of the art and science of testing.

Two initial comments are in order. First, the critics of testing have said nothing new. They offer no unique words of wisdom or new insights. They have not exposed any long-forgotten or hidden psychometric skeletons in the testers' closet. Secondly, criticisms are focused on a perhaps unethical or at least ignorant segment of the psychological profession. Often they represent observations on the self-appointed testers, the small minority of individuals who wish to make a quick profit. The unfortunate result, however, is that the public is

369

likely to assume that these same criticisms apply to tests *and* testers in general. What can be said in support of the "critics"? The potential positive effects of what the critics posit can readily be discerned. First, they reinforce what has long been known about the inadequacy of certain testing practices. Second, their comments should serve to caution both professional and laymen against the misuse of tests. Third, they have really joined their voices with those of the professional tester in calling for better training for those individuals who administer, interpret, and use tests. Lastly, they have made a significant contribution by underlining the certain areas in need of research. This last positive result, however, leads directly to a distinct and unfortunate negative influence. Specifically, that the critics, both directly by their influence on professional educators and indirectly through parents, may tend to deter schools from participating in the much-needed research in testing. Also on the negative side is the fact that the tests, instruments, methods, or devices themselves take the brunt of criticism, when it is all too often the case that it is the *users* who are at fault.

Most observers would agree that the need and responsibility for improving communications between the testing profession and the public are being reawakened and revitalized. Publications by Chauncey and Dobbin (1963), Howes (1964), and the American Psychological Association (1965) attest to this fact. Continued vigilance on the part of professional and lay groups to expose the quacks and incompetents, pressure for higher standards in the test publishing industry, and more intensive pre-service and in-service training in measurement would seem to be in order.

Several of the issues discussed in the foregoing paragraphs are given expanded treatment in the following articles. Dr. Ralph Berdie begins this chapter with a discussion of the motivations evidenced by test users and non-users. He concludes that the need and desirability of scientific rigor in education are not in conflict with a basically humanitarian and wholistic view of man. Underlying Dr. Berdie's presentation is the realization that knowledge is useless unless it is communicated. Just as a teacher has a responsibility for communicating information pertaining to expected and actual classroom performance, so does the testing profession have a like responsibility in communicating with the public about *how* and *why* tests are used.

Dr. Banesh Hoffmann presents in the second paper in this chapter many comments, and offers suggestions that the testing industry should acknowledge if it is really interested in improving practices and communication. His paper contains a detailed analysis of some of the potential shortcomings of multiple-choice tests. The overemphasis on statistical information in test development and the caution that should be taken in relating test use and curriculum are points well made. But to completely negate the use of multiple-choice tests because of the misapplication of a few users or the accessibility of poor commercial or teacher-made tests could not be considered the wisest course of action. But what are the alternatives to the use of "objective tests," or at least multiple-choice tests? Do the critics provide us with any substantive alternatives?

Dr. Marvin D. Dunnette next provides us with a thoughtful analysis of the test critics' basic assumptions and conclusions. His argument may seem to some to be too strong. But the issues raised by Drs. Dunnette and Hoffmann are critical, and forceful presentations are therefore justified. The reader is urged to read these two papers with an open mind, and allow the merits of the respective arguments and points of view determine the final evaluation.

Concluding this chapter is a cogent paper by Dr. Robert L. Ebel. Unlike many commentators on testing, Dr. Ebel provides some suggestions for the improvement of testing practices, particularly with regard to the needed communication between the professional and the public. He also presents some enlightening comments on the consequences of *not* testing that should be given thoughtful consideration.

51   *Science, Values, and Psychometry*

RALPH F. BERDIE

The following comments by Dr. Berdie provide insight into the motivations of individuals who object to the administration and use of standardized tests. They also provide insight into some of the reasons why certain individuals are committed to the use of tests, particularly in educational settings.

In this paper Berdie considers 1) the purposes of education and how tests can be used to implement these purposes, 2) the criticism that behavior cannot be quantified, and 3) the problem of reconciling a commonly encountered fear that tests perpetuate conformity and result in a less humanistic philosophy with the felt need to attain and communicate a rational understanding of behavior.

As important means for social understanding and direction, standardized tests and the uses made of them must constantly be reviewed and examined. Our understanding of tests will be better if we perceive them as parts of our complex culture.

The number and length of affective terms and emotional words in a discussion or report provides a convenient index of the extent to which the participants are concerned with questions of values as opposed to questions of fact. The application of this index to recent discussions of testing in education suggests that we should pay more attention to why people feel the way they do about tests than to the reasoning they use in arriving at their conclusions. The tone of current discussions and disagreements about testing implies that the central issues really

Reprinted with permission of author and publisher from the *Teachers College Record*, 1962, Vol. 64, pp. 199–203.

are not the amount of testing, the fee, and the possible misuse of tests, or the three hours on a Saturday morning, but rather that more basic values and attitudes may be the sources of contemporary criticism.

Two behavioral facts underlie the use of standardized tests in education: (1) individuals differ, and (2) directing growth and change requires understanding.

VARIABILITY AND SOCIALIZATION

Variability of behavior among individuals is not a recent discovery; psychological differences have been recognized and considered important prior to Plato and after Riesman. The extent, stability, nature, and significance of these differences have been appreciated for ages; but only relatively recently has consideration of them been systematically incorporated into social philosophy, and only during the past century have such differences become a matter of scientific inquiry.

Education is a process of establishing individuals in society, a means of making the person a part of his ever-changing culture. The purpose of education is to change behavior, and the desired general direction of these changes is broadly agreed on. Thus, education is an attempt to direct a particular set of behavioral phenomena, and the more known about the phenomena to be directed, the more effective such direction is likely to be. The teacher must understand the pupil.

Most persons, regardless of the extent to which they accept or reject standardized educational and psychological tests, do not attempt to refute these two statements. If a person believed that all people were similar to one another or that education could proceed without knowledge of those to be taught, then the need for educational tests and other methods of observation and understanding could be denied. Persons opposed to the use of standardized tests, however, do not deny these statements. Consequently, their resistance must have other sources.

We will not attempt here to psychoanalyze persons who favor and those who oppose tests. We will not review the relationships between these people and their parents. We will not examine the Oedipal threat of the College Entrance Examination Board Tests; neither will we examine the strands connecting the Minnesota Multiphasic Personality Inventory to the collective unconscious. Rather, we will attempt to discuss briefly some of the personal commitments which cause people to be attracted and repelled by standardized tests.

To begin with, to varying degrees people need to objectify the world around them. Standardized tests facilitate our dealing with the things external to the mind of the observer and provide to their user a sense that he is dealing more explicitly with external reality. Test scores are particularly satisfying to persons with strong needs to deal with things (realities?) as opposed to thoughts and feelings. They provide a medium for transforming intuitive observations and impressions into things of apparent reality.

Somewhat related to and opposed to these needs for objectivity are what appear to be needs for subjectivity. The personal philosophies of some persons strongly lead them to the conviction that knowledge about behavior, like most or all other knowledge, has reality only in the experience of the individual, and knowledge cannot be objectified. To them, the characteristics of others are sensed through intuition, feeling, and inner experience. Knowledge about others loses its true essence when it is systematically observed, analyzed, ordered, and quantified.

TO MEASURE MEN?

The needs for quantification in some people are stronger than in others. At one extreme, quantification is magic; numbers have superstitious connotations. Many persons are impressed by the extent to which mathematical analysis and quantification have aided our understanding of other natural phenomena, and they are eager to apply quantification in a very similar way in their attempts to understand human behavior.

At the other extreme are people whose needs lead them to deny that behavior can be quantified. Some realize the technical difficulties of applying quantitative methods as used in the physical sciences to the behavioral domain and, in the absence of appropriate units of measurement and points of origin, contend that measurement concepts are not appropriate in studying behavior. Others who object to quantifying human behavior do so on more aesthetic grounds, insisting that behavior itself possesses certain characteristics that bar it from quantification.

These two statements about quantification lead to the third attitude present in our discussions of standardized tests. Some persons, because of the nature of their work, and others, because of their own personal needs, place strong emphasis on the communication of information concerning the behavior of others. Information about behavior that is not objectified or quantified is difficult to communicate, and such communication tends to be imprecise, non-rigorous, and easy to misinterpret. The counselor, for example, finds it easier to say (and the college admissions officer finds it easier to understand) that Susan's score on the College Entrance Examination Board Tests is 600 than to say that all of Susan's teachers since the first grade have indicated on cumulative records that Susan is a bright child, that she learns more quickly than most other children in the class, that she obtains good grades in school, that she uses a good vocabulary in school and other conversations, that she understands directions quickly and well, and that she solves many kinds of problems with facility.

Some persons' values lead them to contend that in order to obtain the advantage of easier communication, we have oversimplified our analysis and understanding of behavior. Susan's behavior does not consist of a test score, and the counselor and the college admissions officer should both be interested in more than the number of questions answered correctly on a test and the standard score derived from that number. A related argument contends that test methods are not sufficiently accurate to be used for purposes of such communication; not only does the use of test scores result in oversimplification, but also in excessive error.

Some who favor the use of standardized tests, on the other hand, contend that they force the user to think more rigorously, that they result in more disciplined thought processes and in more exact and accurate conclusions. The authors of standardized tests must define the behaviors of concern to them and logically relate the measurement process to these definitions. Such rigor reduces the probability that the test user will employ terms and concepts loosely and forces him, or at least allows him, to think logically and reasonably. It encourages the test user to apply concepts of specific abilities and traits in his consideration of students and at the same time attend to the differentiated aspects of any given student's behavior.

BUT WHAT OF WHOLISM?

The very characteristics of tests that satisfy certain persons' needs for rigorous thought, however, cause others to fear that standardized tests, through their attempt to analyze behavior, violate what is the essential personality of the individual. These persons conceive of personality as a constellation of forces and energies in constant interaction with one another, and the very act of observing only one segment of the constellation results in the observer's seeing something other than the "real" personality. If personality is to be understood, it must be viewed as a whole, and standardized tests, being analytical, defeat this wholistic perception. Sometimes underlying such arguments is the denial that behavior is caused as are other natural phenomena, and the contention that the theory of personality associated with standardized tests is based on an overly simplified theory of causation borrowed from nineteenth-century natural science. Sometimes this point of view is colored by the fear that such analysis will make the test user forget that man is a social being, and now when more attention than ever must be given to men's relationships to one another, result in our giving them less.

Similarly, some people have strong taxonomic needs; they want to categorize their experiences and perceptions. For these persons, knowledge essentially consists of relating experiences and sensations to other experiences and sensations. Perception is relative, and knowledge is empirical. But some people have less need for such an empirical approach to knowledge and deny that behavior is systematic or perhaps even consistent. For them an attempt to categorize behavior destroys it, and the use of standardized tests to sort out persons on the basis of observed actions is more than a waste of time; it detracts from the very integrity of the individual.

Already implied in our discussion is the need of many to apply the concepts and methods of the other natural sciences to the study and understanding of human behavior. To such people, behavior is caused and orderly, to some extent predictable, and properly subject to analysis and to the methods of observation, taxonomy, prediction, and control used in other sciences. Made anxious by these convictions are persons who fear that such an approach will have us view man as a machine. They fear that the way psychologists, teachers, and society conceive of man will change man, and that approaching behavior as an object of scientific inquiry will result in man's behaving like a machine and losing those humanistic attributes including his aesthetic appreciation, his respect and dignity, and his worship of the unknown. Existentialists and traditional humanists seem to fear that the processes of giving and taking tests may increase the person's self-consciousness and restrict his power to react spontaneously and creatively to himself and others. The student tested may become simply an object instead of a man.

FRIGHTENED BY LEADERSHIP

The ultimate purpose of persons using standardized tests in education is to understand and direct behavior, and it is this that frightens some. The teacher and the counselor are attempting to produce changes in the pupil. The nature of these changes is related to the objectives of the school, and the school's objectives are determined by many persons and groups, including the school board, the Parent-Teacher Association, the superintendent and principal, the editor of the local paper, the students themselves, and—perhaps most importantly—the teacher and counselor who work directly with the student. These objectives sometimes are quite explicit and detailed, e.g., learning how to do differential calculus in the twelfth grade, or they may be general and comprehensive, e.g., attaining intellectual and emotional maturity. Nevertheless, the community assigns to the teacher and counselor the responsibility for producing directed changes in the student, and the school welcomes means for increasing its understanding of the individual boy or girl and for improving its capacity to evoke expected changes in behavior as society requires it to do.

Some persons, perceiving tests primarily as instruments of behavior control, fear their users and interpreters. Perhaps we have in opposition here a need for authority and a need for anarchy. Universally recognized is the necessity for social direction; less agreement is found regarding the amount and nature of such direction.

In a somewhat different vein, fears about aggression and the defensive needs of some of us influence our perceptions of the nature, purposes, and origins of democracy, and testing sometimes is perceived as a threat to the democratic way. Democracy may be equality, and if equality means that people are essentially alike in their characters, rather than that they enjoy equal opportunities, then tests attack the basic assumptions. Tests are used to study differences, and if these differences should not exist, then neither should tests.

Tests themselves, however, are not evaluative, and test scores provide a basis for concluding that persons are "equal but different," just as do measures of physical attributes. Test users, like their opponents, may be democratic or non-democratic.

Additional miscellaneous, although not unimportant forces also influence our different attitudes toward standardized tests. Some of us are more or less willing than others to subscribe to custom, and the extent to which a person has been reared professionally in an atmosphere where standardized tests are accepted and used partly determines his attitudes toward tests. The status that tests have in a person's immediate culture influences how he regards them, as does the prestige attached to persons who use tests or who approve or disapprove of tests. Attitudes toward other means of observation and evaluation are also relevant; a person may be more accepting of standardized tests because he is disillusioned about the usefulness of other observational procedures. Or because he is strongly enthusiastic about other observational procedures, he may think less of tests.

A RECONCILIATION

Reviewing behavior objectively hardly requires one to forego one's humanity. One can understand the nature of art appreciation and at the same time derive satisfaction from viewing a Degas or a Utrillo. One can know and understand another and at the same time respect and love him. In fact, usually such knowledge and understanding increase respect and love. One can test and measure behavior and continue to grant humanity to the one being measured and examined.

Quantification and numbers need not change the realities to which they are applied. The content of thought and understanding is concepts, and numbers and quantification can be applied to concepts. As our concepts become clear and accurate, our contact with reality becomes closer and more satisfying.

Knowledge possessed by a lone individual is satisfying and useful, but knowledge communicated and shared with others provides new satisfactions and gives new uses. If the communication of poor information reduces its potency, so the poor communication of accurate information similarly reduces its power. Scores from standardized tests serve as meaningful symbols to provide a vehicle for more accurate and effective communication.

The understanding of complex personalities demands more careful observation and more rigorous thought than the understanding of simpler structures. As our appreciation of the full complexity of personality increases, so must our demand for rigorous and careful thought and analysis regarding human behavior. No antithesis exists between rigor of analysis and complexity of personality.

Our culture is committed to both an intuitive appreciation of personality and a rational understanding of its products in behavior. Test scores are one means we use to aid in our conceptualizing the person in order to understand him more fully. Test scores do not substitute for behavior. They are not part of the individual; they are part of the thought processes of the persons who use the test.

In conclusion, we accept and we reject standardized tests for many of the same reasons we accept and reject other elements of our culture. We are materialists, and we are human; we are analytical, and we are intuitive. We organize and plan our society; we maximize our freedoms and individualities. We predict behavior, and we attempt to overthrow those predictions. We think and we feel; we know and we fear. To deal effectively with any aspect of complex contemporary life, we must deal effectively with these very human oppositions in ourselves. Standardized tests are no exception.

52   *Toward Less Emphasis on Multiple-Choice Tests*

BANESH HOFFMANN

During the past two decades the critics of educational and psychological tests have become more vocal. One of the more articulate spokesman for the critics has been Dr. Banesh Hoffmann. Through his writings in newspapers, professional journals and magazines, and his book, The Tyranny of Testing *(1962), Dr. Hoffmann has presented informative arguments against the use of multiple-choice tests. Constructive suggestions have also been presented by this author. Although many disagree with Dr. Hoffmann and his fellow critics, by causing the testing profession to take a critical look at itself, the critics influence should ultimately have some positive effects.*

What are Hoffmann's primary criticisms of multiple-choice tests? What kinds of evidence does the author present in support of his contentions? What alternative approaches for the collection of information does he suggest?

A student who took an important test made by one of the leading test makers wrote to me recently that one of the questions on the test read somewhat as follows:

"Among them, Tom and Dick were not able to find enough money." In this question the candidate has to pick the one word, *if any*, that makes the sentence incorrect.

The average student who knows the rules of grammar will doubtless pick the word "among" because when only two people are involved, the appropriate word is "between."

But the deeper student will read less hastily and realize that the word "them" in the sentence is unclear. It might refer to Tom and Dick, in which case picking "among" would be correct. But it might refer instead to a larger group of which Tom and Dick were the financial custodians, or even to a group that Tom and

Reprinted and abridged with permission of author and publisher from the *Teachers College Record*, 1963, Vol. 64, pp. 183–189.

Dick were robbing at gunpoint. If so, the sentence would be correct as it stood, and picking "among" would be wrong. The question is ambiguous. And the ambiguity can be resolved only by making some special assumption, such as that the tester was unaware of the ambiguity and therefore presumably believed that "them" inevitably referred to Tom and Dick. But only the deeper students are likely to recognize the ambiguity, and only they are therefore likely to be disturbed by it. Clearly, then, the question penalizes the deeper students; and the important point is that it does so even if they pick the wanted answer.

PENALTY FOR PERCEPTIVENESS

One may object that the above question was not quoted exactly. Here, therefore, is a question that is taken verbatim from a booklet published by the College Board in 1954 that described its so-called English Composition tests. If the candidate believes that the underlined part of the sentence is correct as it stands, he chooses answer 1; if not, he picks the best substitute from among the other choices:

Cod-liver oil is very good for children. It gives them vitamins they might not otherwise get.

    (1) NO CHANGE.
    (2) , it
    (3) , for it
    (4) ; for it

At first sight this too looks like an ambiguous question, both 1 and 3 being acceptable answers. But it is actually worse than ambiguous. If we were given the context, we might find in it some basis for deciding between two short sentences here or one longer sentence—say, to accentuate a rhythm or to break one that was tending to monotony. But although we are not given the context, we are still expected to choose one "best" answer.

We therefore examine the given words more carefully, seeking some internal clue. And we find two powerful ones. The sentence reads ". . . vitamins they would not otherwise get," not ". . . vitamins *that* they would not otherwise get." Clearly, the style is laconic. Not for it the measured formality of ", for it." The forthright ". It" has the proper tone. And if corroborative evidence is needed that answer 1 is preferable to answer 3, it is found in the word "get." Would not a writer who used the more formal ", for it" be more likely to use "obtain"?

Reasoning thus, a deep candidate would pick answer 1, doubtless with a feeling of delight at the charming subtlety of the question. If he encountered this question on an actual test, he might, fortunately for his peace of mind, never learn that he had picked an unwanted answer. But imagine how he would feel on encountering it as a sample question in a booklet describing the College Board's so-called English Composition tests, and learning that the wanted answer was not 1 but 3!

Such examples suggest some of the things that are wrong with multiple-choice tests. These tests penalize students with deep, subtle, critical minds who see subtle points that others, including the examiners, do not notice.

INVITATION TO THE VAGUE

Do not imagine that ambiguous questions are rare on multiple-choice tests. They are not. See how artlessly Dean Harry N. Rivlin reveals this in the following excerpt from his review, in the *Fifth Mental Measurements Yearbook* (Buros, 1959), of the Graduate Record Examination, Advanced Tests in Education. He is saying kind words about the tests, but note the damning implications of the two words I have emphasized:

"Whenever questions deal with judgment rather than facts, there is a risk that more than one answer can be defended as the best one. There are *remarkably few* items in which the key is challengeable."

What would we infer as to the quality of American college students if an authority praised a first-rate place like Princeton University by saying that it had "remarkably few" illiterate students? Is there not something about Dean Rivlin's statement that recalls that of the character witness who said to the judge, "John is sober on Sundays"?

The multiple-choice format actually invites vagueness and ambiguity. Making a genuinely and honestly difficult multiple-choice question is not at all easy. Too often ambiguity and vagueness are used as substitutes for genuine difficulty. The tests thus become intellectually dishonest; they are reduced to subjective guessing games in which the candidate does not pick the answers he regards as the best, but those he thinks the unknown examiner will believe best.

These tests are concerned solely with the candidate's choice of answer and not with his reasons for his choice. Thus, they ignore that elusive yet crucial thing we call quality. For example, suppose we ask the mailman whether it will rain today, and he says "Yes." And then suppose we ask an expert at the Weather Bureau, and he too says "Yes." They may both turn out to be wrong. Yet the meteorologist's "yes" was of much higher quality than the mailman's, though a statistical-minded, objective, multiple-choice grader might be horrified to hear us say so. As every teacher knows who has not succumbed to the statistical blandishments of the objective testers, a wrong answer for a good reason usually indicates greater ability than does a right answer for a bad reason.

As for the much-vaunted "objectivity" of the multiple-choice tests, it resides in the *process* of grading and not, for example, in the decision as to which shall be the wanted answers. Certain civil service tests are subject to challenge. They are graded objectively, and objective grades are given to the candidates. As a result of successive challenges, successive different sets of grades may be assigned, these all being thoroughly "objective"—as that word is used by the testers.

OBJECTIVITY'S COST

Too much is sacrificed in order to attain this specious objectivity. Essay testers too could achieve comparable objectivity and reliability if they were prepared to sacrifice so much.

Multiple-choice tests by their very nature ignore skill in disciplined expression. Moreover, they are not concerned with the ability to synthesize and carry through major projects—nor even relatively minor projects that require a mere ten minutes. And of course they offer no scope to the imaginative, creative student. An unusual way of looking at things is definitely a handicap, as also is profundity. The tests favor the candidates who read rapidly and are quick-witted and superficially brilliant. Because no explanations are permitted on these tests, the deep students have no chance to show the depth of their reasoning. When their intellectual powers transcend those of the test maker, they are in danger of picking unwanted answers by probing too deeply.

Often one hears the claim that multiple-choice tests are efficient. But their efficiency is of a superficial, statistical sort. Teachers in America used to teach their pupils the themes of symphonies by fitting the themes with childish words—a pedagogical method whose efficiency they could demonstrate objectively and scientifically, and one that they would still be widely using had not musicians, parents, and other non-scientific outsiders somehow opened their eyes to the perils of such efficiency-worship.

Professor John M. Shlien (1958), a psychologist engaged in counseling, discusses this matter of efficiency with wit and wisdom.

> Tests are sold to us on the basis of their "efficiency." Aside from the validity of this claim, the idea of efficiency itself needs to be re-examined. It is often a short-term concept, and a short-sighted one. Suddenly speaking, the most efficient way to get exactly the proteins you need is to take a bite of the nearest person. To get to the ground floor, jump out the window. But these very immediate goals are not our complete or real ones. Until we have thought about these, we cannot use efficiency, even if it can be delivered. Long-term efficiency may rest much more upon people going where and doing what they want than on placing them where tests say they fit best.

STATISTICAL HYPNOSIS

Despite their faults, however, multiple-choice tests are widely used. They are convenient and cheap, and they yield numerical grades with what many people believe to be scientific precision. Their use is fostered by the propaganda of the test makers, which is largely based upon statistics and claims to superior knowledge.

Statistics can have an almost hypnotic effect on the layman. They must be approached warily. Above all, the layman must not fall into the trap of believing that the testers are scientific merely because they use some of the tools that scientists use. Not every person who uses a stethescope is a doctor.

Statistics, for all their scientific aura, can be quite misleading. For example, the usual correlations by which testers measure the validity of their tests treat all people democratically. If in a group of 100 competing for 9 scholarships in science an Einstein is rated tenth from the top, the effect on the validity correlation is just the same as that of a moron being rated tenth from the bottom. This hardly increases one's confidence in the value of the usual correlation coefficient as a measure of practical validity. Mosts tests really have poor validity, a correlation of .60 being usually considered quite good even though it implies an alarming lack of predictive power.

Correlation coefficients do not distinguish between random error and certain kinds of bias. In a school with 449 students, Getzels and Jackson (1962) selected two groups by means of IQ scores and scores on a test of "creativity." The "high creativity group" consisted of the students in the top 20 percent on the creativity test who were *not* in the top 20 percent on IQ; the "high intelligence group" was made up of those in the top 20 percent according to IQ but not in the top 20 percent in creativity. The "high intelligence group" had a mean IQ of 150; the "high creativity group" had a mean IQ of 127—somewhat less than that of the whole school, which was 132. However, the mean scholastic achievement scores were 55 for the "high intelligence group" and 56 for the "high creativity group." Thus, the IQ tests were seriously discriminating against an important group of students. But the usual validity correlation coefficients do not reveal such biases as this. Think of the number of gifted students who are being penalized in America because they lack the IQ knack.

A different experiment yielded even more disturbing results. Professors Robert L. Thorndike and Elizabeth Hagen (1958) made a massive follow-up study of 10,000 members of the US Army Air Force who had been given an elaborate battery of some twenty tests during World War II. Here is how they summed up part of their findings:

> There is no convincing evidence that aptitude tests or biographical information of the type available to us can predict degree of success within an occupation insofar *as this is represented in the criterion measures that we were able to obtain.*

IMPACT ON CURRICULUM

One fact about statistics overshadows all others, though. It is that belief in them corrupts the believer, leading him to belittle and ultimately ignore whatever can not be measured numerically. Thus, all statistics used in testing ignore the non-numerical aspects of testing, especially the deleterious effects of multiple-choice tests on education. For example, the Director of Admissions at Smith College recently said, "Schools are substituting vocabulary drills and word study for meaningful work in reading and writing." And the New York State Teachers Association has passed a resolution urging the State Board of Regents to concentrate on improving essay questions for examinations instead of attempting to develop completely objective tests.

The statistics are thus far from accurate measures of the whole merit or lack of merit of current testing procedures. Reliance on statistics can lead people to do absurd things. For example, the College Board, bemused by certain superficial statistics, gives a so-called English Composition Test that is of the multiple-choice type and has no English composition in it at all! (See Hoffmann, 1962, pp. 112–123.)

As for the action of the National Merit Scholarship Corporation in eliminating all but 2 percent of the candidates by means of a set of multiple-choice tests, it can be condoned only on the basis of expediency; and even then it must be deplored as an unbecoming exhibition of testolatry, glorifying multiple-choice tests and dangerously exaggerating their merits in the eyes of the people. Fortunately, the National Merit Scholarship Corporation is beginning to realize that its multiple-choice tests do not measure creativity, motivation, and other important traits that should loom large in the eyes of the selectors of scholars.

What is to be done about the testing situation? Making general criticisms does not produce significant results. The testers respond by pointing with pride to their superior knowledge and ability, claiming to be as scientific as their critics are romantic, and using what I have elsewhere called their "statistics show" maneuver.

To counter these powerful defensive moves, I have developed a new strategy of exhibiting defective sample questions and challenging the testers to defend them explicitly. It has produced important results, among them evidence (Barzun, 1959, Hoffmann, 1961, a & b) concerning the quality of testers that must be regarded as seriously disquieting. To make a strong case, I have concentrated on the best test makers, principally Educational Testing Service.

The following question, exhibited in 1961 in *Harper's Magazine* (Hoffmann, 1961, b), is taken from a College Board booklet, *Science*, published in 1954, which described the College Board's Science Achievement Tests:

54. The burning of gasoline in an automobile cylinder involves all of the following *except* (A) reduction (B) decomposition (C) an exothermic reaction (D) oxidation (E) conversion of matter to energy.

The wanted answer is E. But the student who is unfortunate enough to understand, even in an elementary way, what $E = mc^2$ is really about finds himself at a distinct disadvantage because he knows that all of the released energy comes from the conversion of matter to energy. He realizes therefore that the question has no correct answer.

RESPONSE IN DEFENSE

It would have been simple, though somewhat embarrassing, for ETS to admit that it had not understood $E = mc^2$ when it made the question. But ETS chose to defend the question instead, and in so doing it put itself in an indefensible position, as will be seen. Here in full is its official defence (Educational Testing Service, 1961):

> *Explanation.* The superior student is as aware of the classical concepts of matter and chemical change as he is of the model of modern physics. He is likely to be more aware than is the average student that the "conversion of matter into energy" has been demonstrated only for nuclear changes. Perhaps he realizes that if the energy freed by the burning of gasoline comes from the conversion of mass to energy, the loss in mass is only about a tenbillionth of the mass of the gasoline burned, a loss too small to be measured by available methods.
>
> When such a student is faced with the above question, he should realize that the classical concepts of matter and chemical change provide the framework in which the question is asked. He also recognizes that the first four processes listed are obviously and immediately involved in the burning of gasoline, and he selects response E as the required answer.

This is not the place for a detailed discussion of this defence (See Hoffmann, 1962, pp. 185–188). ETS tries to give the impression that the question is good despite $E = mc^2$ and that ETS understood $E = mc^2$ when it made the question. But, as I have said before (Hoffmann, 1961 a):

> Note how damaging are the implications if we do assume that ETS was fully aware of the meaning of $E = mc^2$ and deliberately included answer E nevertheless. For we must then ask, What was its motive in doing so? To make a question with no correct answers? Let us hope not. Then what? To penalize the superior student? One doubts that ETS would say so; yet the question is surely easier for the student who does not understand $E = mc^2$ than for the student who does. Is the latter student supposed to compensate for the deficiencies of the test maker by reading possibly hazardous amendments into the question as worded? That way lies chaos—not "objectivity." If the superior student does decide to pick answer E, does he not do so with contempt for the test maker, and with cynical disregard of scientific facts? Should he be rewarded for his willingness thus to place expediency above scientific integrity? If tests are training students to respond in this way, are they not having a deleterious effect on education? Perhaps, after all, it is more charitable to assume that ETS was ignorant of the meaning of $E = mc^2$, even if this does imply a certain lack of candor on its part now.

In defending another science question, ETS not only made elementary scientific errors, but showed that it did not even understand what its own question was asking; and then, in attempting to make a final clinching argument, it cited a scientific fact that actually emphasized the fallaciousness of its own line of defence (Hoffmann, 1962, pp. 189–197).

THE HEART OF THE MATTER

If ETS, the leading educational testing organization, can make such vulnerable questions and can offer no better defences than it does, what shall we think of the quality of the multiple-choice tests made by lesser organizations? And what of those made by individual teachers?

To show that defective questions are far from rare, I have prepared a list of 12 challenge questions, constituting 5 percent of the sample questions in two College Board booklets. The "gasoline" question is one of these. Of the 12 items, 5 are of one kind, and they constitute 24 percent of the supply of that kind in the booklets.

The attack on specific defective questions does not, of course, go to the heart of the matter. It is essentially an attack on a peripheral point. Its purpose is merely to make a *prima facie* case for the setting up of a distinguished and authoritative committee of inquiry that will investigate the whole matter of testing. The minimum concern of the committee would be the problem of policing tests to ensure that they meet high standards. But the committee would also have a more important function. For the professional testers have a restricted set of values. They are primarily statisticians and technicians, and the case they make for their tests, except for matters of cheapness and convenience, is mainly a statistical one. The layman, the business executive, and the school administrator are apt to be overawed by statistical arguments. But the testers' statistics are parochial, touching only the immediate and superficial aspects of testing. The committee of inquiry, with its broad view, would recognize the limitations of these statistics and would weigh against the statistical case (such as it is) for multiple-choice tests the damage that these tests do to education and to the nation. It would realize that the function of tests cannot be confined to that of testing, and it would be well aware, for example, that though a cure for the common cold might be 99 percent effective, this admirable statistic, for all its scientific objectivity, would be a dangerously misleading measure of the value of the cure if the cure invariably left the patient crippled. The committee would be far less willing than the testers to sell our intellectual heritage for a mess of statistical pottage.

53   *An Evaluation of Test Critics and Their Assumptions*

MARVIN D. DUNNETTE

In the previous article Dr. Hoffmann has detailed some specific criticisms of tests and testing. The present paper reviews these allegations and presents counter arguments. Among the issues considered are (1) the relationship of creativity, intelligence, and achievement, (2) the presence of ambiguity in and dubious keying of multiple-choice test items, (3) the use of essay exams, (4) the use of

Reprinted and abridged with permission of author and publisher from an article entitled "Critics of Psychological Tests: Basic Assumptions: How Good?" which appeared in *Psychology in the Schools*, 1963, Vol. 1, pp. 63–69.

statistical techniques in test development and analysis, and (5) the claim that tests constitute an invasion of privacy.

First, let us consider some of the major assumptions made by Hoffmann (1962) in his book, *The Tyranny of Testing,* and consider the relative validity of each. Later, we will comment on some of the broader charges made by other critics and the relative validity of these.

CREATIVITY, INTELLIGENCE, AND ACHIEVEMENT TEST PERFORMANCE

Conveniently, Hoffmann spells out his assumptions on page 150 of his book. The first is as follows:

> "The tests deny the creative person a significant opportunity to demonstrate his creativity and favor the shrewd and facile candidate over the one who has something to say."

I personally know of no evidence to suggest that tests stifle the creative person. The major problem with making such a charge or assumption is that little satisfactory research has been done to define the so-called trait of creativeness. The usual procedure has been simply to call people "creative" who happen to score high on so-called "creativity" tests. Recently Robert Thorndike (1963) has analyzed the relative factorial purity of the content of the standard IQ tests and of the so-called creativity or divergent thinking tests. He finds that tests of creativity actually correlate more highly with convergent thinking tests than they do with themselves. Evidence such as this is hardly sufficient to sustain an argument that the so-called trait or behavior which we label "creative" has been successfully measured by tests now available. Unfortunately, the usual approach is to label persons as creative who score high on these factorially, poorly defined "creativity" tests rather than on the basis of any behaviorally defined reference outside the tests themselves.

Hoffmann cites the study by Getzels and Jackson (1962) described in their book, *Creativity and Intelligence.* Unfortunately the Getzels and Jackson study is a particularly poor example of what I have just discussed. In their study Getzels and Jackson define creativity on the basis of scores on a variety of measures of fluency and divergent thinking. In one part of their study they contrast two groups selected on the basis of high scores on IQ tests and creativity tests, respectively. The average IQ of the students selected on the basis of IQ tests was 150 whereas the average IQ of students selected on the basis of the "creativity" tests was only 127. Getzels and Jackson report that these two groups who differ by 23 points in IQ did not differ on standard multiple-choice achievement examinations. Yet Hoffmann says on page 146 of his book:

> In view of the above how much faith can we have in the IQ as an unbiased predictor of scholastic achievement even when the scholastic achievement is

measured by multiple-choice methods. Think of the number of gifted students who were penalized in our schools because they lack the IQ knack.

It is difficult for me to understand how Hoffmann can use the data of the Getzels and Jackson study to make such a comment. Just the opposite is, in fact, true: the "low ability" (IQ = 127) students were not penalized on achievement examinations; they scored the same as the "high ability" (IQ = 150) students.

Even so there seems to be a widely held misconception that teachers somehow like the highly "creative" children less well than the highly intelligent children. As a matter of fact, Getzels and Jackson are often cited as evidence and they do state that "the high IQ students are preferred over the average students by their teachers, the creativity students are not." The actual facts as shown by the Getzels and Jackson data are that teachers' preferences were in the same direction for both groups and of very nearly the same magnitude. The difference, however, was not statistically significant for the "creative" children. Thus the reader and the public is left by this cavalier treatment of data with the unjustified impression that the teachers prefer the "high IQ's" to the "high creatives." In my opinion this is irresponsible reporting of research data—reporting that is nicely designed to lead people with an axe to grind (such as Mr. Hoffmann) astray.

MISSING THE "DEEP" STUDENT

Let us consider a second assumption made by Hoffmann. He says:

They penalize the candidate who perceives subtle points unnoticed by less able people including the test makers. They are apt to be superficial and intellectually dishonest with questions made artificially difficult by means of ambiguity because genuinely searching questions did not readily fit into the multiple-choice format.

A comment such as this of course ignores the massive amount of careful research which actually goes into the construction and final validation of a test item. For example, it is well known that distractors are purposely written to "fool" the less able person. We know that information about responses made by persons of different levels of knowledge shows without question that the degree of ambiguity perceived by the examinee is inversely related to his knowledge of the subject matter. In other words, in a good test item the less one knows the more ambiguous does the question appear. In spite of this, Hoffmann states on page 67 "and the more one knows about the subject the more glaring the ambiguities become." Hoffmann, of course, has no evidence to support this assumption.

COMMUNICATION PROBLEMS

A further assumption made by Hoffmann may be stated as follows: "They take account of only the choice of answer and not of quality of thought that lead to the choice," and "They neglect skill and disciplined expressions." Hoffmann apparently feels very strongly that objective examinations fail to assess a mysterious entity which he calls "quality of thought" or that they give little opportunity for "disciplined expression." Naturally, he offers no definitions for these mysterious attributes and he certainly suggests no reliable nor valid way of measuring them. In fact Hoffmann seems diligently to resist all references to the concepts of reliability and validity.

In addition to the fact that Hoffmann fails to define quality of thought or disciplined expression, it is noteworthy that he gives in Chapter 3 a series of very convincing arguments for not using essay examinations to measure so-called quality of thought or disciplined expression. For example, Hoffmann states that it is difficult in writing an essay question to choose a topic which will be fair to all examinees. He further states that even if a topic finally is chosen, it is extremely difficult to determine whether the essay is actually relevant to the question, further that it is difficult to overcome the problem of negative halo due to poor handwriting, poor spelling, or poor punctuation. He brings up the problem of different graders of essay examinations using different standards and he even cites the difficulty of the grader changing his standards as he moves through the examinations which he must grade. Hoffmann concludes that essay exams may be unfair, indeed that they are unfair for the testing of the students.

Thus Hoffmann works himself into a corner by criticizing objective exams because they fail to assess quality of thought or disciplined expression; yet he leaves no alternative for assessing these non-defined entities by any other means (such as by essay exams).

In his discussion of this problem he cites a study by the Educational Testing Service showing that a 90-minute essay test was less good than an objective exam, the English Composition Test, for predicting faculty ratings in English Composition. Faced with this evidence that an essay exam is less worthy, Hoffmann simply argues that these results are silly and that they could not possibly have been obtained. He appears to be using logical analysis in order to overcome or to reject empirical results. Essentially, of course, Hoffmann is simply confusing content with predictive or concurrent validity.

THE IDENTIFICATION OF MERIT

Finally, perhaps the potentially most damaging assumption and the one which would be the most difficult for Hoffmann to sustain has to do with the effect of tests in the identification of individual merit. He states, "They have a pernicious effect on education and the recognition of merit." Furthermore he seems to be concerned about the idea that multiple-choice testing might somehow be "efficient" and he feels that efficiency is bad in and of itself. For example, on page 90 he states,

Let us not sacrifice too much for the sake of efficiency. In some respects the dictatorship is more efficient than a democracy and the lie detector more efficient and scientific than the jury. The efficient Nazis made medical experiments directly on men and women.

After reading this I find myself very curious about Mr. Hoffmann's stand on fluoridation of water, which certainly must be regarded as one very efficient way of decreasing the incidence of dental caries. However, lest I be charged with arguing in the same manner as I am accusing Mr. Hoffmann of doing, let me hasten to offer something in a more positive vein.

Today, through objective tests we can identify the many abilities of children and for the first time do a good job of mapping the true individuality of each and every child. In other words, tests provide us with the best means available for assessing individuality and discovering and rewarding individual merit. In my opinion this function is undoubtedly the greatest strength of testing and it is an entirely fallacious and unfounded assumption on the part of Hoffmann that tests are instead working against the recognition of individual merit and the wise and humane utilization of human resources. The creative genius of men such as Terman, Thurstone, Guilford and Strong cannot be nullified by a few Hoffmanns, Packards, Grosses, or Whytes.

Hoffmann argues that statistics should not take precedence over rational analysis of an item's content. I would tend to agree with this statement. Even if empirical validity did show that an item was valid, if a wrong answer were keyed, I would not then proceed to use this wrongly keyed answer. Thus, I would say that empirical validity should not necessarily carry the day over content validity and in so saying I am in essential agreement with Hoffmann. Unfortunately, Hoffmann completely ignores the fact that statistical validation of test items is most often an effective means of discovering poor and ambiguous items. Nowhere in his book does Hoffmann mention that item analysis is primarily a means of identifying poorly keyed and ambiguous items.

A common complaint about psychological testing is that it is an invasion of privacy. It is possible that this criticism may have some merit. This is the point, of course, at which it is incumbent upon the users of psychological tests to demonstrate the validity of any items which might otherwise be regarded as an invasion of privacy. A major point usually ignored by critics of psychological testing when they discuss the invasion of privacy is the distinction between institutional and individual decisions. If a firm is using a test to assess candidates and an individual desires employment with that firm, the use of the test is for the purpose of helping the institution to make a hiring decision; the purpose is not to give guidance or to protect the privacy of the individuals being tested. It is true, but perhaps beside the point, that an increase in the accuracy of institutional decisions will, over the long run, be accompanied by an increasing proportion of accurate or "correct" individual decisions.

Finally, it should be noted that the critics very rarely suggest any alternative to psychological testing. Gardner (1961) in his book, *Excellence*, says the following:

Anyone attacking the usefulness of the tests must suggest workable alternatives. It has been proven over and over again that the alternative methods of evaluating ability are subject to gross errors and capable of producing grave injustices.

I believe that our careful examination of the assumptions by the various critics of psychological testing can lead to only one conclusion: The basic assumptions are erroneous and fallacious; they are based for the most part on lack of information, as apparently is the case for Hoffmann, or more seriously on a refusal to accept the strong evidence showing that individuality can be assessed with accuracy and in such a way as to give better recognition to real merit than has ever before been the case in either our educational or industrial institutions.

54   *The Social Consequences of Educational Testing*

ROBERT L. EBEL

In the following article Dr. Ebel describes the present posture of educational and psychological testing, with respect to both justified and unjustified criticisms by the layman and professional. The author considers four potentially harmful consequences of testing and whether these consequences should legitimately be feared. In discussing means by which these dangers may be eliminated or ameliorated, he also raises the important question of the social consequences of not testing.

Tests have been used increasingly in recent years to make educational assessments. The reasons for this are not hard to discover. Educational tests of aptitude and achievement greatly improve the precision, objectivity, and efficiency of the observations on which educational assessments rest. Tests are not alternatives to observations. At best they represent no more than refined and systematized processes of observation.

But the increasing use of tests has been accompanied by an increasing flow of critical comment. Again the reasons are easy to see. Tests very in quality. None is perfect and some may be quite imperfect. Test scores are sometimes misused. And even if they were flawless and used with the greatest skill, they would probably still be unpopular among those who have reason to fear an impartial assessment of some of their competencies.

Many of the popular articles critical of educational testing that have appeared

Reprinted and abridged with permission of author and publisher from the *Proceedings of the 1963 Invitational Conference on Testing Problems,* Educational Testing Service, 1964, pp. 130–143. (By special arrangement with the American Council on Education)

in recent years do not reflect a very thoughtful, unbiased consideration of its social consequences. Most of them are obvious potboilers for their authors and sensational reader-bait in the eyes of the editors of the journals in which they appear. The writers of some of these articles have paid courteous visits to our offices. They have listened respectfully to our recitals of fact and opinion. They have drunk coffee with us and then taken their leave, presumably to reflect on what they have been told, but in any event to write. What appears in print often seems to be only an elaboration and documentation of their initial prejudices and preconceptions, supported by atypical anecdotes and purposefully selected quotations. Educational testing has not fared very well in their hands.

Among the charges of malfeasance and misfeasance that these critics have leveled against the test makers there is one of nonfeasance. Specifically, we are charged with having shown lack of proper concern for the social consequences of our educational testing. These harmful consequences, they have suggested, may be numerous and serious. The more radical among them imply that because of what they suspect about the serious social consequences of educational testing, the whole testing movement ought to be suppressed. The more moderate critics claim that they do not know much about these social consequences. But they also suggest that the test makers don't either, and that it is the test makers who ought to be doing substantial research to find out.

THE ROLE OF RESEARCH

If we were forced to choose between the two alternatives offered by the critics, either the suppression of educational testing or extensive research on its social consequences, we probably would choose the latter without much hesitation. But it is by no means clear that what testing needs most at this point is a large program of research on its social consequences. Let me elaborate.

Research can be extremely useful, but it is far from being a sure-fire process for finding the answers to any kind of a question, particularly a social question that perplexes us. Nor is research the only source of reliable knowledge. In the social sciences, at least, most of what we know for sure has not come out of formal research projects. It has come instead from the integration of a very large number of more or less incidental observations and accounts of human behavior in natural, rather than experimental situations. There are good reasons why research on human behavior tends to be difficult and often unproductive, but that is a story we cannot go into now.

For present purposes, only two points need to be mentioned. The first is that the scarcity of formal research on the social consequences of educational testing should not be taken to mean that there is no reliable knowledge about those consequences, or that those engaged in educational testing have been callously indifferent to its social consequences. The second is that scientific research on human behavior may require commitment to values that are in basic conflict with our democratic concerns for individual welfare. If boys and girls are used as carefully controlled experimental subjects in tough-minded research on social issues that really matter, not all of them will benefit, and some may be disadvantaged seriously. Our society is not yet ready, and perhaps should never become ready to acquiesce in that kind of scientific research.

HARMFUL CONSEQUENCES

Before proceeding further, let us mention specifically a few of the harmful things that critics have suggested educational testing may do:

1. It may place an indelible stamp of intellectual status—superior, mediocre, or inferior—on a child, and thus predetermine his social status as an adult, and possibly also do irreparable harm to his self-esteem and his educational motivation.
2. It may lead to a narrow conception of ability, encourage pursuit of this single goal, and thus tend to reduce the diversity of talent available to society.
3. It may place the testers in a position to control education and determine the destinies of individual human beings, while, incidentally, making the testers themselves rich in the process.
4. It may encourage impersonal, inflexible, mechanistic processes of evaluation and determination, so that essential human freedoms are limited or lost altogether.

These are four of the most frequent and serious tentative indictments. There have been, of course, many other suggesstions of possible harmful social consequences of educational testing. It may emphasize individual competition and success, rather than social cooperation, and thus conflict with the cultivation of democratic ideals of human equality. It may foster conformity rather than creativity. It may involve cultural bias. It may neglect important intangibles. It may, particularly in the case of personality testing, involve unwarranted and offensive invasions of privacy. It may do serious injustice in particular individual cases. It may reward specious test-taking skill, or penalize the lack of it.

PERMANENT STATUS DETERMINATION

Consider first then, the danger that educational testing may place an indelible stamp of inferiority on a child, ruin his self-esteem and educational motivation, and determine his social status as an adult. The kind of educational testing most likely to have these consequences would involve tests purporting to measure a person's permanent general capacity for learning. These are the intelligence tests, and the presumed measures of general capacity for learning they provide are popularly known as IQ's.

Most of us here assembled are well aware of the fact that there is no direct, unequivocal means for measuring permanent general capacity for learning. It is not even clear to many of us that in the state of our current understanding of mental functions and the learning process, any precise and useful meaning can be given to the concept of "permanent general capacity for learning." We know that all intelligence tests now available are direct measures only of achievement in learning, including learning how to learn, and that inferences from scores on those tests to some native capacity for learning are fraught with many hazards and uncertainties.

But many people who are interested in education do not know this. Many of them believe that native intelligence has been clearly identified and is well understood by expert psychologists. They believe that a person's IQ is one of his basic, permanent attributes, and that any good intelligence test will measure it with a high degree of precision. They do not regard an IQ simply as another test score, a score that may vary considerably depending on the particular test used and the particular time when the person was tested.

Whether or not a person's learning is significantly influenced by his predetermined capacity for learning, there is no denying the obvious fact that individual achievements in learning exhibit considerable consistency over time and across tasks. The superior elementary school pupil may become a mediocre secondary school pupil and an inferior college student, but the odds are against it. Early promise is not always fulfilled, but it is more often than not. The A student in mathematics is a better bet than the C student to be an A student in English literature as well, or in social psychology.

On the other hand, early promise is not always followed by late fulfillment. Ordinary students do blossom sometimes into outstanding scholars. And special talents can be cultivated. There is enough variety in the work of the world so that almost anyone can discover some line of endeavor in which he can develop more skill than most of his fellow men.

In a free society that claims to recognize the dignity and worth of every individual, it is better to emphasize the opportunity for choice and the importance of effort than to stress genetic determinism of status and success. It is better to emphasize the diversity of talents and tasks than to stress general excellence or inferiority. It is important to recognize and to reinforce what John Gardner has called "the principle of multiple chances," not only across time but also across tasks.

The concept of fixed general intelligence, or capacity for learning, is a hypothetical concept. At this stage in the development of our understanding of human learning, it is not a necessary hypothesis. Socially, it is not now a useful hypothesis. One of the important things test specialists can do to improve the social consequences of educational testing is to discredit the popular conception of the IQ. Wilhelm Stern, the German psychologist who suggested the concept originally saw how it was being over-generalized and charged one of his students coming to America to "kill the IQ." Perhaps we would be well advised, even at this late date, to renew our efforts to carry out his wishes.

Recent emphasis on the early identification of academic talent involves similar risks of oversimplifying the concept of talent and overemphasizing its predetermined components. If we think of talent mainly as something that is genetically given, we will run our schools quite differently than if we think of it mainly as something that can be educationally developed.

We should judge the value of the tests we use not in terms of how accurately they enable us to predict later achievement, but rather in terms of how much help they give us to increase achievement by motivating and directing the efforts of students and teachers. From this point of view, those concerned with professional education who have resisted schemes for very long-range predictions of aptitude for or success in their professions have acted wisely. Not only is there likely to be much more of dangerous error than of useful truth in such long-range predictions, but also there is implicit in the whole enterprise a deterministic conception of achievement that is not wholly consistent with the educational facts as we know them, and with the basic assumptions of a democratic, free society.

Prediction has to do with the future, and the future ought to be of greater concern to us than the past. I think that a measurement must be related to some other measurements in order to be useful, and that these relationships provide the basis for, and are tested by, predictions. But these relationships also provide a basis in many educational endeavors for managing outcomes—for making happen what we want to happen. And I cannot agree that precision in language or clarity of thought is well served by referring to this process of controlling outcomes as just another instance of prediction. The etymology and common usage of the word "prediction" imply to me the process of foretelling, not of controlling.

The direct, exclusive, immediate purpose of measurement is always description, not either prediction or control. If we know with reasonable accuracy how things now stand (descriptions), and if we also know with reasonable accuracy what leads to what (functional relations), we are in a position to foretell what will happen if we keep hands off (prediction) or to manipulate the variables we can get our hands on to make happen what we want to happen (control). Of course our powers of control are often limited and uncertain, just as our powers of prediction are. But I have not been able to see what useful purpose is served by referring to both the hands-off and the hands-on operations as prediction, as if there were no important difference between them. It is in the light of these semantic considerations that I suggest that tests should be used less as bases for prediction of achievement, and more as means to increase achievement. I think there is a difference, and that it is important educationally.

LIMITED CONCEPTIONS OF ABILITY

Consider next the danger that a single widely used test or test battery for selective admission or scholarship awards may foster an undesirably narrow conception of ability and thus tend to reduce diversity in the talents available to a school or to society.

Here again, it seems, the danger is not wholly imaginary. Basic as verbal and quantitative skills are to many phases of educational achievement, they do not encompass all phases of achievement. The application of a common yardstick of aptitude or achievement to all pupils is operationally much simpler than the use of a diversity of yardsticks, designed to measure different aspects of achievement. But overemphasis on a common test could lead educators to neglect those students whose special talents lie outside the common core.

Those who manage programs for the testing of scholastic aptitude always insist, and properly so, that scores on these tests should not be the sole consideration when decisions are made on admission or the award of scholarships. But the question of whether the testing itself should not be varied from person to person remains. The use of optional tests of achievement permits some variation. Perhaps the range of available options should be made much wider than it is at present to accommodate greater diversity of talents.

The problem of encouraging the development of various kinds of ability is, of course, much broader than the problem of testing. Widespread commitment to general education, with the requirement that all students study identical courses for a substantial part of their programs, may be a much greater deterrent of specialized diversity in the educational product. Perhaps these requirements should be restudied too.

DOMINATION BY THE TESTERS

What of the concern that the growth of educational testing may increase the influence of the test makers until they are in a position to control educational curricula and determine the destinies of students?

Those who know well how tests are made and used in American education know that the tests more often lag than lead curricular change, and that while tests may affect particular episodes in a student's experience, they can hardly ever be said to determine a student's destiny. American education is, after all, a manifold, decentralized, loosely organized enterprise. Whether it restricts student freedom too much or too little is a subject for lively debate. But it does not even come close to determining any student's destiny, not nearly as close as the examination systems in some countries, ancient and modern.

But test makers have, I fear, sometimes given the general public reason to fear that we may be up to no good. I refer to our sometime reluctance to take the layman fully into our confidence, to share fully with him all information about his test scores, the tests from which they were derived, and our interpretations of what they mean.

Secrecy concerning educational tests and test scores has been justified on several grounds. One is that the information is simply too complex for untrained minds to grasp. Now it is true that some pretty elaborate theories can be built around our testing processes. It is also true that we can perform some very fancy statistical manipulations with the scores they yield. But the essential information revealed by the scores on most educational tests is not particularly complex. If we understand it ourselves, we can communicate it clearly to most laymen without serious difficulty. To be quite candid, we are not all that much brighter than they are, much as we may sometimes need the reassurance of thinking so.

Another justification for secrecy is that laymen will misuse test scores. Mothers may compare scores over the back fences. The one whose child scores high spreads the word around. The one whose child scores low may keep the secret, but seek other grounds for urging changes in the teaching staff or in the educational program. Scores of limited meaning may be treated with undue respect and used to repair or to injure the student's self-esteem rather than to contribute to his learning.

Again it is true that test scores can be misused. They have been in the past and they will be in the future. But does this justify secrecy? Can we minimize abuses due to ignorance by withholding knowledge? We do not flatter our fellow citizens when we tell them, in effect, that they are too ignorant, or too lacking in character to be trusted with the knowledge of their children, or of themselves, that we possess.

Seldom acknowledged, but very persuasive as a practical reason for secrecy regarding test scores is that it spares those who use the scores from having to explain and justify the decisions they make. Preference is not and should not always be given to the person whose test score is the higher. But if score information is withheld, the disappointed applicant will assume that it was because of his low score, not because of some other factor. He will not trouble officials with demands for justification of a decision that in some cases might be hard to justify. But all things considered, more is likely to be gained in the long run by revealing the objective evidence used in reaching a decision. Should the other subjective considerations prove too difficult to justify, perhaps they ought not to be used as part of the basis for decision.

If specialists in educational measurement want to be properly understood and trusted by the public they serve, they will do well to shun secrecy and to share with the public as much as it is interested in knowing about the methods they use, the knowledge they gain, and the interpretations they make. This is clearly the trend of opinion in examining boards and public education authorities. Let us do what we can to reinforce the trend. Whatever mental measurements are so esoteric or so dangerous socially that they must be shrouded in secrecy probably should not be made in the first place.

The testers do not control education or the destinies of individual students. By the avoidance of mystery and secrecy they can help to create better public understanding and support.

MECHANISTIC DECISION MAKING

Finally, let us consider briefly the possibility that testing may encourage mechanical decision making, at the expense of essential human freedoms of choice and action.

Those who work with mental tests often say that the purpose of all measurement is prediction. They use regression equations to predict grade-point averages, or contingency tables to predict the chances of various degrees of success. Their procedures may seem to imply not only that human behavior is part of a deterministic system in which the number of relevant variables is manageably small, but also that the proper goals of human behavior are clearly known and universally accepted.

In these circumstances there is some danger that we may forget our own inadequacies and attempt to play God with the lives of other human beings. We may find it convenient to overlook the gross inaccuracies that plague our measurements and the great uncertainties that bedevil our predictions. Betrayed by overconfidence in our own wisdom and virtue, we may project our particular value systems into a pattern of ideal behavior for all men.

If these limitations on our ability to mold human behavior and to direct its development did not exist, we would need to face the issue debated by B. F. Skinner and Carl Rogers before the American Psychological Association some years ago. Shall our knowledge of human behavior be used to design an ideal culture and condition individuals to live happily in it at whatever necessary cost to their own freedom of choice and action?

But the aforementioned limitations do exist. If we ignore them and undertake to manage the lives of others so that those others will qualify as worthy citizens in our own particular vision of utopia, we do justify the concern that one harmful social consequence of educational testing may be mechanistic decision making and the loss of essential human freedoms.

A large proportion of the decisions affecting the welfare and destiny of a person must be made in the midst of overwhelming uncertainties concerning the outcomes to be desired and the best means of achieving such outcomes. That many mistakes will be made seems inevitable. One of the cornerstones of a free society is the belief that in most cases it is better for the person most concerned to make the decision, right or wrong, and to take the responsibility for its consequences, good or bad.

The implications of this for educational testing are clear. Tests should be used as little as possible to impose decisions and courses of action on others. They should be used as much as possible to provide a sounder basis of choice in individual decision making. Tests can be used and ought to be used to support rather than to limit human freedom and responsibility.

CONCLUSION

In summary we have suggested that those who make and use educational tests might do four things to alleviate public concerns over their possibly adverse social consequences:

1. We could emphasize the use of tests to improve status, and de-emphasize their use to determine status.
2. We could broaden the base of achievements tested to recognize and develop the wide variety of talents needed in our society.
3. We could share openly with the persons most directly concerned all that tests have revealed to us about their abilities and prospects.
4. We could decrease the use of tests to impose decisions on others, and instead increase their use as a basis for better personal decision making.

When Paul Dressel read a draft of this paper, he chided me gently on what he considered to be a serious omission. I had failed to discuss the social consequences of *not* testing. What are some of these consequences?

If the use of educational tests were abandoned, the distinctions between competence and incompetence would become more difficult to discern. Dr. Nathan Womack, former president of the National Board of Medical Examiners, has pointed out that only to the degree to which educational institutions can define what they mean by competence and determine the extent to which it has been achieved can they discharge their obligation to deliver competence to the society they serve.

If the use of educational tests were abandoned, the encouragement and reward of individual efforts to learn would be made more difficult. Excellence in programs of education would become less tangible as a goal and less demonstrable as an attainment. Educational opportunities would be extended less on the basis of aptitude and merit and more on the basis of ancestry and influence; social class barriers would become less permeable. Decisions on important issues of curriculum and method would be made less on the basis of solid evidence and more on the basis of prejudice or caprice.

These are some of the social consequences of *not* testing. In our judgment, they are potentially far more harmful than any possible adverse consequences of testing. But it is also our judgment, and has been the theme of this paper, that we can do much to minimize even these possibilities of harmful consequences. Let us, then, use educational tests for the powerful tools they are with energy and skill, but also with wisdom and care.

REFERENCES

ADAMS, GEORGIA S. *Measurement and evaluation in education, psychology, and guidance.* New York: Holt, Rinehart and Winston, 1964.

ADKINS, DOROTHY C. *Statistics.* Columbus: Charles E. Merrill Books, 1964.

AHMANN, J. S. and GLOCK, M. D. *Evaluating pupil growth.* Boston: Allyn and Bacon. (Second Edition), 1963.

AHMANN, J. S., GLOCK, M. D. and WARDENBERG, HELEN L. *Evaluating elementary school pupils.* Boston: Allyn and Bacon, 1960.

ALLEN, R. M. *Personality assessment procedures.* New York: Harper and Brothers, 1958.

AMERICAN PSYCHOLOGICAL ASSOCIATION. *Standards for educational and psychological tests and manuals.* Washington, D. C.: 1966.

AMERICAN PSYCHOLOGICAL ASSOCIATION. Testing and public policy (Special Issue). *American Psychologist,* 1965, Vol. 20, pp. 857–993.

AMERICAN PSYCHOLOGICAL ASSOCIATION. *Technical recommendations for psychological tests and diagnostic techniques.* Washington, D. C.: 1954 (Also supplement to *Psychological Bulletin,* 1954, Vol. 51, pp. 1–38).

ANASTASI, ANNE. The concept of validity in the interpretation of test scores. *Educational and Psychological Measurement,* 1950, Vol. 10, pp. 67–78.

ANDERSON, E. E. Interrelationship of drives in the male albino rat. 1. Intercorrelations of measure of drives. *Journal of Comparative Psychology,* 1937, Vol. 24, pp. 73–118.

ASTIN, A. W. and HOLLAND, J. L. The environmental assessment technique: A way to measure college environment. *Journal of Educational Psychology,* 1961, Vol. 52, pp. 308–316.

ATKINSON, J. W. Towards experimental analysis of human motivation in terms of motives, expectancies, and incentives. In J. W. Atkinson (ed.), *Motives in fantasy, action, and society.* Princeton, N. J.: Van Nostrand, 1958.

AULD, F., JR., Influence of social class on personality test responses. *Psychological Bulletin,* 1952, Vol. 49, pp. 318–332.

BARZUN, J. *The house of intellect.* New York: Harper, 1959.

BAUERFEIND, R. H. *Building a school testing program.* Boston: Houghton-Mifflin Company, 1963.

BECHTOLDT, H. P. Construct validity: a critique. *American Psychologist,* 1959, Vol. 14, pp. 619–629.

BECHTOLDT, H. P. Selection. In S. S. Stevens (Ed.), *Handbook of experimental psychology.* New York: Wiley, 1951, pp. 1237–1267.

BENNETT, G. K., SEASHORE, H. G., and WESMAN, A. G. *Differential aptitude tests, Manual.* New York: Psychological Corporations, 1947.

BERDIE, R. F. Intra-individual variability and predictability. *Educational and Psychological Measurement,* 1961, Vol. 21, pp. 663–676.

BERNSTEIN, B. Language and social class. *British Journal of Sociology,* 1960, Vol. 11, pp. 271–276.

BITTNER, R. H. and WILDER, C. E. Expectancy tables: a method of interpreting correlation coefficients. *Journal of Experimental Education,* 1946, Vol. 14, pp. 245–252.

BLACK, HILLEL. *They shall not pass.* New York: William Morrow and Company, 1963.

BLOMMERS, P. and LINDQUIST, E. F. *Elementary statistical methods in psychology and education.* Boston: Houghton-Mifflin Co., 1960.

BLOOM, B. S. and OTHERS. *Taxonomy of educational objectives. Handbook I: The cognitive domain.* New York: David McKay Co., 1956.

BLOOM, B. S., and PETERS, F. R. *The use of academic prediction scales for counseling and selecting college entrants.* New York: The Free Press of Glencoe, 1961.

BORISLOW, B. The *Edwards Personal Preference Schedule (EPPS)* and fakeability. *Journal of Applied Psychology,* 1958, Vol. 42, pp. 22–27.

BRADLEY, J. I. and MCCLELLAND, J. N. *Basic statistical concepts (a self-instructional text).* Chicago: Scott, Foresman and Co., 1963.

BRAINARD, P. P., and BRAINARD, R. T. *Manual for the Brainard Occupational Preference Inventory (Form R).* New York: The Psychological Corporation, 1956.

BRAINARD, P. P., and BRAINARD R. T. *Brainard Occupational Preference Inventory (Form R).* New York: The Psychological Corporation, 1945.

BROTHERTON, D A., READ, J. M. and PRATT, K. C. Indeterminate number concepts: II Application to children to determinate number groups. *Journal of Genetic Psychology,* 1948, Vol. 73, pp. 209–236.

BUROS, O. K. *Fifth mental measurements yearbook*. New Jersey: The Gryphon Press, 1959.

CAMPBELL, D. T. and FISKE, D. W. Convergent and discriminant validation by the multi-trait multi-method matrix. *Psychological Bulletin*, 1959, Vol. 56, pp. 81–105.

CATTELL, R. B. *Personality and motivation: structure and measurement*. Tarrytown, N. Y.: Harcourt, Brace and World, 1957. (a)

CATTELL, R. B. A universal index for psychological factors. *Psychologia*, 1957, Vol. 1, pp. 74–85. (b)

CATTELL, R. B. Psychological measurement: ipsative normative and interactive. *Psychological Review*, 1944, Vol. 51, pp. 292–303.

CATTELL, R. B., and RADCLIFFE, J. A. Reliabilities and validities of simple and extended, weighted and buffered unifactor scales. *British Journal of Statistical Psychology*, 1963, Vol. 15, pp. 113–128.

CATTELL, R. B. and TSUJIOKA, B. Orthogenality, homogeneity and other test evils: A plea for structural psychometric concepts and evaluative formulae in personality test design. *Educational and Psychological Measurement*, 1964, Vol. 24, pp. 1–28.

CHAUNCEY, H. and DOBBIN, J. E. *Testing: its place in education today*. New York: Harper and Row, 1963.

CHESHIRE, L., SAFFIR, M., and THURSTONE, L. L. *Computing diagrams for the tetrachoric correlation coefficient*. Chicago: University of Chicago Bookstore, 1933.

COOK, W. W. and LEEDS, C. H. Measuring teacher personality. *Educational and Psychological Measurement*, 1947, Vol. 7, pp. 399–410.

COOLEY, W. W. *Career development of scientists: an overlapping longitudinal study*. Cambridge, Mass.: Harvard Graduate School of Education, Harvard University, 1963.

CRONBACH, L. J. *Essentials of Psychological Testing*. New York: Harper. (Second Edition), 1960.

CRONBACH, L. J. Coefficient alpha and the internal structure of tests. *Psychometrika*, 1951, Vol. 16, pp. 297–334.

CRONBACH, L. J. Further evidence on response sets and test design. *Educational and Psychological Measurement*, 1950, Vol. 10, pp. 3–31.

CRONBACH, L. J. Test "reliability": its meaning and determination. *Psychometrika*, 1947, Vol. 12, pp. 1–16.

CRONBACH, L. J. Response sets and test validity. *Educational and Psychological Measurement*, 1946, Vol. 6, pp. 475–494.

CRONBACH, L. J., and GLESER, GOLDINE C. *Psychological tests and personnel decisions*. Urbana: University of Illinois Press. (Second Edition), 1965.

CRONBACH, L. J., and MEEHL, P. E. Construct validity in psychological tests. *Psychological Bulletin*, 1955, Vol. 52, pp. 281–302.

CRONBACH, L. J., RAJARATNAM, N., and GLESER, GOLDINE C. Theory of generalizability: A liberalization of reliability theory. *British Journal of Statistical Psychology*, 1963, Vol. 16, pp. 137–163.

DAVIS, F. B. *Educational measurements and their interpretation.* Belmont, California; Wadsworth Publishing Co., 1964.

DAVIS, F. B. Item analysis in relation to educational and psychological testing. *Psychological Bulletin*, 1952, Vol. 49, pp. 97–121.

DAVIS, F. B. Item selection techniques. In Lindquist (Ed.). *Educational measurement.* Washington, D. C.: American Council on Education, 1951, (Chapter 9), pp. 266–328.

DREGER, R., and MILLER, K. Comparative psychological studies of Negroes and whites in the United States. *Psychological Bulletin*, 1960, Vol. 57, pp. 361–402.

DRESSEL, P. L. and MAYHEW, L. B. *General education: Explorations in evaluation.* Washington: American Council on Education, 1954.

DRESSEL, P. L. and OTHERS. *Evaluation in higher education.* Boston: Houghton-Mifflin Co., 1961.

EBEL, R. L. *Measuring educational achievement.* Englewood Cliffs, New Jersey: Prentice-Hall, 1965.

EBEL, R. L. Must all tests be valid? *American Psychologist*, 1961, Vol. 16, pp. 640–647.

EDUCATIONAL TESTING SERVICE. *Explanation of multiple-choice tests.* Princeton, New Jersey, 1961.

EDWARDS, A. L. *Edwards personal preference schedule, Manual.* (Rev. ed.) New York: Psychological Corp., 1957. (a)

EDWARDS, A. L. *The social desirability variable in personality assessment and research.* New York: The Dryden Press, 1957. (b)

FARQUHAR, W. W. *Motivation factors related to academic achievement.* Final Report U.S.O.E. Co-operative Research Project #846. Office of Research and Publications, Michigan State University, E. Lansing, Michigan, 1963.

FARQUHAR, W. W. and PAYNE, D. A. A classification and comparison of techniques used in selecting under- and over-achievers. *Personnel and Guidance Journal*, 1964, Vol. 42, pp. 874–884.

FARQUHAR, W. W. and PAYNE, D. A. Factors in the academic-occupational motivations of eleventh-grade under- and over-achievers. *Personnel and Guidance Journal*, 1963, Vol. 42, pp. 245–251.

FINDLEY, W. G. (Ed.) *The impact and improvement of school testing programs.* 62nd Yearbook, Part II, NSSE, Chicago: University of Chicago Press, 1963.

FISK, D. W., and RICE, LAURA. Intra-individual response variability. *Psychological Bulletin*, 1955, Vol. 52, pp. 217–250.

FISHMAN, J. A. and PASANELLA, ANN K. College admission-selection studies. *Review of Educational Research*, 1960, Vol. 30, pp. 298–310.

FLANAGAN, J. C., DAILEY, J. T., SHAYCROFT, M. F., ORR, D. B., and GOLDBERG, I.

Studies of the American High School. Pittsburgh, Pa.: University of Pittsburgh Press, 1962.

FRANDSEN, A. N. Interests and general educational development. *Journal of Applied Psychology,* 1947, Vol. 31, pp. 57–66.

FREDERICKSEN N., and MELVILLE, S. D. Differential predictability in the use of test scores. *Educational and Psychological Measurement,* 1954, Vol. 14, pp. 647–656.

FREEMAN, F. *Theory and practice of psychological testing.* New York: Holt, Rinehart and Winston. (Third Edition), 1962.

FRENCH, ELIZABETH G. Development of a measure of complex motivation. In J. W. Atkinson (Ed.), *Motives in fantasy, action, and society.* Princeton, N. J.: Van Nostrand, 1958.

FREYD, M. The statistical viewpoint in vocational selection. *Journal of Applied Psychology,* 1925, Vol. 9, pp. 349–356.

FURST, E. J. *Constructing evaluation instruments.* New York: Longmans, Green and Co., 1958.

GARDNER, J. *Excellence.* New York: Harper and Row, 1961.

GARRETT, H. E. *Statistics in psychology and education.* New York: Longmans, Green, 1958.

GETZELS, J. W., and JACKSON, P. W. *Creativity and intelligence; explorations with gifted students.* New York: John Wiley & Sons, 1962.

GHISELLI, E. E. Differentiation of tests in terms of the accuracy with which they predict for a given individual. *Educational and Psychological Measurement,* 1960, Vol. 20, pp. 615–684. (a)

GHISELLI, E. E. The prediction of predictability. *Educational and Psychological Measurement,* 1960, Vol. 20, pp. 3–8. (b)

GHISELLI, E. E. Differentiation of individuals in terms of their predictability. *Journal of Applied Psychology,* 1956, Vol. 40, pp. 374–377.

GOODFELLOW, L. D. The human element in probability. *Journal of General Psychology,* 1940, Vol. 33, pp. 201–205.

GOTKIN, L. G. and GOLDSTEIN, L. S. *Descriptive statistics; a programmed textbook.* (Two volumes). New York: John Wiley, 1964.

GROSS, M. L. *The brain watchers.* New York: Random House, 1962.

GUILFORD, J. P. Intelligence 1965 model. *American Psychologist,* 1966, Vol. 21, pp. 20–26.

GUILFORD, J. P. *Fundamental statistics in psychology and education.* New York: McGraw-Hill, (Fourth Edition), 1965.

GUILFORD, J. P. (Ed.) *Printed Classification Tests.* AAF Aviation Psychology Program Research Reports No. 5, Washington, D. C.: Government Printing Office, 1947.

GULLIKSEN, H. *Theory of mental tests.* New York: John Wiley, 1950. (a)

GULLIKSEN, H. Intrinsic validity. *American Psychologist,* 1950, Vol. 5, pp. 511–517. (b)

HAGGARD, E. Social status and intelligence: an experimental study of certain cultural determinants of measured intelligence. *Genetic Psychology Monographs,* 1954, Vol. 49, pp. 141–186.

HANCOCK, J. W. An experimental study of limiting response on attitude scales. In H. H. Remmers (Ed.) *Further studies in attitudes, Series III. Studies in higher education,* 1938, Lafayette, Indiana: Purdue University, Vol. 34, pp. 142–148.

HARRIS, C. W. (Ed.), *Problems in measuring change.* Madison: University of Wisconsin Press, 1963.

HARRIS, D. Factors affecting college grades: A review of the literature, 1930–37. *Psychological Bulletin,* 1940, Vol. 37, pp. 125–66.

HAWES, G. R. *Educational testing for the millions.* New York: McGraw-Hill Book Company, 1964.

HOFFMANN, B. *The tyranny of testing.* New York: The Crowell-Collier Press, 1962.

HOFFMANN, B. Testing. *Physics Today,* 1961, Vol. 14, pp. 38–42. (a)

HOFFMANN, B. The tyranny of multiple-choice tests. *Harper's Magazine,* 1961, March, Vol. 222, pp. 37–44, (b).

HORST, P. A technique for the development of a multiple absolute prediction battery. *Psychological Monographs,* 1955, Vol. 69, (Whole No. 390).

HORST, P. A technique for the development of a differential prediction battery. *Psychological Monographs,* 1954, Vol. 68, (Whole No. 380).

HOYT, C. Test reliability estimated by analysis of variance. *Psychometrika,* 1941, Vol. 6, pp. 153–160.

HUDDLESON, EDITH M. Test development on the basis of content validity. *Educational and Psychological Measurement,* 1956 Vol. 16, pp. 283–293.

JACKSON, R. W. and FERGUSON, S. A. *Studies on the reliability of tests.* Department of Educational Research Bulletin 12. Toronto, Canada: University of Toronto, 1941.

JESSOR, R. and HAMMOND, K. R. Construct validity and the Taylor anxiety scale. *Psychological Bulletin,* 1957, Vol. 54, pp. 161–170.

JOHNSON, G. Meditations on an interest test. *Occupations,* 1952, Vol. 30, pp. 357–358.

JOHNSTON, A. M. *The relationship of various factors to autocratic and democratic classroom practices.* Unpublished doctoral dissertation, University of Chicago, 1948.

KAHN, D. F. and HADLEY, J. M. Factors relatetd to life insurance selling. *Journal of Applied Psychology,* 1949, Vol. 23, pp. 132–140.

KATZ, M. *Selecting an achievement test: Principles and procedures.* Princeton: Educational Testing Service, 1958. (Evaluation and Advisory Service Bulletin No. 3).

KAZMIER, L. J. Cross-validation groups, extreme groups, and the prediction of academic achievement. *Journal of Educational Psychology,* 1961, Vol. 52, pp. 195–198.

KELLEY, T. L. Note on the reliability of a test: A reply to Dr. Crum's criticism. *Journal of Educational Psychology*, 1924, Vol. 15, pp. 193–204.

KELLEY, T. L. and KREY, A. C. *Tests and measurement in the social sciences.* New York: C. Scribner and Sons, 1934.

KLINEBERG, O. *Race differences*, New York: Harper, 1935.

KOGAN, N. and WALLACH, M. A. *Risk taking: a study in cognition and personality.* New York: Holt, Rinehart, and Winston, 1964.

KRATHWOHL, D. R. and OTHERS. *Taxonomy of Educational Objectives. Handbook II: The Affective Domain.* New York: David McKay Co., 1964.

KRUMBOLTZ, J. D. and FARQUHAR, W. W. Reliability and validity of the n-achievement test. *Journal of Consulting Psychology*, 1957, Vol. 21, pp. 226–228.

KUDER, G. F. *Manual for the Kuder Preference Record-Vocational* (Form B). Chicago: Science Research Associates, 1947.

KUDER, G. F. The stability of preference items. *Journal of Social Psychology*, 1939, Vol. 10, pp. 41–50.

KUDER, G. F., and RICHARDSON, M. W. The theory of estimation of test reliability. *Psychometrika*, 1937, Vol. 2, pp. 151–160.

LANGMUIR, C. Cross-validation. *Test Service Bulletin #47.* New York: The Psychological Corporation, 1954, September, pp. 3–6.

LAVIN, D. E. *The prediction of academic performance.* New York: Russell Sage Foundation, 1965.

LENNON, R. T. Assumptions underlying the use of content validity. *Educational and Psychological Measurement*, 1956, Vol. 16, pp. 294–304.

LOEVINGER, JANE A. The technic of homogeneous tests compared with some aspects of scale analysis and factor analysis. *Psychological Bulletin*, 1948, Vol. 45, pp. 507–529.

LORGE, I. Gen-like: halo or reality? *Psychological Bulletin*, 1937, Vol. 24, pp. 545–546.

LOWELL, E. L. The effect of need for achievement on learning and speed of performance. *Journal of Psychology*, 1952, Vol. 33, pp. 31–40.

LUCAS, C. M. Analysis of the relative movement test by a method of individual interviews. *Bureau of Naval Personnel Research Reports*, Contract Nonr-694 (00), NR 131-13 Educational Testing Service, March 1953.

LYMAN, H. B. *Test scores and what they mean.* Englewood Cliffs, N. J.: Prentice-Hall, 1963.

MACFARLANE, JEAN W. Problems of validation inherent in projective methods. *American Journal of Orthopsychiatry*, 1942, Vol. 12, pp. 405–410.

MAGER, R. F. *Preparing objectives for programmed instruction.* San Francisco: Fearon Publishers, 1962. (New printing entitled: *Preparing Instructional Objectives.*)

MAIER, G. E. *The contribution of interest test scores to differential academic prediction.* Doctoral dissertation, University of Washington, 1957.

MASLAND, R., SARASON, S., and GLADWIN, T. *Mental subnormality.* New York: Basic Books, 1958.

MATHEWS, C. O. The effect of the order of printed response on an interest questionnaire. *Journal of Educational Psychology*, 1929, Vol. 20, pp. 128–134.

MAY, M. A. and HARTSHORNE, H. Objective methods of measuring character. *Pedagogical Seminary*, 1925, Vol. 32, pp. 45–47.

McCABE, G. E. How substantial is a substantial validity coefficient? *Personnel and Guidance Journal*, 1956, Vol. 34, pp. 340–344.

McCLELLAND, D. C., ATKINSON, J. W., CLARK, R. A., and LOWELL, E. L. *The achievement motive.* New York: Appleton-Century-Crofts, 1953.

McCOLLOUGH, CELESTE and VAN ATTA, L. *Introduction to descriptive statistics and correlation. (A program for self-instruction).* New York: McGraw-Hill, 1965.

McCOLLOUGH, CELESTE and VAN ATTA, L. *Statistical concepts. (A program for self-instruction).* New York: McGraw-Hill, 1963.

McNEMAR, Q. At random: Sense and nonsense. *American Psychologist*, 1960, Vol. 15, pp. 295–300.

MEEHL, P. E. *Clinical versus statistical prediction (a theoretical analysis and review of the evidence).* Minneapolis: University of Minnesota Press, 1954.

MEEHL, P. E. The dynamics of "structure" personality tests. *Journal of Clinical Psychology*, 1945, 1, 296–303.

MICHAEL, W. B., JONES, R. A. and TREMBLY, W. A. The factored dimensions of a measure of motivation for college students. *Educational and Psychological Measurement*, 1959, Vol. 19, pp. 667–671.

MITCHELL, J. V., JR. An analysis of the factorial dimensions of the achievement motivation construct. *Journal of Educational Psychology*, 1961, Vol. 52, pp. 179–187.

MORGAN, H. H. A psychometric comparison of achieving and non-achieving college students of high ability. *Journal of Consulting Psychology*, 1952, Vol. 16, pp. 292–298.

MOSIER, C. Symposium: the need and means of cross-validation. I; problems and designs of cross-validation. *Educational and Psychological Measurement*, 1951, Vol. 11, pp. 5–11.

MURRAY, H. A. *Explorations in personality.* New York: Oxford University Press, 1938.

NATIONAL BUREAU OF STANDARDS. *Tables of the bivariate normal distribution function and related functions.* (National Bureau of Standards Applied Mathematics Series, No. 50.) Washington: U. S. Government Printing Office, 1959.

NOLL, V. H. *Introduction to educational measurement.* Boston: Houghton-Mifflin Co. (Second Edition), 1965.

NUNNALLY, J. C., THISTLETHWAITE, D. L., and WOLFE, SHARON. Factored scales for measuring characteristics of college environments. *Educational and Psychological Measurement*, 1963, Vol. 23, pp. 239–248.

OWENS, W. A. Item form and 'false-positive' responses on a neurotic inventory. *Journal of Clinical Psychology*, 1947, Vol. 3, pp. 264–269.

PAYNE, D. A. The concurrent and predictive validity of an objective measure of academic self-concept. *Educational and Psychological Measurement*, 1962, Vol. 22, pp. 773–780.

PAYNE, D. A. and FARQUHAR, W. W. The dimensions of an objective measure of academic self-concept. *Journal of Educational Psychology*, 1962, Vol. 53, pp. 187–192.

PHILIP, B. R. Generalization and central tendency in the discrimination of a series of stimuli. *Canadian Journal of Psychology*, 1947, Vol. 1, pp. 196–204.

REICHENBACH, H. *Experience and prediction.* Chicago: University of Chicago Press, 1938.

RORER, L. G. The great response-style myth. *Psychological Bulletin*, 1965, Vol. 63, pp. 129–156.

RUBIN, H. K. *A constant error in the Seashore test of pitch discrimination.* Unpublished masters' thesis, University of Wisconsin, 1940.

SARASON, S. and OTHERS. *Anxiety in elementary school children.* New York: Wiley, 1960.

SAUNDERS, D. R. Moderator variables in prediction. *Educational and Psycholoical Measurement*, 1956, Vol. 16, pp. 209–222.

SEASHORE H. Women are more predictable than men. *Journal of Counseling Psychology*, 1962, Vol. 9, pp. 261–270.

SHAW, M. C. Need achievement scales as predictors of academic success. *Journal of Educational Psychology*, 1961, Vol. 52, pp. 282–285.

SHLEIN, J. M. Mental testing and modern society. *Humanist*, 1958, Vol. 18, pp. 356–364.

SINGER, W. B. and YOUNG, P. T. Studies in affective reaction: III. The specificity of affective reactions. *Journal of General Psychology.* 1941, Vol. 24, pp. 327–341.

SPIELBERGER, C. D. On the relationship between manifest anxiety and intelligence. *Journal of Consulting Psychology*, 1958, Vol. 22, pp. 220–224.

SPIKER, C. C., and McCANDLESS, B. R. The concept of intelligence and the philosophy of science. *Psychological Review*, 1954, Vol. 61, pp. 255–266.

STANLEY, J. C. *Measurement in today's schools.* Englewood Cliffs, New Jersey: Prentice- Hall, Inc. (Fourth Edition), 1964.

STERN, G. G., STEIN, M. I., and BLOOM, B. S. *Methods in personality assessment.* Glencoe, Ill.: Free Press, 1956.

TAYLOR, H. C. and RUSSELL, J. T. The relationship of validity coefficients to the practical effectiveness of tests in selection: discussion and tables. *Journal of Applied Psychology*, 1939, Vol. 23, pp. 565–578.

TAYLOR, JANET A. A personality scale of manifest anxiety. *Journal of Abnormal Social Psychology*, 1953, Vol. 48, pp. 285–290.

TAYLOR, R. A. *Personality factors associated with eleventh grade male and female discrepant achievement.* Unpublished doctoral dissertation, Michigan State University, 1962.

Technical recommendations for psychological tests and diagnostic techniques. *Psychological Bulletin Supplement,* 1954, Vol. 51, 2, Part 2, pp. 1–38.

THORNDIKE, E. L. A constant error in psychological ratings. *Journal of Applied Psychology,* 1920, Vol. 4, pp. 25–29.

THORNDIKE, R. L. Some methodological issues in the study of creativity. In *Proceedings of the 1962 Invitational Conference on Testing Problems,* Princeton, New Jersey: Educational Testing Service, 1963, pp. 40–54.

THORNDIKE, R. L. Reliability. In Lindquist, E. F. (Ed.). *Educational Measurement,* Washington: American Council on Education, 1951.

THORNDIKE, R. L. Critical note on the Pressey interest-attitudes test. *Journal of Applied Psychology,* 1938, Vol. 22, pp. 657–658.

THORNDIKE, R. L. and HAGEN, ELIZABETH. *Measurement and evaluation in psychology and education.* New York: John Wiley. (Second Edition) 1961.

THORNDIKE, R. L. and HAGEN, ELIZABETH. *Ten thousand careers.* New York: John Wiley, 1959.

THORPE, M. D. *The factored dimensions of an objective inventory of academic motivation based on eleventh grade male over- and under-achievers.* Unpublished doctoral dissertation, Michigan State University, 1961.

TIFFIN, J. and LAWSHE, C. H. Examiner manual for the *Adaptability Test.* Chicago: Science Research Associates, 1954.

TRAXLER, A. E. (Ed.) *Measurement and research in today's schools.* Washington, D. C.: American Council on Education, 1961.

TRYON, R. C. Reliability and behavior domain validity: reformulation and historical critique. *Psychological Bulletin,* 1957, Vol. 54, pp. 229–249.

UNDERWOOD, B. J. *Psychological research.* New York: Appleton-Century-Crofts, 1957.

VEROFF, J., WILCOX, S., and ATKINSON, J. W. The achievement motive in high school and college age women. *Journal of Abnormal and Social Psychology,* 1953, Vol. 48, pp. 108–119.

VITELES, M. S. The clinical viewpoint in vocational selection. *Journal of Applied Psychology,* 1925, Vol. 9, pp. 131–138.

WAY, H. H. *The relationship between forced-choice scores and differentiated response scores on the Kuder Preference Record-Vocational.* Unpublished doctoral dissertation, Indiana University, 1953.

WECHSLER, D. *Wechsler adult intelligence scale.* New York: Psychological Corporation, 1955.

WEISS, P., WERTHEIMER, M., and GROESBECK, B. Achievement motivation, academic aptitude and college grades. *Educational and Psychological Measurement,* 1960, Vol. 20, pp. 663–665.

WESMAN, A. G. Expectancy Tables—a way of interpreting test validity. *Test Service Bulletin No. 38.* New York: The Psychological Corporation, 1949.

WESMAN, A. G. Active versus blank responses to multiple-choice items. *Journal of Educational Psychology,* 1947, Vol. 38, pp. 89–95. (a)

Wesman, A. G. The usefulness of correctly spelled words in a spelling test. *Journal of Educational Psychology,* 1947, Vol. 37, pp. 242–246. (b)

Whisler, L. D. Reliability of scores on attitude scales as related to scoring method, in H. H. Remmers, (Ed.), *Further studies in attitudes series III. Studies in higher education,* 1938, Lafayette, Indiana: Purdue University, Vol. 34, pp. 126–129.

SUBJECT INDEX

NAME INDEX

A B C D E F G H I J   5 4 3 2 1 7 0 6 9 8 7